THE
CHALLENGE OF
COMMUNITY POLICING

This book is dedicated to the memory of

Robert C. Trojanowicz

who touched all of our lives with his vision of
community policing and his deeply appreciated
assistance to police and service agencies
around the world

THE
CHALLENGE OF
COMMUNITY POLICING

Testing
the
Promises

Dennis P. Rosenbaum
EDITOR

SAGE Publications
International Educational and Professional Publisher
Thousand Oaks London New Delhi

Grateful acknowledgment is given to the following for permission to reprint:

From "Study Criticizes Community Policing," *The New York Times*, 8 August 1991, p. B2. Copyright © 1991 by The New York Times Company. Reprinted by permission.

From "Revolution at Charter Oak Terrace," *Hartford Courant,* 24 August 1990. Copyright © 1990 *Hartford Courant.*

From "Neighborhood Cleanup Day Caps Year's Effort to Sweep Out Drugs," by R. Stansbury, *Hartford Courant,* 1 March 1992. Copyright © 1992. Reprinted with permission.

For information address:

SAGE Publications, Inc.
2455 Teller Road
Thousand Oaks, California 91320

SAGE Publications Ltd.
6 Bonhill Street
London EC2A 4PU
United Kingdom

SAGE Publications India Pvt. Ltd.
M-32 Market
Greater Kailash I
New Delhi 110 048 India

Printed in the United States of America

Library of Congress Cataloging-in-Publication Data

Main entry under title:

The challenge of community policing: testing the promises / edited by Dennis P. Rosenbaum.
    p.   cm.
    Includes bibliographical references and index.
    ISBN 0-8039-5443-3 (cl.).—ISBN 0-8039-5444-1 (pb.)
    1. Community policing. 2. Community policing—United States.
3. Community policing—Canada. I. Rosenbaum, Dennis P.
    HV7936.C83C668 1994
    363.2—dc20   94-811

94 95 96 97 98 10 9 8 7 6 5 4 3 2

Sage Production Editor: Rebecca Holland

Contents

Foreword

COMMUNITY POLICING is now a household term. With that realization comes an awareness that popular interest and support for a reform movement can be a mixed blessing.

Under the rubric of community policing, progressive police administrators have been trying, for well over a decade, to design and implement a form of policing that is better suited to meet the extraordinary, steadily increasing demands being made of the police. Community policing, as that term has been used among those charting the future of policing, embraces—and intricately webs together—a number of initiatives that have long been advocated for modern-day policing. The current wave of support, expressed by political leaders and the public, generates a welcome impetus for these changes.

The downside of this strong backing and popularity is that the title of the concept, community policing, is often used without concern for its substance. Political leaders and, unfortunately, many police leaders hook onto the label for the positive images it projects, but do not engage or invest in the concept. The meaning of community policing, as a result, is diluted, with consequences that are confusing and troubling for those seriously interested in effecting meaningful change in the police. In many quarters today, "community policing" is used to encompass practically all innovations in policing, from the most ambitious to the most mundane, from the most carefully thought through to the most casual. And in the larger public forum, the label is used in ways that create an expectation that, on implementation, community policing will provide a panacea for not only crime, disorder, and racial tensions but many of the other problems that plague our urban areas.

The varied meanings and high expectations for community policing create enormous difficulties for those actually engaged in implementing such change. They are especially problematic for those committed to *evaluating* its implementation and its impact. Measuring the value of innovations in programs and policies is difficult under the best of conditions. The task is much more complex when, as is true of the community policing movement, there is such variety in the shape, objectives, and depth of the changes being implemented and in the results that are expected.

Within professional policing circles, it is now widely accepted that a commitment to substantial change in direction or strategies carries with it a commitment to learning from the process of change and evaluating its impact. In contrast with the past, there is a welcome readiness to subject innovative programs to evaluation. But one of the many consequences of the widespread popular interest in community policing is that it has generated its own intense pressures for a quick evaluation of impact. Mayors, city managers, local legislators, budget officers, the public, and veteran police officers—among others—ask: "Does it work?" They want some assurance that the changes they are being asked to endorse and finance will meet the claims made for them.

This demand, though understandable, can be intimidating to change efforts. If the taking of new initiatives is conditioned on advanced proof of their effectiveness, there will be no initiatives. Such a demand grossly underestimates the complexity of reform efforts. Recognizing this complexity, both practitioners and those engaged in evaluation have been advocating controlled experimentation with community policing in demonstration projects prior to full-scale implementation. They have been advocating evaluations in which the objective is not to estimate program impact, but to provide feedback to practitioners that can then be used to refine programs. And they have engaged in evaluations of the process of change, so that agencies can learn more about what it takes to change direction and adopt new strategies. Given the complexity of change in large bureaucracies, it is widely recognized by both practitioners and evaluators that sufficient time must be allowed to learn from the earliest experiences, to make the inevitable adjustments required in new programs, and to allow them to take hold. If, in response to public pressures, the ultimate questions about effectiveness are prematurely asked, the results are inevitably likely to be negative. Such a pattern would discourage innovation and stifle the work of innovative police administrators.

The broad meaning and expectations associated with community policing and the hunger for evaluations of it place a heavier than usual responsibility on those who undertake evaluations, for there is bound to be a tendency, in the public forum, to use the results of evaluations in a somewhat indiscriminate manner to unduly promote or unjustly discredit the entire movement. This requires appropriate caution in the claims made for the current capacity to evaluate programs. It requires a high degree of precision and clarity in reporting the results of evaluations. And up front, it requires determining what is appropriately subject to evaluation and in designing evaluations that, in a sensible manner, measure progress in achieving reasonable, incremental, and specifically defined goals. Making this judgment requires some awareness of what it takes, in the form of time allocations, training, staffing, and administrative arrangements, to create a reasonable opportunity that an initiative will succeed, for it makes no sense to invest more in an evaluation than in the programmatic change it is designed to evaluate.

Dennis P. Rosenbaum has performed an extremely valuable service by collecting, in this volume, the work of some heroic souls who have, despite the difficulties identified, ventured forth—attempting as best they could to evaluate specific elements of community policing projects. They have struggled with some of the difficult issues posed here. Their pioneering efforts reflect, in their variety and unevenness, the diversity and fragility of the equally admirable experiments they evaluate. Rosenbaum interleaves these studies with several helpful syntheses of past evaluations and a series of essays offering thoughtful criticisms and raising provocative questions about the community policing movement. Bringing these chapters together in this volume affords interested parties a convenient opportunity to become familiar with the current work on evaluating community policing; provides a good sense for the state of such work and for the complexity of the task; and sets an important benchmark to which the subsequent literature on evaluation can be related.

—*Herman Goldstein*
Madison, Wisconsin

Preface

RESEARCH OVER THE PAST 20 years has underscored the limitations of the "professional law enforcement" model of policing that continues to dominate the practices of most police departments today, but only in the past few years has there been a widespread movement to replace this model with a radically different approach referred to as "community policing." The forces behind this reform movement are numerous, but the visible failure of traditional policing methods to impact permanently the salient problems of violent crime, drug trafficking, gang activity, and police-community relations has only hastened the push to find a more effective and just paradigm for policing in the 1990s. In a nutshell, hundreds of cities have decided that "business as usual"—asking the police to drive around randomly in squad cars and respond to radio calls—does little to address or alleviate persistent community problems.

These same communities have turned to community policing as the promising alternative. In fact, community policing has become so attractive that nearly every politician and police chief today wants to jump on the bandwagon. Unfortunately, as the wagon leaves town, there is one big problem—we don't have answers to the most fundamental questions, including, (1) What is community policing, and how is it superior to the conventional model? (2) Can community policing, however defined, be translated into workable programs, policies, and practices? (3) If implemented, will community policing make a difference; that is, will it have the desired effects on police organizations, police personnel, community residents, and targeted neighborhood problems? The community policing reform movement has created both unwavering advocates and staunch critics, each group believing it has the definitive answers to these questions, based largely on speculation and personal opinion. I proposed this book to address these questions and help facilitate a rational discussion of the "facts" regarding (1) the resources and processes employed under the label of "community policing" and (2) the measurable effects of these organizational efforts both internally and externally. In sum, this collection of empirical works is intended to help the field move beyond "smoke and mirrors," rhetoric, and politics to begin testing the promises associated with genuine police reform efforts.

At this moment in the history of policing, there is no simple or commonly shared definition of community policing, either in theory or practice. Arguably, there is a shared set of theory-based ideas (and philosophical principles) that serve as the impetus for a wide array of changes in police organizations and operations. One of the objectives of this book is to help advance our current thinking about theories of community/problem-oriented policing in the context of numerous experimental efforts to make it happen in the field. Each author has, in his or her own way, helped to sharpen the discourse about community policing and clarify the dimensions of this concept.

Perhaps more importantly, the contributors to this book have sought to document the policies and practices that represent the most current operational definitions of community policing in various communities around the world. The overwhelming popularity of community policing has made it difficult to distinguish rhetoric from reality in the field. Police scholars and administrators suspect (or in some cases, know) that the gap between theory and practice is substantial, but the precise nature, extent, and causes of this discrepancy are often unknown. This is where social science research and program evaluations can play a critical role. The authors attempt to shed light on the nature of this gap by carefully documenting the planning, implementation, and impact of these new initiatives.

Overview of Book Contents

In the Foreword, Herman Goldstein, the widely respected father of problem-oriented policing, provides both encouragement and caution regarding the use of evaluations in this field. In Part 1, Eck and Rosenbaum attempt to establish a theoretical framework to guide researchers, policy makers, and police administrators in their efforts to evaluate community policing. They offer a conceptual framework "for understanding what community policing is and is not in contemporary discourse." By focusing on the dimensions of effectiveness, equity, and efficiency the authors are able to spell out the diverse expectations for community policing (i.e., "the promises") and distinguish this reform movement from previous eras in police history.

Moving from theory to practice, Part 2 offers the reader a clear sense of how community policing is currently being developed and implemented in many cities across the United States and Canada. The studies reported here represent large-scale, multisite assessments that capture the diversity, as well as commonality, of community policing strategies. In Chapter 2, Sadd and Grinc report on their evaluation of the Innovative Neighborhood Oriented Policing (INOP) programs in eight cities—Hayward, California; Houston, Texas; Louisville, Kentucky; New York, New York; Norfolk, Virginia; Portland, Oregon; Prince George's County, Maryland; and Tempe, Arizona. Relying on qualitative data from their site visits, Sadd and Grinc describe the programs, issues in implementation, and apparent impact on several community-related outcomes. Noteworthy is their attention to interagency cooperation and community involvement. In Chapter 3, Weisel and Eck describe their evaluation of community policing programs in six cities—Las Vegas, Nevada; Edmonton, Alberta; Philadelphia; Santa Barbara, California; Savannah, Georgia; and Newport News, Virginia. Unlike Sadd and Grinc in their evaluation of the INOP programs, Weisel and Eck were free to select jurisdictions where community policing was already in place as a defining characteristic of the agency. Although case study methods were also employed in this evaluation, the authors use the results of a standardized police officer survey to document convergence and differences among agencies with regard to planning, operational practices, and police attitudes toward community policing. Individual factors related to internal resistance to change are given particular attention.

Part 3 further advances our understanding of the internal workings of organizational reform by giving the reader a more in-depth analysis of how individual police agencies have grappled with key issues and obstacles during program development and implementation. Using both quantitative and qualitative methods, these site-specific studies document the processes involved in planning and implementing community policing, as well as the impact of these activities on the police organization and its employees. In Chapter 4, Wycoff and Skogan report findings from their quasi-experimental evaluation of the widely touted program in Madison, Wisconsin. The authors describe the development of new management strategies in Madison, known as "quality policing," and report the impact of these reform efforts on both police personnel and community residents. In Chapter 5, Greene, Bergman, and McLaughlin describe the evolutionary process of organizational and cultural change within a much larger agency—the Philadelphia Police Department. The authors give particular attention to the origins of the change agenda, the impact of the police culture on the reform process, and the community partnerships that developed as a result of these initiatives. In a similar vein, Wilkinson and Rosenbaum (Chapter 6) describe a comprehensive effort to plan and implement community policing programs in two midwestern cities—Aurora and Joliet, Illinois. The authors explore how each agency's organizational structure and commitment to participatory management facilitated or inhibited the implementation of community policing and problem-solving initiatives.

In Chapter 7, Capowich and Roehl take a close look at problem-oriented policing in San Diego, focusing on the nature and effectiveness of police officer behavior as officers attempt to resolve drug, crime, and disorder problems. The authors describe and evaluate the actions of San Diego police officers in the context of the four-step SARA model—scanning, analysis, response, and assess-ment—and illustrate the nature and effectiveness of police actions with three problem-solving case studies. In Chapter 6, Lurigio and Rosenbaum attempt to eliminate some of the present ambiguity about "what works" by reviewing the available research literature concerning the effects of community policing pro-grams on police personnel. Their view was motivated by the argument that "police departments will not be prepared to achieve effective problem solving and community partnerships until the beliefs, perceptions, attitudes, and behav-iors of individual officers become more compatible with the redefinition and enlargement of their jobs as described by the community policing model."

Part 4 gives primary attention to the impact of community policing on neighborhoods and individual residents. The community policing literature is replete with rhetoric and theorizing about how these new forms of policing can improve the quality of life in urban neighborhoods, yet there have been few good evaluations that address this hypothesis. In Chapter 9, Skogan pulls together some of the major studies to examine the implementation and impact of various community policing strategies on community residents and their local environ-ment. Through his reanalysis of community data in six U.S. cities—Oakland, California; Birmingham, Alabama; Baltimore, Maryland; Madison, Wisconsin; Houston, Texas; and Newark, New Jersey—Skogan is able to contrast commu-nity policing initiatives with intense enforcement programs in terms of their effect on fear of crime, assessments of police service, neighborhood disorder, victimization, and drug availability. In Chapter 10, Cordner evaluates a public housing foot patrol program in Lexington, Kentucky, that more closely resem-bles a crackdown than community policing. Because foot patrol continues to be the backbone of many community policing operations, Cordner's chapter is important for reviewing the foot patrol literature and highlighting the fact that foot patrol, per se, is not necessarily synonymous (or even consistent) with either community policing or problem-oriented policing. Finally, in Chapter 11, Tien and Rich describe their evaluation of the COMPASS program in four Hartford, Connecticut, neighborhoods. COMPASS was a "weed and seed" anti-drug partnership involving the police, other city agencies, and the community in an effort to reclaim and then stabilize target neighborhoods. Through a combination of data sources, the authors illustrate the difficulty of going beyond successful enforcement activities (i.e., "weeding") to establish long-term plans and work-ing relationships among agencies that can stabilize the neighborhood (i.e., "seeding").

Part 5 gives the reader an international perspective on community policing. Leighton provides an overview of developments in Canada and summarizes the findings from the two major evaluations. He also discusses some of the key issues that have emerged in Canada and future directions for community polic-ing. Bennett assesses community policing in Britain, covering theory, public policy, operational strategies, and evaluation data. He examines the extent to which the philosophies of "community policing" (although rarely described in these terms in Britain) are apparent in public policy and police practice, and examines the effectiveness of these actions from an evaluation perspective. Both Leighton and Bennett discuss the role of community in these innovations. (For additional insights regarding practices around the world, including Singapore and cities in Australia and Japan, see Bayley's chapter in Part 6.)

Part 6 of this book is unique because it does not focus on the findings from empirical studies (although some are discussed). Rather, this section was included to give leading scholars and community experts an opportunity to discuss key issues and concerns about community policing at this point in the reform movement. The authors manage to cover a wide range of issues that are relevant to either program policy or program evaluation. Roberg articulates a variety of obstacles within the police organization that must be addressed before community policing can be effectively implemented. Trojanowicz discusses the future of community policing, identifies many barriers that must be removed, and proposes a new partnership/coalition between the "Big Five" (police, community, social agencies, political leaders, and the media). Similarly, Friedman underscores the importance of developing "problem-solving partnerships" in which the community plays a critical role as an active, informed partner with the police rather than serving as a passive observer or recipient. Offering a divergent perspective, Buerger explores several possible roles for the community and questions whether current community activities can live up to the promises and produce any real impact on neighborhoods. The two closing chapters in this section have direct implications for evaluators. Weisburd examines the tensions that are inherent in the roles of evaluators and practitioners, especially in the political environment of community policing reform. Bayley draws on his experiences around the world to question the feasibility of evaluating community policing when the operational definitions are so different from one country to the next and from one city to the next.

In Part 7, Moore tackles the difficult task of synthesizing and assessing the research findings and commentaries presented in this book. He draws out key observations and implications and explores the challenges that lie ahead for both researchers and practitioners. Moore examines what we have learned from this collection of works about the concept of community policing, the feasibility of community policing reform, and the effectiveness of these initiatives. Because his assessment of the current state of affairs is optimistic on the whole, Moore also recommends actions to accelerate the present movement toward community policing.

Acknowledgments

I would like to acknowledge the National Institute of Justice and the Bureau of Justice Assistance (Office of Justice Programs, U.S. Department of Justice) for their roles in funding many of the demonstration and evaluation projects reported in this book. Developing, testing, and disseminating innovative ideas is very difficult in the absence of adequate external funds, and these agencies in particular should be applauded for their commitment to police reform. Last, but certainly not least, on behalf of the contributors, I want to thank the many police departments, community groups, service agencies, and community residents who participated in this research and gave so generously of their time. Because of their participation, others have the opportunity to learn from their experiences.

—Dennis P. Rosenbaum
Chicago, Illinois

PART

I

Community Policing in Theory

1

The New Police Order

Effectiveness, Equity, and Efficiency in Community Policing

JOHN E. ECK

DENNIS P. ROSENBAUM

COMMUNITY POLICING has become the new orthodoxy for cops. Simultaneously ambitious and ambiguous, community policing promises to change radically the relationship between the police and the public, address underlying community problems, and improve the living conditions in neighborhoods. One reason for its popularity is that community policing is a plastic concept, meaning different things to different people. There are many perspectives on community policing, and each of them is built on assumptions that are only partially supported by empirical evidence.

This chapter will establish a conceptual framework for understanding what community policing is and is not in contemporary discourse. By articulating some of the central (although sometimes conflicting) expectations that we hold for community policing, we are able to distinguish this reform movement from previous initiatives and make its unique features more amenable to critical policy analysis and scientific evaluation.

In both theory and practice, the dominance of the community policing movement is evident. First, there is a large and growing literature on this topic. The

AUTHORS' NOTE: This chapter is supported, in part, under award 91-IJ-CX-K0007 from the National Institute of Justice. Points of view in this chapter do not necessarily represent the official position of the U.S. Department of Justice.

growth of this literature began in the mid-1980s, but exploded with the publication of Greene and Mastrofski's (1988) anthology, *Community Policing: Rhetoric or Reality*. There are at least six other books on this subject (Goldstein, 1990; McElroy, Cosgrove, & Sadd, 1993; Skolnick & Bayley, 1986; Sparrow, Moore, & Kennedy, 1990; Trojanowicz & Bucqueroux, 1989; and Toch & Grant, 1991). Police executives also have written extensively on this subject (Brown, 1985, 1989; Couper & Lobitz, 1991; Stamper, 1992; Wadman & Olson, 1990; Williams & Sloan, 1990).

At the conferences of major police executive organizations—Police Executive Research Forum (PERF), International Association of Chiefs of Police (IACP), and National Sheriff's Association (NSA)—sessions on community policing are prominent and well attended. In fall 1992, four national conferences were held on community policing. In 1993 at least three such conferences were held. The Federal Government has recognized the emergence of community policing by funding various projects through various branches of the Department of Justice.[1] Presidents Bush and Clinton have made community policing a key element in their administrations' efforts to fight crime and rebuild cities.

Proponents of community policing can no longer claim to be fighting the battle alone against a sea of opposition. Although internal resistance to such innovation continues to be formidable in many departments, the fact remains that community policing is the only form of policing available for anyone who seeks to improve police operations, management, or relations with the public. The reason for this is simple. Community policing is part of a larger set of changes in progress throughout the United States. Many of the management practices that community policing advocates—decentralizing decision making, problem-solving teams, attention to customer needs, and others—are used widely in industry. Racial fairness, another theme in community policing, is a resurgent theme throughout society. Community policing is only one manifestation of a larger social concern with quality of life issues. And renewed faith in community empowerment and self-help pervades discussions of how to address virtually any social problem. In short, there are many forces in society that support the full-scale adaptation of community policing and discourage the decline of this reform movement.

With all this interest and activity, one might assume that community policing is a well-defined idea. As early as 1985, however, concern was being expressed that community policing was not a unitary concept (Murphy & Muir, 1985). Bayley (1988) expanded on this concern:

> Despite the benefits claimed for community policing, programmatic implementation of it has been very uneven. Although widely, almost universally, said to be important, it means different things to different people—public relations campaigns, shopfronts and mini-stations, rescaled patrol beats, liaison with ethnic groups, permission for rank-and-file to speak to the press, Neighborhood Watch, foot patrols, patrol-detective teams, and door-to-door visits by police officers. Community policing on the ground often seems less a program than a set of aspirations wrapped in a slogan. (p. 225)

The diversity of police programs that fit under the community policing umbrella can be seen in the programs operating under a single Bureau of Justice Assistance initiative, the Innovative Neighborhood Oriented Policing (INOP) program. The eight sites initiated a variety of projects within this program, including ombudsmen, coordinating councils, mobile and stationary mini-stations, enforcement crackdowns, advertising campaigns, problem-solving efforts, and foot patrols (see Sadd & Grinc, Chapter 2, this volume). This range of approaches to community policing is indicative of the flexibility of the concept as well as the difficulty of defining what it is. The diversity and the lack of definition of community policing has generated critical discussion. Manning (1988), Mastrofski (1988), and Klockars (1988) attack the vagueness of community policing and question whether it can result in substantive changes in the performance of the police. Weatheritt (1988) describes how this vagueness was used by police in Great Britain to enhance their public image without having to change their organizations or the behavior of their constables.

Organizing the diverse views on community policing into a coherent whole is a daunting and possibly futile task. So much has been said by so many police officials, policy analysts, researchers, and theoreticians that one sometimes wonders if they are talking about the same thing. So many claims have been made about community policing—with and without evidence—that one wonders if it is possible for community policing to deliver on all or even most of them.

Framework for Understanding
Community Policing Expectations

The public asks a number of things of the police. First, it asks that the police be effective at carrying out their function. This question requires us to determine what the police function is. Some of the discussions of community policing, and all of the discussions of problem-oriented policing, are concerned primarily with the effectiveness of police services. The next question we ask is that these services be equitably distributed. That is, that the police act in a fair and responsive manner while carrying out their functions. Equity issues are at the core of many forms of community policing, especially those advocated in response to serious crises resulting from police abuses of force. Finally, we ask that effectiveness be achieved at minimal cost or that the resources provided the police be used in the most productive manner possible. Efficiency concerns are about the means of policing: hiring, training, performance measurement, organizational structure, technology, integrity, morale, policies, and procedures. Efficiency dominates most discussions of community policing, just as it has dominated discussions of the styles of policing that preceded it.

Community policing developed in response to increased realization that established forms of policing were far less effective, equitable, and efficient than had been imagined. But discussions of community policing seldom distinguish effectiveness, equity, and efficiency, in part because these are often inseparable. Attempts to redress one deficiency, say equity, are often seen as addressing the other two. For example, it has been asserted, with little hard evidence, that involving members of the community in police decision making (equity) simultaneously makes people feel that the police are responsive (equity), helps reduce neighborhood crime (effectiveness), and can reduce the police workload (efficiency). Similarly, it has been claimed that decentralizing decision making (efficiency) makes officers better able to address community problems (effectiveness), makes officers more accountable to citizens (equity), and makes better use of police resources (efficiency).

By not distinguishing among these three requirements, and by not clearly separating the means of policing from the ends it serves, community policing advocates have made it more difficult to achieve meaningful improvements in policing and have made it easier for some police administrators to enact cosmetic changes disguised as fundamental reforms. Confusing these conceptually distinct requirements also has led to exaggerated claims that have the potential of undermining legitimate claims. Finally, confusing effectiveness, equity, and efficiency makes it more difficult to evaluate the successes of community policing.

In this chapter we will examine community policing in terms of effectiveness, equity, and efficiency. In doing so, we will compare how earlier forms of policing have applied these three concepts to how they have been applied in community policing. This will reveal those features that distinguish community policing from the forms of policing that it grew out of. We will also use these concepts to critically examine a number of claims for community policing. Finally, we will describe how these three concepts can be used to measure the performance of community policing so that the claims can be empirically verified.

Effectiveness and the Police Function

The function of policing always has been a subject of discussion and policing has undergone several changes in function (Fogelson, 1977; Monkkonen, 1992). Community policing is, in part, the latest attempt to answer the question, Why do we have a police force and what services should it deliver? There are a number of histories of policing and this chapter is not the place to recount past debates over the appropriate role of policing in society. To understand how community policing departs from police practice of a decade ago, however, we need to examine the principal functions the police performed.

First, police are a part of society's attempts to control crime. The fact that much of what police do appears to have little to do with crime (Reiss, 1971) does not diminish the fact that police agencies are the principal arm of local government that have crime control as one of its mandates. The traditional approach to carrying out this function is through the criminal justice system. There are three traditional methods the police could use to control crime in this manner, and each requires the apprehension of criminal offenders. First, through the application of deterrence, potential offenders might be frightened into keeping to the straight and narrow, and active offenders might be scared into abating their criminal careers. Second, locking the most active offenders away for prolonged periods could prevent them from preying on members of the public. Or, third, once caught, offenders could be rehabilitated to lead more socially acceptable lives.

A series of National Academy of Sciences studies has cast doubt on the efficacy of each of these traditional means of crime prevention and control (Blumstein, Cohen, & Nagin, 1978; Blumstein, Cohen, Roth, & Visher, 1986; Sechrest, White, & Brown, 1979). Police-specific studies questioned whether the standard police strategies of random patrolling, rapid response, and follow-up investigative work resulted in more arrests and less crime (Greenwood, Chaiken, & Petersilia, 1977; Kelling, Pate, Dieckman, & Brown, 1974; Spelman & Brown, 1984). Despite evidence that police are unlikely to have a great impact on crime on a large scale, crime control has remained an important function of policing.

A second function of policing is the rendering of immediate aid to people in crisis. The emergency response function is related to crime control, but can be considered independent of its impact on crime. Even if arriving rapidly at the scene of a crime or other emergency does not prevent future reoccurrences of that type of event, police can provide aid and assistance to people in trouble. A 911 system may not frighten offenders, but it probably gives comfort to members of the public who feel that if something goes terribly wrong they can get assistance quickly.

Also related to the crime control function, but conceptually distinct, is the police role in serving justice. Again, even if arresting a suspect does not reduce future criminal acts, it is important that people who misbehave are given some measure of punishment. The saturation of the criminal justice system with offenders has undermined this important function of the police, but the function still exists and is unlikely to be removed from the police.

The fourth and last traditional function of policing is the delivery of a variety of nonemergency services. These include such tasks as giving directions to lost tourists, controlling traffic, helping motorists whose cars have broken down, and so forth. These services are often placed in secondary importance to crime related functions, but they occupy a great deal of police time. Nevertheless, the police have slowly divested themselves of many of these services as other specialized agencies of government have taken them over (Monkkonen, 1992).

These functions—crime control, emergency aid, nonemergency services, and justice—have not been discarded by community policing advocates. Instead, community policing rearranges priorities among functions and adds new ones.

Nonemergency services take on greater importance. Crime control, emergency aid, and justice become less prominent relative to nonemergency services for four reasons: They make up such a small portion of police work that police organizations should not be organized around these functions; research has shown that the police are not particularly effective in carrying out these functions; when asked, the public is more frequently concerned about noncriminal, nonemergency quality-of-life problems; and researchers have suggested that the presence of social and physical disorder, if left unchecked, can lead to more serious neighborhood problems, including criminality (Skogan, 1990).

For some police executives community policing has to do with their beliefs (and social science theories) about the role of community in preventing crime. Community theories suggest that social order is maintained primarily by informal social processes within the neighborhood and not by police activity, thus underscoring the importance of citizen participation and the utilization of available community resources for preventing crime (Bursik & Grasmick, 1993; Byrne & Sampson, 1986; Rosenbaum, 1988). Because police have been given the public resources and mandate to fight crime, however, they have been encouraged to take a leadership role in stimulating community action and developing partnerships with community organizations and agencies (Lavrakas, 1985; Rosenbaum, Hernandez, & Daughtry, 1991). A fundamental objective of this community engagement perspective is to help create self-regulating, self-sufficient communities where levels of crime and disorder are contained by the efforts of local residents and local institutions.

Unfortunately, there is limited evidence that informal social control processes and collective crime prevention behaviors can be "implanted" in neighborhoods characterized by social disorganization and the absence of these behaviors, although comprehensive efforts certainly hold some promise (see Rosenbaum, 1986, 1988; Skogan, 1990). Furthermore, there is concern on the part of both the police and community leaders about whether police should be in the business of organizing communities, given the complex politics represented by diverse ethnic and racial needs.

A community's ability to regulate and defend itself is in part related to individuals' perceptions about crime. So community policing added fear of crime to the portfolio of police concerns. The rational behind this was twofold: Research had shown that fear of crime was influenced by many factors other than objective risks of crime (Rosenbaum et al., 1991; Skogan & Maxfield, 1981), and it was suggested that fear of crime undermined neighborhood cohesiveness and led to the deterioration of communities (Skogan, 1990; Wilson & Kelling, 1982). Making fear of crime a center piece of community policing presents two difficulties. First, police do not claim expertise on factors that contribute to fear or effective methods of reducing fear. Second, because fear of crime is often associated with the presence of racially or ethnically dissimilar groups within the community (Anderson, 1990; Heitgerd & Bursik, 1987; Merry, 1981; Suttles, 1968; Taub, Taylor, & Dunham, 1984), police can find it difficult simultaneously to reduce fear, respond to divergent community desires, and provide equitable services (Gottlieb, 1993). Nevertheless, there is some evidence that increased contact with the public can have a fear-reducing effect (Pate, Wycoff, Skogan, & Sherman, 1986; Skogan, 1990).

When the Baltimore County Police Department added fear of crime to the problems it would address, it took a problem-oriented approach (Cordner, 1986; Goldstein, 1979). A problem-oriented approach does not start with a tactical solution to a problem and seek to apply it to all occurrences of the problem. Instead, it begins with the peculiar circumstances that give rise to the problem and then looks for a situational solution (Clarke, 1992; Goldstein, 1979, 1990). That this solution may be unique—and never used again—is of little concern. The situational strategy of problem-oriented policing is a radical departure from the generic posture of traditional policing and some forms of community policing (Eck, 1993). Community policing experts should not be concerned by the repeated application of police tactics or methods to *identify or analyze* local problems (e.g., interviews, meetings, or door-to-door visits with citizens), but rather by their repeated application as *solutions* to local problems.

When one examines the fear-fighting experiments that are associated with community policing, some of these efforts represent a departure from traditional means-oriented policing, while others do not (see Pate et al., 1986; Police Foundation, 1981; Skogan, 1990). The decision to operationalize community policing as foot patrol, for example, would not be a departure from means-oriented policing unless officers were specifically instructed to gather information about possible fear-inducing problems or the police department was responding to a known fear problem. Whenever problem-oriented goals and objectives are built into this process, a police organization cannot be accused of engaging in foot patrol "for the sake of foot patrol"—a motivation that is all too common these days.

Problem-oriented policing reorganizes the police role. Emergency aid and justice are still important functions, but crime and nonemergency services are now seen as two broad classes of problems, as are fear of crime and quality of life concerns. The problem is a primary unit of police work (for the justice function the offender or victim is the unit of work and for emergency aid the event or incident is the unit of work). Goldstein (1990) defined a problem as

a cluster of similar, related, or recurring incidents rather than a single incident; a substantive community concern; a unit of police business. (p. 66)

This definition emphasizes the importance of the public in defining a problem. Ideally, problem solving needs a high level of community engagement to identify problems, to develop an understanding of the particular circumstances that give rise to them, to craft enduring preventive remedies, and to evaluate the effectiveness of the remedies. Without community engagement many problems will be difficult to detect, it will be hard for the police to learn about the circumstances that give rise to them, solutions will be harder to craft, and police will have limited means for determining their effectiveness (Eck & Spelman, 1987). In reality, the extent to which police agencies have solicited community input and participation in the problem-solving process varies significantly from one jurisdiction to the next, and community leaders sometimes complain about having limited input (see Sunset Park Restoration Committee, 1993). The nature, extent, and productivity of community participation in community policing is an important question for research and policy analysis.

Goldstein's definition of problems also emphasized that they are made up of events and events are potential symptoms of problems. An incident that occurs once and has little chance of occurring again is not a problem. The implication is that the purpose behind addressing problems is not to redress past wrongs but to prevent future harmful events.

Problem handling represents a departure from the past in another way. The theoretical basis for traditional police crime control has been deterrence, incapacitation, or rehabilitation. All three rely on the application of the criminal law, and as noted above, the efficacy of such a strategy of crime control is dubious. A problem-oriented approach adds a variety of ways to control crime that do not rely on the application of the criminal law. Some might be classified as situational crime prevention (Clarke, 1992). Other tactics could be classified as social prevention, addressing the root causes of crime, and relying on education and redirection of potential offenders before they get into trouble (see Rosenbaum & Lurigio, in press). And other tactics rely on the use of the civil law to change behaviors.

Community policing changes the way effectiveness is measured. Numbers of arrests and prosecutions may be crude measures of how well the police contribute to achieving justice, and response time may still be a useful gauge for measuring police handling of emergency incidents, but other measures take on greater importance. In particular, two effectiveness questions are critical: Do the police detect problems that are important to most members of the community? And do the problems the police handle decline in magnitude or seriousness as a result? If the police do not detect important problems, then they cannot address them. But even if they address them, they may not reduce the harmful effects of the problems.

Equity and the Engagement of the Public

Another long-standing concern to policing is the relationship between the police and the public. This concern was central to the debates leading to the formation of the first uniformed civil police force in London (Critchley, 1979), it shaped the form policing took when the London model was adapted to the United States (Miller, 1977), and it is a central theme in recent reform commission reports calling for community policing (Independent Commission on the Los Angeles Police Department, 1991; Philadelphia Police Study Task Force, 1987).

There are two common methods of judging the equity, or fairness, of modern policing. The first is based on legal principles. Here, police are judged to be fair if they follow the rules, that is, due process based on constitutional principles as interpreted by court decisions, legislatures, and legal authorities (the local prosecutor, city attorney, or department legal advisor). If a citizen or group of citizens complains about the fairness of police actions, then the police defend themselves by claiming that officers are simply enforcing the laws and following the procedures laid down by others. Wilson (1968) describes the extreme reliance on this way of justifying police action as the "legalistic" form of policing. Skolnick (1966) points out that the ideals of due process often run counter to other demands on policing, principally efficiency. The second method of judging equity involves the distribution of resources or outcomes. A complaint that a community does not receive the same level of police service might be met by a police claim that response times, the number of officers per capita, the number of officers per crime, or the number of crimes per resident is the same across all communities.

These approaches to equity may be acceptable if the population is homogeneous or no group feels excluded from local politics. If, however, a sizeable group feels that the local political system and its government bureaucracies are unresponsive, then appeals to procedure or statistics will not address claims of inequitable treatment. Community policing is sometimes a response to the inadequacy of these methods for judging equity. Though steeped in euphemistic rhetoric, the "community" in community policing often, but not always, refers to groups who have not traditionally been in the mainstream of society.

Following recent crises in public confidence in large city policing, public commissions have called for the implementation of community policing (Independent Commission on the Los Angeles Police Department, 1991; Philadelphia Police Study Task Force, 1987). Though reports of commissions established to investigate policing address effectiveness, the precipitating events that created a sense of crisis have little to do with effectiveness. Instead they almost always involve the use of force against a nonwhite citizen and a long history of complaints by minority groups about unresponsive and inequitable treatment by the police. For some cities, though not all, community policing is an attempt to forge links between police and previously excluded communities. In this context community policing can be viewed as an outgrowth of the civil rights movement and the ascendancy to power of non-European groups in large cities. And in this sense community policing is a professional approach to Wilson's (1968) watchman style of policing, in that fairness in both styles is particularistic and personal, rather than rule bound and bureaucratic.

Equity is no longer simply defined as adherence to due process or numerical parity. Instead, community policing seeks to build trust and change the perceptions of communities toward the police, and of police officers toward communities. The principal means for achieving a sense that the police are fair and responsive is through personal contacts. The methods for community engagement vary from the deployment of foot officers to community organizing. Apart from any substantive impact on problems, one of the central objectives of these efforts is to place police employees in close prolonged contact with the same group of residents. This contact is intended to close the physical and psychological distance between the police and the community. Unless there is an explicit emphasis on addressing other problems, however, community empowerment does not necessarily require that problems be addressed or solved. Thus working directly to achieve equity will not necessarily produce more effective police, but working to solve community problems may build partnerships and improve equity as a by-product (cf. Goldstein, 1990).

Regardless of whether high-crime neighborhoods can be "turned around" through community empowerment initiatives, on a more limited scale the community perspective calls for greater citizen involvement in police decision making and problem-solving efforts. Equity concerns typically imply a passive role for citizens ("Did we get our fair share of police service?"), but in a growing number of urban communities with active neighborhood groups, equity is more about participatory management and power sharing ("Did the police ask us which problems are the most important for our community?" or "Did the police demonstrate a desire to work with us as equal partners in developing anticrime and antidrug initiatives?"). In sum, although equity efforts in the context of community policing are typically limited to increasing the number of police-citizen contacts, the community outreach perspective can be, and has been, taken to another level. New police-community relationships (established by additional contact) can be used to enhance citizen involvement in decision making, problem solving, community self-defense, and various community empowerment actions. The popular methods for communication with the public (e.g., door-to-door interviews, foot patrols, community meetings, mini-stations) can provide vehicles for attacking specific local problems if police management will use them as such.

The appropriate measure of equity changes with a move to community policing. Traditional measures such as compliance with due process, use of force, and the distribution of services remain important gauges of equity. However, the most relevant measures are the perceptions of the various publics served by the police. How people feel about the police is as critical, if not more critical, than other measures of equity. Both the quantity and quality of police-citizen contacts are considered important measures of police performance under many community policing programs. It is for this reason that police agencies in Reno (NV) and Madison (WI) routinely use surveys to assess public opinion about their services. Periodic samples of public opinion can show changes in community concerns about the police and show how perceptions vary by neighborhood, age, race, gender, and other characteristics. Large stable differences among groups may be indicators of perceptions of inequity.

Efficiency in Resource Deployment and Control

Finally, there is the concern with police organization and management. Whether based on the management principles of the British military (Critchley, 1979), Taylorist theories (Wilson, 1950), or current management styles (Moore &

Stephens, 1991), how the police mobilized their resources to fulfill their mission has been a recurring theme within the writings on policing. Given demands to deliver services effectively and equitably, which management procedures help achieve these goals with the minimal cost? In particular, two concerns are paramount: How should resources be deployed in a police organization? and how should the behaviors of officers be controlled so these resources are put to use in the most effective and equitable manner?

Until recently, the resources of concern to the police could be itemized within the police operating and capital budgets. These resources included equipment, facilities, and most importantly, its personnel. If the people, equipment, or facilities were not included in the police organization, then police managers did not view them as assets. The police saw themselves as self-contained and did not ask assistance in carrying out their functions. The primary task for police managers was to allocate their resources among various divisions and deploy their personnel geographically and functionally. The decision to decentralize or centralize commands was based on whether it would reduce costs for the same results or achieve more results for the same costs.

The Achilles' heel of this approach is readily appreciated when one looks at the actual number of officers deployed on the street at any given time. Out of every 100 sworn personnel, seldom are more than 60 in the uniform patrol division (Police Executive Research Forum, 1981). Once these personnel are divided among three shifts and allowing for time off, weekends, and holidays, few are on duty at any given time. This number is further reduced because some of these officers are managers who are not engaged in street work, and many of the street officers may be in court or other off-street activities. Of the remaining officers, many others will be handling calls (Levine & McEwen, 1985). This leaves very few officers patrolling the street as a deterrent to crime. The simple arithmetic of policing suggests that in any neighborhood it is not the police who are keeping the peace, it is the public. So for the purposes of controlling crime, the assets of the police extend far beyond the police organization. The same is true of the other functions of the police; in order to pursue justice and provide emergency and nonemergency services, the police rely on citizens to report events and pass on vital information.

At the same time as the police discounted their assets they ignored their limits for taking on more work. To an individual considering whether to request police help, policing is free. Though the public does pay for policing through their taxes, people can consume unlimited amounts of police services without their individual tax bill being affected. As with all free services, customers will use much more of it than they would if there was a cost for its use. By making it easier to get this service, the telephone, radio, and squad car increased the demand for it. Without a phone, a citizen with a problem would have to seek out an officer. The inconvenience of going to a police station kept the demand for policing down prior to the widespread access to telephones and the adoption of two-way radios and cars. Call handling would be effective and efficient if answering calls prevented future calls from the same location, but recent studies of repeat calls indicate that responding to events does little to control them (Pierce, Spaar, & Briggs, 1986; Sherman, Gartin, & Buerger, 1989). So from the standpoint of simple economics, there is no staffing level for policing that would ever keep the call workload in check, as long as calling is free and easy.

Community policing departs from previous styles of policing by the way resources are counted and the methods by which control over officer behavior is exerted. Many of the assets needed to address problems are outside the boundaries of police organizations. These assets are the powers and resources of other government agencies, businesses, and the community itself. Bolstering the capacities of others can help the police become more effective without requiring proportional increases in police controlled resources. When officers of the Baltimore County police discovered that the county needed a detoxification center to handle chronic alcoholics to address a panhandler problem around a shopping center, the department requested that the county establish such a facility. When San Diego police officers found that violent crimes at a trolley stop were facilitated by the station's physical design, they asked the trolley authority to make the required changes. When a Newport News police detective wanted to reduce domestic homicides he established a multiagency task force involving local hospitals, the prosecutor, the newspaper, women's groups, military bases, and various other stakeholders in the problem. The common theme to these examples is that the police expand their capacity to address community concerns by using the resources of other groups. This stands in stark contrast to the standard practices of trying to carry out the police function with existing police resources or by requesting greater resources.

Community policing advocates have advanced the idea that organized citizens can control crime and improve neighborhood conditions, and therefore police should mobilize neighborhood groups. As noted earlier, the empirical support for this idea is limited (Rosenbaum, 1988; Skogan, 1990). The weak empirical support may be because insufficient research has been conducted on the precise mechanisms by which organized communities could control crime and improve the quality of community life. There are five means by which citizens can help accomplish these ends. First, they can watch and report suspicious behavior and other information to police officials. Police have promoted passive involvement through the formation of Neighborhood Watch groups. Second, citizens can patrol areas, confront suspicious people, and ask that they leave the area or change their behaviors. Active involvement is less common than passive involvement, and police agencies often try to thwart active involvement because of safety concerns. Nevertheless, some police have encouraged such actions. Third, citizens can change their own behavior to reduce their chances of becoming victims of crime or inadvertently contributing to a deterioration of the quality of life in a neighborhood. Police crime prevention programs frequently promote personal safety precautions. Fourth, citizens can put pressure on others to act: They can demand more police resources, they can pressure businesses to change their practices, they can lobby local government agencies to obtain services and get favorable rulings from regulators, and they can threaten property owners and organizations with civil suits to change behaviors and physical conditions. Unlike the first and third methods, here citizens do not directly confront the problem with their own resources, but use their legal and political powers to gain external resources. Exerting pressure is a tactic that has been highly effective for many community organizations, as documented in case studies (Rosenbaum, 1993). Fifth, citizens can authorize the police to act on their behalf. Knowing this, community police officers will meet with community members and gain their acquiescence, thereby allowing the police to act. By building a rapport with neighborhood residents, officers can carry out enforcement actions that would be otherwise unacceptable (Eck, 1993; Weisburd, McElroy, & Hardyman, 1988).

Though these methods of contributing to neighborhood safety are important, many of these actions are indirect, operating through the police or other organizations. This is because to take direct action on problems one must have resources and special powers, which community organizations often lack. For example, the residents of an apartment complex may want a drug dealer to leave the complex, but only the landlord can evict him. A community may want a local liquor store to stop selling fortified wine to chronic alcoholics, but only the owner of the store can curtail this behavior. Citizens can pressure the landlord or the liquor store owner (threatening a rent boycott, picketing, adverse publicity, or a suit), or they can get the police or a regulatory agency to apply pressure for them. In either case, the actions of the citizen group are to get others to act on their behalf. Sometimes, these pressures can be very effective if the community has the necessary organizing skills or clout. Other times, community frustrations are not translated into action.

Therefore, when the police go to a community to help address a problem, there are limits on what the community can deliver and what the police can realistically expect. If police feel that community consent is not problematic, they think that they understand the problem, and they believe that they can get the help of other city agencies, the police often will handle the problem without community help (e.g., threaten the landlord with a nuisance abatement proceeding that could result in the confiscation of the apartment building unless the drug dealer is evicted, or threaten the liquor store owner with the revocation of his license to sell alcohol unless he controls whom he sells to). It can be more efficient not to involve the community. Police are especially likely to act this way in disorganized neighborhoods with little political clout and where knowledge of how to access government agencies is limited. Interestingly enough, research suggests that *if* the police were to invite community input in these neighborhoods, many, if not most, residents would support aggressive (and sometimes unconstitutional) enforcement actions by the police (Rosenbaum, 1993).[2]

Organizing resources to cope with demands for service presents one set of problems for efficiently running a police agency. Another set of problems involves control over police employees. To be effective and deliver services equitably, police officers must use their powers for the ends of the organization. Miller (1977) shows that the police in the United States have always been endowed with more discretion than their British counterparts, in large part for efficiency reasons; to save costs police agencies in the United States hired fewer officers and gave them wider latitude to make decisions while police forces in Great Britain hired more constables and gave them less discretion. Police organizations attempt to limit the discretionary authority of police officers through rules and procedures and a system of command and control. This approach is top-down and rule driven. The limits of this approach to controlling officer behavior have been widely documented (Brown, 1981; Davis, 1975; Krantz, Gilman, Benda, Hallstrom, & Nadworny, 1979; LaFave, 1965; Punch, 1983). Officers operate out of sight of their supervisors and make decisions that seldom can be directly monitored (Goldstein, 1960). Rules and procedures are more likely to proscribe behaviors than to help officers determine the appropriate behavior (Goldstein, 1977). Further, the police organization often makes demands on officers that cannot be fulfilled without violating some rule or procedure (Skolnick, 1966).

At the same time that community policing advocates promote the idea that networking with other organizations and communities is important, they also promote the idea that police organizations need to make better use of the experience and knowledge of street officers. This has taken a variety of forms from decentralization of decision making from headquarters to substations and the establishment of fixed beat assignments (Brown, 1989; Koller, 1990; Sparrow, 1988) to experiments in replacing rule-based/top-down decision making with bottom-up/value-driven decision making (Couper & Lobitz, 1991; Sparrow, 1988; Wasserman & Moore, 1988). The rationale for these changes is that to be responsive to community members and to address problems, decision makers need more information than is usually available to high-level commanders, and the police need to be more flexible than is possible by following the chain of command. These changes will bring officers closer to the communities they serve and provide them with the authority to act on their behalf.

In the process of attempting these organizational changes, police administrators and researchers recognize that community residents are not the only clients (or targets) of community policing and that internal changes may benefit police personnel as well. Authors have suggested that decentralization and participatory management, for example, will improve the morale of officers (Trojanowicz & Banas, 1985; Wycoff, 1988), despite internal resistance to change. These ideas are well grounded in organizational theory (e.g., Hackman & Oldham, 1976), but there is a paucity of well-designed studies capable of testing these and other hypotheses (see Lurigio & Rosenbaum, Chapter 8, this volume). For the most part, community policing efforts are relatively new and the officers involved are either specially selected for special assignments or the officers decided to get on board early. In either case, it is difficult to determine if changes in the administration of the department had an effect on the behavior and attitudes of the officers or whether the officers were predisposed to this type of work and already had a different view of their work as police officers before their involvement in community policing.

As community policing becomes more pervasive within police agencies, and officers do not have the option of keeping away from it, these management concepts will be put to a more rigorous test. It seems unlikely that police agencies will be able to abandon totally their many rules and procedures in deference to a mission-driven organization, or that police agencies will become fully democratic institutions instead of command bureaucracies. Instead, these newer management ideas may be layered on top of more traditional management techniques.

A major barrier to newer management ideas is the political environment that police departments must work within. Local officials with authority over the police will have to give police agencies broad authority to work with communities, address problems, and adopt a mission-driven perspective. But the police, with their monopoly on the use of force, 24-hour responsibilities, and broad mandate, will always be the center of conflicting demands. The uncertain nature of the police chief's job will maintain a demand for rules that curtail officers' authority and centralize decision making.

Because efficiency is a gauge of how well resources are used to obtain a given level of effectiveness, two yardsticks for efficiency are appropriate for community policing. First, given two equally effective community policing agencies, the agency that makes the greatest use of resources beyond its direct control should be viewed as the most efficient. These resources include those of other government and private organizations and citizens' groups. By this measure of efficiency, police agencies that are well integrated into local government service delivery systems, have extensive networks with private institutions, and have well-developed partnerships with community groups should be able to leverage their resources more than police agencies that operate autonomously. One would expect, if proponents of community policing are correct, that police agencies that have extensive collaborative arrangements will need fewer resources to achieve a given level of effectiveness than police agencies that do not.

Second, given comparable levels of effectiveness, police agencies with the fewest internal layers of bureaucratic control are more efficient than police agencies with a greater number of ranks. The parts of a police agency that directly serve the public are those parts that have direct contact with people outside the organization. The greater the ratio of service deliverers to administrators, the more services that can be provided or leveraged for a given level of resources. Agencies that find ways to guide officers to activities that are effective and equitable, with few levels of supervision, will be more efficient than agencies that are equally effective and equitable, but have more layers of supervision.

Future of Community Policing

We began this discussion by noting that a reason community policing is so difficult to define is that different proponents emphasize different aspects while using the same terminology. We have shown that organizing a discussion of community policing around effectiveness, equity, and efficiency helps clarify the concept by highlighting the aspects of community policing that are different from previous practices and suggesting methods for gauging performance.

This discussion raises the question of priority among the three concerns. Does it matter if community policing is framed in terms of efficiency, equity, or effectiveness? Which concern—effectiveness, equity, or efficiency—should be the starting point for implementing community policing? Or will beginning with any one of these concerns naturally and inevitably lead to addressing the other two? Will a police agency that starts by changing the decision-making processes of the organization also end up improving trust between the police and the public and effectively addressing problems? Will a department that starts by building trust between members of the public and the police inevitably come to addressing problems, developing partnerships with other organizations, and decentralizing decision-making authority? Will a police agency that begins by promoting effective problem solving have to engage members of communities, decentralize authority, and develop collaborative arrangements with other organizations? The answers to these questions are unclear, but we suggest three related hypotheses.

Historically, police have emphasized efficiency and equity concerns relative to effectiveness. This emphasis on means over ends was the basis for Goldstein's (1979) critique of policing and led to his development of problem-oriented policing. If a police agency begins by focusing on substantive community problems, the need to improve relationships with the public, decentralize decision-making, and create networks with other groups may become rather obvious. Most problems cannot be successfully addressed without the involvement of others and collaboration requires a level of trust. Effective problem solving also seems to require a high level of delegation of authority to line personnel. Further, the process of working on problems is likely to build trust between the police and community. Therefore, a police agency that begins by focusing on effectiveness and continually looks for ways of making the agency more effective, is likely to address equity and efficiency concerns as well. There is nothing that is inevitable about this, but if communities, other agencies, and officers' experiences are crucial to effective problem solving, then beginning with effectiveness will lead to the more equitable and efficient policing.

An agency that begins by focusing on equity may not make fundamental changes to improve the effectiveness of the police. One could reduce conflicts between the police and the public by hiring more minority officers, conducting cultural sensitivity training for officers, reducing police use of force, developing open citizen-complaint handling processes, creating stable beat assignments, and enacting a host of other policies and procedures. As important as these changes may be, none of them require the police to change their basic functions. It is not difficult to imagine a police force that focuses exclusively on handling emergency and nonemergency calls and making sure offenders are brought to justice and is seen as responsive and trustworthy by the communities it serves. In such instances, other institutions may handle community problems, with or without police assistance. A responsive police agency can easily increase the level of patrolling when community groups ask. A responsive police agency can enlist the help of local organizations to make sure officers handle incidents better. If the police are particularly good at building trust, it is quite likely that they will be able to use their support in the community to increase staffing and resources, resulting in a decrease in efficiency. In short, a focus on equity concerns without a major effort to improve effectiveness and efficiency may only change how the police are perceived by members of the public.

This improvement should not be taken lightly in inner-city neighborhoods where massive distrust between the police and the community may prohibit the development of a problem-solving partnership. But even here, our point is that unless a plan is eventually developed to attack specific crime and disorder problems, the improved attitudes about the police are unlikely to portend any major improvements in the quality of neighborhood life.

Finally, addressing efficiency issues alone is unlikely to lead to changes in police effectiveness or improvements in equity. For example, a police agency that changes the way nonemergency calls are handled—from a rapid response by an officer to taking a report over the telephone or a follow-up by a civilian employee—may reduce officers' workloads and reduce costs. But unless the time officers no longer have to spend on these calls is used to address problems, there will be no improvement in effectiveness. Neither are such policies likely to project a feeling of responsiveness to community needs. Officers may be delegated a great deal of decision-making authority but unless they are directed to address problems, and unless they are shown the appropriate ways to interact with the public, effectiveness and equity will not be addressed.

Though effectiveness is unlikely to be improved without improving equity and efficiency also, it is possible to make improvements in equity or efficiency and leave the other two areas untouched. If this is true, then three forms of community policing may develop in U.S. cities. Equitable community policing agencies would seek to improve the way police are perceived by minority communities and groups that have been traditionally left out of the mainstream. Such agencies may not necessarily be more effective or efficient than police agencies are today. Efficient community police agencies would have a few highly trained officers carry out the police function without layers of management. These agencies also could have highly developed networks with other organizations. The officers would use these networks to divert cases and shift workload. Because this may be accomplished without preventing the incidents that create the workload, efficiency would improve but effectiveness would remain unchanged. In these agencies police community relations might not be appreciably different than we see them today. Effective community policing, or problem-oriented policing agencies could be more preventive and thereby improve their effectiveness. But because prevention would require them to be responsive to communities, to collaborate with other agencies, and to decentralize decision making, these agencies might have to make strides in all three areas.

Developing performance measures for community policing and stronger evaluations will allow the testing of these hypotheses. By longitudinally measuring effectiveness, equity, and efficiency in police agencies we could determine how police agencies change and if changes in one domain influence changes in the other two. These measures would allow us to determine if community policing substantially improves police effectiveness, the equitable distribution of police services, or the efficient use of police resources.

Notes

1. In 1992 the Bureau of Justice Assistance funded a consortium of the IACP, PERF, Police Foundation, and NSA to develop a model community policing strategy and deliver technical assistance to four demonstration sites to be selected in 1993.

2. We should note that although police often act without community involvement or total consent, the reverse is also true when residents have lost confidence in the ability of the police to solve their local problems. Citizen patrols and direct actions against drug dealers have become common occurrences in neighborhoods where drug markets have emerged and citizens have come to realize that no one outside the neighborhood is going to rescue them (see Davis, Lurigio, & Rosenbaum, 1993).

References

Anderson, E. (1990). *Streetwise*. Chicago: University of Chicago Press.

Bayley, D. H. (1988). Community policing: A report from the devil's advocate. In J. R. Greene & S. D. Mastrofski (Eds.), *Community policing: Rhetoric or reality?* (pp. 225-238). New York: Praeger.

Blumstein, A., Cohen, J., & Nagin, D. (Eds.). (1978). *Deterrence and incapacitation: Estimating the effects of criminal sanctions on crime rates*. Washington, DC: National Academy of Sciences.

Blumstein, A., Cohen, J., Roth, J., & Visher, C. (1986). *Criminal careers and "career criminals"* (Vol. I). Washington, DC: National Academy of Sciences.

Brown, L. P. (1985). Community-policing power sharing. In W. A. Geller (Ed.), *Police leadership in America: Crisis and opportunity* (pp. 70-83). New York: Praeger.

Brown, L. P. (1989). *Community policing: A practical guide for police officials* (Perspectives in Policing No. 12). Washington, DC: National Institute of Justice.

Brown, M. K. (1981). *Working the street: Police discretion and the dilemmas of reform*. New York: Russell Sage Foundation.

Bursik, R. J., & Grasmick, H. G. (1993). *Neighborhoods and crime: The dimensions of effective community control*. New York: Lexington.

Byrne, J. M., & Sampson, R. J. (Eds.). (1986). *The social ecology of crime*. New York: Springer.

Clarke, R. V. (Ed.). (1992). *Situational crime prevention: Successful case studies*. New York: Harrow & Heston.

Cordner, G. W. (1986). Fear of crime and the police: An evaluation of a fear-reduction strategy. *Journal of Police Science and Administration, 14,* 223-233.

Couper, D. C., & Lobitz, S. H. (1991). *Quality policing: The Madison experience*. Washington, DC: Police Executive Research Forum.

Critchley, T. A. (1979). *A history of police in England and Wales.* Montclair, NJ: Patterson Smith.

Davis, K. C. (1975). *Police discretion.* St. Paul, MN: West.

Davis, R. C., Lurigio, A. J., & Rosenbaum, D. P. (Eds.). (1993). *Drugs and the community.* Springfield, IL: Charles C Thomas.

Eck, J. E. (1993). Alternative futures for policing. In D. Weisburd & C. Uchida (Eds.), *Police innovation and control of the police* (pp. 59-79). New York: Springer.

Eck, J. E., & Spelman, W. (1987). *Problem solving: Problem-oriented policing in Newport News.* Washington, DC: Police Executive Research Forum.

Fogelson, R. M. (1977). *Big city police.* Cambridge, MA: Harvard University Press.

Goldstein, H. (1977). *Policing a free society.* Cambridge, MA: Ballinger.

Goldstein, H. (1979). Improving policing: A problem-oriented approach. *Crime and Delinquency, 25,* 236-258.

Goldstein, H. (1990). *Problem-oriented policing.* New York: McGraw-Hill.

Goldstein, J. (1960). Police discretion not to invoke the criminal process: Low-visibility decisions in the administration of justice. *Yale Law Journal, 69,* 543-594.

Gottlieb, M. (1993, July 21). Crown Heights study finds Dinkins and police at fault in letting unrest escalate. *The New York Times,* p. 1.

Greene, J. R., & Mastrofski, S. D. (Eds.). (1988). *Community policing: Rhetoric or reality?* New York: Praeger.

Greenwood, P. W., Chaiken, J. M., & Petersilia, J. (1977). *The criminal investigation process.* Lexington, MA: D. C. Heath.

Hackman, J. R., & Oldham, G. R. (1976). Motivation through the design of work: Test of a theory. *Organizational Behavior and Human Performance, 16,* 250-279.

Heitgerd, J. L., & Bursik, R. L., Jr. (1987). Extra-community dynamics and the ecology of delinquency. *American Journal of Sociology, 92,* 775-787.

Independent Commission on the Los Angeles Police Department. (1991). *Report of the Independent Commission on the Los Angeles Police Department.* Los Angeles, CA: Author.

Kelling, G. L., Pate, T., Dieckman, D., & Brown, C. E. (1974). *The Kansas City preventive patrol experiment: A technical report.* Washington, DC: Police Foundation.

Klockars, C. B. (1988). The rhetoric of community policing. In J. R. Greene & S. D. Mastrofski (Eds.), *Community policing: Rhetoric or reality?* (pp. 239-258). New York: Praeger.

Koller, K. (1990). *Working the beat: The Edmonton neighborhood foot patrol.* Edmonton, Alberta: Edmonton Police Service.

Krantz, S., Gilman, B., Benda, C., Hallstrom, C., and Nadworny, E. (1979). *Police policymaking.* Lexington, MA: D. C. Heath.

LaFave, W. R. (1965). *Arrest: The decision to take a suspect into custody.* Boston: Little, Brown.

Lavrakas, P. J. (1985). Citizen self-help and neighborhood crime prevention policy. In L. A. Curtis (Ed.), *American violence and public policy* (pp. 87-116). New Haven, CT: Yale University Press.

Levine, M. J., & McEwen, J. T. (1985). *Patrol deployment.* Washington, DC: National Institute of Justice.

Manning, P. K. (1988). Community policing as a drama of control. In J. R. Greene & S. D. Mastrofski (Eds.), *Community policing: Rhetoric or reality?* (pp. 27-46). New York: Praeger.

Mastrofski, S. D. (1988). Community policing as reform: A cautionary tale. In J. R. Greene & S. D. Mastrofski (Eds.), *Community policing: Rhetoric or reality?* (pp. 47-68). New York: Praeger.

McElroy, J. E., Cosgrove, C. A., & Sadd, S. (1993). *Community policing: The CPOP in New York.* Newbury Park, CA: Sage.

Merry, S. F. (1981). Defensible space undefended: Social factors in crime prevention through environmental design. *Urban Affairs Quarterly, 16,* 397-422.

Miller, W. R. (1977). *Cops and Bobbies: Police authority in New York and London, 1830-1870.* Chicago: University of Chicago Press.

Monkkonen, E. (1992). History of urban police. In M. Tonry & N. Morris (Eds.), *Crime and justice: Vol. 15. Modern policing* (pp. 547-580). Chicago: University of Chicago Press.

Moore, M. H., & Stephens, D. W. (1991). *Beyond command and control: The strategic management of police departments.* Washington, DC: Police Executive Research Forum.

Murphy, C., & Muir, G. (1985). *Community-based policing: A review of the critical issues.* Ottawa: Solicitor General of Canada.

Pate, A. M., Wycoff, M. A., Skogan, W. G., & Sherman, L. W. (1986). *Reducing fear of crime in Houston and Newark: A summary report.* Washington, DC: Police Foundation.

Philadelphia Police Study Task Force. (1987). *Philadelphia and its police: Toward a new partnership.* Philadelphia: Philadelphia Police Department.

Pierce, G. L., Spaar, S., & Briggs L. R. (1986). *The character of police work: Strategic and tactical implications.* Boston: Center for Applied Social Research, Northeastern University.

Police Executive Research Forum. (1981). *Survey of police operational and administrative practices.* Washington, DC: Author.

Police Foundation. (1981). *The Newark foot patrol experiment.* Washington, DC: Author.

Punch, M. (Ed.). (1983). *Control in the police organization.* Cambridge: MIT Press.

Reiss, A. J., Jr. (1971). *The police and the public.* New Haven, CT: Yale University Press.

Rosenbaum, D. P. (1986). *Community crime prevention: Does it work?* Beverly Hills, CA: Sage.

Rosenbaum, D. P. (1988). Community crime prevention: A review and synthesis of the literature. *Justice Quarterly, 5,* 323-395.

Rosenbaum, D. P. (1993). Civil liberties and aggressive enforcement: Balancing the rights of individuals and society in the drug war. In R. C. Davis, A. J. Lurigio, & D. P. Rosenbaum (Eds.), *Drugs and the community* (pp. 55-82). Springfield, IL: Charles C Thomas.

Rosenbaum, D. P., & Lurigio, A. J. (in press). *Fighting back: Two sides of citizen reactions to crime.* Pacific Grove, CA: Wadsworth.

Rosenbaum, D. P., Hernandez, E., & Daughtry. S., Jr. (1991). Crime prevention, fear reduction, and the community. In W. A. Geller (Ed.), *Local government police management* (Golden Anniversary ed.) (pp. 96-130). Washington, DC: International City Management Association.

Sechrest, L. B., White, S. O., & Brown, E. D. (Eds.). (1979). *The rehabilitation of criminal offenders: Problems and prospects.* Washington, DC: National Academy of Sciences.

Sherman, L. W., Gartin, P. R., & Buerger, M. E. (1989). Hot spots of predatory crime: Routine activities and the criminology of place. *Criminology, 27,* 27-55.

Skogan, W. G. (1990). *Disorder and decline: Crime and the spiral of decay in American neighborhoods.* New York: Free Press.

Skogan, W. G., & Maxfield, M. (1981). *Coping with crime: Individual and neighborhood reactions.* Beverly Hills, CA: Sage.

Skolnick, J. (1966). *Justice without trial: Law enforcement in a democratic society.* New York: John Wiley.

Skolnick, J. H., & Bayley, D. H. (1986). *The new blue line: Police innovations in six American cities.* New York: Free Press.

Sparrow, M. K. (1988). *Implementing community policing* (Perspectives on Policing No. 9). Washington, DC: National Institute of Justice.

Sparrow, M. K., Moore, M. H., & Kennedy, D. M. (1990). *Beyond 911: A new era for policing.* New York: Basic Books.

Spelman, W., & Brown, D. K. (1984). *Calling the police: Citizen reporting of serious crime.* Washington, DC: Government Printing Office.

Stamper, N. (1992). *Removing managerial barriers to effective police leadership.* Washington, DC: Police Executive Research Forum.

Sunset Park Restoration Committee, Inc. (1993). *The model precinct: A community review of the 72nd Police Precinct.* Brooklyn, NY: Author.

Suttles, G. D. (1968). *Social order of the slum: Ethnicity and territory in the inner city.* Chicago: University of Chicago Press.

Taub, R. D., Taylor, G. S., Dunham, J. (1984). *Patterns of neighborhood change: Race and crime in urban America.* Chicago: University of Chicago Press.

Toch, H., & Grant, J. D. (1991). *Police as problem solvers.* New York: Plenum.

Trojanowicz, R. C., & Banas, D. (1985). *Job satisfaction: A comparison of foot patrol versus motor patrol officers* (Community Policing Series No. 2). East Lansing: Michigan State University, National Neighborhood Foot Patrol Center.

Trojanowicz, R. C., & Bucqueroux, B. (1989). *Community policing: A contemporary perspective.* Cincinnati: Anderson.

Wadman, R. C., & Olson, R. K. (1990). *Community wellness: A new theory of policing.* Washington, DC: Police Executive Research Forum.

Wasserman, R., & Moore, M. H. (1988). *Values in policing* (Perspectives in Policing No. 8). Washington, DC: National Institute of Justice.

Weatheritt, M. (1988). Community policing: Rhetoric or reality. In J. R. Greene & S. D. Mastrofski (Eds.), *Community policing: Rhetoric or reality?* (pp. 153-176). New York: Praeger.

Weisburd, D., McElroy, J. E., & Hardyman, P. (1988). Challenges to supervision in community policing: Observations on a pilot project. *American Journal of Police, 7,* 29-59.

Williams, J., & Sloan, R. (1990). *Turning concept into practice: The Aurora, Colorado story* (Community Policing Series No. 19). East Lansing: Michigan State University, National Center for Community Policing.

Wilson, J. Q. (1968). *Varieties of police behavior.* New York: Atheneum.

Wilson, J. Q., & Kelling, G. L. (1982, March). Broken windows: The police and neighborhood safety. *The Atlantic Monthly,* pp. 29-38.

Wilson, O. W. (1950). *Police administration.* New York: McGraw-Hill.

Wycoff, M. A. (1988). The benefits of community policing: Evidence and conjecture. In J. R. Greene & S. D. Mastrofski (Eds.), *Community policing: Rhetoric or reality?* (pp. 103-121). New York: Praeger.

PART

II

Community Police in Practice:
Multisite Assessments

Innovative Neighborhood Oriented Policing

An Evaluation of Community Policing Programs in Eight Cities

SUSAN SADD

RANDOLPH GRINC

COMMUNITY POLICING has become an increasingly popular alternative to what many police administrators see as the failure of traditional policing to deal with increases in crime and drug trafficking and deteriorating relationships between the police and the communities they serve. Late in 1990, the Bureau of Justice Assistance (BJA) awarded funds to eight jurisdictions to implement Innovative Neighborhood Oriented Policing (INOP) programs. The purpose of INOP was to provide police departments with funds to implement community policing approaches to drug demand reduction. In June 1991, the Vera Institute of Justice was awarded an 18-month grant from the National Institute of Justice to conduct an evaluation of the INOP programs. The research on these projects was designed to be both descriptive and analytic and relied heavily on qualitative research methods. The research data were collected by having two researchers visit the sites three times for a week each. During these visits, researchers observed program operations; conducted semi-structured interviews with project

AUTHORS' NOTE: The information presented in this chapter was collected under a grant awarded to the Vera Institute of Justice by the National Institute of Justice (award 91-DD- CX-0012), Office of Justice Programs, U.S. Department of Justice. Points of view in this chapter are those of the authors and do not necessarily represent the official position of the U.S. Department of Justice.

managers and staff, community residents and merchants, and personnel from
government and private agencies involved in the programs; and conducted focus
group interviews with members of these groups.

The analyses of research data focused on the effectiveness of the programs
with regard to drug-demand reduction, drug-related crime, quality of life, and
police-community relations. Although the research focused on the eight INOP
programs, the project raised important issues with regard to community policing
in general. These are discussed below, under the three general headings of
policing, interagency cooperation, and community involvement. Common problems among the eight project sites are discussed and their implications for basic
policy issues are considered.

The Purpose and Nature of
the BJA-Funded INOP Programs

The eight jurisdictions that received INOP funds are Hayward, California;
Houston, Texas; Louisville, Kentucky; New York, New York; Norfolk, Virginia; Portland, Oregon; Prince George's County, Maryland; and Tempe, Arizona. These projects vary greatly in terms of the size of the localities and in the
size of the police departments in which they have been developed, and in their
prior experience with community policing. In some of the cities the INOP project
represents the first effort at community (or neighborhood-oriented) policing
(Louisville, Prince George's County, Portland, and Tempe). In others (Hayward
and Norfolk), the INOP project is a small component of a new, city-wide
community policing initiative. And in Houston and New York the INOP projects
are small, new efforts in departments with well-established community policing
programs.

Although each of the eight sites received between $100,000 and $200,000 for
their first year of INOP activities, the ways in which each used those funds varied
widely. For example, in Houston and Norfolk the primary emphasis was on
enforcement, with secondary drug prevention activities. Other cities placed
greater emphasis on provision of community-based services, such as drug
prevention, education, and treatment. Several of the cities (Norfolk, Portland,
Prince George's County, and Tempe) used satellite offices for their INOP
efforts. Hayward and New York used their funds to purchase motor homes; these
vans were intended to provide a place for community organizations to hold
meetings, for residents to obtain information about available services, and, it
was hoped, would provide a police presence to deter drug trafficking.[1]

Tempe. With a population of 145,000 residents and a police force of 234 sworn
officers, Tempe was one of the smallest of the INOP cities. The Beat 16 project
(Tempe's INOP project) was the city's introduction to community policing. This

pilot project was conducted in one of the city's beats and was staffed by a squad of 10 patrol officers and a sergeant, under the supervision of the lieutenant for that area. The Beat 16 squad was made up of volunteers who received special training in the philosophy of community policing and the strategies of problem-solving policing. Beat 16 officers differed from regular patrol officers in that they were responsible for answering calls for service only within their beats and they worked overlapping shifts.

The project's target area was a subsection of the beat of about a half square mile in area, which included a business district with motels, bars, and commercial outlets; a park, which is adjacent to the local elementary school; and residences. The population is racially mixed (white and Latino), with most residents in the low- to moderate-income range. The primary crime and quality-of-life problems identified by residents were burglary, drugs, juvenile crime, and graffiti. Prostitution was a primary concern among business leaders; both business leaders and residents identified specific bars and motels that they considered to be problems. The local drug problem was heroin trafficking within the commercial and residential streets of the target area.

Norfolk. Norfolk has a population of more than 250,000 and a police force of 684 sworn officers. In contrast to the project in Tempe, Norfolk's INOP project was city-wide and virtually indistinguishable from its new community-policing effort, Police Assisted Community Enforcement (PACE). Although the PACE program (which began in January 1991) operates city-wide, its efforts are focused on specific target areas, most of which are public housing complexes. PACE is characterized by a very heavy enforcement component involving undercover operations and saturation patrol, which is supposed to be followed by increased involvement of the community and decreased involvement of the police.

One of the most notable characteristics of the PACE program is its extensive interagency coordination. This is achieved through the PACE Support Services Committee, which has representatives from all city departments and meets monthly. In addition, this committee has two subcommittees that provide neighborhood-focused services to the PACE target areas.

New York. New York is a city of more than 7 million people, living in five counties (known as boroughs) that cover 319 square miles, and has a population density of more than 25,000 people per square mile. The NYPD has more than 30,000 sworn officers and is in the process of a department-wide transition to community policing. The New York INOP project, however, represented a tiny portion of the NYPD's ongoing community policing effort.

The INOP project consisted of three target areas in three different boroughs, with a large van in the center of each target area. Each of the vans was parked in the vicinity of an elementary school or a junior high school, and the blocks around the van were designated drug-free zones. The vans, known as Neighborhood Resource Centers (or NRCs), were the central component of New York's

INOP project. The NRCs were staffed by volunteers drawn from the neighborhoods and contained information on services in the area. In addition to providing information, the vans were intended to serve as a deterrent to drug trafficking in the immediate area. The connection between community policing in New York City and the INOP project was tenuous—the community patrol officers in whose beats the vans were located patrolled the area around the van, but had little additional contact with the project.

Hayward. With a population of 120,000, Hayward was the smallest of the INOP cities and had the smallest police department, 156 sworn officers. Like the Norfolk project, the Hayward INOP project was difficult to separate from its city-wide community policing effort.[2] The Hayward INOP project had as its central component a large van (very similar to those in New York) known as the Neighborhood Access Vehicle. The Neighborhood Access Vehicle was staffed by the police officer funded by the INOP project, and was available for community meetings and also served as a police substation. Another central feature of the Hayward INOP project, and of the COPPS (Community Oriented Policing and Problem Solving) project, was an extensive network of Neighborhood Watch organizations.

Portland. With a population of 418,000 and an area of 145 square miles, Portland is a medium-sized city. The Portland Police Bureau employs 850 sworn officers. Like Hayward and Norfolk, Portland is in the process of a department-wide transition to community policing. But unlike these two cities, Portland focused its INOP resources on one small housing project—Iris Court—which was home to some 159 people, nearly 40% of whom were children; about 85% of the adult residents were single women.

The goals of the Iris Court project were to improve the quality of life and health of the residents of Iris Court, reduce their fear of crime, and reduce the actual incidence of crime in the complex. Although the project changed over time, it originally relied upon several interrelated components, including (1) a street enforcement/high-visibility patrol unit; (2) a "Neighborhood Response Team" consisting of two uniformed patrol officers; (3) a community health nurse; (4) a community policing contact office located in the Iris Court complex; (5) community partnerships established with the residents of Iris Court and various social service providers from the city, county, state, and private organizations; (6) the use of Crime Prevention Through Environmental Design (CPTED); and (7) resident organizing and empowerment.

Prince George's County. Prince George's County covers nearly 500 square miles and has more than 700,000 residents. The police department has 1,230 sworn officers; the county is divided into six police districts and 10 patrol sectors. The Prince George's County INOP project, the Community Oriented Policing Squad (COPS), began in one sector and was later expanded to a second sector. The District in which the program operated is a "line" district; that is, it shares a border with Washington, D.C., and shares a number of problems with it—drug trafficking, drug-related violence, prostitution, poverty.

The COPS program was the county's first experience with community policing. The project had satellite offices in problem-ridden apartment complexes in each of the beats. Squad members had office hours in these satellite offices, each equipped with an answering machine to receive calls at other times. A notable feature of the COPS program was problem solving through use of the SARA model (Scanning, Analysis, Response, and Assessment). Approaches used by the COPS program include an active Explorer program for youth between the ages of 14 and 25; literature distributed through the satellite offices; a "knock and talk" program; attempts by the officers to encourage the formation of Neighborhood Watch groups; and the use of civil abatement procedures.

Houston. Occupying more than 600 square miles, Houston was the largest of the INOP sites, at least geographically, and the second largest in terms of population, with 1.7 million residents. There are 3,950 sworn officers in the Houston Police Department.

Operation Siege was implemented in two target areas—Frenchtown and the Near Northside BOND area (Blocks Organizing Neighborhood Defenses, a Neighborhood Watch group). The major problems identified by members of the Frenchtown Community Association were prostitution, crack cocaine dealing, abandoned buildings used by crack dealers, and trash-filled vacant lots. BOND area residents identified their greatest problems as cantinas and criminal activities associated with the cantinas.

Operation Siege was unique among the INOP projects because its approach was strictly enforcement. Its goals were to improve the quality of life by preventing crime at the neighborhood level; introduce crime prevention strategies (e.g., target hardening); and reduce fears associated with crime. The project was to be implemented in six stages: (1) a series of meetings held with community groups to identify problems and plan a crime prevention strategy; (2) heavy enforcement activity; (3) saturation patrol and Zero Tolerance; (4) neighborhood cleanups; (5) crime prevention surveys; and (6) target hardening and senior citizen home repair.

Louisville. Louisville is a city of approximately 300,000 people with 671 sworn police officers. There are six police districts in Louisville; the INOP project began in one of these (the Fourth). All 66 officers in the Fourth District received training on problem solving; however, participation in the INOP project, Community Oriented Policing (COP), was voluntary. Officers who did not wish to participate in problem-solving activities continued to answer calls for service (and saw themselves as facilitating the COP program by allowing those officers who wished to participate the opportunity to do so).

The Fourth District has the highest volume of violent crime of the six police districts in Louisville. Ninety-one percent of its residents are African American, and assessed housing values are considerably lower than in the city as a whole. This District also has the highest concentration of public housing in the city, including four developments that are either the locus of or adjacent to many of the quality-of-life problems within the District.

Louisville was unique among the INOP projects in that crack cocaine was not a problem; rather, the major drug problems were marijuana and powder cocaine. At three community forums held in April 1991, residents identified some 43 problems that were divided into 13 categories: random shootings; street-corner drug dealing; loitering around liquor stores; other congregations of loiterers; congregations of youth; burglary; auto theft; police-community interactions; loud music; vandalism; traffic problems; illegal dumping; and stray dogs.

Vera's Evaluation Design

The INOP research began in June 1991, several months after the start of most of the INOP projects, and the data collection period ended in August 1992 while most of the projects were ongoing. As a result of the timing of the research (which was dictated by NIJ), it was not possible to design what might be considered the typical and desirable evaluation, involving the collection of quantitative data in a "pre/post" design. Furthermore, the INOP projects were quite varied in design and stage of implementation, and statistics were not available in many of the sites. Therefore, the research was confined to qualitative data, collected and analyzed systematically.

During the three sets of week-long visits to each site, Vera research staff collected observational data and conducted semi-structured interviews with police personnel, employees of city agencies involved in the projects, and community members. These interviews were conducted both with individuals and in homogeneous focus groups (i.e., focus groups did not combine community members with police, police with employees of other city agencies, etc.). In each case, interviewees were asked questions that probed their knowledge of the INOP program and about community policing in general; perceptions of the project's effectiveness; personal definition of community policing; perceptions regarding the role of the community in community policing; and expectations for the future of community policing. These interviews were tape-recorded (unless any of the participants objected) and later transcribed.

Data were interpreted qualitatively, using systematic, computer-assisted analysis. Transcribed interviews were entered into personal computers using a free-form text database manager (*askSam®*), which made the data accessible for coding and analysis. A set of codes were developed from the interview protocols and then modified empirically (when the coding process revealed a consistent set of responses that was not previously included among the codes). Once the data had been coded, *askSam®* was used to produce sets of text receiving the same code;

research staff then analyzed these data and developed conclusions regarding the effects of the programs and their implications for community policing in general.[3]

Effects of the INOP Programs

As was indicated above, the effects of the INOP projects were measured in terms of perceptions of residents, police officers and administrators, and other agency personnel, as expressed in individual interviews and focus groups. Although the research intended to measure the effects of the INOP programs in terms of the goals of the particular projects, in reality these effects were measured in terms of the respondents' perceptions of both goals and outcomes. In each instance, interviewees were asked to discuss the effects of the program on drug use and drug trafficking, drug-related crime, fear, quality of life in the area, police-community relations, and level of community organization and involvement.

Drug Trafficking. The general impression in the INOP sites was that the projects had displaced drug trafficking either geographically, from street-level to indoors, or temporally. In Hayward, Houston, and New York, however, there were some respondents who believed the INOP project had no effect on drug trafficking. At the other end of the spectrum were Portland and Tempe, where most respondents perceived the project to have been extremely effective with regard to drug trafficking, either by moving it out of the target area or by making it less visible. In the other INOP sites, respondents also believed drug trafficking had been displaced; there was just less agreement on the extent of that displacement.

Drug-Related Crime. Respondents had more trouble assessing the effects of the INOP projects on drug-related crime and often indicated that they were unable to determine which crimes were drug related. In Hayward, Houston, and New York there appeared to be few effects on crime: New York respondents reported no effects on crime; in Houston the effects appeared to be temporary, at best; and in Hayward some respondents thought the program had reduced drug-related crime while others did not. Respondents in Portland, Norfolk, Tempe, and Prince George's County believed their INOP programs had been very effective in reducing crime, while in Louisville sentiments were mixed.

Fear of Crime. Theorists in the area of policing suggest that physical and social disorder and crime are linked to fear of crime (Kelling, 1992; Moore & Trojanowicz, 1988; Skogan, 1986, 1990; Wilson & Kelling, 1982), and one would therefore expect that in those sites where the INOP program was perceived to have had an effect on crime, it should also be perceived to have had an effect on fear levels. This relationship was certainly evident in New York,

Houston, and Hayward, where few respondents thought fear had decreased. This same relationship was present in the other INOP sites, where respondents were more positive about the projects' effects on crime. In Portland, Tempe, and Prince George's County, respondents were very positive about their INOP project's effects on fear. Norfolk respondents were also generally positive, although more respondents perceived fear to have been reduced at the time of the second site visit than at the time of the third visit.[4] In Louisville, police administrators and officers believed their INOP project had been very effective in reducing fear in the target areas, but residents were less certain.

Police/Community Relationships. Most respondents in the INOP sites also reported improved relationships between the police and community residents. Even in those sites where perceived effects on drugs, crime, and fear were minimal (Hayward, Houston, and New York), respondents believed that the relationship between the police and the community had improved. Some respondents qualified their responses, however. The most important qualification was that many respondents indicated that the improvement was limited to relationships with specific officers or to certain segments of the community. As will be seen below in the discussion of Issues in Implementation, in many of the communities in which the INOP programs were implemented, there was a long history of poor relations between the police and the community, fear of the police by many residents, and mutual distrust. These historically negative factors are not easily overcome.

Community Organization and Community Involvement. Although they were not always certain that the INOP program was responsible for this effect, most respondents believed that levels of community organization and community involvement had increased since the start of the INOP program. One site in which this effect was very pronounced was Hayward, which had very well-organized citizens' groups. And although the community policing program (of which INOP was a part) was very supportive of community organization, in fact, this increased community organization was due to a grassroots effort that predated community policing in Hayward.

Other cities in which INOP was credited with improving community organization or involvement were Portland, Norfolk, Tempe, Prince George's County, and Louisville. In Portland and Louisville, this increase took the form of improved attendance at tenants' meetings. In Prince George's County, respondents indicated that residents had become more involved in problem solving. Although there was little evidence of community organization in Norfolk, police administrators and officers believed their community policing effort had had positive effects on community involvement. This *involvement* often took the form of providing the police with information. The INOP project in Tempe was thought to have facilitated communication among preexisting community organizations and helped to form some new organizations. By the end of the research, however, community support and involvement in Tempe's INOP project had declined precipitously.

Respondents in Houston offered varied perceptions; some believed the program had been responsible for increased attendance at community meetings, while others attributed the increase to efforts from the community. There was virtually no response to this question in the New York INOP sites, which is illustrative of the failure of this program to involve the larger community. The few residents who volunteered in the vans were the same people who were involved in many other precinct activities. Despite some efforts to involve other residents in the project, implementation problems and fear of retaliation by drug dealers or of traveling at night to get to the volunteer training, limited involvement to a very small group of community activists. In addition, the project seemed unable to attract many people to use the services available on the vans. Indeed, participation by residents was so limited in New York that the only community residents identified for the research staff to interview were those involved as volunteers.

Issues in Implementation

Police Support for INOP and Community Policing

The difficulties associated with the implementation of community policing are a product of the ambitious nature of its mission. Community policing seeks to create a new role for the patrol officer ("problem solver") and forge new working relationships with the public ("partnerships"). Because restructuring these fundamental elements of policing will have important consequences for police work, community policing requires that police personnel support or "buy into" its goals and means. The implementation of community policing is thus a fight for the "hearts and minds" of the ordinary patrol officer. Data from the INOP research show that police researchers and policy makers may have gravely underestimated the difficulty of gaining the support of these groups and suggest strongly that police departments must make the education of police officers in the theory and practice of community policing a priority.

The research found that patrol officers are particularly resistant to the transition to community policing because community policing seeks to redefine their role and the way they perform their duties. The paramilitary structure of most police departments has also produced a well-documented antagonism between the "two cultures" (management and line officers) of policing (Ianni & Ianni, 1983). Because community policing is a management initiative instituted from the top down, and because its success is dependent on the support of patrol officers, the resistance of the average patrol officer to community policing is a major obstacle to its successful implementation. As we shall see, the level of enthusiasm for community policing among patrol officers in all eight sites was weak, at best. Even in those cities where community policing is at present nothing more than an experimental unit, patrol officers generally had serious doubts about its potential for success.

Knowledge of INOP and Community Policing Among Patrol Officers. One of the primary reasons for the lack of support for both the INOP projects and community policing in general among patrol officers was a simple lack of adequate knowledge about either. Because the majority of the INOP projects consisted of pilot or experimental community policing units distinct from the larger patrol division, the level of knowledge about the goals of the INOP projects or community policing possessed by the average officer was low even among officers involved in the INOP projects, although these officers possessed higher levels of knowledge about the projects and the goals of community policing than other officers. Interviews with police officers showed that this lack of knowledge could be traced in every instance to inadequate efforts on the part of police administrators to communicate the philosophy, goals, and tactics of community policing to their officers. For example, in Houston (the city with the longest history of community policing among the eight INOP sites), even those officers involved in INOP project activities had a minimal understanding of "Operation Siege" and almost unanimously defined the project as a means to increased overtime pay. When asked if they had received a briefing or any training on the purpose of the INOP project, one officer in a Houston focus group, reflecting a consensus, replied, "No. At least I wasn't. I remember them just saying that they had money for overtime." Indeed, most of the officers there had not even heard of the INOP grant. The Houston experience, of course, represents an extreme case of lack of communication. However, by their own accounts, even those officers selected for the INOP projects in the other sites had little, if any, training in community policing or problem solving. After a year of regular involvement in Louisville's INOP project, one officer, when asked about the goals of the INOP project, said, "I'm not sure. I thought when I came into the community-oriented police program that I understood what it was about, where we were going, what we wanted to do. Now, I'm more confused than ever."

Most commonly, when asked about INOP project goals or for their definition of community policing, officers (both in and outside of the INOP projects) would emphasize the community outreach role of the patrol officer. Only occasionally did officers mention problem-solving activities or interagency cooperation in problem-solving efforts. One officer from Louisville, for example, offered a typical definition of community policing as, "[Better] interactions with the public." In most cases officers believed that the role of the public in community policing should be as "the eyes and ears of the police." One administrator in Norfolk said:

> To me it's [i.e., community policing] just simply working very closely with your citizens. . . . You're not out there . . . to take a hard approach with folks. You enforce the law as you're supposed to, but you also have to be sensitive. . . . So it's just working hand in hand with the folks and knowing you're out there to be their friend.

One of the bases, however, for officers' skepticism of community policing is the community itself. For many officers, the community outreach and partnership creation role was central to community policing. Yet few officers believed that community residents would be willing to get involved in community policing. The present study suggests that community policing is not understood well by community residents, and community leaders are guarded in their assessments of how the average resident will react to community policing's planned role for the public. Indeed, many officers were discouraged by their perception that police administration seemed more interested in including citizen input in their planning than in the input of their own officers. In defining it almost exclusively in terms of community outreach, many officers labeled community policing as "social work," "smile and wave," or "Officer Friendly" policing (all derogatory labels).

Because most officers had little knowledge of community policing beyond its "social work" aspects, those bent on pursuing traditional policing had few qualms about rejecting community policing in its entirety. Indeed, many police officers believed that community policing did not involve "real" police work (i.e., tasks involving the apprehension of criminals). Officers not involved in the INOP projects often viewed INOP officers as "empty suits" who do little if anything to reduce the incidence of crime. One INOP officer in Louisville attributed such perceptions to a lack of understanding of community policing within the department:

> [Patrol officers] don't understand what actually [INOP officers] are doing, so of course they're going to say, "[INOP officers] couldn't have [reduced 911 calls] because . . . all they do is have office hours; all they do is attend meetings, and that's it!" But it goes well beyond that; it's not just office hours and meetings and things like that, and they just don't know it. So they say, "What I know about community policing—they can't reduce [crime]. . . . The only thing that they can do is reduce the IQ level when they walk into the room!"

It is thus important for those in community policing units to convince their colleagues in patrol that they are still "real" police officers. Indeed, from both a police and a community perspective, community policing will attain legitimacy only when it is perceived as effective in controlling and preventing crime. When asked how most patrol officers perceive community policing, for example, a supervisor in one of New York's Community Policing Units said:

> They think it's a joke! I go to one precinct where I used to work and they say: "Oh, you're a supervisor [in the Community Policing Unit] now? . . . Oh, they're a bunch of do-nothings!" And I defend my guys. I said: "No. You may do that in your precinct, it may be true [of the Community Policing Unit] in your precinct. But my guys are happy to be in the conditions unit. They're into making arrests!"

Only by claiming that the Community Policing Unit is "into making arrests" does this supervisor hope to win the admiration of other patrol officers. One major hurdle that community policing must overcome is the value placed on the arrest as *the* measure of prestige and success. Changing such subcultural norms and values will prove difficult.

In failing to provide adequate education in problem solving community policing to officers involved and those not involved in the INOP projects, police managers have made it easier for them to see only those parts of the projects that they are bound to dislike, such as community outreach. Most administrators, citing a lack of funds for training, said that they preferred to concentrate their training efforts on INOP officers. Given the small budgets with which the INOP projects were launched, restricting training to INOP officers was a reasonable decision.

Because most of the INOP projects were conceived of as experimental units within patrol, and because so little effort was made to educate non-project officers, it is not surprising that officers outside of INOP knew so little about it or about community policing. The special unit status of most of the INOP projects was a major factor perpetuating distrust between police managers and patrol officers and provided fertile ground for the growth of resentment between traditional patrol officers and INOP officers.[5] Patrol officers' objections to community policing stemmed from the belief that community policing is a less productive and less labor-intensive form of policing than traditional patrol. Within the universal context of strained police resources, the supposedly less productive INOP units come up for special criticism from officers involved in traditional patrol. One administrative officer in Norfolk, for example, reported:

> The community police officer seems like a selective unit; they are a special unit in the department. The other officers resent that; they have a problem with that and [they say], "How do we reconcile [the expenditures for the INOP units] when we have resource problems?" . . . We hear a lot of that.

A particularly sensitive resource issue among patrol officers focused on their ability to respond to 911 calls. In several of the sites, INOP officers were not required to respond to 911 calls in their beats—a fact that led non-INOP officers to conclude that the community policing projects were safe havens for those officers who did not wish to work very hard. One patrol officer in Prince George's County described INOP officers as not wanting to be "active" in making arrests because community police officers there were not required to answer 911 calls:

> I mean, they don't take calls; they're probably not going to be doing many reports. They're kind of on their own. If [dispatchers] run out of cars because we're (i.e., patrol officers) all tied up in court, they're not going to give [911 calls] to the COPS officers!

That the ability of community police officers to respond to 911 calls is of major importance to other patrol officers may be found in two examples. In Prince George's County, for instance, an officer involved in the community policing unit funded under BJA's first-year INOP funding wondered whether members of the newer community policing unit (created with second-year funds) were making a concerted effort to take more emergency calls to gain acceptance from the larger patrol force:

> I get a feeling that [officers in the new INOP unit] are not going in quite the same direction as [officers in the old INOP unit]. . . . And I don't know if this is right or not, but it seems as if they're trying to . . . I don't know if they're trying to be accepted because they take all these [911] calls.

Patrol officers in Tempe also felt that INOP officers should respond to emergency calls in their beat. This was an issue even though Tempe's Beat 16 officers responded to roughly half of all emergency calls in the project beat. Indeed, it was such an important issue because many officers believed that Beat 16 officers were "not carrying their weight" with regard to emergency calls, and this perception adversely affected the morale of both INOP officers and non-project patrol officers. Beat 16 administrative officers lobbied their Chief for an increase in human resources that, coupled with a reorganization of work shifts, they hoped would allow INOP officers to respond to all emergency calls in the beat.

There are other reasons why patrol officers were cautious to accord any legitimacy to the INOP projects specifically or to community policing as an organizational philosophy. Many officers, for example, reported that enthusiastic administrators ("true believers") have overestimated the potential positive effects of the INOP projects and community policing. According to many officers, project administrators often described their project's potential effects too broadly and optimistically, and thus unintentionally gave resistant officers (and, in some cases, police union representatives) a clear opportunity for criticism if the projects failed to deliver the promised effects. One Portland officer, for example, argued that administrators may have been overzealous in their claims for community policing:

> I don't think that people should teach that community policing is going to fix everything. Community policing is just another way of addressing a continuing problem . . . crime. And it is not something that we are going to look at in 5 years and say, "I told you it wasn't going to fix our neighborhood." It was never designed to do that; it was designed to . . . address these many problems that are going to happen instead of slapping everyone in jail . . . I think a lot of officers and people are looking at it as, "That will fix the problem."

As with community residents, police officers display a healthy skepticism about new innovations or organizational changes. Without question, a significant portion of patrol officers in all eight sites labeled community policing as a "management reorganization of the week." Many officers are old enough to have survived many such reorganizations that, they say, come with each new police chief. In addition, officers with many years of experience claimed that these periodic restructurings and redefinitions of the police role have actually had little impact on the way policing gets done. Thus, a long history of fleeting police "programs" has made police officers highly skeptical of new reforms. Community policing, they believe, will also pass as an organizational philosophy.

In one of the largest police departments, Houston, officers argued that given scarce resources, community policing was impossible to implement. So low was the average officers' regard for the concept of community policing (or Neighborhood Oriented Policing—NOP, as it is called in Houston) that officers had taken the NOP acronym and renamed it "Nobody on Patrol" and "Not Our Problem." The newly installed Chief had decided that, by not using the NOP acronym while still carrying out NOP's mission, he could overcome the institutional resistance to NOP:

> The words NOP are no longer used in the Houston Police Department because they became a curse word to the officers, or to a good many of them. . . . We don't use NOP, as everyone knows . . . it came to mean here, "Never On Patrol." And so I don't use the word, I don't use the word at all and we don't use it in our documents.

Indeed, it was the hope of most patrol officers in Houston that the new Chief would move the police department away from community policing and back to the "basics"—crime fighting and law enforcement.

In sum, patrol officers in all eight INOP sites had little understanding of the goals of the INOP projects or community policing and were particularly resistant to the transition to community policing that their police departments are making. There are a number of reasons for this resistance. First, community policing seeks to redefine the role of the patrol officer from crime-fighter to problem-solver. Many officers also expressed displeasure with their perception of community policing's emphasis on community outreach ("Officer Friendly"). For such officers, community policing does not constitute "real" policing, which is concerned with the apprehension of criminals. Also common to all sites was the perception that community policing was being "shoved down the throats" of patrol officers without their input into the process. Thus, the transition to community policing is in many cases exacerbating the historical antagonism between the "two cultures" (management and line officers) of policing. The lack of knowledge about INOP and community policing generally can be traced to inadequate efforts of police departments to train sufficiently officers involved and those not involved in the INOP projects. If police administrators have not underestimated the resistance of the average patrol officer to the concept of problem-solving community policing, they have grossly underestimated the level of training and information exchange that it will take to achieve support for community policing among patrol officers.

Interagency Involvement

Interagency involvement is probably the least discussed and perhaps the least well-implemented component of community policing in the INOP sites and in other cities around the country. Even in those cities where the INOP project was well integrated into the department or sector in which the project was implemented (e.g., Prince George's County), involvement of other city agencies or private agencies was minimal. But for community policing to be successful, it must incorporate problem-solving policing into its design, and no police department can do effective and efficient problem solving without the active involvement of other city agencies. The only exception to that rule was Norfolk; in fact, it is the involvement of all city agencies that makes Norfolk's PACE program notable.

Traditionally, police are reactive and respond to calls for service with the tools in their police arsenal; these are primarily enforcement—file a report, make an arrest, issue a summons, and so forth. But problem-solving policing requires police officers to be proactive, identify problems (with the help of the community), analyze the problems, devise strategies, and implement those strategies (Goldstein, 1977, 1979, 1990). In the absence of comprehensive training in problem-solving methods, the strategies police officers choose tend to be the methods they are most comfortable with, such as conducting high visibility patrol, issuing summonses, and making arrests (see, for example, McElroy, Cosgrove, & Sadd, 1993.) These types of strategies do not involve other city agencies and often do not even involve other units within their own department. But many problems cannot be solved through traditional means alone and require the involvement of other agencies (and residents of the community, as well). This is especially true of quality-of-life problems, for which traditionally structured police departments do not take responsibility.

The data that are accruing from community policing experiments around the country suggest that if community policing is an isolated change within the police department it will not work. Police in a number of the INOP sites complained that residents do not distinguish police work from issues that should be the responsibility of other city agencies. Residents call the police to report abandoned vehicles, barking dogs, overgrown lots, and health hazards, as well as crime and disorder problems. If the change to community policing involves the entire city government *from the beginning,* then police and citizens alike can be educated regarding how to deal with quality-of-life conditions that do not fall within the purview of the police department. Furthermore, if all city agencies make the transition to what might be thought of as "community governing," then they too can work together with the police and with the public to ensure that the appropriate agencies are involved in problem solving from the beginning.

Although most of the INOP sites made some attempts to involve city agencies in addition to the police, none had *formal* interagency agreements. And only in Norfolk was the support from the city government strong enough to be, in fact, a mandate that every city agency be involved. As will be seen in the section on Community Involvement below, with the exception of community leaders, most residents of Norfolk, including those in PACE areas, were unfamiliar with the structure of the program. Thus they would not know which agency to call to repair a street light or clear a vacant lot of trash, and therefore continued to rely on the police to handle such problems for them.

The problem was substantially worse in the other INOP sites where the interagency involvement was minimal and much more informal than that in Norfolk. Police agencies around the country are jumping on the community policing bandwagon without having a clear conception of what community policing is all about. This is reflected in failures to mobilize the community, lack of interagency involvement, and a lack of understanding among police officers regarding their own roles. One problem common to all the INOP sites was that the police had to take the lead and other agencies *might* follow along. What is clear from a review of interagency involvement across the eight INOP sites is that the interagency involvement was informal, and business continued to be conducted the way it always had been. When the police encountered a problem for which they needed the help of another city agency, they called the person in that department with whom they had a *personal* relationship. If that person were to leave the agency, a new relationship would have to be cultivated with his or her replacement.

Community Involvement in the INOP Projects

Although there is little agreement among theorists and practitioners on the precise definition of *community policing,* one element common to all definitions is the idea that the police and the community must work in concert both to define and to develop solutions to problems affecting the community. Increasing contact among police officers, individual community residents, and existing community organizations to enlist their aid in this task is thus central to all definitions of community policing. Indeed, where formal community organizations do not exist, the police ought to help develop and support them (Goldstein, 1987, 1990, p. 21).

Police departments, however, have little experience in organizing communities, and how to unleash the potential for effective organization lying dormant in the community may prove to be the greatest challenge facing community policing. As one police administrator in Norfolk observed:

> Our biggest problem is community partnerships. . . . [We institute community polic-
> ing] in mostly low-income areas where they have a high incidence of crime, and a
> lot of the residents are not well educated. . . . We have to *teach* those civic leaders
> and those residents, those concerned residents how to become empowered, how to
> seek out resources that are available . . . the [law enforcement] stages of PACE are

easy . . . the community partnership stage is the most difficult, time consuming, and resource draining.

Norfolk's problem in stimulating community involvement and building partnerships is not unique; all eight INOP sites experienced great difficulty in establishing a solid community infrastructure upon which to build their new community policing programs.[6]

Levels of Knowledge About INOP Project Structure and Goals. Respondents' knowledge of a project's existence, goals, and tactics varied greatly. Interviews strongly suggest that the level of understanding people have about INOP, or community policing in general, is closely linked to their status in the community. Thus community leaders who had close and frequent interaction with the police had a higher level of knowledge about INOP or community policing than ordinary residents who did not belong to any organized community group. Even the most enlightened community leaders in all eight sites, however, had only a limited understanding of INOP project goals and tactics. For example, few community leaders in any of the sites knew of other agencies involved in their projects.

A second level of knowledge existed among "ordinary" (i.e., those not members of any formal community organizations such as a block watch, residents' council, etc.) area residents, members of community groups, and employees of city agencies other than the police. These people knew that there was a "program" present in specific neighborhoods (or, more frequently, that there was an increased police presence in their area), but few of them were able to specify much detail about the INOP projects or community policing in general. In Norfolk, for example, a community leader said:

> I think the average person, if you said "PACE," they'd say, "Yeah, that's some kind of program that the police department has to get the community involved." But when you start getting more specific than that in your questions, I don't think that they [know].

The final, and lowest, level of knowledge was found among respondents (usually "ordinary" community residents with no community group affiliation) who had no idea that any police program had been operating in their neighborhood. In all the sites, these people were most likely to be senior citizens who present an especially difficult challenge for officers engaged in community outreach.

Given the finding that few police officers knew many details about the INOP projects, it would be unreasonable to expect that members of the community would know much. According to most community leaders and individual residents in all the INOP sites, their respective police departments did not adequately inform or *educate* the general population affected by the project in the goals and objectives of the projects or the role of the community resident.

Indeed, when asked whether they thought the larger community was aware of the INOP project, or community policing in general, people familiar with the INOP projects answered that they did not think either was known to the communities affected by the projects.

Putting the "Community" Into Community Policing: Issues in Stimulating Community Involvement. The assumption is often made, by both practitioners and theorists of community policing, that because community policing offers such clear benefits to the community, once they are educated about these benefits community residents will actively aid community policing efforts. It is often an explicit or implicit assumption that community policing should also actively organize the communities it serves. The experience of the INOP projects suggests, however, that such assumptions largely ignore and underestimate the hostilities that have existed between the police and members of poor and minority communities who have often borne the brunt of police indiscretions. In light of the historical relationship between the police and minority communities that are most often the targets for new community policing initiatives such as the INOP projects, practitioners and theorists alike would be better off asking, "Why *should* community members be willing to involve themselves in community policing?" Data collected from the eight INOP sites strongly suggest that community residents generally may *not* want to become involved in the community policing effort. At the very least, exploratory data suggest the need for further research focusing on these issues.

Fear of Retaliation From Drug Dealers. Across all eight sites, the most frequently given explanation for a lack of community involvement in the INOP projects (and community policing in general) was residents' fear of retaliation from drug dealers. One Neighborhood Alert leader in Hayward, for example, said:

> People on this block will not get more involved because they are afraid. It's difficult for us to even advertise that we're with the Neighborhood Watch or to pass out flyers, because when they (i.e., drug dealers) see us on the street passing out flyers, they automatically harass us, we're automatically labeled . . . as snitches. . . . People are afraid of that and they don't want to get involved in anything that's going to upset the street anymore than it already is, and they are just afraid of retaliation. . . . The fear is so strong that it's going to take the street being patrolled [by police officers] 24-hours-a-day before the people are actually going to feel better.[7]

Many of the INOP projects (Houston, Norfolk, Tempe, Portland, and Hayward) realized it was necessary to reduce residents' fear to obtain their participation, and began their projects (or preceded their projects) with intensive traditional law enforcement efforts. To reduce fear in Houston, for example, two districts initiated "zero tolerance" whereby all crime and disorder become the target of enforcement. In Portland, the police department prefaced its INOP project (consisting almost entirely of social service delivery) with an intensive enforcement effort to evict drug-using or -trafficking tenants in the Iris Court public housing target site. The Portland police, in association with the Housing Authority of Portland, also implemented a "trespass" enforcement effort whereby nonresidents guilty of engaging in criminal behavior or causing other problems would be "excluded" from the project site. In Tempe, the INOP project included "Sweep 16," in which all major drug dealers in the target area were arrested.

Such efforts, however, may well serve to produce unintended negative effects. Residents almost unanimously applaud police efforts to increase the level of enforcement in their neighborhoods (for almost all residents, the more police in their neighborhood, the better). During such "crackdowns" residents report feeling safer. However, many of these heavy enforcement efforts are short lived and therefore do not have the desired effect of reducing residents' fears in the long run. When this is the case, it may actually create an additional crisis of legitimacy for the police as residents begin to define community policing as "just another program" in which services are "here today, gone tomorrow."

The Historically Poor Relationship
Between the Police and the Community

Common wisdom among police officers holds that, "Ninety-five percent of the community is good and law-abiding. These are the people with whom we must work." However, one of the untested assumptions of community policing is that residents want closer contact with the police and, further, want to work actively with the police to reduce the incidence of crime in their neighborhoods. Exploratory data collected in interviews with residents, however, casts some doubt on these assumptions.

According to a large number of community residents, a major reason why residents do not get involved with community policing projects is the histori-cally poor relationship between the police and the residents of poor communi-ties. Such poor relationships, most common in those areas of the city usually chosen as the target sites for community policing demonstration projects, will not be easily changed. One resident in Louisville, for example, explained:

> There has been such a negative view of the police. People don't trust them. . . . And most of those who are policing us do not live in our area so, therefore, they don't un-derstand what we're going through. . . . So, there's a lot of misunderstanding—no communication at all. . . . That's the kind of attitude [distrust of the police] that the community has. . . . Attitudes are learned. . . . So for 20 years they're taught that the police are no good. . . . You know, it's a lot of hard work to get somebody to change their perspective of something like the police department all of a sudden when you've been taught all your life to think a certain way about them.

At the very least, these findings call into question the assumption that even "good" people desire a closer relationship with the police and are willing to participate in the community policing process.

"Apathy." In interviews with police administrators and police officers assigned to the INOP projects, it appeared that many police officers had become increasingly hostile toward residents who, because of a perceived "apathy," or lack of interest in "bettering their own lives," refused to get involved in community policing efforts. Such a perspective, however, fails to appreciate the depth of distrust and fear of the police among residents where community policing projects are often initiated. Such areas are typically poor, disorganized areas of the city where residents have for generations borne the brunt of police abuses. The apparent unwillingness of residents to involve themselves with the police may thus be less a product of apathy than of fear and suspicion grounded in their past experiences with the police. In addition, people in poorer communities also have vast experience with seemingly endless government programs designed to improve their quality of life. It is little wonder then that residents in these communities often label community policing "just another program" that will come and go.

Police officers across sites often reported *increased* hostility toward community residents who, because of their apathy, refused to involve themselves in the INOP projects. These officers, often extremely enthusiastic at the beginning of the INOP project, found themselves demoralized because of the lack of community enthusiasm and involvement.[8] For example, one administrative officer in Norfolk said:

> There's maybe three or four people in each community involved and the rest are apathetic. They are either hopeless or they have no hope. They don't think it can work and aren't doing anything to make it work—maybe because they don't feel safe yet . . . or they feel it's just another scam. And then, some are just bad people. There's a whole bunch of bad people. . . . But the community. I say the community is like a bunch of baby birds, "Gimme, gimme, gimme, gimme!" And they . . . oughta start getting out there and getting their own stuff. Until they do that, this program won't work. The officers will just have disdain for them.

From a residents' perspective, however, there are a number of rational reasons why it is difficult to inspire the community to trust and help the police in their efforts. It is unlikely that the long history of fear and distrust that exists between the police and communities served by the INOP projects will be soon forgotten. A lesson learned from all the INOP projects is that community policing practitioners (whether at the administrative or beat level) must take far more seriously the need to narrow the gap between police and ordinary community residents in poor neighborhoods.

The Fleeting Nature of "Projects" to Help Poor Communities. Another reason for a lack of community involvement was the feeling among many residents that projects (not only police projects, but others as well) "come and go" all the time in poor communities. Why should community policing be any different? There exists, in short, a healthy skepticism in poor communities that projects designed to help them are going to be anything but short lived. Residents of neighborhoods targeted by the INOP projects have empirical experience with projects that are designed to help them, but disappear when funding runs out. One volunteer in the New York INOP project, for example, claimed that outreach efforts had largely failed because:

> What normally happens in the community is that something [i.e., a "project"] comes in and you just start to get the feel of it, and then it's pulled out. You know, it's pulled out because it wasn't doing what anyone thought it should be doing. . . . But what normally happens in the East Harlem community is that programs come in and you start to warm up to them, and you start to develop a relationship to them, but they get pulled out. So that creates skepticism in the community, because you don't know if you want to participate or not because you don't know how long it's going to be there.

In addition, many respondents felt that the police were "pulling out" of their communities too soon after delivering an initially high level of services. In Portland, for example, several residents' council members reported that at the inception of the INOP project they had two officers who walked through the housing project every day. Officers often drove through the complex as well. By the time of the third Vera site visit in the summer of 1992, however, they claimed that the level of police service had declined dramatically. Many residents, they claimed, felt that the police had withdrawn too soon. The level of personal contact with residents had also declined.

These perceptions were most apparent in projects that had strong enforcement efforts at the outset of the project. In theory, such crackdowns (e.g., "sweeps" in Norfolk, "trespass" enforcement in Portland, "zero tolerance" in Houston) are designed to reduce the level of fear in a community to the point where they can actively organize and "reclaim their streets." In practice, the duration of such crackdowns is generally far too short for fear to be significantly reduced. When a high level of enforcement is provided and then withdrawn suddenly, the general response of most residents is anger.[9] In such instances the police lose credibility and the project legitimacy in the eyes of the community.[10]

Although intensive enforcement efforts such as those seen in many of the INOP projects may make clear and immediate impacts on the levels of crime in any given community, their long-term impacts are highly suspect. It is less clear whether such crackdowns can (either alone or in concert with other agencies) inspire the level of community organization and participation that is necessary to maintain those effects. Without a solid infrastructure of community support and organization, it is unlikely that such enforcement measures can have any enduring value.

Lack of Community Outreach Means That People Do Not Understand Community Policing or Their Role in It. If, as community leaders report, most residents are unfamiliar with the INOP projects specifically, or community policing generally, it is difficult to see how residents could be inspired to organize around and participate in these efforts.

All of the INOP sites were hampered in their attempts to generate community organization and involvement by a lack of fundamental resources and *experience*.[11] Though these departments recognize the immediate need to train their officers in the philosophy, strategy, and tactics of community policing, none has taken steps to provide the same "training" to members of the community. As Goldstein (1990, p. 114) has observed, "conveying sound, accurate information is currently one of the least used, but potentially most effective, means the police have for responding to a wide range of problems." Although the preferred method for conveying information to the public has been meetings with community groups, Goldstein notes, little attention has been given to the *type* of information that is presented or the most effective way to present it (1990, pp. 114-118).

Certainly, one type of information that members of the community need is training on the fundamentals of community policing and the role of the community.[12] A major problem encountered in all eight INOP sites was that while community leaders had some notion of what community policing was, ordinary *residents* had limited knowledge about the INOP efforts specifically, and community policing generally. The possibility for success of these projects and community policing in general will ultimately be limited if major commitments to community education and training are not forthcoming. Thus far, police departments have de facto viewed community policing as a *police department* phenomenon. When police departments make the decision to adopt community policing philosophy and tactics, they take the logical step of training and educating their officers in the new approach. The education of the organized community is often an afterthought. Departments rely upon the officers who have been trained to pass on information to the community, but the INOP experience clearly indicates that this approach is inadequate. One community leader in Hayward, for example, believed that few people in the city had any knowledge of the COPPS program and argued that, even as a well-informed community activist, she was unsure of what the police meant by "partnership" and what the community's role was in community policing:

> Well, I just think that the average person doesn't have a clue what it [i.e., community policing] means, all they know is that if you call the police, somebody pays attention. . . . But the one question that never gets answered to my satisfaction by the police department is—they want this "partnership," right? But I still can't figure out exactly what we are supposed to do in the "partnership." I don't think that question has been thought through . . .

This position was a common one across the sites. Although most of the INOP projects attempted to involve residents in some manner (e.g., volunteers in Tempe and New York; helping residents form councils in Portland; allowing residents to take part in interagency problem-solving sessions in Norfolk), even community leaders are unsure about the fundamental role of the community in community policing. All respondents, for example, were asked what the police in their city meant when they asked the community for "help" under the new banner of community policing. Without question, the most frequent response was that the police wanted residents to be the "eyes and ears" of the police. When the police ask for "help" according to residents, they are asking for information on crimes. Similarly, police officers involved in the INOP projects generally defined *help* as the community providing information on criminal activity.

When asked how this was different from the "help" police had requested under "traditional" policing, most respondents were hard pressed to answer. Those who did answer generally thought that under community policing the police were "nicer" in their request and also seemed more willing to help residents and community groups.

At least three of the INOP sites—Tempe, Hayward, and Prince George's County—have instituted "citizens academies" that can provide at least one avenue for education of the public in community policing. The idea of training the community may at first appear strange, but police departments have offered training to the public in a variety of forms in the past (in CPTED or crime prevention strategies, for example). Too often, however, such citizens' academies focus on introducing the public to the *police role* and thus emphasize "ride alongs" with officers so that the public may develop a better appreciation of that role. Such programs are fine as far as they go. However, if these academies do not properly instruct residents in the *community role* in community policing they will not help advance the effort to institutionalize community policing.

It must be remembered that community residents have been conditioned for more than a century and a half to view the police officer as crime-fighter. During the era of "professional" policing, the police *actively* discouraged any community participation in order maintenance and problem solving in their own neighborhoods. The lack of participation and enthusiasm in the INOP projects and community policing in general is thus not so much a manifestation of "apathy" or "laziness" as it is a historical product of the era of professionalism. If the police are genuine in their appeal for help from the public, it will be the responsibility of the police to educate and train the public.

Conclusions

Like those in other jurisdictions around the country, police administrators in the INOP sites were eager to implement community policing. Indeed, some expressed the notion that more traditional approaches to policing had failed to stem the tide of increasing crime and drug trafficking and that community policing represented their last, best hope. The lack of evidence regarding the effectiveness of community policing has not kept many police administrators from proclaiming that community policing is "policing for the 21st century." The results of the INOP research suggest, however, that these forays into community policing produced only minimal, and often transient, effects on drug trafficking, drug-related crime, and fear of crime. And perhaps even more important were the findings that these eight sites experienced common implementation problems that hampered their ability to have the desired impacts.

In all eight sites the police administrators were the initiators and formulators of the community policing programs. The involvement of police officers, city agencies, and community residents in program design was generally minimal and, as a result, knowledge of the structure and goals of the program and of community policing in general was lacking in all of these groups. In part, because of their lack of knowledge and input into the community policing efforts in these cities, there was considerable resistance on the part of police officers to the substantial role changes being required of those officers involved in the programs. There was even less knowledge and greater skepticism and resentment on the part of officers who were not involved in the programs. Many officers were critical of the community outreach and "social work" role of community policing and criticized it as not involving "real" police work.

Similarly, community residents (even those living in the INOP target areas) were generally unaware of the goals of the INOP projects. Although respondents in most of the INOP sites believed that community organization and involvement had increased since the start of the INOP program, this involvement was limited either in number or nature (i.e., in some INOP sites "involvement" meant simply providing the police with information about crime). The INOP projects did not solve the problem of how to get the community truly involved in community policing. Nor was it clear in these sites that the police knew what the community wanted from their community policing programs.

Too often, community policing is defined and implemented as a *police initiative* alone to the virtual exclusion of other city agencies and, perhaps even more importantly, the communities it hopes to serve. One of the most significant findings of the INOP research is that the education and training of community residents in their roles in community policing is almost nonexistent. Without meaningful involvement of patrol officers in the planning process, participation by all city agencies, and true community involvement, community policing will fail to realize its potential. Thus among the most difficult tasks for the future are educating and training police officers and administrators about the goals and techniques of community policing; obtaining the cooperation of other city agencies in the community policing effort; building trust between the police and residents of communities where there is a history of antagonistic relationships; and stimulating community involvement in the planning and implementation of community policing from the outset.

Notes

1. Space does not allow for complete descriptions of the eight projects here; these descriptions may be found in Vera's report on the project (Sadd & Grinc, 1993a).

2. The 5-year Community Oriented Policing and Problem Solving (COPPS) implementation process began on July 1, 1991.

3. The discussion that follows is necessarily brief. For a more complete discussion of effects and implications of the INOP projects, see the final report of this research, submitted to NIJ in summer 1993 (Sadd & Grinc, 1993a).

4. One of the things that changed between the two research site visits was that the PACE program had expanded considerably and added a number of target areas, and as a result, police administrators and officers (as well as residents of the target areas) felt that one of the problems with the program was that their resources were being stretched thin because of the rapid expansion.

5. In several of the INOP sites it was clear that patrol officers objected to the special unit status of the INOP project officers. In an effort to diffuse such tension, some administrators in Norfolk, for example, insisted that, "All Norfolk police officers are PACE (i.e., community police officers)!" This statement backfired and caused the average patrol officer to distrust the administration to an even greater degree.

6. It is significant that even the two INOP sites with the greatest experience with community policing, Houston and New York, experienced difficulty in stimulating and maintaining community involvement. Houston, however, made extensive use of existing community groups (the BOND group in the Northeast target area, and the Frenchtown Neighborhood Association in the Fifth Ward target site).

7. This Hayward resident was one of only two residents on her block involved in Neighborhood Alert. By all accounts, her street was one of the worst drug areas in Hayward—supporting both local and drive-through drug trafficking. By the time researchers returned to Hayward for their third and final site visit, this woman had decided to leave Hayward. This left the Neighborhood Alert on this block with one member (a senior citizen).

8. According to community policing theory, officers assigned to regular beats should develop better relationships with the population because of greater one-to-one interaction. This interaction gives officers an opportunity to develop personal relationships with community residents that leads the officers to "care" more about the community. It is possible, however, if the residents of the community do not respond enthusiastically to community policing, that relations between the community and the police may not improve, leading officers to feel alienated from residents.

9. Because heavy enforcement actions enjoy high popularity among the public, police departments are usually under heavy political pressure to provide such action to a large number of communities. However, because police departments have limited resources, communities receive limited enforcement intervention (i.e., the level of "treatment" received by the community in the form of the crackdown effort is of relatively short duration), the net result being that the level of illegal activity returns to normal soon after the intervention is withdrawn and moved to another community.

10. The Vera Institute's recent analysis of the New York City Police Department's Tactical Narcotics Teams (TNT) showed that heavy short-term, street-level drug enforcement did not significantly affect the level of fear in three Brooklyn communities. In addition, the level of community organization and community participation did not change. Residents interviewed for the study generally argued that the short duration of TNT (3 months in any one target precinct) made little, if any, difference in the level of street-level drug dealing. In addition, residents claimed that as soon as the crackdown ended, drug dealing almost always resumed at its former level.

11. There were two exceptions; Hayward and Houston had strong block watch community groups in their target sites prior to the implementation of INOP. These groups were helpful in outreach efforts.

12. Portland's Landlord Training is an example of how the police department can educate the public on their role in community policing. However, even Landlord Training participants in Portland had little idea about what community policing is and why their participation in it is critical to its success.

References

Goldstein, H. (1977). *Policing a free society.* Cambridge, MA: Ballinger.

Goldstein, H. (1979). Improving policing: A problem-oriented approach. *Crime and Delinquency, 25,* 236-258.

Goldstein, H. (1987). Toward community oriented policing: Potential, basic requirements and threshold questions. *Crime and Delinquency, 33,* 6-30.

Goldstein, H. (1990). *Problem-oriented policing.* New York: McGraw-Hill.

Ianni, E. R., & Ianni, F. A. J. (1983). Street cops and management cops: The two cultures of policing. In M. Punch (Ed.), *Control in the police organization* (pp. 251-274). Cambridge: MIT Press.

Kelling, G. (1992, Spring). Measuring what matters: A new way of thinking about crime and public order. *The City Journal,* pp. 21-33.

McElroy, J. E., Cosgrove, C. A., & Sadd, S. (1993). *Community policing: The CPOP in New York.* Newbury Park, CA: Sage.

Moore, M. H., & Trojanowicz, R. C. (1988). *Policing and the fear of crime* (Perspectives on Policing, No. 3). Washington, DC: National Institute of Justice and Harvard University.

Sadd, S., & Grinc, R. (1993a). *Innovative neighborhood oriented policing: Descriptions of programs in eight cities.* New York: Vera Institute of Justice.

Sadd, S., & Grinc, R. (1993b). *Issues in community policing: An evaluation of eight innovative neighborhood oriented policing projects.* New York: Vera Institute of Justice.

Skogan, W. G. (1986). Fear of crime and neighborhood change. In A. J. Reiss, Jr., & M. Tonry (Eds.), *Crime and justice: An annual review of research* (Vol. 8). Chicago: University of Chicago Press.

Skogan, W. G. (1990). *Disorder and decline: Crime and the spiral of decay in American neighborhoods.* New York: Free Press.

Wilson, J. Q., & Kelling, G. L. (1982, March). Broken windows. *The Atlantic Monthly,* pp. 29-38.

Toward a Practical Approach to Organizational Change

Community Policing Initiatives in Six Cities

DEBORAH LAMM WEISEL

JOHN E. ECK

THERE IS CURRENTLY widespread interest in community policing. Whether one reads the extensive literature on the subject or reviews current practices, however, there is no single articulated form of community policing. Instead police agencies are engaged in a diverse set of practices united by the general idea that the police and the public need to become better partners in order to control crime, disorder, and a host of other problems. Although numerous police agencies are practicing some form of community policing, little is known about the variations of community policing being practiced or the reasons for these variations, the relative impact of these variations upon the objectives being sought, or the ways in which the behaviors of police personnel are altered in order to carry out the community policing efforts. One cluster of questions that has dominated practitioner discussions on community policing is how does one change an organization in order to get personnel to carry out the prescribed activities? Practitioners have been searching for guidance on the mechanisms useful for putting a particular form of community policing into place.

AUTHORS' NOTE: This chapter was supported under award 91-IJ-CX-K007 from the National Institute of Justice, Office of Justice Programs, U.S. Department of Justice. Points of view in this chapter are those of the authors and do not necessarily represent the official position of the U.S. Department of Justice.

This chapter discusses one aspect from the findings of a comprehensive study of community policing that began with an extensive review to identify common measurable attributes and activities thought to be associated with community policing. These attributes were used to frame a study of community policing in six municipal agencies. Detailed information was collected on the actual practice of particular styles of community policing in Las Vegas, Nevada; Edmonton, Alberta; Philadelphia; Santa Barbara, California; Savannah, Georgia; and Newport News, Virginia. Although the variations cannot be fully addressed within the confines of this chapter—more fitting instead for the lengthier and descriptive case studies being developed as a primary product of this research—community policing initiatives varied among these sites. Some of the factors observed to be relevant in shaping the form of a city's community policing initiative included the precipitating motivation for community policing, such as tenuous race relations and potential for racial conflict; the political structure and dynamics of the city including the relationship between elections and crime rates; police organizational culture and style including leadership, openness, and degree of hierarchical structure; and the history of the city, including its approach to service delivery, among other factors.

This chapter looks primarily at the activities that police agencies used to enjoin, cajole, or direct uniformed police officers to carry out community policing efforts. These activities ranged from strategic planning that involved line officers, training efforts, and changes in promotional practices and performance evaluation. The chapter evaluates the impact of these various activities upon the outlook of line officers toward the future of community policing in their agency.

Research Methods

The agencies selected for study were all self-defined as engaged in some form or variation of community policing. As detailed later, these forms of community policing varied enormously and it should be emphasized here that there is no single model of community policing being identified, advocated, or studied. Consequently, a cross-site comparison of these highly variable programs represented a major research challenge. The primary method of research used was a case study method, employing experienced mid-ranking police practitioners teamed with researchers to collect background, programmatic, and other information. A comprehensive protocol was developed to ensure standardization of data collection across sites. The case study collection of extant documentation and interviews with key individuals was supplemented by a survey of line officers. The survey was intended to validate much of the qualitative data collected through other methods and to inform the cross-site analysis. The instrument was administered to all line personnel in Newport News, Santa

Barbara, and Savannah (with response rates ranging from 68% to 86%) while a random sample of officers in Philadelphia, Edmonton, and Las Vegas were surveyed. Response rates for the identified samples ranged from 65% to 74%. Overall, a 75% response rate was achieved with a total of 866 surveys completed. Although attempts were made to quantify much of the data for the cross-site analysis, it should be noted that the richest findings from this study include both observations and impressions of the on-site researchers. Standardized case study protocols and other means do not obviate these impressions, which, although a product of a single point in time data collection effort, represent years of accumulated experience in the field of community policing. Thus, throughout this chapter, much emphasis is placed upon both the line officer survey and the opinions of researchers regarding the relative merit of important issues in each site.

Specifically, the study documented a number of community policing issues including how each of the agencies defined community policing, identifying any changes in activities and responsibilities for patrol officers; determined the stimulus for the implementation of the effort; and developed a full description of the organizational mechanisms used to support or encourage community policing within and external to the organization. Data were collected through several methods including review of supporting documentation and direct interviews of patrol officers and supervisors engaged in community policing, police managers, and police executives as well as a limited number of city officials and community members.

One important element of the cross-site evaluation looked at the extent to which police agencies were able to implement their efforts successfully as reflected by the attitudes of each agency's patrol officers toward community policing. The research adopted a basic assumption that community policing involves an activity or embodies a philosophy of policing that, regardless of the form of the community policing effort, is reflected at the level of the line officer. In other words, most police agencies dedicated to community policing are primarily interested in modifying the way in which their primary point of contact with the public—patrol officers—conducts their business with citizens. This change is consistent with what Skolnick and Bayley (1988) identify as a "change in the practices but not the objectives of policing" (p. 90). The resultant behavioral change could range from addressing problems that officers or citizens identify, the way or form in which officers interact with citizens (such as through foot patrols or citizen reporting stations), or other patrol officer activities. It should be acknowledged that most community policing initiatives clearly are not defined by how officers view the approach. But many community policing efforts are defined de facto by the change in the conduct of most officers as reflected by their behaviors and activities. In this sense, officer behavior might be identified as the intermediate product while the ultimate product might be citizen attitudes to police, crime reduction, fear reduction, or other varied objectives, depending upon the organizational goals. Thus research about community policing efforts might suggest the following inquiries:

What proportion of an officer's time is uncommitted? How are officers spending their uncommitted time that is not involved in answering calls for service? Where are officers spending this time?

How do officers follow up on calls for service? Are calls handled as isolated incidents?

How interactive are officers with members of the community? In what ways does the interaction occur—through meetings, door-to-door contacts, while on foot patrol, or in other ways?

How interactive are officers with other agencies? How does this interaction occur?

How are officers identifying and resolving crime, disorder, or fear issues with which they must deal?

In the context of this line of inquiry, a great many of the community policing implementation efforts of police agencies were specifically directed toward improving the skills and abilities of officers to carry out the specific community policing efforts desired. For example, many departments used formal mechanisms such as training, participative management, and modifications of performance evaluations and promotional structure in order to change or modify officer behavior. To what extent do these various implementation activities or tools have an impact on the acceptance by officers of the community policing initiative? This is a major research question that this chapter addresses.

Based on the assumption of officer behavior as the intermediate product of community policing (and because of research resource constraints), this research is absent any structured insight into the perceptions of citizens. If community policing behavior is indeed reflected primarily by officer actions, the absence of citizen input is not critical. It is only when behavioral actions are not sought as part of the process that the absence of citizen input becomes critical. It should be noted that one police agency in this study achieves its community policing goals primarily through the interaction of patrol captains with community residents. This department nonetheless has a valid claim that it is engaged in community policing. Citizens may feel safer, have greater access to police resources, and have other positive feelings that one might anticipate with a line officer-based community policing initiative. Nonetheless, because of the absence of line officer involvement, little can be said about the impact of such a program based on the research methods used in this study. This is a limitation of the study.

Overview of Study Sites

The six cities and their police departments in the study varied dramatically in their approach to community policing, a variance most apparent in the nomenclature used in each agency. There was no evidence of a single model of community policing. The Santa Barbara Police Department primarily uses a

TABLE 3.1 Demographic Characteristics of Study Cities

	Savannah	*Phila-delphia*	*Las Vegas*	*Edmonton*	*Newport News*	*Santa Barbara*
City population	138,000	1,500,000	742,000	620,000	170,000	86,000
Total sworn personnel	326	6,523	1,162	1,095	263	138
Percentage of sworn personnel representing persons of color	38	26	13	N/A	17	15
Sworn personnel per 1,000 population	2.4	4.4	1.6	1.8	1.6	1.6

SOURCE: Crime in the United States, 1990, Washington, D.C.: U.S. Department of Justice, Federal Bureau of Investigation.

special unit although virtually all of the agency's sworn and nonsworn personnel are engaged in the department's COPS (community-oriented problem solving) effort. The Metropolitan Las Vegas Police Department also uses a special unit known as Line Solution Policing, but the form looks significantly different from Santa Barbara's. The units take sole responsibility for problem-solving activities.

The police departments of Savannah (with its COP/POP initiative) and Newport News (with its Neighborhood Oriented Policing effort) developed generalist approaches to community policing based on a decentralization of dedicated police beats throughout each city. The community policing approach of the Edmonton, Alberta, Police Service is also decentralized, involving the development of service centers throughout the city. A different approach is embodied by Philadelphia, which conducts its community policing effort primarily at the captain level.

The cities varied in terms of geographic location, including one international city, Edmonton, Alberta, Canada, and five diverse U.S. cities. The cities included a variety of sizes, although three were clearly smaller cities with less than 200,000 population, and the remaining three ranged from more than half a million residents to three times that number.

The number of personnel varied widely, ranging from Philadelphia's 7,354 personnel to Santa Barbara's 228. The ratio of sworn personnel to population also indicated the variation among the agencies. As indicated in Table 3.1, the number of sworn personnel per 1,000 population ranged from Philadelphia's 4.4 to the 1.6 mark of Santa Barbara, Newport News, and Las Vegas. (The ratio was an important issue for community policing, for most agencies raised the issue of having an insufficient number of personnel to carry out the desired community policing tasks. These issues were as evident in departments with higher officer-to-citizen ratios as in departments with much lower ratios.)

Personnel varied in other ways. The ethnic composition of all sworn personnel in agencies ranged from Savannah's 38% representing persons of color to the 13% persons-of-color composition of the Las Vegas agency. (Persons of color in the departments were underrepresentative of the population in every city studied, although no data was available for Edmonton.) Regarding educational level of officers, in Santa Barbara, 95% of all patrol officers reported having more than a high school diploma (43% had a college degree or more education) while in Philadelphia, 45% of patrol officers reported having only a high school diploma. The educational level of the other four agencies fell within these endpoints.

Santa Barbara

Santa Barbara is a relatively sleepy but picturesque city of less than 100,000 formal residents, overlooking the Pacific Ocean. Some 100 miles north of Los Angeles and 250 miles south of San Francisco, the community is sheltered from the urban woes that have challenged its larger neighbors. The city has a reputation for being an enclave to the rich and famous, although its largely working-class population struggles with a high cost of living (particularly for real estate) and problems related to incorporating and serving a large and unofficial immigrant population. Officially, the city's population is 39% nonwhite, but unofficial estimates are that much more of the city's population consists of undocumented Mexicans, which contributes to latent ethnic tensions and significant language barriers with which the police department's mostly Caucasian force must often struggle.

The city's police department is led by the ebullient Richard Breza, a product of the city's own police force. Since taking the helm as chief in 1987, Breza, guided by a philosophical commitment to the idea of problem solving and community interaction, has molded the organization of 138 sworn personnel into an agency that is more integrated in community activities, from working with small business groups to the local housing agency and a host of other city agencies.

The department's approach to community policing includes the use of a team of six officers, known as beat coordinators, who focus their attention on specific problems within the six geographic beats that constitute the city. The beat coordinators are supplemented by other patrol officers and special units (such as the bicycle patrol) that alternately provide resources to the beat coordinators or conduct their own problem-solving efforts, using the beat coordinator for guidance and coordination. The beat coordinators are organizationally located within the department's Patrol Division in order to coordinate information and cooperation better among the beat coordinators and other patrol officers. Despite their existence as a special unit, the beat coordinators routinely handle calls for service for a portion of their shift.

Las Vegas

In stark contrast to Santa Barbara, Las Vegas is a town that never sleeps. The gambling industry, the city's economic foundation, operates around the clock.

But few of the city's crime problems are related to gambling, at least partially because the casinos maintain strict security systems and take steps to ensure the perceived and actual safety of their patrons.

The strong racial tension in Las Vegas between the city's black and white populations is palpable. During the aftermath of the Rodney King incident in Los Angeles, the city of Las Vegas was poised for massive protests and civil disorder among the minority residents. Indeed, a period of civil disorder with rioting, fires, and attendant violence occurred in the spring 1992. The tensions exist within a large and growing metropolitan area. With nearly three quarters of a million in population, the city is located in one of the fastest growing metropolitan areas in the United States, expanding by approximately 5,000 persons per month.

Policing in the metropolitan Las Vegas area occurs under a political umbrella. The agency is headed by an elected sheriff, who is reportedly retiring prior to the next election, and three political command-level appointees, who serve at the pleasure of the sheriff. The consolidated city-county jurisdiction provides a huge geographic service area; one can drive 2 hours down major highways and still be within the confines of the agency's service area.

The Las Vegas Police Department has also used a relatively decentralized special unit approach in its community policing effort. The department's Line Solution Policing (LSP) effort provides teams of officers to police area commands throughout the city who have the latitude to engage in proactive activities to address specific community problems—especially those related to gangs, drugs, and burglaries. The units were suspended in mid-1993 in an effort to expand the approach to all patrol officers within the agency. This change occurred following the conclusion of on-site data collection.

Savannah

The historic Spanish-moss-swathed city of Savannah is nestled on the banks of the Savannah River near its mouth at the Atlantic Ocean. The narrow streets and numerous public squares as laid out by the city's founder, James Oglethorpe, in 1733 constitute the core of one of the nation's largest historic districts. Although tourism is not the city's major industry, it is a growing and important part of the local economy.

The city has been troubled by severe crime problems in recent years, including a high rate of violent crime and concomitant fear among the city's residents and businesses, particularly for the possibility of its adverse impact upon tourism. The city is predominately black (51%) with little other ethnic diversity, but most political power positions appear to be held by whites. The police department has made great efforts to include black representation; 36% of the department's personnel are black and blacks appear well represented throughout the command structure.

Ethnic tensions did not directly motivate Savannah's community policing initiative. It was driven instead by political sensitivity to the growing violent crime problem, which crested in 1991. The problem threatened the reelection and subsequently resulted in the loss of the mayor's seat by a 20-year incumbent. The political instability during the election period provided a forum for the city's manager and sitting mayor, in league with the chief of police, to craft and fund a full-fledged community policing effort. The department previously had implemented elements of such a community policing effort; the election-motivated initiative provided teeth and funding to buoy the previously ad hoc effort.

The Savannah Police Department's approach to community policing is based upon the decentralization of patrol activities to each of four precincts in a geographic area commanded by a captain. Each captain is responsible for using resources and encouraging officers to engage in problem-solving efforts. There appear to be some differences in the level in which problem-solving or community involvement activities occur within the city, based upon competing demands (such as heavy call loads) in each precinct and the personal approach of the patrol captain in carrying out the mandate in his area command. Savannah's most visible implementation activity in fulfilling the community policing initiative is a commitment to formal training of all personnel, civilian and sworn. Fully 95% of officer survey respondents indicated they had received formal training, and a third of those had received more than 17 hours of training in Community Oriented Policing/Problem Oriented Policing (COP/POP). This was significantly more training than occurred in any other agency.

Newport News

The approach to community policing in Newport News is similar to that of Savannah, for the department is utilizing generalist officers assigned to relatively fixed beats. The department has divided the city into geographic areas based upon workload factors; officers are assigned to permanent beats. Unlike Savannah, the patrol areas are much smaller and are designed to increase an officer's knowledge and familiarity with an area. Although the department has struggled with issues related to beat integrity—particularly in terms of limiting cross-dispatching of officers to other beats—additional resources were being sought in 1993 in order to alleviate the resource problem. In addition to the beat reconfiguration, patrol lieutenants (rather than captains) were given 24-hour responsibility for patrol areas. The city consists of two geographically distinct patrol divisions dividing the 22-mile-long city; a main headquarters and a patrol station serve as the focus of patrol functions for the department. In addition, efforts were being made to develop several community storefronts to serve citizens directly.

Newport News is a blue-collar city dominated by the shipbuilding industry and strongly influenced by the military installations in the adjacent city of

Norfolk. Located on a peninsula jutting out into the southern end of the Chesapeake Bay of Virginia, Newport News is part of a huge metropolitan area of more than 1.4 million people.

Newport News was an interesting city for inclusion in this study because it represented something of an anomaly among community policing agencies. The department first experimented with and adopted the concept of problem-oriented policing in the mid-1980s under the leadership of its previous chief of police. The agency achieved something of a national reputation for its approach and became a model for departments implementing problem solving. Despite its perceived success, however, the approach examined in this study was the department's newer Neighborhood Oriented Policing effort, circa mid-1992. Although the department had not abandoned its problem-oriented policing approach, the agency's current chief, Jay Carey, had envisioned the department's problem solving effort as being carried out at a highly decentralized level in order to provide greater and more systematic interaction between police officers and area residents. Carey, chief since 1986, believes the decentralized approach will also enable officers to become more familiar with particular problems that cause citizens concern in their neighborhoods. The reconstituted Neighborhood Oriented Policing (NOP) effort in Newport News represented the "youngest" of the community policing initiatives studied.

Edmonton

More than 600,000 citizens live in Edmonton, the capital city of the province of Alberta in western Canada. Located roughly due north of Missoula, Montana, Edmonton is a city whose economy is built upon the oil and petrochemical industries and is sometimes referred to as the Houston of Canada. Following a boom period in the late 1970s and early 1980s, Edmonton suffered an economic slump with the decline of the oil business. The resultant financial pressure within the city resulted in major belt tightening in the city's police agency and contributed to pay cuts and a freeze on hiring.

By the early 1990s, restricted police growth had become incompatible with the city's burgeoning calls for service. The agency developed a unique form of community policing in order to get a handle on the excessive number of calls for police service that had burdened the agency and improve operating efficiency. The initiative was also developed as a means to bring police officers closer to the community and to address specific community problems. The department created customer service centers scattered throughout the jurisdiction, which were designed to encourage citizen reporting as well as increase interaction with the police.

This service-oriented approach to citizens occurred at the behest of the Edmonton Police Commission, a policy-making group appointed by the mayor to provide direction to the police. The board used its major policy-making role—hiring the police department's chief—as a means to direct the department's future specifically toward community policing.

Philadelphia

Philadelphia is a traditional East Coast city and, like many of its sister cities, it was suffering from economic woes during the 1980s. Economic difficulties caused the police force to shrink dramatically during the period although the city still maintains a 4.4 officer per 1,000 population ratio, a staffing reinforced by the strong police union, the deep political roots of the police agency, and a steeply vertical organizational structure. The department is run by a commissioner of police who is appointed and serves at the pleasure of the city's mayor. There is no city manager form of government here; the elected mayor operates all of city government and key appointees serve at his will.

Philadelphia's community policing effort can be traced to a destructive bombing related to the urban cult group MOVE in 1985 that destroyed two city blocks and caused major conflict between the citizens and police. Commissioner Kevin Tucker, formerly of the Secret Service, was appointed as a reform commissioner. Serving from 1986 to 1988, Tucker was the first and only outside police commissioner ever to serve in that position.

The form of community policing in Philadelphia occurs primarily under the direction of police captains who command the dozens of patrol districts within the jurisdiction. In addition to patrol officers and detectives, each captain supervises what is known as a Five Squad, consisting of specialized officers who deal with community problems. Within a district, the Five Squad includes Community Relations, Victims Assistance, Crime Prevention, Sanitation, and Abandoned Auto officers—each with specialized responsibilities and assigned to deal with common community problems. Regular patrol officers and detectives have not yet been integrated into community policing. However, the community policing effort is also structured to utilize Police District Advisory Panels, citizens groups that meet regularly and provide input to the district captains. The panels were created under Tucker and strengthened under Commissioner Willie Williams, who succeeded Tucker and served as commissioner until taking the helm of the Los Angeles Police Department.

Convergence and Variation

Six diverse cities and six unique approaches to loosely clustered objectives related to enhancing crime prevention, increasing police accountability, and coproduction of public safety produced community policing initiatives with wide variation but with some noteworthy issues of convergence. Based primarily upon the perceptions of researchers, the following issues emerged.

Catalyst. All six departments developed and implemented their community policing efforts for different but specific reasons. Some of the stimuli for community policing initiatives were apparent and reinforced through subsequent data collection; others were fleeting and desultory, reflecting only perceptions of researchers on site. Nonetheless, the perceived stimulus or precipitating event for implementation ranged from new leadership and adapting an agency for organizational efficiency to advancement of a philosophical commitment to the approach as an effective system for delivery of services to an effort to resolve potential or existing racial conflict within the community. The latter theme simmered in each agency to varying degrees. Each city, from Edmonton with its Aboriginal (equivalent of the United States' Native American) population to Santa Barbara with its influx of Latino immigrants to more traditional problems such as the relative isolation of blacks in Newport News, Savannah, Las Vegas, and Philadelphia, wrestled with the issues of developing police departments whose ethnic composition would be reflective of the community being policed; ensuring that patrol officers exhibited cultural sensitivity to ethnic groups; securing full access to police services for all populations; and addressing the potential for violence or disorder between ethnic communities and the police.

Regardless of the catalyst, the presence of a catalyst and the variation among cities suggests that different approaches to community policing efforts might be developed in order to address the varying objectives implicated by the variation in the catalyst. For example, a community policing effort designed to ease racial tension might look quite different from a community policing effort designed to reduce violent crime.

History. The departments in this study faced a set of organizational options defined by political and other systemic structures within their cities. Chief executives serving at the will of the mayor or publicly elected faced an entirely different set of constraints than those serving appointments under a council-manager form of government. At-large elections of city council members posed different political concerns than occurred in cities with single member districts whose representatives were in a position to lobby and demand additional resources for certain districts. Indeed, several cities anticipated transitions from at-large elections to single member elections in the future, all suggesting that such a move might have significant implications for their deployment of resources.

In several of the cities, an element of decision making about community policing was imposed on the department from outside. In Edmonton, the city's police commission formally tasked the department with implementing community policing; in Savannah an election-oriented mayor and his city manager pushed for and funded the city's COP/POP effort; and in Newport News, a decision to accept a federal grant kicked off efforts to implement the original POP efforts. These measures appear to have created a certain amount of demand or legitimacy for a concept that was already being advocated by leaders within the agencies.

It is important to note that the agencies were at different points in their evolution of community policing. This temporal dimension was not just chronological; some agencies with fewer years of experience appeared to be "further along" in their evolution than did others. But these agencies were "headed" different places to achieve different goals under varied circumstances. Most acknowledged that fully implementing a community policing initiative (whether the initiative was constituted as a program, a philosophy, or a hybrid variation) takes a long period of time. However, almost all of the agencies had previous experience with concepts related in form to community policing: citizen liaison groups; park, walk, and talk activities; Neighborhood Watch meetings; foot patrol; storefronts; bike patrol units; and other activities. For many of the agencies, adopting community policing meant integrating these and additional activities within a broader conceptual framework, expanding the concept and activities beyond special units, or establishing procedures to ensure that the activities would not terminate based upon political whim or funding constraints. Because of this evolving nature of community policing, one difficult dimension of the research was identifying the starting point of an agency's community policing effort. Indeed, based on the survey, officers within an agency were seldom in agreement on when their department's community policing effort actually began.

Leadership. Data collection efforts revealed a wide variation in the amount and type of leadership and the intensity with which such leadership was used to promulgate community policing efforts. For example, the chief of police in Santa Barbara routinely and consistently reiterated the messages of community policing, and officers, even those at patrol level who may be distant from directives of the chief executive, left no doubt that the vision touted by the chief was well understood. In other agencies, the chief executives routinely incorporated the language of community policing into public statements, which were not of the depth to consistently reach to the troops. Several of these agencies had de facto community policing leaders at mid or upper ranks who assumed responsibility for pushing the concept of community policing within the agency. One agency even informally designated its mid-ranking leader as the "Community Policing Czar."

Implementation Activities

Given the wide variety of community policing efforts implemented, the variation in city size and location, and other important factors, it is not surprising that the police departments used a wide variety of strategies in order to implement community policing.

None of the agencies were directly involved in formal decentralization by flattening their organizations, although there were some efforts to increase accountability and responsibility at ranks deeper within agencies. In all of the agencies, there was a heavy emphasis placed upon establishing geographic responsibility and accountability to police officers, establishing relatively permanent shifts and beats for personnel assignments, and limiting cross-dispatching of officers away from assigned areas—all within the general rubric of increasing an officer's familiarity with residents and knowledge of conditions and problems within specific areas.

Overall, there appeared to be only slight modifications in recruitment and selection practices as methods to increase hires of officers oriented toward community policing. Often these practices were informal and difficult to document. For example, in both Santa Barbara and Savannah, the chief of police routinely interviews all new police recruits. The interview provides an opportunity for department leaders to assist in selecting the "type" of officers who will fit in the direction the organization is headed. Many of the agencies had an increase in hires of college-educated officers and officers who were locally based or had some familiarity and connection with the local area.

Departments used various forms of internal communication to get the word out about the agency's community policing efforts. In Savannah, the agency's problem-solving committee included representatives from all the patrol areas in order to facilitate the dissemination of information. In Santa Barbara, white boards featuring efforts of the beat coordinators were prominently displayed in the patrol roll call room and beat coordinators routinely attended roll call to update other patrol officers about problem-solving efforts.

Across all six agencies, the most pervasive attention was given to four organizational approaches to getting community policing initiatives into action by altering or reinforcing officer behavior. These organizational approaches included:

- Using participative management styles, including seeking input from line officers into development of the community policing effort
- Changing promotional practices to reinforce officer involvement with community policing efforts
- Changing performance evaluation systems to support community policing
- Providing formal training to personnel

To one extent or another, every agency studied used these approaches to advance its community policing initiative (see Table 3.2). For example, based on the officer survey, Newport News and Santa Barbara ranked the highest for their involvement of patrol officers in planning of the community policing effort. Fully 41% and 57%, respectively, of patrol officer respondents felt officers had been included in the planning process. By contrast, only 13% of Philadelphia officers believed patrol officers had been involved in the planning process.

TABLE 3.2   Use of Implementation Tools, Percent of Officers Responding Affirmatively

	Savannah	Phila-delphia	Las Vegas	Edmonton	Newport News	Santa Barbara
Involved officers in planning	25	13	30	34	41	57
Formal training	95	35	47	79	36	66
Affect promotion potential	95	45	73	87	68	84
Community involvement in beat as a factor in performance evaluation	45	16	37	53	49	50
Number/quality of arrests as factor in performance evaluation	57	73	76	68	74	92

NOTE: Figures do not sum to 100 because respondents were allowed to select multiple answers.

As mentioned previously, the Savannah Police Department extensively used formal training of its personnel in order to further community policing efforts. Some 95% of patrol officers indicated they had been trained. In contrast, 35% and 36% of respondents in Philadelphia and Newport News, respectively, felt they had received formal training in the community policing effort.

Philadelphia was also the low agency out in terms of the degree to which patrol officers felt that involvement in community policing affected promotional opportunities. This is likely a result of the positioning of the community policing effort at the captain level rather than at the patrol officer level. By contrast, however, nearly 95% of Savannah's patrol officer personnel thought COP/POP involvement affected promotional opportunities, while fully 87% and 84%, respectively, for Edmonton and Santa Barbara agreed that community policing involvement affected opportunities for promotion.

Changes in the performance evaluation systems of the departments studied did not indicate that this mechanism was widely used to reward officer involvement with the community. Indeed, arrests, technical skills (such as report preparation), and personal appearance were the most highly rated factors used in performance evaluations in every department. Problem solving, ability to relate to citizens in the officer's beat, citizen complaints, and community involvement rated lowest as factors actually used for evaluation purposes. In Table 3.2, the figures reflecting an officer's evaluation based upon his or her involvement with the community in the beat are included only to show the range of differences between agencies. For example, it is clear that community involvement of patrol officers is much less important in Philadelphia than in the other cities.

The continued emphasis on traditional performance measures (such as arrests) is noteworthy. Officers did not perceive, despite community policing efforts, that arrests had become a less important part of their work. Instead, in some agencies, other factors such as community involvement by officers may have become relatively more important. This distinction is critical, for many practitioners articulate a view that community policing suggests a lessened focus on

TABLE 3.3 Police Perception of Future of Community Policing in Their Departments (in percent of respondents)

	Savannah	Phila-delphia	Las Vegas	Edmonton	Newport News	Santa Barbara
Community policing is here to stay	68	79	80	78	73	64
Community policing fad/on way out	32	21	20	22	27	36

NOTE: Columns are adjusted to 100 percent by eliminating nonresponses.

arrests. Clearly, in the agencies in this study a reduced emphasis on arrests has not occurred or, at least, community involvement has not supplanted arrests as an evaluation criterion based upon officer perceptions.

The agencies in this study demonstrated a wide range in the use of the various implementation activities in order to encourage officer participation in community policing efforts. Because of that variation, an important question is, To what extent did the degree of departmental involvement in these various organizational activities affect the attitudes of officers? For example, did the strong commitment of the Savannah Police Department to train its personnel formally and extensively create more support for community policing? Did the involvement of officers in the planning process in Santa Barbara win officer support? Did the promotional opportunities in Edmonton, Santa Barbara, and Savannah win officer support for community policing? Or did the relatively weak involvement by Philadelphia in officer participation in planning, formal training, and use of promotional practices and evaluations negatively affect the extent of officer support in that city?

Despite the wide variation in implementation activities, the officer survey revealed remarkable consistency in the attitudes of officers toward community policing. At least two thirds of personnel (68%-80%) in each agency believed community policing, as currently practiced or in a varied form, was there to stay in their agency. (For convenience, this category of response is subsequently referred to as "positive view of community policing.") Only about 25% (20-32) felt community policing was either a fad connected with current political leadership or on its way out. (For convenience, this category is subsequently referred to as "negative view of community policing.") The positive views of the future of community policing were as strong in Philadelphia as in any other city despite the fact that Philadelphia rated lowest on all the measured implementation activities. The specific differences between departments in terms of officer perception of the future of community policing are detailed in Table 3.3.

The consistency of positive views of community policing among officers—in light of the variations in not only implementation activities but also in length of time involved with community policing, department-wide versus special unit approach, and other distinguishing programmatic characteristics—is surprising. One would anticipate that a much wider variation in officer attitudes would emerge among departments.

TABLE 3.4 View of Community Policing by Years of Service (in percent responding)*

	Less Than 1 Year	1-3 Years	4-5 Years	6-10 Years	11-15 Years	16-20 Years	20+ Years
Here to stay	86	78	71	64	69	77	63
On way out	14	22	29	36	31	23	37

*Responses of all departments are consolidated.

Why has this consistency emerged and what factors might account for the absence of variation between agencies in terms of officers' views about community policing?

One might anticipate that desistance from those with a negative outlook about the future of community policing would reflect certain demographic characteristics. The literature and popular practitioner opinion suggest that age of officers, length of service, and educational level may play a major role in their support or opposition to community policing efforts (see, e.g., Carter, Sapp, & Stephens, 1989; Skolnick & Bayley, 1988). Instead, this research shows that consistency of positive views of community policing remain regardless of years of service (partially a surrogate variable for age), education, race, sex, or experience in a fixed beat area. Positive views of community policing—disaggregated by demographic factors but consolidated across departments—fall, with only one exception, within the same percentage parameters (64%-80%) as did general support for community policing within the individual police agencies studied.

The one exception to the consistency of positive views occurs in the endpoints of length of service (Table 3.4): Those officers with less than one year of service in policing exceeded the highest percentage of positive views in individual departments, while those officers with more than 20 years of experience in policing fell below the lowest level of positive views. This variation is consistent with the scant literature on the topic, indicating that support for community policing is higher among newer or younger officers and declines for personnel in subsequent years of service. This research shows, however, a marked about face among positive views over increasing years of service. Following a decline of positive views following the first year of service, a positive outlook for the future of community policing increases after the mid-career point of 6-10 years of service. Again, this upward trend remains consistent except for the 20+ years service group.

Other demographic variables in the study show far less variation than years of service in their impact on views of community policing. Educational level (Table 3.5) showed no impact on support for community policing. Those personnel with only a high school degree were as likely to support community policing as were those with additional years of education, perhaps debunking the popular myth that officers with college educations might be more likely to embrace community policing.

Neither race nor sex was more likely to be identified with support of community policing (see Tables 3.6 and 3.7). White, black, and other persons of color

TABLE 3.5 View of Community Policing by Educational Level (in percent responding)*

	High School Only	Some College	College Degree or More
Here to stay	79	71	74
On way out	21	29	26

*Responses of all departments are consolidated.

TABLE 3.6 View of Community Policing by Race (in percent responding)*

	White	Black	All Other Races
Here to stay	73	80	72
On way out	27	20	28

*Responses of all departments are consolidated.

TABLE 3.7 View of Community Policing by Sex (in percent responding)*

	Male	Female
Here to stay	75	66
On way out	25	34

*Responses of all departments are consolidated.

TABLE 3.8 View of Community Policing by Fixed Beat Assignment, in Last 4 Months (in percent responding)*

	No fixed beat	Fixed beat
Here to stay	75	72
On way out	25	28

*Responses of all departments are consolidated.

were equally as likely to feel positive about the future of community policing in their agencies. Female and male officers shared similar attitudes; although the attitudes of females were slightly less positive, the percentage still falls within the range of positive views established earlier.

The assignment of an officer to a fixed beat assignment within his or her police jurisdiction (within the last 4 months) also indicated little variation in terms of affecting views of community policing. Although some practitioners speculate that a fixed beat assignment contributes to an officer's understanding of problems in the area and increases the officer's contact with citizens, this factor did not appear to affect officers' views about the future of community policing efforts.

Implications

The consistently positive views of the future of community policing within and across police agencies might lead a researcher intentioned with providing useful information to police practitioners in myriad directions. The research might reflect a general basic level of support for an apple-pie-and-baseball issue such as community policing. Perhaps a norm exists in policing, and the communication of information within the broader criminal justice field provides similar information to police officers despite the decentralized approach to policing that exists in this country. Perhaps, in fact, the concept of resistance to change is overrated and is less pervasive than widely assumed.

The research, however, does beg the issue of what kind of effort it takes to get a uniformed police officer to buy into a new concept such as community policing and embrace or carry out such a change. Must a police department develop a remunerative system that financially rewards the officer for his or her support? Is educating the officer about the benefits of the effort sufficient to overcome potential resistance? Will involvement in the process of change ensure support? These are the questions that police agencies throughout the country are exploring as many agencies move toward implementation of the concept of community policing.

Despite the widespread variation in the form of community policing being implemented, questions related to implementation largely dominate many organizational efforts, particularly as related to their ability to address officer resistance to change. The concept of resistance to change frequently rears its head in community policing literature, although there is little description of such resistance in the literature on police organizational change (a noteworthy exception is Guyot, 1979). In community policing, individual-level factors such as age of personnel, tenure on job, and educational level and organizational characteristics such as police hierarchy, proliferation of rules, and centralization are often cited as factors contributing to resistance (Williams & Sloan, 1990).

In fact, this study showed that neither tenure, education, sex, race, nor assignment to a fixed beat affected the proportion of officers who felt positively about the future of community policing in their agency. An important dimension of implementation may be the existence of different types of police personnel within organizations. Goldstein (1990), for example, suggests that within police agencies, new concepts will have a range of employees including supporters, pacifists, and resisters or saboteurs.

> Many officers, whether experienced and set in their ways or new and recruited with certain expectations about policing, find it difficult to alter how they think about their jobs. If one sets out to effect changes that depend for their success on a change in attitude of all members of a police agency, the task is enormous; many people must be reached, and the effort is bound to be diluted by those who are either passive or—as is likely to be true especially of middle management—actively resist and

perhaps even attempt to sabotage the efforts. Undertaken in this manner, planned change requires a long time frame, consistent and persistent efforts, facilitated by a gradual turnover in personnel. (p. 173)

Goldstein's typology is consistent with those heard from the field and described in less academic prose. One police supervisor with more than two decades of experience in policing described police personnel as falling clearly into three flavor categories: vanilla, chocolate, and strawberry. (It should be noted that these "flavors" have nothing to do with skin color but are intended to represent different personality types of police officers that may be found within an organization.)

Vanilla officers are those personnel who are compliant, willing to follow direction, and, with sufficient training, will carry out to the best of their abilities the tasks that are sought by police administrators. Chocolate officers are a bit more complex: These officers need to be sold upon the merits of any organizational change. They are outspoken and may be critical until convinced of the value and logic of the change. Once convinced, however, these officers are stalwart supporters of the concept. The final flavor in the ice cream trio are the strawberry officers who are present in every organization. The strawberries are stubborn and resistant; no amount of training, inducements, direction, or other strategies will dislodge their position of resistance.

To the extent that these specific types of police officer personalities exist, these personalities contribute to the "culture" of the police agency. Sparrow, Moore, and Kennedy (1990) identify police culture as the single biggest obstacle facing those who desire to implement a new strategy of policing. But, importantly, the disaggregation of personality types as delineated suggests that there is not a single type of officer characterized by Skolnick's (1966) classic view of the "working personality" of the police officer as characterized by his or her distinctive way of looking at situations and events.

These types may affect the attitude of police officers so that, indeed, resistance may be limited to a small number of police personnel. If so, resistance may be overrated and the vast majority of officers will be willing to go along with new approaches to police work.

To the extent that different personality types such as those described occur naturally within organizations, there are implications for implementing any type of organizational change. The data in this research suggest that regardless of type and longevity of community policing effort, and the variety and intensity of implementation activity, a solid core of personnel (about 75%) believe community policing is here to stay and their behaviors are likely to reflect that perception. Indeed, one might expect to see a concurrent increase in the behaviors sought within community policing. Such an observation could be significantly informed via a pretest-posttest study of officer behavior. Without such research, we can only speculate about changes in the conduct and deportment of line personnel.

What does the research suggest about the solid core of individuals—the strawberries or saboteurs who may be obstructionists for community policing initiatives? In a practical sense, perhaps the best approach for advocates of community policing is to simply ignore or wait out the detractors and move ahead with community policing efforts. Because the relative importance of different implementation efforts in overcoming resistance to change appears minimal, an organization's time may be better spent by forging ahead. As the German physicist Max Planck observed: "A new scientific truth does not triumph by convincing its opponents and making them see the light, but rather because its opponents eventually die, and a new generation grows up that is familiar with it." The observation is consistent with the approach advocated by some management analysts as a bias for action, suggesting that the most important activity in implementing change may be simply to move forward and avoid laboriously concentrating on process variables. Indeed, the single most important activity for changing the police agency and institutionalizing community policing may be simply to move ahead and get new people on board the community policing agency.

References

Carter, D., Sapp, A. D., & Stephens, D. W. (1989). *The state of police education: Policy direction for the 21st century.* Washington, DC: Police Executive Research Forum.

Federal Bureau of Investigation. (1990). *Crime in the United States.* Washington, DC: Department of Justice.

Goldstein, H. (1990). *Problem-oriented policing.* New York: McGraw-Hill.

Guyot, D. (1979). Bending granite: Attempts to change the rank structure of American police departments. *Journal of Police Science and Administration, 7*(3), 253-384.

Skolnick, J. H. (1966). *Justice without trial.* New York: John Wiley.

Skolnick, J. H., & Bayley, D. (1988). *Community policing: Issues and practices around the world.* Washington, DC: National Institute of Justice.

Sparrow, M., Moore, M. H., & Kennedy, D. M. (1990). *Beyond 911: A new era for policing.* New York: Basic Books.

Williams, J., & Sloan, R. C. (1990). *Turning concept into practice: The Aurora Colorado story.* East Lansing: University of Michigan, National Center for Community Policing.

PART

Police Organizational Reform:
Planning, Implementation,
and Impact Within the Agency

Community Policing in Madison

An Analysis of Implementation and Impact

MARY ANN WYCOFF

WESLEY G. SKOGAN

BETWEEN 1987 AND 1990 the Police Foundation, with funding from the National Institute of Justice, observed the process by which the Madison, Wisconsin, Police Department fostered community policing. This chapter reports observations on the change process and presents significant findings about the impact of the process and the products of that change effort on both the officers in the department and the citizens served by it.

After an implementation period of 2 years, it was determined that:

- a new, participatory management approach was successfully implemented in the experimental area;
- employee attitudes toward the organization and toward their work improved; and
- physical decentralization was accomplished.

For citizens, these changes were associated with:

- a reduction in citizens' perceptions that crime was a problem in their neighborhood, and

AUTHORS' NOTE: Preparation of this chapter was supported in part by Grant 87-IJ-CX-0062 to the Police Foundation from the National Institute of Justice, Office of Justice Programs, U.S. Department of Justice. Opinions expressed in this chapter are those of the authors and do not necessarily represent the official position of the U.S. Department of Justice or the Police Foundation.

- an increase in the belief that police were working on problems of importance to people in the neighborhood.

Quality Policing in Madison

The importance of Madison's undertaking and of the research conducted there rests in substantial part on the fact that Madison was one of the first agencies to assert that there must be an internal foundation for the successful external application of community policing, or "Quality Policing,"[1] as the concept is known in Madison.

Since 1987 the Madison department has believed three conditions are necessary for the development of Quality Policing. The first is the implementation of a new management approach that supports employee participation in organizational decisions. The management philosophy is known as "Quality Leadership," an approach that emphasizes the role of managers as facilitators whose job it is to improve systems, involve employees in decision making, employ database problem-solving approaches, promote team work, encourage risk-taking and creativity, and give and receive feedback from employees.

The second necessary condition is a healthy work environment for employees. In Madison this means treating employees as "internal customers" whose problems should be identified and resolved. Quality Leadership is the means of creating the healthy workplace and is defined in Madison by the department's Twelve Principles of Quality Leadership.

1. Believe in, foster, and support *teamwork.*
2. Be committed to the *problem-solving* process; use it and let *data,* not emotions, drive decisions.
3. Seek employees' *input* before you make decisions.
4. Believe that the best way to improve the quality of work or service is to *ask* and *listen to* employees who are doing the work.
5. Strive to develop mutual *respect* and *trust* among employees.
6. Have a *customer* orientation and focus toward employees and citizens.
7. Manage on the *behavior* of 95% of employees and not on that of the 5% who cause problems.
8. *Improve systems* and examine processes before blaming people.
9. Avoid "top down," *power-oriented* decision making whenever possible.
10. Encourage *creativity* through *risk-taking* and be tolerant of honest *mistakes.*
11. Be a *facilitator* and *coach.* Develop an *open* atmosphere that encourages providing and accepting *feedback.*
12. With teamwork, develop with employees agreed-upon *goals* and a *plan* to achieve them.

Physical decentralization is the third necessary condition. A small work group (the consequence of physical decentralization) is viewed as essential to being able to identify and improve conditions in the workplace. At the same time, the closer physical proximity to citizens resulting from decentralization is necessary in order for police to know citizens and be aware of their problems.

The relationship of these three conditions to the goal of Quality Policing is reflected in the motto of the Madison department:

CLOSER TO THE PEOPLE:
QUALITY FROM THE INSIDE, OUT

The operational relationship among these ideas was to be developed and tested in what Madison called its Experimental Police District (EPD), one sixth of the department that was established in 1987 as the organization's laboratory for new ideas. Its initial charge was to promote innovation and experimentation in three areas:

1. employee participation in decision making about the conditions of work and the delivery of police service;
2. management and supervisory styles supportive of employee participation and of community-oriented and problem-oriented policing; and
3. the implementation of community-oriented and problem-oriented policing.

The EPD was to work through the problems of physical decentralization and create closer relationships with area residents for the purpose of solving problems in the community.

The Experimental Police District

Planning Process

In 1986 Chief David Couper proposed creation of the Experimental Police District.[2] Following an open departmental meeting to discuss the EPD idea, a selection committee of interested employees chose 10 members of the organization to serve as a planning team that represented all functions and ranks of the department. The Chief appointed a coordinating team that consisted of the Chief, four captains, and the president of the officers' union.[3]

The planning team selected an area that constituted approximately one sixth of the city[4] to serve as the project area. The group designed a facility to be built in the district and determined the numbers of personnel to work in the EPD, the means by which they would be selected, their basic responsibilities, and guidelines for their management.

The team identified organizational problems in need of correction, such as lack of meaningful involvement with the community, lack of teamwork and/or team identity among officers, inflexible management styles and resulting loss of creativity, and lack of communication and information exchange among ranks. Team members then met in small groups with all department employees to hear what they felt needed to be done.

To get citizens involved, the team held eight community meetings in the EPD area, two in each alderperson's district. Citizens were asked about their knowledge of and satisfaction with police services, neighborhood problems and concerns, and how they felt police could work with them in responding to problems. At each meeting the problems identified were rated by priority.

EPD Personnel

Officers and sergeants who wanted to work in the EPD bid for the assignment and their shift on the basis of seniority during the department's annual bidding process. More than enough officers bid for the 22 patrol assignments. This was not the case among detectives, who generally were opposed to being decentralized; at least three of the six original EPD detectives were assigned on the basis of their low seniority (i.e., inexperience). The lieutenant and captain for the EPD were chosen from among the applicants for these jobs by a vote of the project team and the personnel who had elected to work in the area.

The Experimental Police District opened for business in April 1988 with 40 sworn employees: 22 patrol officers, 3 neighborhood officers,[5] 6 detectives, 3 parking monitors, 4 sergeants, 1 lieutenant, and 1 captain. The captain has responsibility for all patrol and investigative operations at the station. He reports to the department's deputy chief of operations but has substantial flexibility in running the EPD. In addition to the sworn personnel, the EPD has a civilian stenographer and makes occasional use of volunteers and student interns.

EPD Training

All members of the department received Quality/Productivity training. In addition, EPD personnel received four additional days of training. Professor Herman Goldstein, from the University of Wisconsin Law School, spent a day discussing problem-oriented policing with the group. Much of the rest of the training focused on decentralization issues and the development of a team approach. Trainers also discussed the use of data for problem analysis and ways of measuring success at problem resolution.

One of the advantages of the EPD, resulting from the ease of making arrangements in a small work group, has been the frequency of in-service training. Training sessions are held whenever necessary to address issues that arise. Alderpersons from the area and personnel from other agencies may be invited to attend. Occasionally, the EPD invites personnel from the department's central station to attend training sessions dealing with problems between EPD and other department personnel. Although the formal training function will continue to be based in the central station, EPD managers feel that having their own training sessions facilitates teamwork and the handling of area problems.

EPD Facility

The building is visible and accessible on a heavily traveled, primarily residential street, a block from the main artery through the EPD area. Its external appearance is more like that of a professional office than a traditional police facility.

In the report to the National Institute of Justice on the evaluation of the EPD (Wycoff & Skogan, 1993), the building is described in detail because the evaluators concluded that the size and design of the work space played a central role in creating a sense of "team" at the EPD—an opinion shared by several officers and managers. A large briefing room serves multiple formal and informal functions, and its location in the center of the work space requires personnel of various functions and ranks to pass through it to reach the exit or other offices. It is a comfortably appointed area in which officers gather before their shift and where they can be found after shift conversing with colleagues who are coming to work. It functions as the EPD "family room" as well as the core operations space.

Observations of the use of this building suggest that other organizations planning to encourage closer working relationships among employees should give serious consideration to the design of the workplace.

EPD Management Style

The principles of Quality Management outlined previously have influenced managers throughout the Madison department but, during the evaluation period (1988-1990), were given greater emphasis in the EPD where the captain and lieutenant clearly viewed themselves as facilitators of officers' efforts to identify and solve problems. They reported their goal to be that of becoming coaches and teachers who allow and encourage creativity and risk-taking among officers. They gave officers substantial latitude to decide their own schedule, determine their work conditions, and decide how to address neighborhood problems. They sought and considered the input of employees before making managerial-level decisions.

EPD managers encouraged problem solving by offering ideas, information, and alternatives to traditional work schedules. They avoided directing officers to do specified neighborhood problem-solving activities. Initially, the EPD project team had planned for EPD personnel to work together to develop community policing strategies and plans for the station. However, it was decided after the station opened that EPD officers should individually, or in small teams, identify neighborhood problems and plan responses. Although things moved slowly at the beginning, by 1989 the managers reported an increased use of problem-solving approaches among officers.

Officers who identified problems were free to consult other officers and their supervisors to make arrangements for the necessary time and resources to address the problems. (This means ensuring that enough people are working, enough cars are available, etc.) Several officers worked cooperatively, switching days off or changing schedules to accommodate colleagues. Managers provided support by arranging teamwork across shifts and coordinating the efforts of officers who wanted to address the same problems.

To help arrange time for problem solving and for shift meetings, the sergeants, lieutenant, and captain occasionally would work the streets. EPD managers called their street work "management participation" (rather than participatory management) and felt that this involvement contributed to the team spirit.

Supervision and discipline deliberately were more informal at the EPD than in the rest of the department. Managers attempted to accept honest mistakes as mistakes. As indicated previously, officers were given wider latitude for carrying out problem-solving activities and were encouraged to seek innovative solutions and take risks. To support this, managers were more likely to begin a disciplinary case by examining it to determine whether it involved honest operational mistakes or blatant wrongdoing. In the case of apparently honest mistakes, they would attempt reconciliation between citizen and officer.

By sharing decision making with officers, managers appear to have fostered supervision among peers. Rather than always depending on sergeants to handle problems among officers, EPD officers were more likely to handle issues through informal discussions and through group discussions at briefings.

Work in the EPD

Although the research project included no systematic observations of officers, some of them reported in conversations with researchers their increased levels of interaction with citizens. When answering calls for service, officers might ask citizens if there were problems, other than the subject of the call, about which officers should be aware. Officers also might make more efforts to talk informally with citizens, visit businesses and schools, and attend neighborhood meetings. These activities reflected an emphasis on what managers at the EPD and in the rest of the department call "value added service." Basically, this means going the extra distance to do a good job: spending more time at calls; making follow-up visits or calls to problem addresses; analyzing calls for service to identify problems and proactively contacting those involved to seek a solution; and, in general, taking more time to understand the problems and concerns of citizens.

Officers from the EPD cooperated with a neighborhood association, for instance, to correct a speeding problem in one of the district's neighborhoods. In a community meeting with EPD officers, area residents had identified speeding on a particular street as a significant concern. Together officers and some citizens spent a day stopping cars speeding in the area. Instead of issuing tickets, officers issued warnings to the speeders and residents delivered personal pleas to them. The drivers were given a flyer explaining the speeding problem and displaying the fine that could have been levied.

Patrol officers at the EPD were allowed to develop individualized patrol strategies. Getting officers involved in problem solving was a gradual process; managers encouraged problem solving but did not require it. Some EPD officers requested their assignment for reasons other than eagerness to do community-oriented policing (e.g., the chance to work a better shift), but more active problem-solving officers did, in several instances, draw these other officers into community-oriented work by asking for their help on specific projects.

The flexibility given EPD officers to pursue interests and to work as teams was the major force motivating changes in service delivery. If, for example, a patrol officer wished to work plainclothes on a burglary problem, she or he was free to work out the arrangements with the supervisor and any other officer who might appropriately be involved in the effort. In another police setting, such a request from a patrol officer might be denied out of concern for the precedent it would set. At the EPD, this *was* the desired precedent.

Research Design and Methodology

There were three objectives of the Madison evaluation:[6]

1. document the process of developing the Experimental Police District;
2. measure the internal effects of change on officers; and
3. measure the external effects of change on citizens.

Objective One: Document the Implementation Process

Over the 3-year period of the evaluation, the Project Director, who was off site, monitored the implementation process through regular review of reports, memos, and newspaper articles; through direct observation of the EPD during site visits; by frequent telephone contact with EPD managers; and conversations with two University of Wisconsin faculty members who are long-term observers of the relationship between the department and the community.

Three annual administrations of a police personnel survey provided opportunity for numerous informal conversations with personnel throughout the organization concerning the perceptions of the change process.

During the summers of 1988 and 1990, the Project Director, assisted by George Kelling, conducted lengthy interviews with all members of the department's management team and, in 1990, with 14 lieutenants and eight detectives.

Objective Two: Measure the Internal Effects of Change

It was expected that successful implementation of Quality Leadership and the orientation of the department to community- and problem-oriented policing would have an impact on personnel that would be reflected in their attitudes toward:

- the organization, management, and supervision;
- the nature of the police role; and
- the role of the community in policing.

It was further expected that change in employee attitudes during the evaluation period would occur primarily in the Experimental Police District. The design for testing this assumption was a quasi-experimental one in which changes in attitudes of EPD employees would be compared over time with attitude changes of employees in the rest of the department. Exposure to the impacts of the changes in the EPD was to be controlled by analyzing changes for employees who had been in the EPD for the entire evaluation period of 2 years in comparison to those of employees who were never in the EPD during this period.

The conditions of a true experiment did not exist because the program site (the service area of the Experimental Police District) was not randomly selected but was selected by the department, based on a number of indicators of need. Officers were not randomly assigned to work in the EPD but were allowed to bid for assignment there just as they annually bid for other assignments.

Personnel Survey

Employee attitudes were measured by the administration of a written survey to all commissioned personnel three times during the evaluation period: December 1987, prior to the opening of the Experimental Police District; one year later in December 1988; and again in December 1989. Survey participation rates ranged between 97% in 1987 and 86% in 1989. The participation rate for the panel, on which most of the analysis is based, was 79%.

Analysis of Personnel Survey Data

Both within-group analysis and regression analysis were conducted. Within-group analyses were used to determine whether statistically significant change occurred *among* EPD officers and *among* Non-EPD officers; this was of interest because change clearly was occurring throughout the department. Regression analyses were conducted in which group assignment (EPD or Non-EPD) was the independent variable and the pretest score was controlled. These regression analyses are the most stringent measures of program effect.

Objective Three: Measure the External Effects of Change

Citizen Survey

It was expected that residents of Madison who were served by EPD officers would, over time, interact more frequently with police, perceive that they were receiving better service, and believe that police were addressing problems of concern to the community. These assumptions were tested using the quasi-experimental design that compared attitudes and perceptions of residents in the EPD service area with those of residents in the rest of the city. The same respondents were surveyed twice. The first survey was conducted in person in February and March 1988, just prior to the opening of the EPD station; the second was conducted by telephone in February and March 1990.

The total number of completed interviews at Time 1 was 1,170. The response rate in the EPD area was 77.8%; it was 75.1% in the rest of the city. For the posttest (1990) survey, 772 interviews were completed for a panel completion rate of 66.2%. Attrition analysis found the main outcome measures to be unrelated to attrition, either in general or within the program and comparison areas. In addition, there were no consistent differences between the areas in how rates of attrition were related to social and demographic factors.

Analysis of Citizen Survey Data

As with the officer data, analysis of the citizen surveys involved both within-group and regression analysis of the panel data. In the regression analysis, the following covariates were controlled: area of residency, number of adults in household, whether employed, education, residency in Madison in 1988, gender, U.S. citizenship, length of time in Madison, months lived in current residence, number of children in household, student status, race, whether employed full or part time, home ownership, income, whether living alone or as a couple, number of adults in household over 60 years of age, and respondent's age. Whenever appropriate, multiple items were used to measure a given construct.

The Findings

The Implementation Process

Observations and interviews confirmed that decentralization was accomplished successfully and that Quality Management was implemented in the Experimental Police District. Officers interacted as members of a team and participated with their supervisors and managers in work-related decisions.

The Internal Effects of Change

The following outcomes were considered important possible effects for employees of the efforts at internal change:

- *sense of participation in organizational decision making
- sense of cooperation among employees
- *feedback about work from other officers
- *frequency of contacts between officers and detectives
- *frequency of officer participation in investigations
- availability of time for proactive work
- *ease of arranging time off
- *perceived availability of backup support
- *satisfaction with physical working conditions
- satisfaction with kind of work on job
- *satisfaction with department as place to work
- *satisfaction with supervision
- sense that job is significant
- sense of wholeness of task
- *sense of autonomy in job
- satisfaction with potential for personal growth

- belief in working on neighborhood problems
- belief in citizen involvement in problem solving
- belief in noncrime problem solving
- belief in strict enforcement
- *belief that patrol function develops community support
- sense that citizens have high regard for police
- belief that people are altruistic
- belief that people are trustworthy
- *belief in benefits of change
- willingness to support change
- *belief in decentralization

In analyzing the effects of the changes on officer attitudes and reported behaviors, within-group analyses were used to assess the magnitude and patterns of change and regression analyses were conducted to test the strength of the proposition that the observed changes are the result of the approaches to management and operations used in the Experimental Police District.

Among these variables were 14 outcomes for which the regression coefficient was significant ($p < .05$), indicating that the outcome was positively and significantly associated with assignment to the Experimental Police District. These significant outcomes are indicated in the list above with an asterisk (*).

The within-group analyses produced a picture across these 27 outcomes of the entire department, moving generally toward goals of the change program. On 15 of these measures, scores for each group indicated movement (although not always statistically significant) in the direction of positive program effects. For 8 of these outcomes the regression coefficient was not significant, suggesting that the lack of demonstrated program (EPD) effect on these outcomes may have been the result of both the program and the control groups moving in the same direction over time. This finding of positive movement in both groups is a highly desirable result for an organization that is attempting a department-wide reorientation toward police service; it is a problem only for the evaluators who are looking for the measurable differences. In addition to showing that the entire department is moving toward goals of the change program, the data indicate that efforts made in the Experimental Police District are producing the desired changes to a greater extent or, perhaps, at a faster rate.

Insofar as it can be determined from attitudinal questionnaires, the data used to assess the internal effects of the change process strongly suggest that substantial progress has been made in the Madison Police Department, and especially in the Experimental Police District, toward the implementation of Quality Leadership.

The attitudes toward management and working conditions (the internal aspects of the job) changed more dramatically than did attitudes toward community involvement and the nature of the role. Nevertheless, there was a pattern of change within the EPD toward greater belief in community policing and prob-lem-oriented policing. The apparently greater strength of the organization-related attitudes suggests support for the two-stage model of change in Madison that calls for creating greater quality on the inside of the organization before it is manifested on the outside.

The External Effects of Change

The variables used in the citizen survey to measure the effects of the change process on the community included:

- seeing an officer in the area in past 24 hours
- *seeing an officer walking patrol in past week
- seeing an officer engaged in friendly conversation with neighborhood people in past week
- police came to door to inquire about problems
- *citizen attended meeting at which officer was present
- belief that lack of police contact is a problem
- citizen knows name of officer
- satisfaction with most recent citizen-initiated contact

Police perceived as . . .

- . . . attentive in last contact
- . . . helpful in last contact
- *. . . working with citizens to solve problems
- . . . spending enough time on right problems
- . . . good at preventing crime
- . . . good at keeping order
- . . . controlling speeding and careless driving
- . . . good at helping victims

Belief that . . .

- *. . . robbery or attack are problems (decreased)
- . . . adult drug use/sales is a problem
- . . . residential burglary is a problem
- . . . speeding and careless driving are problems
- . . . police are police
- . . . South Madison is a good place to live

- *. . . crime is a problem in South Madison (lower in EPD)
- . . . feeling of being unsafe in neighborhood at night

Worry about . . .

- . . . being robbed
- . . . burglary
- . . . theft outside at night

Having experienced . . .

- . . . robbery
- *. . . burglary (decreased)
- . . . knowing a burglary victim

There is some evidence among these external outcomes that the work of EPD officers is having a positive impact on residents in the area. Among the 30 outcomes listed above, there are 7 for which a significant regression coefficient suggests that improved attitudes or conditions may be attributable to the EPD efforts. These outcomes are marked with an asterisk (*).

Undesirable outcomes associated significantly with residing in the EPD service area are:

- increased belief that drug use and sales are big problems in the area, and
- increased belief that the violation of parking rules is a big problem.

It is the case that the external benefits are not as numerous as the internal benefits that were measured, and there are not as many that are as clearly attributable to community policing as the department had hoped. Constraints listed below (and discussed in detail in Wycoff & Skogan, 1993) may have limited the ability to find more evidence of community benefits. These include:

- the possible inadequacy of measures of impact. More development and testing of appropriate outcome measures specifically designed for community-oriented and problem-oriented policing needs to be done.
- the fact that community policing began to emerge late in the test period. The two-stage process of change in which the EPD was involved required more time and energy for the first stage (internal change) than had been anticipated; the second stage (improved external service) was not sufficiently developed at the time of measurement to show as much impact as had been expected when the evaluation was designed.
- too many changes were occurring at once. Ironically, the process of developing Quality Leadership, a goal of which is better service for the customer, may have

interfered initially with efforts to create a new external orientation. To guarantee that they were not being traditional, order-giving commanders, EPD managers began their new roles by taking a position of "allowing" community policing to occur rather than directing that it occur. Over time they realized that some officers were motivated by the sense of permission while others were more comfortable when receiving more explicit direction. Quality Management, like any effective management approach, may need to be tailored somewhat to each employee.

• attitudes of the EPD managers toward research. They knew what could be done to produce positive outcomes in the citizen surveys (e.g., door-to-door contacts just prior to the second survey) but deliberately chose not to induce an artificial effect, preferring the long-term benefits of changes that grew naturally out of the process of "permitted" or "facilitated" change.

• characteristics of the personnel who were the first members of the EPD. Because of seniority rules, some of those most interested in community policing and problem-solving policing worked the late shift where they were least able to work on problems with the community.

• citizen satisfaction levels already so high that efforts to raise them would have to be dramatic before changes would register as statistically significant. This was the case for several measures of citizen satisfaction with police service.

• the EPD was not changing in isolation from the rest of the department. The entire organization was being affected by the transition to Quality Leadership and was exposed to the ideas of community policing and problem-oriented policing.

The impacts of these various conditions cannot be measured and cannot be teased apart. They can only be noted as possible alternative explanations for findings or the lack of significant findings.

The most serious constraint may have been the time frame within which the evaluation had to be conducted. In any department, community policing is a slow organizational sea change from which measurable external effects perhaps should not be expected in less than several years. In the case of Madison where the change process was a two-stage one, the internal moves to decentralization and Quality Management required more time than initially had been predicted. The department was beginning to concentrate on the external changes at about the time this study had to be completed. Crime data and informal reports from the department 3 years later indicate that the magnitude of the external effects continues to grow.

Discussion

Surely the most dramatic finding indicated in this chapter is that it *is* possible to "bend granite" (Guyot, 1979); it is possible to change a traditional, control-oriented police organization into one in which employees become members of work teams and participants in decision-making processes. The Madison Police Department has changed the inside to the benefit of employees. This research suggests that associated with these internal changes are external benefits for citizens, including indications of reductions in crime and reduced levels of concern about crime.

Are these relationships causal? Or do they occur together in these data because they result from a variety of efforts, all of which were undertaken in the Experimental Police District at the same time? It is impossible to say. What can be said is that it is possible to implement participatory management in a police department, and that doing so is very likely to produce more satisfied workers.

Is the Quality Leadership approach a necessary condition for community-oriented and problem-oriented policing? This research cannot say with certainty that it is. Many managers and employees in Madison believe that it is, as do some theorists who write about these approaches to policing. Employees who are treated as internal customers, the logic goes, are better able to understand what it means to treat citizens as external customers. Employees whose input is valued learn to value the input of others (e.g., citizens). Employees who are invited to work in team relationships to solve internal problems learn in this way to work with citizens in team relationships to solve problems. People closest to the problems (officers and citizens) have the most information about those problems, and their input is critical for problem definition and resolution. Finally, students of change have long argued that organizational change is more readily accepted by employees who participate in the process of creating it. All of these arguments appear to have been supported in the Experimental Police District. If our data cannot prove a necessary relationship between the management style of Quality Leadership and the new approaches to policing, they do indicate that they were highly compatible in the Experimental Police District.

The data *do* indicate that officers' attitudes can shift from more traditional views of policing to ones that are more in line with police-community involvement in problem identification and resolution, even among officers with many years of service.

The data also cannot prove that decentralization is a necessary condition for community-oriented policing. Madison Police Department managers now tend to agree that it is. As observers, we believe that decentralization contributed significantly to the creation of the new management style. It also contributed to the development of team spirit and processes, conditions that should facilitate problem-solving policing. Officers who work in the EPD believe the decentralized station enhances relationships with the public; they report increased numbers of contacts with citizens in the community and an ever-increasing number of citizens who come to the station for assistance.

The scale on which decentralization occurred was important. The small physical space of the EPD station and its floor plan made close interaction among officers, detectives, supervisors, and managers unavoidable.

Our data also cannot prove that changing one part of the organization before proceeding with department-wide implementation is the best way to move toward decentralization and community policing. However, after more than 3 years of experience with this approach to change, the managers of the Madison Police Department, all of whom have experienced the various costs of changing in this way, tend to agree that this way *is* the right approach. Further, as the data indicate, special attention to one part of the organization did not block change elsewhere.

Finally, it must be emphasized that the changes that occurred in the Madison Police Department did not begin within the time frame of the study reported here. This study was a window into one relatively brief period in the much lengthier process of change. This research project did not begin at The Beginning, and we have no idea when to expect the full impact of the changes that are under way. The changes that are documented here have occurred and are occurring in a context of organizational history and community culture that may determine, to some unmeasured degree, the ability to implement the changes and the magnitude of the impact of the changes. The department began the change discussed in this chapter after nearly 15 years of ongoing experimentation with new ideas and the development of a commitment to seek better ways of conducting policing. Also, during this same period, continual efforts were made to recruit educated officers whose backgrounds, life experiences, and attitudes may increase their tendencies to support these changes. This observation is offered merely as a caution against unrealistic expectations for departments in which change is attempted in a different context.

Notes

1. "Quality Policing" is, for the Madison department, a broad concept that encompasses community policing. It is a philosophy that emphasizes quality of service delivery based on responsiveness to the customer, quality of life in the community, quality of life in the workplace, the Quality/Productivity/Quality Leadership processes advocated by Edwards Deming, and the Madison department's commitment to continual improvement. The link to "community policing" is the belief that, although the commitment to constant improvement means the department may one day work to implement other approaches to police service than ones now used, these will evolve out of current efforts to develop a community orientation to police service.

2. This discussion is indebted to the work of Chris Koper, a doctoral student at the University of Maryland in summer 1989 when he worked on this project as an intern with the Police Foundation.

3. The historical context of this planning effort is important. It was not the first time employees of all ranks had participated in organizational decision making. In 1981 the Officers' Advisory Council (OAC) was created. Twelve peer-selected employees who meet monthly with the Chief advise the management team about problems that need to be addressed and then participate in decisions about these issues. The OAC has selected both vehicles and weapons for the department. In 1984 a Committee on the Future of the department, broadly representative of the department, was created to establish long-range organizational goals. This study of Madison's change process, conducted between 1987 and 1990, provides only a narrow window onto a process that occurred over a 20-year period that began with Chief Couper's appointment in 1973 and continued after the evaluation project ended.

4. The project area has a diverse population including whites, blacks, Asians, Native Americans, and Hispanics. In 1986 the EPD area accounted for 20% of the city's reported crimes. It received 15,761 calls for service, which were 16% of total calls to the department.

5. In Madison, neighborhood officers are patrol officers who have responsibility for a neighborhood area that has been identified as needing more intensive service. Not required to respond to calls for service (although they often do), these officers have more time for community organization activities and problem identification and resolution than do other officers. At the time of this study, there were eight such officers in Madison, three of whom were assigned to the EPD area.

6. The detailed discussion of the methodology, analysis, and findings and the data collection instruments are available in the technical report for this project (Wycoff & Skogan, 1993).

References

Guyot, D. (1979). Bending granite: Attempts to change the rank structure of American police departments. *Journal of Police Science and Administration, 7*(3), 253-384.

Wycoff, M. A., & Skogan, W. G. (1993). *Community policing in Madison: Quality from the inside out. An evaluation of implementation and impact* (Tech. Rep.). Washington, DC: Police Foundation.

Implementing Community Policing

Cultural and Structural Change in Police Organizations

JACK R. GREENE

WILLIAM T. BERGMAN

EDWARD J. McLAUGHLIN

Community Policing as the Study of Organizational Change

In recent years a new "style" of policing has emerged in American law enforcement, a style emphasizing greater police and community interaction, increased managerial autonomy and accountability, and improved service delivery (Eck & Spelman, 1987; Goldstein, 1990; Kelling & Moore, 1988). Known generally as "community policing," this style of policing is argued to be a paradigmatic shift in public law enforcement wherein police organizations are to become "flatter" (less hierarchical), more product as opposed to process oriented, and less driven by reactive responses to citizen mobilizations (Skolnick & Bayley, 1986; Sparrow, Moore, & Kennedy, 1990).

In both the academic and practicing circles of American policing a new jargon, core principles, and a service rhetoric have accompanied this community policing discussion. Topics such as developing values and missions statements, advancing training and human resource development, and improving customer services and customer relations have been central features of the "new" language of American policing. Generally rooted in the "excellence movement" in the business sector (see, e.g., Peters & Waterman, 1982), community policing discussions resonate with ideas about "getting closer to the customer," "sticking to the knitting," and creating an internal organizational culture emphasizing "autonomy and entrepreneurship."

Although much attention in the literature on community policing has concentrated on police-public contact and cooperation and the need for an improved focus in service delivery, the organizational medium through which this "new wave" policing is to take shape is essentially under-studied (see Greene, 1993a). That is to say, for community policing to become a central feature of American law enforcement, the institutional framework and organizational apparatus of police organizations must be altered if they are to accommodate the sweeping changes implied by community policing proponents. The success or failure of community policing, then, is in large measure affected by the organizational structures and processes that characterize modern-day policing. Moreover, the internal culture of these organizations, together with structural and technological considerations, is also expected to greatly shape the success or failure of community policing implementation efforts (see Greene, 1993a, 1993b). This is true for several reasons.

First, by all accounts, police organizations have been some of the most intractable of public bureaucracies, capable of resisting and ultimately thwarting change efforts (Guyot, 1979). The rise and fall of "team policing" in the early 1970s is illustrative of the capacity of police organizations to deny change (see Sherman, Milton, & Kelly, 1973).

Second, the history of police organizational change has generally favored the police organization over other institutions bent on changing it. Organizational adaptation in police bureaucracies has tended to be one way: the change efforts adapt to the organization, rather than the organization adapting to the intended change. Confirmation of this proposition rests in the observation that American policing is more or less organized and implemented as it was at the turn of the century. Police organizations are rank and power centered, they maintain an emphasis on control, and they remain rooted in the call-response-call technology developed with the introduction of the motor car and police radio in the early 1900s. Culturally, police organizations remain inward looking; they are often distant from their clients and they shun most civic oversight attempts.

Third, although many have suggested the importance that police organizations play in shaping police responses (Manning, 1977; Rubenstein, 1973; Wilson, 1968), there are only a few studies that have examined police organizations empirically (see Langworthy, 1986). Detailed understanding of organizational change dynamics within police organizations, particularly as they relate to organizational culture considerations, is at best fragmented (see Greene, Alpert, & Styles, 1992).

The study of the adoption of community policing, then, is the study of organizational structure, culture, and service delivery change. Assessments of community policing, by consequence, must account for the structural, normative, and cultural dimensions of organizational life in American police departments.

This chapter briefly examines selected aspects of organizational change and cultural adaptation within the Philadelphia Police Department. It is a process that has taken at least 7 years to germinate, and it is a process that has yet to culminate in a reinvented police department. Philadelphia's experience, we believe, is not atypical. It has involved a series of starts, stops, and restarts. It has become an evolutionary rather than a revolutionary process. The process of changing the Philadelphia Police Department from a traditional police department to one emphasizing community policing goals and aspirations has been a process of selective adaptation.

Organizational Dynamics and Changing Organizational Culture

Classical views of organizational dynamics emphasize structure to the near exclusion of culture. Early theories tended to downplay the role that organizational culture has in shaping bureaucracies. Weber (1947) separated the professional and personal lives of his bureaucrats, in part as a means of leaving the issue of culture at the doorstep, rather than within his "ideal" organization. Early structural and managerial theories of organizations more often treated the internal culture of the organization as highly susceptible to manipulation by those in authority (Fayol, 1925; Taylor, 1911). For all practical and theoretical purposes the culture of an organization was the object rather than the source of organizational change.

The normative and cultural aspects of organizational life saw light briefly in the work of the early human relations movement, most notably the work of Mayo (1933), Barnard (1938), Roethlisberger and Dickson (1939), and reemerged in the 1950s and 1960s in the work of Argyris (1953, 1957), Drucker (1954), and McGregor (1960). The theoretical focus shifted from structure to process and from managers to workers. Work group culture dominated much of the analysis, and managerial focus shifted from control to co-optation and cooperation. The social-psychological dynamics of organizational life gained greater credibility, providing a foundation for the analysis of organizations as cultural systems (see Morgan, 1986). Other applied and theoretical work in organizational linguistics, semiotics, and semantics (for a review, see Ott, 1989) provided a rich set of constructs for investigating the qualitative aspects of organizational life.

In policing, many of these concepts were "arrested" in the era of managerial thought emphasizing unitary cultures and managerial control of those cultures. The writings of O. W. Wilson (1950) and the International City Management Association (Eastman, 1969), among others, greatly shaped thinking and practice of police managers throughout the 1960s and into the 1970s. Top-down management prevailed, command and control systems were emphasized, a style of detached police professionalism was advocated, and police work group norms were assumed to be inoperative or at least unimportant.

In the early 1950s and continuing to the present, police research began to focus on the interactions among the police, inside and outside of police organizations. The work of Skolnick (1966), Bittner (1967), Neiderhoffer (1967), Westley (1970), Black (1970), Reiss (1971), Manning (1977), Muir (1977), Van Maanen (1974), Klockars (1985), and others supported the idea of a police occupational culture that oftentimes thwarted attempts to have the police behave lawfully and/or change the basis of their social interactions with the public. As early studies of police culture, these works set the stage for the current assessment of the organizational culture of the Philadelphia Police Department and attempts to change that culture through the introduction of community policing.

The Impetus for Changing the Philadelphia Police

For many years the Philadelphia Police Department had earned, and often enjoyed, a reputation for being a "tough" police department. Despite its tough image, most Philadelphians typically supported the police. A tough police in a tough city, perhaps, or rather a local view that although the police had made mistakes in the past, the system of policing was reasonably intact. Although there had always been minor problems with the police and the citizenry, particularly in minority communities, there was a general feeling that the police were committed to public safety and upholding the law. And even though there were always to be "rotten apples" within the Police Department's ranks, the barrels—or the system of policing in Philadelphia—in which the apples were contained was generally sound.

The events surrounding the Philadelphia Police Department from 1983 throughout 1985 were to shatter even the most ardent support. A major corruption scandal, reaching the foremost top of the police hierarchy in the person of Deputy Police Commissioner Martin, and the public spectacle of the MOVE incident, where Philadelphia Police were accused of "bombing" an urban neighborhood, focused the perception of significant police department problems and provided the impetus for organizational introspection and purposeful change. Scandal and reform are intimately linked in policing throughout America (Sherman, 1978) and in Philadelphia.

Faced with a challenged internal ethic and the public display of MOVE, the Philadelphia Police Department had "bottomed out" in terms of public trust and confidence. Being a "cop" in Philadelphia had an onerous and negative public connotation in 1985.

A review of the department by an external "blue-ribbon" study group summarized the Philadelphia Police Department as being "unfocused, unmanaged, under-trained, under-equipped, and unaccountable" (Police Study Task Force, 1987, p. 16). The system of policing, not police officers, was under fire.

The Philadelphia Police Department's organizational style had been fundamentally shaped in the 20 years preceding MOVE and Martin. During this period the dominant ethos of the department emerged, an ethos that emphasized toughness, power, and dominance, and an ethic that would later lead the department into its crisis of confidence. As in many social institutions, the problems of the Philadelphia Police Department in the mid-1980s were the cumulative result of years of institutional neglect, an obliviousness to a changing world, and an institutional arrogance that pitted the police against those policed.

Case Study Overview

Invariably police services are produced through police organizations. In big cities these organizations are complex bureaucracies that continually spawn and mediate changes. As an organizational strategy in Philadelphia, "community policing" has come to mean the implementation of a philosophy and processes that: (1) encourage a police-community partnership in setting the local crime control and order-maintenance agenda; (2) strengthen a managerial culture focused on group decision making, inclusion, and reasoned analysis; and (3) rebuild the internal "thinking systems" of the police department so as to sustain long-term adaptation and growth.

Such a change agenda has had some modest successes and some unqualified failures over the 7 years of its development. This chapter presents a brief case analysis that addresses three interdependent questions:

1. How did the change agenda within the Philadelphia Police Department emerge, who were its champions, who were its detractors, what issues separated supporters from detractors, and how has support and conflict been mediated within the organization?

2. How did the internal organizational culture of the Philadelphia Police Department affect the assimilation or resistance to organizational change implied by this community policing strategy, and has the culture changed sufficiently to support the community policing agenda outlined for the department?

3. What are the community partnership outcomes of this change strategy in Philadelphia? Did they occur, with what degree of success, and with what effect?

Shaping the Change Agenda in Philadelphia

Changing the Philadelphia Police Department, like changing any large-scale bureaucracy, is a process of shaping the change agenda among command officers and other personnel, as much as it is a process of restructuring power and authority or changing the organization's structure. In late 1985 the Philadelphia Police Department was ripe for such change, given its poor showing in the Martin and MOVE scandals.

Despite the acknowledged need for change within and outside the Philadelphia Police Department, internal coalitions composed of ranking officers in liaison with external local politicians had a stake in preserving the traditional order of the department. These coalitions were a continual source of resistance, as the "old guard" made way for the new.

In January 1986 Philadelphia's then mayor, W. Wilson Goode, appointed the first police commissioner from outside the police department. The move toward an "outside" police commissioner gave the mayor the opportunity to distance this change effort from the department's historical malaise. At the same time, having an "outsider" direct the actions of an inwardly focused, control-centered bureaucracy proved to be a great liability for the incoming police commissioner. Without internal credibility, the new police commissioner was immediately confronted with hostile coalitional arrangements that were well steeped in the traditions of the Philadelphia Police Department. Figure 5.1 depicts the coalitional arrangements within the Philadelphia Police Department in 1986, as well as the Commissioner's efforts to rearrange coalitional forces.

The coalitions within the Philadelphia Police were of three orders. First, the three deputy commissioners appointed to the new police administration came with different agendas. Each had his own power base within the organization, an attachment to the department's traditions and beliefs, and enough power to effect or defeat change efforts. The deputy commissioners' interests were at best only partly in support of the police commissioner's views on organizational reform. More often than not the shifting power struggles among deputy commissioners impeded the rate of change anticipated under this "new" administration.

At a second level within this coalitional network were senior, old-line commanders (Chief Inspectors) who had been the leadership of the Philadelphia police in the prior 20 years. They retained control of vital organizational functions and they served as a buffer between the policies and pronouncements of the police commissioner and the deputy commissioners and the day-to-day activities of the rest of the department.

The poly-decisional and authoritative nature of the Philadelphia police at that time proved to increase coalitional conflict. Each of the senior commanders was an island unto himself. Each had considerable power and had grown up in the Philadelphia Police Department; they knew how to get things done and how to prevent them from being done. They were a formidable obstacle to change.

At the next coalitional level were upper and middle-level police commanders who had a more long-term stake in the reform of the Philadelphia police. Unlike their chief inspector counterparts—often referred to as the department's dinosaurs—these lesser ranked commanders were most likely to want change: They had only moderate investment in maintaining the historical past, they had been exposed to more ideas about police reform, they had more time to remain within the department, and they were more likely to feel the long-term consequences of the tainted image

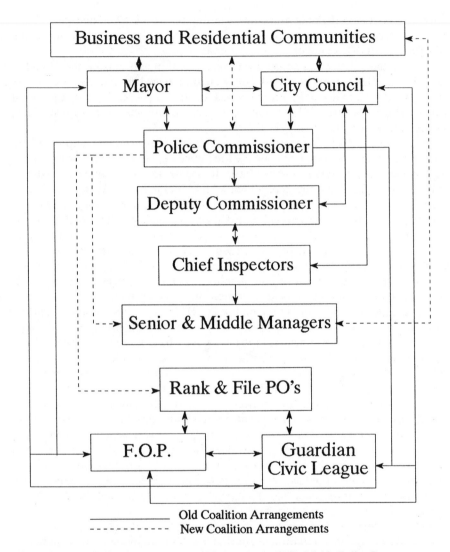

Figure 5.1. Coalition Environment for Changes in the Philadelphia Police Department

of the Philadelphia police. While there were certainly several individuals within these upper and middle management ranks who had allegiances to senior commanders and to chief inspectors, a significant number of others did not. As a result, this stratum of management within the department appeared more willing to adopt the change agenda of the police commissioner. Some of this acceptance was due to an acknowledged need for change, some was political—trying to be on the right side—while others joined the change effort without a clear alternative.

A final stratum within the coalitional arrangement was at the operational level. Here the rift was between two prominent labor-based groups, each with internal coalitions of its own. The Fraternal Order of Police (FOP), the recognized bargaining unit for Philadelphia police officers, had developed a combative, litigious posture toward the police administration. Although this posture preceded the change administration, the FOP became a more feverish advocate for stopping change efforts than for facilitating them. Virtually all attempts to reinvent the Philadelphia police involving personnel changes were resisted by the FOP, and much of the resistance was effective. The FOP resisted uniform changes, shift changes, personnel assignment changes, wage and salary changes, and changes aimed at improving the system of employee evaluation.

In addition to the FOP, a coalition of minority group officers had been formed in earlier years to increase pressure for equitable treatment for the department's minority officers. The Guardian Civic League, although not formally charged with contract negotiations, effectively used the civil courts, or threats of civil action, to cajole police administrators into taking minority officer interests into policy considerations. More often than not the position of the League was diametrically opposed to the position taken by the FOP, introducing yet another level of coalitional conflict into what was already a dense coalitional environment.

In this political and social "mix" of internal police coalitions, the new police commissioner was faced with a dilemma: how to bring the department along in a change process within an administrative culture designed to resist change? The initial solution to this dilemma was to introduce more complexity into coalition networks. By forming a coalition of upper and middle-level managers with active external business and community support, the commissioner sought to encourage a linkage among the long-term reform interests of the external community with the long-term capacity of those within the police department likely to be its future.

Related to this coalition building was the need to build managerial confidence and competence among subordinate commanders who were used to being told what to do, rather than being self-directed. For years upper and middle-level police commanders in Philadelphia had been managerially impotent. Decisions were made at the top of the organizations. Middle-level managers were not thinkers and policy makers, they simply carried out policy directives. To shift the practice and confidence of middle- and upper level managers several emphases, discussed below, were established.

Changing the Organizational Culture and Structure of the Philadelphia Police

From Implicit to Explicit Values

Since 1986 the Philadelphia Police Department has designed and implemented several emphases to make explicit a strategic vision for the department, its membership, and its community. Cumulatively, these efforts have resulted in two major developments. The first is the explication of a set of departmental ethics and a mission statement. The second is the adoption of a departmental strategic plan, the first of its kind in Philadelphia (see Williams, Greene, & Bergman, 1992).

In 1986 the Philadelphia Police Department commissioned the Philadelphia Police Study Task Force, a blue-ribbon panel of experts to assess all aspects of the police department. The Task Force's effort was to become a major "stock-taking" effort, explicating the resources available to the department, the goods and services produced by the department, and public recognition and acceptance of those goods and services.

In all, the Task Force made 92 recommendations for massive and far-reaching change within the Philadelphia Police Department (Police Study Task Force, 1987). Among its major findings, the Task Force noted that:

1. Philadelphia compared favorably to other big cities in respect to overall ratios of police officers to citizens, but that overspecialization in the department had stripped it of its general capacity to respond to calls for service.
2. The police department was under-managed and ill equipped in comparison to standards of common practice; police facilities were dilapidated and managerial initiative was nonexistent.
3. Performance evaluation within the department was generally lacking, and while police officer entry-level salaries were comparable to other large cities, over time police salaries, most particularly those of managers, became noncompetitive.
4. The police enjoyed some support in the community, but that support was tempered by a community belief that the police were sometimes brutal, drank on duty, and were themselves uncivil to citizens. This perception was more strongly held in minority communities.

Prior to the publication of the panel's report, *Philadelphia and its Police: Toward a New Partnership* (Police Study Task Force, 1987), the police department did not have an explicit strategic emphasis nor did it have a clear mission and set of organizational value statements. It was an organization in strategic drift.

By virtue of needing to improve the community focus of the department, an effort to create a mission statement and statement of ethical principles was successful early in the program. By the end of 1987 the Philadelphia Police Department had begun the process of overcoming negative public response to the MOVE incident and to perceptions that many of its 6,000 officers were corrupt. For perhaps the first time, the department and its community had two documents making a strategy of community partnership ascendent in Philadelphia.

The explication of departmental values and ethics together with a mission statement is important for three fundamental reasons. First, such statements make clear to those within and outside the organization what the organization values and has set for its goals. Second, such public pronouncements provide a yardstick for the assessment of the organization. That is to say, such documents create expectations about what the organization will and will not do and what services the public should expect from the organization. Third, such statements provide the formal basis for changing the informal culture of the organization through formal training and other socialization and value transmission activities.

Whereas in the past the Philadelphia Police Department lacked formal statements about purposes and expected services, throughout the 1986-1989 period the department began the process of better defining itself, its cultural underpinnings, and its attachments to its wider constituents.

From Shunning the Community to Community-Based Participation

The environments surrounding police agencies can be either hostile or friendly, they can be aggressive or passive, and they can be affected by whether the police organization is environmentally dependent or autonomous (Cordner & Greene, 1983; Sherman, 1978; Wilson, 1978). In turn, the internal dynamics of the agency can respond to or try to rebuff these environmental pressures. The extent to which rejection of the environment is possible depends on an autonomy-dependence relationship between the focal organization and the environment, the strength and persistence of environmental demand, and the coping mechanisms available within the agency for resisting external influence. Co-optation of the environment is often a strategy for reducing environmental pressures (Selznick, 1957).

In 1987, the community in Philadelphia was at once apathetic toward and demanding of police services. In 1985 the department responded to 3 million calls for service, roughly two calls for service for each resident. The community used the police for all kinds of services, 218,000 of which were "hospital cases," transportation of individuals to local hospitals.

A community survey conducted in conjunction with the Police Study Task Force reported favorable citizen evaluation of police service. The most positive evaluations came from white residents living in the Northeast section of the city, many of whom are blue-collar workers (Police Study Task Force, 1987, p. 164). Least positive ratings came from black and Hispanic residents, who are primarily concentrated in the North Central, West, and Southwestern sections of the city.

Among the most visible complaints about the Philadelphia police was the belief that minorities were treated more negatively by the police (4 out of 10 residents saw minorities being treated differently, and 87% of these respondents saw minorities as being treated less fairly) (Police Study Task Force, 1987, p. 167). Also striking was the finding that nearly 5 out of 10 residents saw the police as being unfair, discourteous, not caring about people's welfare, and lazy (p. 169). These distinctions were similarly defined by area of the city and by race.

Police and community relations have often been strained in Philadelphia. While citizens globally evaluate the department as effective, the department's reputation for aggressive law enforcement has often pitted the community against the police.

As previously indicated, cultures within complex organizations are difficult to change. Philadelphia's police had come to think of themselves as the "thin blue line" between civilization and chaos. All too often their actions further disengaged contact with the community.

In January 1986 the incoming police commissioner announced a policy of "community policing" to engage the police department and the citizens of Philadelphia in a dialogue about the quality of police services that were being provided. Of course the senior leadership of the department saw little reason for such a dialogue; they were convinced that with a little more manpower and greater resource commitment they could improve services and be more crime effective. Besides, community policing, they argued, was "soft on crime," something that the Philadelphia police did not take lightly.

An important component to establishing the premise for community policing, and the inherent partnership it implies for civic involvement, is the establishment of points of contact between the police organization and its wider service environment. This too is an important aspect of strategic management in that creating a vision for the organization and its constituents is a major task of the chief executive (see Reiss, 1985, pp. 61-69).

As part of the creation of the Police Study Task Force Study and the subsequent assessment of the Philadelphia Police Department by that group, an external Police Commissioner's Advisory Committee was convened with the explicit purpose of providing advice and council to the police commissioner on matters of strategic purpose. This advisory group, composed of several notable business, civic, and religious leaders, assisted the department in crafting the beginnings of a strategic vision throughout 1986 and 1987.

The central role of the Commissioner's Advisory Committee was to be a sounding board for proposed strategic changes within the police department. Given the business and community expertise represented by the members of this committee, responses to proposed changes could be immediately marshaled and subsidiary technical assistance could be more readily acquired. The Commissioner's Advisory Committee in its early stages (1987-1988) was primarily concerned with creating a supportive external environment within which a strategic emphasis for the police department might be developed. Later (1988-1990) the Commissioner's Advisory Committee focused on the design of a strategic plan, while in the most recent years (1990-1993) the committee is focused on evaluating progress toward the implementation of the strategic plan.

The Commissioner's Advisory Committee proved to be a powerful tool in maintaining pressure for change outside of the police department. The committee ultimately spawned 23 Police District Advisory Councils, each of which provides direct input into the management of local police services. These Police District Advisory Councils, involving nearly 300 residents and business persons, were originally created by the police. In 4 years they have come to take charge of their own affairs to the extent that they have created their own citywide

TABLE 5.1 Philadelphia Police Department: Shifting of Resources from a Specialized to a Generalized Police Department

Year	Patrol	Special Units	Investigation	Administration	Total Personnel
86	55.9	19.8	*15.9	**8.4	(6791)
87	51.7	15.1	15.3	17.9	(6753)
88	55.1	15.1	19.8	12.5	(6429)
89	53.9	12.6	16.3	18.6	(6014)
90	52.2	11.2	17.3	18.9	(6356)
91	56.9	11.6	16.4	14.4	(6479)
92	54.9	11.1	19.4	14.6	(6478)
93	64.5	10.2	14.0	11.3	(6175)

*Includes civil affairs, internal investigation, detective bureau personnel.
**Includes training and other support services.

charter and have become a potent force in lobbying the central administration of the police department for more efficient and effective police services.

In addition to expanding police department-community contact on a strategic level, the Philadelphia police also began to open the relationships between police and citizens on a service delivery and interpersonal level. In 1985, with the exception of a traditional "public relations" function, there was little contact between the department and its constituents. In 1986 the department implemented what were to become the equivalent of "community policing teams" in each of the patrol districts within the city. A Police Community Relations Officer, Victim Assistance Officer, Crime Prevention Officer, Abandoned Auto Officer, and Sanitation Officer were incorporated into this "neighborhood order-maintenance team." More than 100 officers are directly assigned to these positions. These officers report to the captain of the police district, who, in concert with the Police District Advisory Councils, directs these officers to resolve persistent order maintenance and crime problems.

These community-based efforts have been supported in the gradual reallocation of police officers from specialized functions within the department to more generalized functions. As shown in Table 5.1, police staffing decreased in Philadelphia between 1986 and 1993. At the same time, resources committed to patrol services have steadily increased, while specialized unit functions have gradually receded.

Increased resources to community-based police patrol services are further evidenced in the implementation of police mini-stations throughout the city. In 1985 there were no such neighborhood police services; by 1988, 14 mini-stations had been opened and by 1993 a total of 31 mini-stations were in operation. These stations typically deploy from two to four patrol officers to provide foot patrol services in neighborhood and business corridor settings. In addition to the opening of neighborhood mini-stations, in 1990 the Philadelphia Police Department opened a larger mini-station within the city's central business district.

TABLE 5.2 Philadelphia Police Radio/Calls for Service

Year	9-1-1	*231-3131	Total Calls	Actual Dispatches
83	2,462,631	620,576	3,083,207	3,719,603
84	2,389,309	622,271	3,011,580	3,612,148
85	2,497,421	643,699	3,141,120	3,655,811
86	2,845,550	628,483	3,444,033	3,655,811
87	3,097,044	41,418	3,138,462	3,582,938
88	3,015,480	0	3,015,480	2,506,987
89	3,028,893	0	3,028,893	2,552,209
90	2,981,384	0	2,981,384	2,496,748
91	2,857,089	0	2,857,089	2,491,417
92	2,753,274	0	2,753,274	2,372,205

*Police administrative telephone numbers.

Fifty-seven patrol officers, accompanied by approximately 60 Community Service Officers and 115 street cleaners, all function together to improve the "quality of life" in the central business district of Philadelphia (see Greene, Seamon, & Levy, 1993).

The upshot of much of the community policing efforts in Philadelphia has been an impact on calls for police service. Calls-for-service impacts have been largely conditioned through the district and center city level community policing efforts and through a conscious effort to increase differential police response systems. Table 5.2 provides data on calls for police services in Philadelphia from 1983 to 1992. As indicated in the table, total calls for service declined by about 300,000, while patrol dispatches have decreased by nearly 1.4 million. Much of the initial decline in calls for service is attributable to a reduction in calls received through an administrative line (as shown in the table). Nevertheless, both the total calls for service and the number of police dispatches have declined, most dramatically since 1986.

A third potential indicator of the increased community focus of the Philadelphia Police Department is related to abandoned vehicles. Abandoned vehicles increase public wariness about crime, while at the same time providing additional locations for criminal activity. As such they are neighborhood hazards.

Table 5.3 provides information on the number of abandoned vehicles towed in Philadelphia from 1985 through 1992. As shown, the number of abandoned vehicles towed doubled during that period. The vast majority of these vehicles are abandoned in residential neighborhoods; their removal contributes to neighborhood demands for order maintenance services.

Collectively, the efforts described above have opened the police department to greater civic attachment. Nevertheless the department has continued to resist the formation of a citizens' review process, and recently Philadelphia's City Council passed such legislation over the objection of the department and the mayor.

TABLE 5.3 Philadelphia Police Department

Year Abandoned	Vehicles Towed
FY 85	13,077
FY 86	10,011
FY 87	21,938
FY 88	24,475
FY 89	23,385
FY 90	27,785
FY 91	28,035
FY 92	26,516

From Top-Down To Decentralized Management

The central command staff within the department was itself divided. Long-tenured commanders and those who grew up in the former police system in Philadelphia more often than not sent mixed messages about their support of the changes sought. As previously indicated, the Commissioner developed a cadre of middle-level command officers to assume some of the programmatic responsibilities anticipated in the change program.

In 1986 the Commissioner announced that South Police Division would become an "experimental" police command for the purposes of building a decentralized model of police service delivery. After many starts and stops, South Police Division became a model of decentralized police services. In this experimental division, repeat call analysis, problem-oriented policing, and a host of other programs were implemented (see Davis, Smith, Lurigio, & Skogan, 1991; Greene & McLaughlin, 1993).

The South Division experience ultimately influenced the department's understanding of and approach to decentralization issues. In 1992 the department decentralized police operations, including patrol, juvenile investigations, general investigation services, and some tactical functions.

From Doing to Thinking First

Another important ingredient necessary for the support and continuation of a change emphasis within the Philadelphia Police Department was changing the internal "learning curve" of the managerial corps. As expected, this has proved to take the longest amount of time, given the state of managerial development among police executives in Philadelphia prior to 1986.

Prior to 1986 police supervisors and managers within the Philadelphia Police Department received little in the way of information regarding strategic planning, management, or leadership. To be sure, some of those commanders independently pursued training and education that would have brought them into contact with such matters. Nonetheless, up to and including 1986 there was no systematic effort on the part of the department to upgrade its managerial personnel and to make them conversant in strategic issues.

By 1987 and throughout 1989 the leadership of the department arranged to finance the first of several "brain-trust" developments by sending nearly 100 managerial personnel to two independent executive-level managerial training programs. The first program was conducted by Harvard University, in conjunction with the Police Executive Research Forum. A total of 44 police managers from Philadelphia participated in this program.

Upon returning from the Harvard experience, these police managers, Harvard coffee cups and T-shirts in hand, had begun to develop a change ideology and a change vocabulary. They became a core element of police managers to spearhead change efforts within the Philadelphia police. They were formed into policy committees producing recommendations for changing the service delivery, organizational, and managerial systems within the Philadelphia Police Department. Although it ultimately took a few years for these "policy reports" to take hold, the "seeds" of changing the internal administrative culture had been placed. The "Harvard 44" nevertheless labored under a continuous bombardment of senior-level commander control, in part because these senior managers had been consciously excluded from participation in the Harvard program. And, despite the formation of this core of change agents within the administrative apparatus of the Philadelphia Police Department, it ultimately took several years before any of these officers had the administrative rank to adequately fend off challenges for control from the "dinosaurs."

These efforts initially created the pretext and later the context of change within the Philadelphia Police Department. The legacy of these initial efforts is found in the department's official policy as well as its unofficial practices.

In early 1989, another executive-level training program was germinating in a local university in Philadelphia. By 1990 the Public Service Management Institute was up and running and seeded with persons who were seen as on "the fast track." The Temple program, similar to the program designed at Harvard, had several distinguishing features of its own. First and foremost, the Temple program was designed from the onset to produce a strategic plan by introducing group decisional processes into the police department. Widespread management group involvement in the crafting of the department's first strategic plan went a long way in facilitating its internal acceptance. Furthermore, this developmental process assisted the department in better grounding an internal capacity to conduct similar planning exercises in the future.

This personnel development process has also served to support the decentralized approach to service delivery now operant in Philadelphia. Managerial personnel, most particularly those in line-command functions, now have greater autonomy than they did in the past.

Concluding Remarks

The change process in Philadelphia described here is yet to be completed. And, in many respects, this change process will continue as part of the evolution of this complex police organization. The Philadelphia Police Department has moved considerably from its status in 1985; still, it has considerable distance yet to travel. Much of the effort to date has been focused on managerial development and improved use of line personnel. Internal communications and analytic systems are much less developed. In such an analytically transitional state, the department struggles to maintain a community focus.

Structurally, the Philadelphia Police Department has experienced at least four reorganizations since 1985. Some were cosmetic, while others were substantive. At present many of the department's operational functions have been decentralized; police training has more substance than it did in the past, and the rhetoric of community policing is beginning to become more prominent in departmental discussions. On the other hand, as part of the transitioning of the organization, there are more chief inspectors today than ever before in the department's history, giving the department the perception and reality of being top-heavy.

Externally, the community (civic and business) has come to expect a different service-based style of policing in Philadelphia. This is perhaps the most important of all the changes, in that such expectations will continue to press the department toward greater community involvement.

Community-based policing is a dramatic departure for most traditional police agencies in America. It involves building trust within and outside the police department, and it involves power sharing. As such it requires thorough consideration of police organizations and their internal cultures, to the extent that these structures and cultures can inhibit such institutional change.

References

Argyris, C. (1953). *Executive leadership.* New York: Harper & Bros.

Argyris, C. (1957). *Personality and organization.* New York: Harper & Bros.

Barnard, C. I. (1938). *The functions of the executive.* Cambridge, MA: Harvard University Press.

Bittner, E. (1967). The police on skid-row: A study of peacekeeping. *American Sociological Review, 32*(October), 699-715.

Black, D. (1970). The production of crime rates. *American Sociological Review, 35*(August), 733-740.

Cordner, G. W., & Greene, J. R. (1983). Policy and administration in criminal justice organizations. In W. Jones (Ed.), *Criminal justice administration* (pp. 101-133). New York: Dekker.

Davis, R. C., Smith, B. E., Lurigio, A. J. & Skogan, W. G. (1991). *Community responses to crack: Grassroots anti-drug programs.* Washington, DC: National Institute of Justice.

Drucker, P. F. (1954). *The practice of management.* New York: Harper & Bros.

Eastman, G. D. (Ed.). (1969). *Municipal police administration.* Washington, DC: International City Management Association.

Eck, J., & Spelman, W. (1987). *Problem-solving: Problem-oriented policing in Newport News.* Washington, DC: National Institute of Justice and Police Executive Research Forum.

Fayol, H. (1925). *Administration industrielle et generale.* Paris: Dunod.

Goldstein, H. (1990). *Problem-oriented policing.* New York: McGraw-Hill.

Greene, J. R. (1993a). Civic accountability and the police: Lessons learned from police and community relations. In R. Dunham & G. Alpert (Eds.), *Critical issues in policing* (2nd ed.) (pp. 369-394). Prospect Heights, IL: Waveland Press.

Greene, J. R. (1993b). Community policing in the United States: Historical roots, present practices and future requirements. In D. Dolling & T. Feltes (Eds.), *Community policing—Comparative aspects of community oriented police work* (pp. 71-92). Holzkirchen/Obb.: Felix Verlag.

Greene, J. R., Alpert, G. P., & Styles, P. (1992). Values and culture in two American police departments: Lessons from King Arthur. *Contemporary Criminal Justice, 8*(3), 183-207.

Greene, J. R., & McLaughlin, E. (1993). Facilitating communities through police work: Drug problem solving and neighborhood involvement in Philadelphia. In R. C. Davis, A. J. Lurigio, & D. P. Rosenbaum (Eds.), *Drugs and the community* (pp. 141-161). Springfield, IL: Charles C Thomas.

Greene, J. R., Seamon, T. S., & Levy, P. (1993, March). *Merging public and private security for collective benefit: Philadelphia's Center City District.* Paper presented at the meeting of the Police Futurist Society, Baltimore, MD.

Guyot, D. (1979). Bending granite: Attempts to change the rank structure of American police departments. *Journal of Police Science and Administration, 7*(3), 253-284.

Kelling, G. L., & Moore, M. H. (1988). From political to reform to community: The evolving strategy of police. In J. R. Greene & S. D. Mastrofski (Eds.), *Community policing: Rhetoric or reality?* (pp. 3-26). New York: Praeger.

Klockars, C. E. (1985). *The idea of police.* Beverly Hills, CA: Sage.

Langworthy, R. H. (1986). *The structure of police organizations.* New York: Praeger.

Manning, P. K. (1977). *Policework: The social organization of policing.* Cambridge: MIT Press.

Mayo, G. E. (1933). *The human problems of an industrial civilization.* Boston: Harvard Business School.

McGregor, D. (1960). *The human side of enterprise.* New York: McGraw-Hill.

Morgan, G. (1986). *Images of organization.* Beverly Hills, CA: Sage.

Muir, W. K., Jr. (1977). *Police: Streetcorner politicians.* Chicago: University of Chicago Press.

Neiderhoffer, A. (1967). *Behind the shield.* Garden City, NY: Doubleday.

Ott, J. S. (1989). *The organizational culture perspective.* Pacific Grove, CA: Brooks/Cole.

Peters, T. J., & Waterman, R. H., Jr. (1982). *In search of excellence.* New York: Warner Books.

Police Study Task Force. (1987). *Philadelphia and its police.* Philadelphia: Philadelphia Police Department.

Reiss, A. J., Jr. (1971). *The police and the public.* New Haven, CT: Yale University Press.

Reiss, A. J., Jr. (1985). Shaping and serving the community: The role of the police chief executive. In W. A. Geller (Ed.), *Police leadership in America* (pp. 61-69). New York: Praeger.

Roethlisberger, F. J., & Dickson, W. J. (1939). *Management and the worker.* Cambridge, MA: Harvard University Press.

Rubenstein, J. (1973). *City police.* New York: Farrar, Straus & Giroux.

Selznick, P. (1957). *Leadership in administration.* Evanston, IL: Row, Peterson.

Sherman, L. W. (1978). *Scandal and reform: Controlling police corruption.* Berkeley: University of California Press.

Sherman, L. W., Milton, C. H., & Kelly, T. V. (1973). *Team policing: Seven case studies.* Washington, DC: Police Foundation.

Skolnick, J. H. (1966). *Justice without trial: Law enforcement in democratic society.* New York: John Wiley.

Skolnick, J. H., & Bayley, D. H. (1986). *The new blue line: Police innovations in six American cities.* New York: Free Press.

Sparrow, M. K., Moore, M. H., & Kennedy, D. M. (1990). *Beyond 911: A new era for policing.* New York: Basic Books.

Taylor, F. E. (1911). *The principles of scientific management.* New York: Harper & Bros.

Van Maanen, J. (1974). Working the street: A developmental view of police behavior. In H. Jacob (Ed.), *The potential for reform of criminal justice* (pp. 83-130). Beverly Hills, CA: Sage.

Weber, M. (1947). *The theory of social and economic organization.* Oxford: Oxford University Press.

Westley, W. A. (1970). *Violence and the police.* Cambridge: MIT Press.

Williams, W. L., Jr., Greene, J. R., & Bergman, W. T. (1992). Strategic leadership in a big-city police department: The Philadelphia story. In K. E. Clark, M. B. Clark, & D. P. Campbell (Eds.), *Impact of leadership* (pp. 107-118). Greensboro, NC: Center for Creative Leadership.

Wilson, J. Q. (1968). *Variety of police behavior.* Cambridge, MA: Harvard University Press.

Wilson, J. Q. (1978). *The investigators: Managing FBI and narcotics agents.* New York: Basic Books.

Wilson, O. W. (1950). *Police administration.* New York: McGraw-Hill.

The Effects of Organizational Structure on Community Policing

A Comparison of Two Cities

DEANNA L. WILKINSON

DENNIS P. ROSENBAUM

THE FUNDAMENTAL QUESTION about community policing in the 1990s is not "should it be implemented?"—the concept is already extremely popular with policymakers—but rather "How should it be implemented?" With any sizeable programmatic or organizational change there is always the risk of serious setbacks or delays in achieving the optimum level of implementation due to poor planning, employee or community resistance, or other factors. In theory, community policing represents a fundamental change in the basic role of the police officer, including changes in his or her *skills, motivation,* and *opportunity* to engage in problem-solving activities and to develop new partnerships with key elements of the community. Therefore, the primary responsibility for achieving these basic changes in police attitudes and behaviors rests with the officer's employer. Police departments, led by a growing number of talented and progressive chiefs, must face this task head-on if they want to go beyond the labels and buzz words of the 1980s to see an impact on community problems.

AUTHORS' NOTE: The research discussed in this chapter was supported by a grant from the Illinois Criminal Justice Information Authority to the University of Illinois at Chicago. Points of view expressed in this chapter are those of the authors and do not necessarily represent the official position of the ICJIA or the University of Illinois at Chicago.

Determining what changes in the police organization are needed to achieve real changes in policing on the street is a matter of opinion, but some consensus exists on the larger issues. Allowing officers the freedom to be creative problem solvers and resource facilitators will require a less rigid, less hierarchical organization with a new set of performance standards and rewards. In addition, giving officers the necessary skills and motivation to excel in their new role will require radically different training programs at all levels of the organization, including new approaches to supervision. Beyond this, there is little agreement about the prescription for organizational reform, and hence, individual police departments have pursued a wide range of initiatives under the umbrella of community policing.

This chapter tells the story of two cities in Illinois that received sizable grants to develop and implement community policing as demonstration programs. Our evaluation of these demonstration programs focused on the planning and implementation processes during the first year and how these changes were received by police personnel.

Problem-oriented policing provided the theoretical foundation for these demonstration programs, as the planning process was heavily influenced by the work of Goldstein (1979, 1990) and the problem-solving model articulated by Eck and Spelman (1987). This adherence to the problem-solving approach carries important implications for the order in which specific changes are introduced on the road toward full-scale community policing. Seeking to eliminate police dependency on the *means* of policing and to focus their attention on the *ends* or goals of policing, Goldstein (1979) argues that addressing specific community problems should take precedent over "improvements in the internal management of police departments" (p. 236). More specifically, he suggests that:

Improvements in staffing, organization, and management remain important, but they should be achieved—and may, in fact, be more achievable—within the context of a more direct concern with the outcome of policing. (1979, p. 236)

A problem-oriented approach, with its greater appeal, has the potential for becoming a vehicle through which long-sought organizational change might be more effectively and more rapidly achieved. (1979, p. 257)

Indeed, many departments have heeded this advice and have focused their efforts on identifying and solving community problems. For the demonstration programs studied here a key question is: How has the introduction of problem-oriented policing affected the organizational structure that supports the many demands of modern policing? Has the structure changed to meet the demands of problem solving? Conversely, how does the initial organizational structure influence the department's ability to implement problem-oriented policing? More generally, what efforts are made to reduce any incompatibility or dissonance between the organizational structure and the new police role? Although many departments have struggled with these change issues, few have had their experiences documented by outside researchers.

The Foundation for Organizational Reform

Previous reform efforts have concentrated more consistently on changing the underlying organizational structure under which police departments operate (see Angell, 1971; Bayley, 1988; Goldstein, 1979, 1987, 1990; Kelling & Moore, 1988; Wilson, 1950). "Professional law enforcement" promoted an organizational design, based on classic organizational theory, that is highly centralized, formally hierarchical, and quasi-military (Moore, 1992). Modern police agencies have relied heavily on bureaucratic means of control including: close supervision, orders given from the top down, information flow from the bottom up, extensive use of record keeping or documentation of activity (Kelling & Moore, 1988), promotions based on impersonal evaluations by supervisors, and managerial control maintained "through a monocratic system of routinized superior-subordinate relationships" (Angell, 1971). This structure has been viewed as a successful approach to control police discretion, promote fairness, avoid misuse of authority, and protect the individual rights of citizens. It has also been blamed for many of the existing problems in modern police organizations, including a 911 system that makes officers prisoners of endless nonemergency calls, an impersonal system of performance evaluation, and other factors that lead to low officer morale, high levels of cynicism, and an inability (and lack of opportunity) to work closely with the community in a problem-oriented framework. Whether or not problem solving is the best vehicle for changing the role of police in society or whether it can even precede substantial organizational reform remains uncertain.

In their essay on the history of policing, Kelling and Moore (1988, p. 11) describe the dominant organizational design for the "community problem-solving era" as having five central characteristics that distinguish it from the reform or professional law enforcement era: (1) workers can have substantive interest in their work; (2) officers' discretion can be encouraged and supported through community engagement, problem solving, and other strategies; (3) decentralization of decision making to line personnel in neighborhood specific assignments can be effective; (4) increased participatory management; and (5) more involvement of top executives in strategic planning and implementation. While these are considered defining characteristics of organizations during the current community problem-solving era, we are quick to point out that few if any police organizations have fully implemented this model.

Moore and Stephens (1991) take a closer look at organizational issues in their paper on the strategic management of police departments, and they offer the following recommendations for improvement: Organizational structure would need to change from a functional orientation to a geographic one, decision making would need to be decentralized to line-level personnel, the emphasis of training would need to shift from academy based to field based, and control of officers would need to rely on "a system of values supported by the organization's culture and evaluation of officers' actions after the fact" rather than a rule-based system emphasizing close supervision and prior authorization (Moore & Stephens, 1991, p. 103).

Moore and Stephens describe a variety of organizational structures and operating styles that exist in police departments that are considered traditional organizations. The uniqueness of police organizations may be determined largely by the rigidity of the bureaucratic structures and by various contextual factors. These important variations may affect the level of success when implementing community policing.

In sum, many hypotheses and theoretical suppositions have been articulated about the relationship between community policing and organizational structure and the effects this fit may have on job satisfaction, community confidence, and use of police resources (see Goldstein, 1979, 1987, 1990; Greene, 1989; Hackman & Oldham, 1976; Moore & Stephens, 1991; Rosenbaum, 1988; Skogan, 1990). Despite numerous expectations, the empirical literature is scant in this area. Many important process questions have not been fully addressed. How do organizational structure and cultural climate influence the overall planning and implementation process? How do different police departments, with a variety of pressures both internally and externally, cope with efforts to institute structural, programmatic, and attitudinal changes? What mechanisms are necessary or useful to promote the shift from a traditional operating mode to a problem-oriented or community policing approach? It is hoped that the field research reported here will shed some light on this issue.

Setting and Methods

The findings reported here are the product of field research conducted at two medium-sized police departments in Illinois. The cities of Aurora and Joliet had received a large grant to develop and implement community policing strategies in their communities. The University of Illinois at Chicago was funded to conduct a process and impact evaluation of this program, referred to as the Aurora-Joliet Neighborhood-Oriented Policing and Problem Solving Demonstration (NOP) project (see Rosenbaum & Wilkinson, 1993; Wilkinson & Rosenbaum, 1993).[1] The two sites were similar on a number of dimensions, including the type of population served, the size of the police force, a joint proposal to implement similar community problem-solving programs, the type of outside technical assistance received, the content of the training program, and the level of external funding. However, the organizational structures and styles were different in several ways, as described below. Hence this was a unique opportunity to observe the implementation of similar community policing plans in two settings where many variables were held constant and key organizational factors varied.

The goals of the NOP demonstration were to improve the quality of life, reduce criminal activity, reduce fear of crime, and increase community confidence. In addition, the departments sought to target gang and drug activity through a problem-oriented policing approach.

The description below provides a general overview of the context in which police reform efforts coalesced during the early phases in two cities.

The Aurora Program. The City of Aurora, a metropolitan area approximately 40 miles away from Chicago, serves as a center for surrounding communities in Kane and DuPage counties. Of the nearly 100,000 residents, 64% are white, 23% are Hispanic, and 12% are African American (according to 1990 U.S. Census data). Approximately 74% of the housing is owner-occupied with a median rent of $425 per month. Aurora is physically divided by the Fox River, separating the city into two distinct areas. The target areas were located on the east side of town, which has a higher concentration of lower income residents and subsidized public housing. An emerging gang problem over the past 5 to 10 years and the subsequent increase in violent crime had become a major community concern.

Like many other police forces, the Aurora police department operated under the professional law enforcement model. In the 1990s the organization could be described as having three general characteristics: hierarchical structure with rigid centralized control, functional distribution of resources (highly specialized), and dependence on bureaucratic procedures to regulate performance. The department had approximately 210 sworn personnel, with about 20% ranking at sergeant or above. Experimentation with community policing strategies began within the department nearly 2 years prior to the award of grant monies under a progressive chief hired in 1989 from outside the organization.

The program was commonly referred to as the Neighborhood Action Base Station (NABS) and officers assigned specifically to a neighborhood were called NABS officers. The concept behind NABS was to utilize a transportable police substation that could be placed temporarily in high-crime, high-fear neighborhoods, thus enabling the station to follow displaced or newly emergent problems. Once the project goals were met in a particular area and the neighborhood was stabilized, the idea was to move the unit to another targeted area. The main NABS objective was to help the police department serve as a "catalyst to renew community involvement and positive police-citizen interaction."

Organizationally, a specialized unit approach was used for program implementation. Fifteen officers representing all four shifts were assigned to five program target areas. Officially, NABS officers were considered part of the Patrol Bureau—they reported to patrol supervisors and attended daily roll call meetings. Unofficially, all guidance and support for program officers came from the Research and Planning Unit within the Administrative Services Bureau, the unit responsible for managing the community policing grant. All police personnel were exposed to the problem-oriented policing concepts in a 12-hour training seminar conducted by the Police Executive Research Forum.

The Joliet Program. The City of Joliet is located approximately 40 miles southwest of Chicago and is typically described as a working-class, blue-collar town. The population, according to the 1990 U.S. Census, is 76,836 persons, of which 65% are white, 22% are African American, and 13% are Hispanic. The percentage of owner-occupied households is nearly 63% and the median rent is $331 per month. Like Aurora, the Des Plaines River provides a natural boundary and divides the city into two distinctive communities. Community problems described by key informants related to gang activity, drug dealing, and poor economic conditions.

The Joliet police department was found to be an organization with a long history of traditional policing. Within this organization of nearly 200 sworn personnel (19% at the rank of sergeant or above), professionalism had been defined by aggressive enforcement and reactive patrol. Although the department relied heavily on an organizational structure with clearly defined roles regarding command and control, unlike that in Aurora this structure was not strictly executed. The structure was less rigid and a more relaxed climate prevailed. Police personnel were laid-back in style, relationships were personal in nature, and informal mechanisms were used to achieve desired results. Bureaucratic procedures—including paper work—were avoided whenever possible. In contrast, paper work was a central feature of the Aurora organization.

In Joliet, seven target areas were identified for implementation during the first phase of the Neighborhood-Oriented Policing program. The NOP unit, although technically part of the patrol division, was very specialized and separate from regular patrol officers. Eighteen NOP officers were primarily responsible to two sergeants assigned to the program and had a limited amount of interaction with other street sergeants. NOP officers were allowed to have flexible schedules and oftentimes used this option (e.g., worked the day shift for one day, afternoons the next day, etc.). Department-wide training was conducted on three important topic areas: problem-oriented policing, cultural awareness, and crime prevention.

Methodology. A multimethod approach was used to document the planning and implementation process of the NOP program in both Aurora and Joliet. Extensive field work provided the bulk of the data. The field work was completed between October 15, 1991, and October 14, 1992, with more intensive data collection during the first 3 and last 3 months of the study. Frequent site visits were made, with as many as four visits per week during the most intensive period of the evaluation. Several field methods were employed, including in-person interviews with key participants, focus group interviews, observations, and a comprehensive review of documents.

Each process methodology served a particular purpose in the overall research design. Generally speaking, the field protocols were directed at organizational and work issues related to the implementation of community policing strategies. The study sought to describe the organizational and program structure, program planning and resources, the types of strategies attempted, program coordination and management, and factors affecting implementation. Comparisons were made between the two departments by identifying both the common and unique experiences with regard to program development and implementation.

On average 45 police department personnel from each department were interviewed one or more times. Both purposeful and random sampling procedures were used to select respondents for in-depth interviews, focus groups, and observations (see Henry, 1990; Patton, 1987). Both program and nonprogram personnel at all ranks were represented in the sample. In addition to the structured interviews, numerous informal interviews, observations, and reviews of documents helped shape the overall impression formed by the researchers.[2]

The Planning Process

The NOP programs in Aurora and Joliet were conceptualized by the two police chiefs with input from PERF advisors and various police personnel within each department. The initial plan for both departments was to develop the program incrementally, beginning with a small specialized unit, and then implement it throughout the department.

Aurora Planning. For the most part, planning and decision making in Aurora were highly centralized prior to the introduction of community policing. The NOP planning process attempted to remedy this situation, at least with regard to the NOP initiative. Upon the recommendation of the technical assistance provider, a committee was established to oversee the general direction of the NOP program and deal with issues and concerns that arose during implementation. The need for a healthy representation of patrol officers on the committee was emphasized. Eight patrol officers (including many assigned to NABS) were selected by the chief and NABS supervisors to be part of the 14-member committee. The implementation team, under the direction of one sergeant and/or one lieutenant, completed a 5-month planning phase during the early months of 1992. While the committee was active, participating officers complained about being excluded from the decision-making process. Some officers felt that management was controlling the meetings, setting the agenda, and limiting the level of participation/input from the rank and file officers.

In addition to the implementation team meetings, NABS program officers and a sergeant from the Research and Planning Bureau met informally on a semi-regular basis (monthly) to discuss problem-solving initiatives and other implementation issues. In most cases these meetings were an opportunity to exchange strategy information, brainstorm on alternative problem-solving approaches, discuss community and agency involvement, and plan for collective problem-solving efforts. Oftentimes, the meetings became a forum to air complaints and frustrations.

A command-level committee was also established to plan for the future of the department. The Strategic Planning Committee (STRAP) met on a regular basis and was designed to be an ongoing mechanism to evaluate the strengths, weaknesses, and long-range needs of the department. It also created a forum to monitor the progress of NABS and other activities.

In sum, despite the use of committee and unit meetings, adequate representation of rank and file in the planning and decision-making process never occurred in Aurora. Several program officers were distressed about the lack of commitment to seeking input from line officers. The following example illustrates this frustration. In spring 1992, two bicycles were purchased for summer use by the NABS unit. The use of bicycles was a cause for concern among several NABS officers who felt they should have been consulted on such an important decision. From the officers' point of view, supervisors were simply making decisions for them without seeking their input. As a result, some felt bitter about the lack of inclusion and were cynical about using the bikes on patrol.

Joliet Planning. The planning process in Joliet occurred at several levels. The original plan was developed by the chief of police and others within the department. The first planning committee[3] consisted of command-level personnel only. This body, which met on a monthly basis, was primarily responsible for selecting program target areas but was involved in other implementation issues.

A second planning committee, the Implementation Team, was established to incorporate the views of rank-and-file personnel. It consisted of a more representative slice of police personnel, as well as individuals from other city departments. This group met at least monthly from November 1991 until April 1992. A rotating "chair" approach was selected to ensure that all committee members were included in the planning process. On at least one occasion the planning and the implementation committees held a joint meeting to share ideas. During the ensuing months, however, meetings were less regular and in general the interest in sustaining a large planning committee seemed to wane.

Although department-wide planning for community policing was on the decline in Joliet, the NOP unit (including sergeants) met as a group on a regular basis to discuss implementation issues and problem-solving projects. Planning at the officer level for problem-solving projects was intense and diverse. Essentially, officers were assigned to an area in pairs and were given the freedom to plan their own problem-solving projects. The two NOP supervisors regularly discussed with officers any proposed projects prior to implementation.

Overview of Planning Results. The above observations suggest that the planning processes used in each department—which were influenced by the organizational histories—played an important role in determining the line officers' receptivity to change and ultimately impacted the department's success with implementing community policing. The centralization of decision making at the command level in Aurora upset the department's efforts to promote community policing among non-command personnel. The heavy reliance on existing mechanisms for planning restricted input from officers most likely to be affected by the new program, thus creating resentment and some degree of withdrawal from the process. In contrast, the use of participatory management principles in Joliet was effective in stimulating officers' participation in the planning and problem-solving process.

NOP Structure

Community policing is often brought to life through an organizational arrangement involving special units or bureaus that function with relative autonomy. Small-scale implementation is a common first step by police chiefs who want to move slowly and avoid "upsetting the apple cart." This strategy also allows administrators to be responsive to the often-heard call to decentralize the police bureaucracy, while at the same time test the waters of change. Aurora and Joliet were no exception, as each created specialized units to implement the program. The unit configuration, however, was different in each department and each claimed unique advantages and disadvantages. Indeed, the repercussions of these distinctive attributes were felt by the police personnel, although not always as expected.

Joliet Structure. In Joliet, the unit was highly specialized and organizationally isolated from the rest of patrol. This gave the organization an opportunity to develop community policing strategies within the "incubation chamber" of a specialized unit. The NOP officers had little interaction with regular patrol and the two NOP sergeants had only limited contact with other sergeants. NOP officers were allowed to have flexible schedules so they could become familiar with neighborhood concerns at different times of the day. Their responsibility for handling calls was limited to their assigned target area.

Although the creation of a special unit served to protect these NOP officers and their supervisors from the usual demands of professional policing and allowed them time to develop problem-solving projects, this organizational structure also served to isolate NOP officers from the rest of the department, in effect creating a "split force." This created some predictable problems. With regard to problem solving, NOP officers experienced limited success working with regular patrol officers who were assigned to the zone car that encompassed the NOP target area. Regular patrol officers felt that some NOP officers were taking advantage of their special status in an unstructured environment. They also expressed concern about whether NOP officers were getting adequate supervision. Although the relationship between regular patrol and NOP officers improved over time as the former became more familiar with the objectives of the NOP program, some of the standard problems associated with specialized units continued to hinder further improvements (e.g., misperceptions about roles, responsibilities, and performance evaluations).

Aurora Structure. In Aurora, the use of a specialized unit (NABS) looked quite different than in Joliet. NABS was initially perceived by regular patrol as a separate, elite unit, but significant efforts were made to prevent its isolation and the development of other problems known to be associated with specialized units. For example, frequent interaction with regular patrol officers (during daily roll call), placement of the unit on the shift level, and the maintenance of call handling responsibilities (albeit limited) were among the steps taken to avoid the perception of an "elite squad of problem solvers." NABS officers reported to the patrol shift supervisor and were responsible to that individual. These efforts to prevent the perceived formation of an elite team, while effective, had serious untoward consequences for the program. Most importantly, this organizational placement contributed to the lack of interest or involvement in community policing exhibited by first-line supervisors. NABS officers were quite critical of their supervisors. The officers recalled numerous instances where supervisors were, in essence, barriers to effective problem solving. First and foremost, many NOP officers reported that their supervisors placed too much emphasis on responding to calls for service, suggesting that problem solving was secondary to handling specific incidents.

The supervisors' lack of interest in community policing was apparent to the NABS officers. During a ride-along interview, one officer explained a recent and rare occurrence in which the direct supervisor had actually read one of the problem-solving project worksheets and had asked a question about it. The officer's reaction was one of astonishment in light of past experiences with first-line supervisors in the department. Most of the officers attributed their supervisors' attitudes and behavior to an inability to deviate from "the way things were"—a time when responding to calls for service was the highest police priority. The following comments from two officers convey their concerns:

> Even if you have something that's really important that you want to get done—[something] that's going to save a lot of man hours in the future—they [supervisors] still think that you've got to answer that radio call, whatever it is. Until we get over that hump in this program, it's going to be slow going.

> . . . back in the 1970s and even the early 1980s, the big thing was the response time in handling every call that came into the police department. And they're still stuck on that mode of thinking. And they don't want to leave that. The call is more important than actually doing the job out there. We have to get away from that mentality. . .

Recognizing this lack of management support, the Research and Planning Bureau stepped up to provide most of the supervision and support for the NABS program during the first year. One sergeant single-handedly shouldered the responsibility for the day-to-day operational needs of the program, including coordinating officers assigned to NABS, getting the substations operational, promoting the program among department personnel, and assisting officers with problem-solving projects. The original plan was that NABS activities should be developed and sustained with the support of patrol operations. Clearly, this support mechanism never evolved; instead, the program was sustained by an informal structure in administrative services.

Our analysis of Aurora suggests that this outcome was due to the strong opposition of a rigid bureaucracy, a professional policing climate, and the availability of a charismatic leader to salvage the program. The sergeant in

Research and Planning was able to work around bureaucratic obstacles and exploit strong personal relationships to achieve his objectives. As a respected leader in the department, he was able to convince some of the most resistant personnel to participate in community policing activities. Oftentimes he used a crisis management approach to pressure them or to remove obstacles.

The implementation of the community policing grant was far behind schedule when he was assigned to the unit. Furthermore, there was a widely held belief that community policing efforts would be unsuccessful, based on prior experiences with the concept. In the face of this skepticism, the sergeant was committed to making NABS a success and used his position well to get *some* of the NABS activities moving forward. The emergence of an informal structure to support the Aurora initiative was effective for averting program failure and even guaranteed some degree of success with implementation. However, this informal structure—and the program activities it spawned—had little impact on the rigidly formal structure of the organization. For the remainder of the department it was "business as usual." In fact, constant effort was necessary to maintain even a low level of cooperation and interest in community policing with certain personnel. Street sergeants claimed no responsibility for the NABS program and resented the loss of control over NABS officers. In addition, those sergeants who were persuaded by the charismatic NABS sergeant to become more involved simply did not see the benefit of endorsing the community-oriented policing philosophy. Although the NABS unit was able to make some progress on problem-solving activities, the organizational arrangement prevented sustained implementation.

The experiences of these two departments show that the operationalization of specialized units can take different forms and result in different outcomes. In Joliet, the intentional segregation of problem solvers from regular patrol officers created a split force with relationship problems. Over time frictions lessened, as many nonprogram personnel saw the benefits of problem-solving activities in the troubled areas. In Aurora, efforts to prevent the appearance of a split force created its own set of problems, including ambiguous reporting lines and lack of organizational support for NABS activities. In addition, the heavy reliance on informal support mechanisms weakened any attempt to transform the existing structure. The Aurora experience illustrates how a department with rigid lines of command and control can be unwilling to make a drastic departure from this style of management for the sake of community policing.

Program Implementation

In many ways program implementation in Aurora and Joliet looked quite similar. Specialized units, storefronts or substations, beepers, cellular telephones, foot patrols, and bicycles were part of the community policing operations in both cities. Technical assistance and one major component of the training were also provided by the same source. Despite these similarities, time lines and planning mechanisms for the programs varied dramatically during the first year. Also, the departments had different organizational arrangements, problems, and resources that either facilitated or inhibited program implementation. In both cases certain administrative changes that occurred were disruptive and delayed implementation progress.

Our fieldwork suggests that one of the major differences in implementation process between the two cities was the level of emphasis on bureaucratic operationalization of the program. The more formal the bureaucracy, the slower the implementation of community policing. The documentation of problem-oriented policing projects is one example of how this difference is played out. A second illustration can be found by comparing the types of problem-solving projects that emerged under different levels of formality.

Example 1: Documentation of Problem Solving. In January 1992, Aurora's Implementation Committee and one of its subcommittees developed a formal system for documenting problem-solving projects in Aurora. After studying several examples from other departments across the country, the committee developed a problem-solving activity worksheet that was tailored to the needs of the organization. Many issues had to be addressed before this paperwork could be finalized. Committee members were concerned that information about specific problems would not be properly disseminated throughout the department, thus precluding the possibility of several officers working together as a problem-solving team. Hence, they decided that a formal paperwork system was needed to process all problem-solving projects and that such a system would engender department-wide participation in the program. The subcommittee developed and pilot tested a five-part carbon-copy form designed to achieve maximum involvement and allow the organization to monitor the status of individual problems.

Unfortunately, the documentation process (i.e., the "means") became the focal point of the Aurora program rather than problem solving itself (i.e., the "ends"). Consistent with the organization's strong bureaucratic style, the committees revised the original form many times to satisfy those involved in the planning process and to create what they considered the best database. Because of this concern with paperwork and process, less time was spent discussing problem-solving strategies per se. Although one might expect this documentation process to encourage supervisory participation and involvement of nonprogram officers in the problem-solving process, this did not happen for the structural and cultural reasons stated earlier.

In Joliet a totally different attitude about documentation was prevalent. Joliet police officers repeatedly stated that they "hate paperwork." For this reason, the development of a formal system to document problem-solving projects was not considered a priority. The administration felt that unnecessary paperwork would discourage officers from getting involved with problem solving. Documentation was considered a low priority and officers were encouraged to keep records of their efforts using mechanisms already in place. Some documentation, however, was considered a "necessary evil" to enhance accountability and provide a basis for officer recognition. A less formal system was employed whereby NOP officers submitted a one-page project description to their immediate supervisor for review and feedback. The emphasis in Joliet was on effective problem-solving activity, whereas Aurora paid considerably more attention to developing an effective means of documenting problem-solving activity.

Example 2: Types of Problem Solving. A cross-site analysis of problem-solving projects provided additional insight regarding the effects of organizational structure on the daily practice of community policing. Generally the problem-solving projects in Joliet were much more involved than those in Aurora. Officers exhibited a more thorough understanding of the first three stages of the problem-solving model (see Eck & Spelman, 1987, for an outline of the four-stage problem solving model). Furthermore, the problems identified in Joliet were more complex and more likely to require the application of multiple resources than the problems targeted in Aurora. Although Joliet officers were granted the autonomy to develop their own ideas, guidance, support, and accountability for problem solving was provided by the two NOP sergeants. The guidelines for problem solving were defined rather loosely allowing officers the opportunity to be creative and unconventional. Being creative and unconventional, however, does not necessarily guarantee effectiveness. In many cases, officers did not decompose large, complex problems into smaller, more manageable issues, thus making it difficult to develop effective solutions.

In one target area, for example, NOP officers identified a number of problems including open-air drug dealing, gang activity, drive-by shootings, fear of crime, vandalism, and other disorder problems at an apartment complex. The officers defined the entire complex (consisting of several 6-8 story buildings) as their problem-solving project. Because the problems at the target location were multifaceted, a comprehensive approach was attempted. Officers worked with the property management company to begin to address problems affecting building tenants and nearby residents. As a first step, officers implemented a number of enforcement strategies to stabilize the area. Trespass agreements were signed enabling the police to regulate visitors to the properties. Off-duty police officers assumed responsibility for the security of the properties (at the expense of the management company). These actions were an impressive start, but NOP officers became frustrated trying to identify additional strategies that would get to the underlying causes of the problems at this location. They realized that enforcement strategies alone would not solve the fear and disorder problems that plagued the area. Officers encouraged building managers to get more involved in maintaining the properties, getting residents more involved in self-protection, and screening prospective tenants but detailed, intensive programs were not developed. Other strategies were planned and had yet to be implemented. Officers monitored the status of the problem through the analysis of citizen calls for service from that location. This example illustrates the difficulty police officers can encounter when analyzing large complex problems. The NOP team did not have a comprehensive plan for improving the area or attacking specific problems, despite the best of intentions. Nevertheless, they were able to bring closure to a number of smaller problems.

In Aurora, a major problem was bringing closure and completeness to the process. Although NABS officers tackled many problem-solving initiatives during the first year (with the exception of about 10 to 15), most were left incomplete or are best described as one-time responses to persistent problems. Many of the original problem-solving cases were closed out administratively without checking the status of target problems. In Aurora, officers were most concerned with identifying problems and proposing possible solutions. Unfortunately, many proposed responses had not been fully implemented or were abandoned midpoint. One source of the problem was apparent from our fieldwork, namely, that problem-solving efforts were lacking in support, supervision, guidance, and accountability. Consistently throughout the first year NABS officers reported that their primary support and assistance came from one sergeant and one watch commander. A review of the formal documentation database revealed that officers would initially identify the problem, outline a strategy, and project the results. The actual strategy used and the results achieved were rarely recorded in the file. Also, we did not find that closed problem-solving initiatives had been reevaluated with any regularity.

Lack of administrative support for the program in Aurora goes a long way toward explaining the absence of full-blown problem solving. Many times officers reported that they were not, in fact, "freed-up" to do problem-solving work during the first year. As a result cases were often initiated but strategies were not implemented. Some officers (both program and nonprogram) expressed concern about the department's support of problem-solving efforts and wondered how long the "few good people" involved would continue to "carry the ball."

Clearly, some of the difficulties experienced in Aurora were due to an enduring police culture and the absence of leadership (with regard to community policing values and philosophy) at high levels of the administration. Nevertheless, structural arrangements still played a critical role in limiting the implementation of effective problem solving. For example, as a result of the documentation procedure created in Aurora, officers' behavior was measured by the number of problem-solving cases initiated rather than the quality of their problem-solving work. Inevitably, this will increase the quantity of work at the expense of quality.

Conclusion

The literature on community policing is replete with speculation and theorizing about the type of organizational structure and work environment that is needed to implement these new initiatives successfully. While agreeing on the need for organizational reform to fit community policing strategies better, there is little consensus about the urgency or importance of specific changes or the manner in which change should be instituted. For example, will problem-solving strategies necessarily lead to the organizational changes discussed in the literature or must organizational changes be implemented first to create an environment where problem-solving activities will thrive? Although definitive answers to these questions are not available, the present research in two midwestern cities does shed some light on these and other issues.

On the basis of extensive field work during the first year of planning and program implementation, several conclusions can be drawn from the experiences with community policing in Aurora and Joliet. First, a police organization that is heavily invested in the professional model of policing—with a centralized, hierarchical, and bureaucratized command structure—will have difficulty creating an environment that is conducive to community policing strategies and that encourages creative problem solving. This is not to suggest that community policing initiatives cannot survive in these conditions, but doing so may require the creation of an informal support structure within the organization or a completely isolated unit with its own set of rules, regulations, and performance standards for some period of time.

Second, to survive is not the same as to thrive. Although community policing can survive within the constraints of special units, this does not mean that such activities will flourish or even survive for an extended period of time given the cultural and organizational forces that continue to work against this arrangement. The level of success is likely to depend on the degree of isolation from these forces and the level of management support among other factors. In one of the present case studies, management support went beyond the immediate needs of the special unit to include the development of plans for department-wide implementation. By advising all officers in the organization that community policing is here to stay and will become a part of their everyday work experience, some opposition can be nipped in the bud. Given that immediate department-wide implementation seems unmanageable (and has never been attempted to our knowledge), this may be the only feasible approach.

Third, the field data suggest that "participatory management" is not an empty concept. When commanders and supervisors exclude line officers from the decision-making process, resentment and withdrawal can follow. When they are included, officers can emerge as motivated planners and problem solvers.

Fourth, the depth of an organization's commitment to bureaucracy appears to be inversely related to the speed at which it is able to implement community policing. Too much concern with accountability and control can lead to significant program delays as new systems and procedures must be created and tested. Furthermore, the results suggest that problem solving can become means-oriented policing if officers get lost in the bureaucracy of paperwork and forget the larger objective. Having said this, we should also say that we believe that some amount of record keeping is critical to the problem-solving process and should not be discarded for the benefit of efficiency or short-term employee morale. The type of supervisory feedback and reinforcement that is considered essential to encourage a new behavioral repertoire for police officers will require good documentation of employee activities.

Fifth, with regard to the policy question about whether bureaucratic reform should precede or follow the implementation of community policing strategies, we found little evidence that the implementation of problem-solving strategies had any significant impact on the police organization structure or police culture as a whole (while the reverse was certainly true as noted above). When a department demonstrates a rigid adherence to the professional model of policing, it seems unwilling to give up this command and control for the sake of community policing. When the style of management is less rigid and more informal, the door is opened slightly for a gradual breakdown in the prevailing bureaucracy, especially when change is presented by the chief as inevitable. Of course, it is important to note that our evaluation took place in the first year of these programs, and one might choose to argue that the repeated application of the problem-solving approach will eventually modify the way business is conducted and change the culture that maintains it. We are more inclined, at this point, to conclude that in rigid organizations, community policing initiatives will be snuffed out before this happens unless the professional model is attacked from all sides and from the top and the bottom. Special units with a "few good officers" do not have the clout to change the larger organization, as the history of team policing so vividly illustrates.

Finally, on a related note, we would be remiss not to mention that the constraints on new community policing programs reached far beyond organizational structure to police culture. Although we did not address police culture in any depth here, certainly we observed the forces of resistance at all levels of these departments— forces that appeared to stem from officers' beliefs and philosophies about the legitimate role of police in society, their fear of punishment, and so forth. Clearly, organizational structure and police culture are closely linked and mutually reinforcing; strategies for reform may need to approach them differently. Regardless, our observations suggest that the chief of police and the leadership he or she demonstrates plays a critical role in changing both the culture and the organization.

Today, police chiefs and researchers on the cutting edge have their attention focused almost exclusively on the goals of policing rather than the means of policing. While this change of focus is laudable, perhaps there has been too little attention paid to the means of reform. We all seem to know where police organizations should be headed, yet our knowledge of how to get there remains quite limited. The continued reporting of research findings and individual experiences should help to correct this state of affairs.

Notes

1. Funds for the demonstration and evaluation were provided by the Illinois Criminal Justice Information Authority.

2. The typical structured interview approach used in qualitative evaluation was modified significantly in this study to provide a richer database (see Dorr-Bremme, 1985, for a discussion of the advantages of less structured depth interviews with observation built into the design). A majority of the interviews of (program and nonprogram) officers were conducted during ride-along observations. Members of the research team spent part or all of a shift out on the street with the officers. This approach promoted a more relaxed environment in which officers could be interviewed and observed simultaneously.

3. Committee on Problem-Oriented Policing (CPOP).

References

Angell, J. E. (1971). Alternative to police organization. *Criminology, 9,* 186-206.

Bayley, D. (1988). Community policing: A report from the devil's advocate. In J. R. Greene & S. D. Mastrofski (Eds.), *Community policing: Rhetoric or reality?* New York: Praeger.

Dorr-Bremme, D. W. (1985). Ethnographic evaluation: A theory and method. *Educational Evaluation and Policy Analysis, 7*(1), 65-83.

Eck, J. E., & Spelman, W. (1987). *Problem-solving.* Washington, DC: Police Executive Research Forum.

Goldstein, H. (1979). Improving policing: A problem-oriented approach. *Crime and Delinquency, 25,* 236-258.

Goldstein, H. (1987). Toward community-oriented policing: Potential, basic requirements, and threshold questions. *Crime and Delinquency, 33*(1), 6-30.

Goldstein, H. (1990). *Problem-oriented policing.* New York: McGraw-Hill.

Greene, J. (1989). Police officer job satisfaction and community perceptions: Implications for community-oriented policing. *Crime and Delinquency, 36*(2), 168-183.

Hackman, J. R., & Oldham, G. R. (1976). Motivation through the design of work: Test of a theory. *Organizational Behavior and Human Performance, 16,* 250-279.

Henry, G. T. (1990). *Practical sampling.* Applied Social Research Methods Series, Vol. 21. Newbury Park, CA: Sage.

Kelling, G. L., & Moore, M. H. (1988). *The evolving strategy of policing* (Perspectives on Policing, No. 4). Washington, DC: National Institute of Justice and Harvard University.

Moore, M. H. (1992). Problem-solving and community policing. In M. Tonry & N. Morris (Eds.), *Crime and justice: A review of research: Vol. 15. Modern policing.* Chicago: University of Chicago Press.

Moore, M. H., & Stephens, D. (1991). *Police organization and management: Towards a new managerial orthodoxy.* Washington, DC: Police Executive Research Forum.

Patton, M. Q. (1987). *How to use qualitative methods in evaluation.* Newbury Park, CA: Sage.

Rosenbaum, D. P. (1988). Community crime prevention: A review and synthesis of the literature. *Justice Quarterly, 5,* 323-395.

Rosenbaum, D. P., & Wilkinson, D. L. (1993). *Aurora-Joliet neighborhood-oriented policing and problem solving demonstration project: Impact on police personnel and community residents: Vol. 2. Draft final report.* Chicago: Center for Research in Law and Justice.

Skogan, W. (1990). *Disorder and community decline: Crime and the spiral of decay in American neighborhoods.* New York: Free Press.

Wilkinson, D. L., & Rosenbaum, D. P. (1993). *Aurora-Joliet neighborhood-oriented policing and problem solving demonstration project: Process evaluation: Vol. 1. Draft final report.* Chicago: Center for Research in Law and Justice.

Wilson, O. W. (1950). *Police administration.* New York: McGraw-Hill.

Problem-Oriented Policing

Actions and Effectiveness in San Diego

GEORGE E. CAPOWICH

JANICE A. ROEHL

PROBLEM-ORIENTED POLICING (POP) is part of the family of reforms generically referred to as community policing. The development of problem-oriented policing occurred simultaneously with the development of community policing (Goldstein, 1990), yet these two policing strategies are just as often combined (Goldstein, 1987; Wilson & Kelling, 1989) as separated (Eck & Spelman, 1987b; Trojanowicz & Bucqueroux, 1989). Although problems—drug dealing, burglaries, mischief-making teenagers—are the common focus of both, the way the community is defined differs. In a community-oriented approach, a geographically based *community* with particular problems is first and foremost the policing target. In a problem-oriented approach, a specific *problem* is targeted, with the community of interest involved in problem analysis and resolution. In addition, community-oriented policing is probably best viewed as a guiding philosophy for police, whereas problem-solving is one means of enacting a community-based philosophy at the street level.

Problem-oriented policing is based on the idea that police need to focus their attention on the *ends* of policing and move away from their traditional emphasis

AUTHORS' NOTE: This research was funded by grant number 90-DD-CX-0058 from the National Institute of Justice. The views and opinions expressed are those of the authors and do not represent the policies of the National Institute of Justice, the Office of Justice Programs, or the U.S. Department of Justice.

on the *means* (e.g., rapid response, arrest) of policing. The ends of policing, according to Goldstein (1979), are the vast array of problems the public expects the police to resolve, or at least control. For this shift to occur, police need to harness the informal experiences of street officers and apply this knowledge to the substantive concerns of the public. Problem-oriented approaches to police work are based on the assumption that careful analysis of problems will enable police agencies to create policies and procedures that provide useful guidance for officers in their efforts to address neighborhood problems.

Addressing substantive problems is a more substantial change for police agencies than might appear at first because it implies a different focus and role for police and portends changes for the organization. It is well known that police have always addressed a wide array of problems in their communities—violent felonies, missing children, loud parties, and homeless people. A fundamental difference between POP approaches and traditional police work is that POP directs officers away from viewing individual occurrences as unrelated incidents and toward a focus on the underlying factors that account for the repetitious nature of some incidents. This requires that police de-emphasize their responses to incidents (the means of policing) in favor of addressing the underlying problems. Shifting to POP approaches is a major change for police departments because this demands that police

> go beyond taking satisfaction in the smooth operation of their organization; it re-
> quires that they extend their concern to dealing effectively with the problems that
> justify creating a police agency in the first instance. (Goldstein, 1990, p. 35)

The systematic implementation of problem-oriented policing as a specific form of policing is generally attributed to the Police Executive Research Forum (Eck & Spelman, 1987a, 1987b). Its roots may be traced to the Madison Police Department's problem analysis methods (Goldstein & Susmilch, 1982), Baltimore County Police Department's COPE units (Cordner, 1986), New York City's CPOP officers (McElroy, Cosgrove, & Sadd, 1989), the systems approach to community crime and drug problems (Roehl, Capowich, & Llaneras, 1991), as well as to the work of the London Metropolitan Police (Hoare, Stewart, & Purcell, 1984). Problem-oriented policing emphasizes identifying and analyzing problems (criminal, civil, or public nuisance) and implementing solutions to resolve the underlying causes of the problem. Community residents, local businesses, and governmental agencies may be central participants in the analysis and resolution steps. Problem-oriented policing emphasizes proactive intervention rather than reactive responses to calls for service, resolution of root causes rather than symptoms, and use of multiparty, community-based problem solving rather than unilateral police response. Problem-oriented policing focuses on a problem in a long-term, comprehensive manner, rather than handling the problem as a series of separate incidents to be resolved via arrest or other police action.

The research described here, which was part of a larger study of POP in Tulsa as well as San Diego, focuses on two major areas: (1) the actual behaviors of police officers when they are resolving problems; and (2) the effectiveness of these strategies in resolving drug, crime, and order maintenance problems. In this chapter we use all of the cases we examined to describe and review the behaviors and strategies used by officers. We then highlight three cases in which we describe the officers' activities and examine evidence of impact.

Methodology

Research Site. Crime rates, drug-related emergency room admissions and deaths, and citizen fear of crime increased rapidly in the mid-1980s in San Diego, a city with an international border and a mobile, heterogeneous population of 1.1 million. In 1988, with the help of a federal grant from the Bureau of Justice Assistance (BJA) and the Police Executive Research Forum (PERF), the San Diego Police Department initiated problem-oriented policing approaches to drug problems, particularly street-level sales of crack and cocaine and the violence associated with such dealing. Early departmental steps included developing an inventory of the target area's drug problems, forming a management committee to guide POP techniques, and hiring on-site coordinators to provide technical assistance and ensure communication within and outside the department. Two-day training sessions involving 30-40 officers, first-line supervisors, and command staff were conducted by PERF and on-site coordinators. Much of it relied on the case study approach, in which participants read about problems, analyzed them in groups, and developed preliminary responses. The training emphasized a four-step SARA model as a guide to problem solving.

- Scanning: The initial identification of the problem, which occurs in a variety of ways, including police recognition of a problem due to the number of calls for service or reported crimes, repeated citizen or business complaints, knowledge acquired from the community, and so forth.
- Analysis: An in-depth analysis of the problem and its related and underlying causes and the development of a strategy for resolving the problem.
- Response: The implementation of the problem-solving strategy, including the roles and activities of the police, citizens, businesses, local government agencies, and others.
- Assessment: An ongoing review and assessment process to monitor the success of the response. May include maintenance activities.

Problem-oriented policing techniques were implemented initially by a special squad of uniformed foot patrol officers in a 12-square-block neighborhood in southeastern San Diego with 1,300 residents and a violent crime rate five times the city average. Since 1990, POP has been promoted throughout the department, supported by a full-time coordinator, regular meetings of a Problem Analysis

Advisory Committee (PAAC), and a cadre of training staff who regularly reach others through in-service training.

When our study of problem-solving behavior began in 1991, POP was an accepted part of police practice. During 1989 when the BJA grant began, 32 officers applied POP principles in 50 cases. There were approximately 135 active cases when our study got under way, and by the end of this study, approximately 400 problem-solving cases were open at any given time and about 325 officers engaged in problem-oriented policing in the course of their routine work.

Methods. Twenty problems were selected for study over a 6-month period in San Diego, varying by type of problem (i.e., legal, order maintenance, service) and officer characteristics (i.e., experience levels, age, sex, and ethnicity) to present a reasonable cross-section of the department. In addition, at least one problem was selected from each of the department's patrol divisions. The data for each case study were collected by locally recruited on-site analysts who reviewed project files, interviewed officers four times during the problem-solving process, observed police actions and the problem sites directly, and interviewed citizens and business owners and managers at the problem sites.

Using the problem as the unit of analysis, measures of effectiveness were tailored to each case in order to assess whether specific problems appeared to be resolved following the cessation of problem-oriented activities. Where possible, unobtrusive measures such as customer counts were used. Interviews with those affected by the problem—such as nearby residents, business owners and managers, workers, and others—were also used to gather outcome data. Official data on reported crime and calls for service in the problem area also were collected to analyze immediate effects and problem resolution over a 6-month period.

Description of Problems and Problem-Solving Activities

In its textbook form, problem-oriented policing begins with the identification of a crime or nuisance problem. An in-depth analysis of the problem and its related and underlying causes is completed, followed by the development of a strategy for resolving it. Whether and how these processes occur and who (police, neighborhood residents, business owners, etc.) is involved in each step were critical questions in our study. Below we present a summary of the 16 complete cases we studied.[1]

Types of Problems. Of the 16 complete problem-oriented policing cases we followed, all involved multiple problems. The *primary* problem in each of the 16 cases was identified as drug dealing (6 cases), public nuisance (6 cases), or serious crime other than drugs (4 cases). In the cases involving drug dealing, it was also common to find instances of violent crime, burglary and robbery, environmental problems, transients and/or illegal alien problems, and gang activity. Public nuisances typically involved transients loitering in public places and creating nuisances via drinking, panhandling, drug use, public indecency, and theft. In 3 of the 4 cases involving serious crime, drug dealing and gang activity also were implicated.

Problem Identification. In 9 of the 16 problems, official police data or officers were the central means of identifying the problem. Six of the problems were recognized because of the inordinately large number of calls for service and/or reported crime. In 3, patrol officers were well aware of problem spots and made a decision to tackle them via problem-oriented policing. Despite this substantial reliance on traditional means of identification, which resulted primarily in the selection of crime and drug problems, 6 of the 16 problems were brought to the attention of the police by complaints from neighborhood residents or business owners. Five of these 6 cases are the nuisance problems. One nuisance case was referred to the police by the city's abatement office.

In the cases studied it was difficult to distinguish between problem identification and the processes of analysis and response formulation. Similarly, it was difficult to distinguish between discussions of how to resolve problems and involving the discussants in actual problem solving. For example, identifying and contacting the owner of a troubled apartment complex typically had several steps, including gathering information, discussing potential solutions to the problem, and enlisting the owner in resolution steps. In reality, the processes of identification, analysis, and response do not follow the four steps of the SARA model in linear or separable fashion. Rather, the steps in the problem-solving model tend to either occur simultaneously or in a fashion in which officers move back and forth between scanning, analysis, and responses. It is typical that discussions leading to responses or efforts to implement a response bring new problems to the surface, which are then analyzed and acted upon.

Analysis and Response Formation. In the cases studied, decisions related to strategies to resolve a problem were, in the main, made by the POP officers, often in consultation with others. There were three major sources of guidance and feedback used by officers as they addressed problems: (1) the civilian POP coordinator, whose office acted as a clearinghouse for officers seeking information; (2) the squad sergeant, as first-line supervisor, usually became involved because the officer needed relief from the demands of calls for service in order to attend to the problem; and (3) the Problem Analysis Advisory Committee (PAAC)—a group made up of officers from all ranks who acted as informal advisers to officers using POP strategies. Officers wishing PAAC guidance would voluntarily attend the group's regular meeting and present issues or ask questions emanating from their POP problem for discussion. It was common for the POP officers to discuss the problem and potential solutions with others within the police department, particularly supervisors, other patrol officers, the POP coordinator, and specialized units (e.g., vice, crime analysis, narcotics). In six cases, crime analysis was used to analyze patterns and trends, build suspect profiles, and obtain maps. In all but three of the cases, police officials were consulted in some capacity.

In addition to tapping various sources of information within the department, officers using POP in the studied cases often sought information from the public. In all but four cases, citizens (e.g., business owners or managers, residents, workers, etc.) were consulted during the information gathering and response formation stages. Officers used formal surveys in only two of the cases. In the remainder, officers relied on their own contacts with people in the target area for information.

Yet, interviews with the POP officers and the case records indicate that little in-depth, objective analysis was done as part of the problem-solving process. Officers tended to move quickly into implementing responses, as though believing they *knew* without exploration which strategies would be effective. The officers' actions appear to be based on their original classification of the problem. That is to say, once an officer made a conclusion about the nature of the problem (e.g., drugs and disorder), this conclusion apparently led directly to ideas about appropriate or necessary responses. This may explain why certain patterns of POP behavior emerge. With regard to combating drugs, for example, there was a pattern to the problem-solving activity. The officers would contact owners, managers, businesses, and/or city agencies to implement obviously needed environmental design changes, such as fences and increased security. If applicable, the officers would work with managers of housing complexes in order to evict troublesome residents. At the same time the officers would intensify enforcement efforts.

Problem-Solving Activities. The problem-solving responses engineered by the POP officers varied tremendously across the cases because of the unique characteristics of each problem. Nevertheless, it is possible to count and categorize the problem-solving responses applied in the 16 cases. Table 7.1 summarizes the different categories of responses used by officers. Unsuccessful attempts to make changes (e.g., to have pay phones modified) were included, and multiple responses from the same actors were counted separately (e.g., if police officers instituted foot patrols and detectives conducted undercover investigations, two traditional law enforcement efforts were recorded).

To address the 16 problems, 112 responses were noted, an average of 7 responses per problem. Virtually all of the responses, regardless of the actor (apartment manager, vice squad, building inspection department, etc.), were instigated by the officer or officers who initiated the problem-solving effort. The most numerous responses came from owners and managers of houses, apartment complexes, and businesses; 35% of the responses were implemented by this group. Two thirds of them were environmental in nature, such as increasing lighting or security, cutting brush, cleaning up an area, installing fencing, and posting signs. The others have been labeled "social control," referring to a

TABLE 7.1 Problem-Solving Profile in San Diego, 1989

POP Stage	Variable	Percentage (Number of Cases)
Scanning	Problem type:	
	Crime	82 (41)
	Environment	39 (19)
	Disorder	22 (11)
	Other	4 (2)
	Services	2 (1)
	Personal dispute	0
	Business dispute	0
	Rental dispute	0
	Traffic	0
	Alarms	0
	Prevention	0
Analysis	Awareness:	
	Citizen	34 (17)
	Repeat calls	28 (14)
	Observation	20 (10)
	Records	16 (8)
	Supervisor	16 (8)
	Citizen group	6 (3)
	Survey	4 (2)
	Hunch	2 (1)
	Other agency	2 (1)
	Call pattern	0
	Other offices	0
	Media	0
	Other	
Response	Solution:	
	Enforcement	64 (32)
	Other department	52 (26)
	Other groups	50 (25)
	Referral to P.D.	42 (21)
	Input	38 (10)
	Government referral	36 (18)
	Regulatory	20 (10)
	Community referral	8 (4)
	Halted	8 (4)
	CJ	6 (3)
	Civil	6 (3)
	Citizen Mobil.	4 (2)
	Change	4 (2)
Assessment	Officers	30 (15)
	Department	2 (1)

variety of actions that aim to evict drug dealers or problem tenants, screen customers or tenants better, and the like.

Responses from municipal and county agencies formed the second most common response to problems (25%). Environmental changes (e.g., hauling away abandoned cars, installing street signs and lighting, etc.) and code enforcement actions represented the majority of this work. The agencies are generally brought into the problem-solving activity by the POP officers in charge. In these 16 problems alone, the following agencies and local government officials were involved: Building Inspection, Housing, Vehicle Abatement, Zoning, Eviction Attorney, Litter Abatement, Graffiti Control, District Attorney's Office, City Attorney, Trolley officials, Adult Protective Services, Child Protective Services, County Mental Health Department, Health Department, Meals on Wheels, the Chamber of Commerce, and the American Civil Liberties Union.

Traditional law enforcement tactics were found in nearly a quarter of the problem-solving cases. Such tactics include undercover drug investigations, increased patrol, investigations by vice and narcotics units, and field interviews, and were usually found in concert with other responses. In 3 of the 16 cases studied, traditional law enforcement was clearly the predominate response, as illustrated by the responses in the street robberies case discussed later.

Problem-solving actions by police include a wide range of responses. It is important to reemphasize that *all* the responses referred to above were instigated by the POP officer(s); this category includes actions taken directly by the officers. Included are actions such as improving departmental communication, changing dispatch responses, working with military authorities, organizing business watches, identifying and contacting owners, trying to form a tenant's association, and talking to local residents and businesses.

Notably, citizens were involved actively with the problem-solving effort in only one case. In this case, involving serious street crime and other problems around an apartment building, citizens observed and reported problems to the police. Otherwise, the role for citizens in the problem-solving process was fairly limited in the cases we examined. For the most part, citizens were tapped as sources of information or as an avenue for accomplishing a certain objective, such as an eviction.

Effectiveness. Although the three examples below focused on impact associated with specific POP strategies, we want to make a general point about the effectiveness of the POP cases we examined. Knowing something about the global findings in the study will, besides informing you of the results, help put the findings we present below in perspective. Because our unit of analysis was the problem, the measures we used varied according to each problem. In some cases personal and photographic observation over time was the only sensible measure given the specific target (e.g., an unkempt yard), while in others calls for service and reported crime rates were appropriate. Taken together, we conclude that 11 of the 16 cases were successful (Capowich, Roehl, & Andrews, 1993).

Problem-Oriented Policing: Three Examples

Three brief case studies of POP presented below provide examples of the central elements of the approach, along with evidence of its effectiveness. Portions of each case study also highlight situations in which elements of problem-oriented policing gave way to traditional policing tactics.

The Cucas Apartment Complex

The POP project at the Cucas apartment complex in northeastern San Diego began in May 1991 and continued through mid-1992. According to the lead officer, drugs and related problems such as residential and commercial burglaries, auto thefts, car burglaries, and domestic disputes were endemic throughout the entire Northeastern Division. Drugs were a particular problem in the Cucas, with inadequate lighting and poorly marked streets facilitating the drug trade while hindering police enforcement efforts. Communication problems within the department also limited enforcement. Narcotics complaints (e.g., information on the location of drug houses) typically bypassed the patrol level to go directly to the Narcotics Division. In addition, needed information was often bypassed by the officers who patrolled the area.

The need for a problem-oriented approach in the Cucas was recognized by two officers, who brought it to the attention of a supervisor. They and other patrol officers were aware that the Cucas apartment complex generated more calls for service than most of the other apartment complexes in the Northeastern Division. The solutions proposed for the Cucas were based on information from crime analysis and discussions with other officers (such as the POP coordinator), the management company, and apartment security. As time passed and new developments occurred in the Cucas, the officer who led the problem-solving effort reported he was constantly rethinking and developing alternative solutions. After 7 months, however, the central strategies had not changed substantially.

The officer initiating the project felt that fighting the narcotics problem in the Cucas first required resolving several related problems. In order to improve communication within the department, the POP officer proposed a coordinated flow of information in which the Narcotics Street Team would share information with patrol. He also requested contacts and information related to the Cucas from other patrol officers, via a line-up book.

The officer also contacted the San Diego Housing Commission, which provided information and assistance and informed him that they planned to install additional lighting and new street signs. California Properties and AMP Property Management, the companies responsible for maintenance and property management of the Cucas, worked with the officers on the location of the street lighting, provided the detailed street maps, and approved the removal of abandoned cars after police officers enforced vehicle code violations. The officers worked with apartment management to enforce Section 8 housing regulations that, in part, expedite the eviction process of tenants implicated in drug activity. The owner of a local gas station where drug dealers loiter and wait for orders from the pay phone was very cooperative and instructed his employees to watch the area and call the police when people loitered by the phone. In addition, the pay phone was modified so that it could no longer receive incoming calls.

Police enforcement efforts also were focused on the Cucas. Plainclothes officers were assigned to the area to identify the source of drugs, conduct undercover investigations, and increase arrests of dealers. Other officers and the Narcotics Street Team also assisted in this POP project by providing narcotics information directly to the POP officer and the others working in the area. Supervisors provided support, advice, and feedback and helped circulate information about the project through the department. According to the POP officer, the need for information brought an excellent response from other divisions in the department. He even obtained information on traffic citations and parking tickets as part of regular reports he received from the crime analysis section.

At the last observation point 7 months after this POP project began, resolution efforts were continuing and no formal assessment had been done by the officer or the department. The street lights were installed, but the street signs had not yet been erected. Drug dealing was perceived to be reduced by the officer, but the decrease may be attributable to the death of a major Cucas drug dealer after a high-speed police chase. According to the POP officer working on the project, the general disorder at the complex had lessened and he reported receiving positive comments from residents. The complex managers were very enthusiastic about the problem solving and positive in their assessment of how these steps had improved conditions at the apartments. They also expressed hope that this type of cooperative effort could be maintained in the future.

Several steps were taken to assess the effects of this POP project. First, we obtained data on the number of narcotic arrests made at the complex during the time the case was active. Despite statements that enforcement had intensified, there is no evidence that this occurred. According to department records, only one narcotics arrest was made in the complex between January 1991 and June 1992, the 18 months surrounding the project time period. It does not appear that this part of the POP plan was ever implemented.

Calls for service at the complex were tracked from 3 months before the start of the POP project through June 1992, when the project was still active. As Graph 7.1 illustrates, calls for service seemed to be unaffected by the POP project. By the end of June 1992, calls for service were at the same level as when the project began in May 1991.

Thirty residents whose apartments had a direct view of the courtyard area where the outdoor drug trafficking was most evident were interviewed in May 1991. Most were aware of the drug activity. Seventy percent (21 people) cited drugs and related disorder (e.g., fights, noise) as the most serious crime problems facing the complex. In May 1992 a second survey was completed with 33

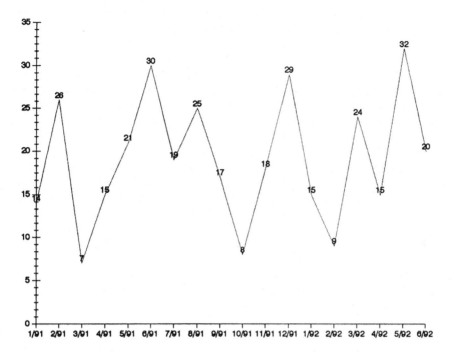

Graph 7.1. Calls for Service, Cucas Apartment Complex, January 1991-June 1992

residents of the same apartments. Only 30% (10 residents) stated that drug activity on the grounds was still a serious problem. However, a majority of these residents (77%) stated that general disorder and noise continued to be a serious problem. The public drug activity appears to have diminished, but the problems with disorder persisted.

Street Robberies in the Eastern Division

The problem-oriented policing project concerning street robberies in the Eastern Division was concentrated in a large area along a 20-block corridor of a major thoroughfare. In some respects this project was actually several POP projects led by individual officers working on certain streets or at specific residences. Like the Cucas apartments project, the project was opened in May 1991 and was still active in July 1992. Several patrol officers were involved in this problem-solving effort, however.

These three areas were experiencing a large number of street robberies, problems with gangs, residential and commercial robberies, and high rates of auto theft. The POP officers chose to focus on street crimes because they were viewed as serious problems that contributed to the public's fear. The thrust of the strategy used to resolve the street robbery problem in this general vicinity was to focus on very specific problem spots in hopes of affecting the entire target area.

The target area was identified when the beats gained the dubious honor of hosting the largest number of robberies in the city in a month; in fact, 80 street robberies were recorded in a 2-week period. Other indicators of the need for intervention in this area of the city were statistical reports from Crime Analysis, officer-to-officer and citizen-to-officer conversations, officer observations, and information contained within a division logbook that documented "hot crimes"— crimes that were of a serious or important nature.

The central strategies applied in the target area were traditional law enforcement tactics. Suspect profiles and their crime methods were analyzed. The majority of robbery suspects were young black males (probably gang members, according to the police), who lived, or at least spent most of their time, in the neighborhoods in which they were committing crimes. Young Hispanic males also were implicated. To get these criminal elements out of the target area, the officers decided to target known drug houses. They worked with citizens to get information on illegal activity and individuals and obtained maps and statistical information from crime analysis, to relate suspects' addresses to crime locations.

As the project evolved, a street robbery task force was created. This task force included members of the newly formed Neighborhood Policing Team, patrol officers and sergeants, a robbery detective, two bike officers, and a storefront community service officer. The members had biweekly meetings and also met with area property owners, business managers, and representatives from various city agencies including housing, zoning, an eviction attorney, litter and waste, and graffiti control. Citizens were asked to identify specific problems and participate in problem solving by submitting Citizen Referral Forms to the storefront officers.

The officers originally planned on working with the adult and juvenile specialized gang unit, a collaboration of police and probation officers proactive in enforcing probation restrictions on selected offenders, to gather intelligence on known adult and juvenile probationers and parolees in the target area. They then planned to go to the addresses where the problems were occurring, talk to residents and neighbors, and learn the identities of the true residents. This unit was supposed to ride with a uniformed officer through the target area simply to show offenders that both entities were working together and cooperating. Officers also wanted to do the same with representatives from the Serious Habitual Offender Program, then make arrests for parole violations. Although initial contact was made between the entities, nothing was pursued and these coordinated activities were never implemented.

There are three noteworthy aspects of this POP project. First, this project was directed by a sergeant who coordinated the work of several officers from the patrol division and other divisions within the department. Second, the officers relied heavily on traditional police methods such as saturation patrol and targeted field interviews based on a suspect profile. Third, the officers relied

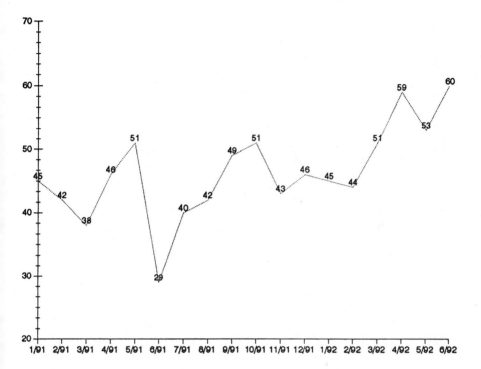

Graph 7.2. Reported Robberies, Eastern Division, Beat 413 (0.2 mile radius), January 1991-June 1992

heavily on crime analysis for information. Although robberies were occurring throughout the area, the officers concentrated their efforts in three areas where the robbery activity was most pronounced.

To assess the effectiveness of the POP approach in this instance, reports of robberies and calls for service were tracked from 3 months before the project began through June 1992. Because this POP project encompassed a larger area that surrounded the three primary target areas, crime data for a 0.2 mile radius around the target area were tracked.

As Graph 7.2 illustrates, reported robberies remained fairly stable throughout the project period, although reported incidents increased dramatically near the end of the time we traced this project. Reported incidents ranged from a low of 29 just after the project began to a high of 60 by the end of June 1992. Calls for service (see Graph 7.3) also increased through the project's period. There were 408 calls in January 1991 and they climbed to a plateau of around 550 for the period between April and June 1992 when the observation period ended. This undoubtedly reflects the increased police activity in the area.

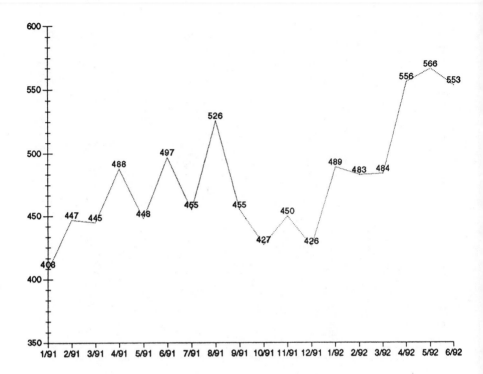

Graph 7.3. Calls for Service, Eastern Division, Beat 413 (0.2 mile radius), January 1991-June 1992

Surveys of business establishments and pedestrians in the area were conducted at the start of the project and again in May 1992. The responses from citizens and businesses showed high levels of fear associated with a perception of violence. Eighty-seven percent (46 respondents) stated that general violence (e.g., hearing shots fired, fights, usually attributable to drugs) was a serious problem in the area. These perceptions did not change over the life of the project. When asked without prompting, none of the respondents viewed robbery as a problem. Instead, most people (40) focused on the general level of violence as well as the disorder and unkempt environment that contained trash and graffiti.

Drugs and Gangs on the Trolley Line

This one-year case began in June 1991 and focused on gangs, violence, and drug dealing on the trolley line between 12th and Market and 12th and C Streets, including the trolley stations. Officers first noticed a problem when they started receiving numerous calls for service and complaints from area businesses. The 12th Street Gang, consisting of migrants from Tijuana and Ensenada, Mexico, was engaged in turf wars with other gangs. In addition to the drug dealing and turf wars, there were homicides, vandalism, assaults with deadly weapons, drive-by shootings, rapes, loitering around the trolley stops, people riding the trolley without paying for tickets, and street robberies.

Enforcement efforts such as surveillance, making arrests, and increasing patrols to eradicate the gangs and drugs were initiated before the POP file was opened. Officers chose to conduct a POP project because they hoped to address long-term solutions. In order to pursue the POP project, two officers made contact with the Narcotics Street Teams and patrol officers who handle the downtown area, requesting assistance and ideas about the problem.

The POP officers also sought assistance from the Border Patrol (who increased patrols in that area, enforcing immigration laws), Crime Analysis (for statistical information), and the department's Gang Unit. The officers also relied on assistance and information from citizens who lived and worked in that area. Some businesses allowed officers to have keys and access codes so that they could use their stores and offices for surveillance. Police supervisors were very supportive during this project by allowing officers to adjust their schedules in order to attend meetings and allowing them to use their time on the POP project between radio calls. One response was to increase the number of officers on foot patrol in the area who did not answer radio calls. This step allowed a concentrated effort in the target area that is rare for POP cases. This factor is likely a key ingredient to this project's ultimate success.

The POP officers met with San Diego trolley officials to discuss ideas for decreasing the number of loiterers and the number of people riding the trolley without paying for their tickets. The trolley administrators agreed to eliminate bleachers at one of the trolley stops to make it uncomfortable to loiter there, and also suggested that saturation checks be conducted more often at the problem stops. In a saturation check, officers and trolley security guards check for tickets from every passenger, issuing citations to those who have none.

As the project evolved, the officers also requested the removal of some of the pay phones near the trolley stations, which were being used for drug sales. They contacted the owner of many of the phones, but he did not see the need for removing them based on the fact that the phones can only be used to make outgoing calls.

In February 1992 a third officer was recruited to join their project. He contacted area businesses in order to set up a "Business Alert" program. Several businesses were cooperative, except for one market owner; his market provided a great deal of drug paraphernalia and fortified wine to the neighborhood transients.

Within the first 6 months of the project, feedback from residents and business owners within the community to the POP officer indicated that the project had a positive impact. Although a formal assessment does not appear to have been

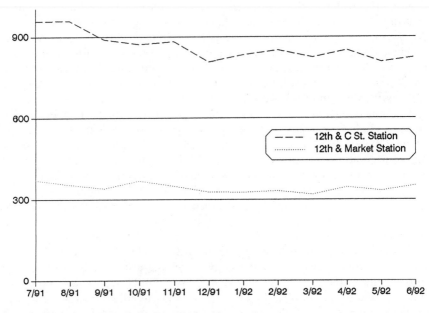

Graph 7.4. Average Daily Trolley Ridership

conducted by the officers, and despite the fact that gangs and drugs were still a part of this community as of the final interview, officers perceived that the problems in the area were more manageable as a result of the POP effort.

To assess the resolution of this problem, the average daily usage of the trolley stations in the target area was one of the indicators we examined to gauge whether changes occurred in the regular activity of those who live and work in the area. As shown in Graph 7.4, the number of riders using the station at 12th and C Streets surged in the summer months then declined through the year. Ridership at the station at 12th and Market Streets remained fairly stable through the year, with the number of riders going from 371 in July 1991 to 352 in June 1992.

During the project, the increase in enforcement activity was accompanied by an increase in narcotics arrests. In the 3 months before the project began, narcotics arrests averaged 1.3 a month at the two stations; during the 12-month project, 4.88 narcotics arrests were made per month. Similarly, other police activity increased noticeably. Monthly field interviews increased from 14 in the month prior to the project to 38 each month, and misdemeanor citations increased from 12 to an average of 28 a month during the project.

Decreases in both calls for service and reported crime at the two stations were noted. Graph 7.5 illustrates how the monthly calls for service went from a high of 38 in June 1991, and after fluctuating on a downward trend through the project, leveled off at 14 calls for service in June 1992 (a 63% decrease). Reports of crime follow a similar, though less dramatic, downward trend. The number

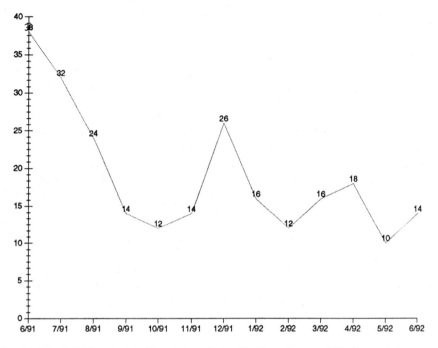

Graph 7.5. Calls for Service, Target Area Trolley Stations, January 1991-June 1992

of reported public disorder incidents[2] rose dramatically from 22 in June (the month the project started) to 79 in September 1991. There also was a sharp increase in the number of field interviews (37 in June, 60 in September), certainly a reflection of officers' activities. During this same time period, reports of Part I offenses decreased slightly from 22 to 17. Reports of public order offenses decreased to 40 by December when the project ended, and dropped further to 20 by March 1992. Part I offenses remained almost level in December 1991, with 16 reported incidents and then decreased further to 12 in March 1992.

Discussion and Summary

The case studies presented here illustrate three different crime and public disorder problems where there were differing results. The Cucas apartment complex was targeted because of disorder that was assumed to be associated with drug activity, and the evidence shows mixed results. The officers targeted certain people, among them drug dealers, in an effort to alleviate the drug problem and reduce the level of disorder. The key intervening event was the accidental death of a well-known drug dealer in the area. Calls for service were unaffected, and it does not appear that the level of disorderliness was reduced. Residents' perceptions and the stable level of calls for service support this contention. In this respect, the POP effort at the Cucas did not reduce the workload for officers.

Reducing the level of drug activity within the apartment complex arguably improved the situation by reducing the level of harm associated with the problem. Residents' perceptions concur with officers' impressions that the level of drug dealing had decreased. However, the death of a major drug dealer was a key confounding event that probably accounts for the decreased drug activity because nothing else about the complex changed. The rowdiness and loud noise continued to be a problem, and the workload for police did not diminish.

The street robberies project did not result in positive effects. The project was specifically targeting street robberies in an area that encompassed several beats, yet did not reduce the robbery rate. Similarly, there is no evidence that calls for service decreased over the one-year period. Most of the activity was traditional police work directed at the robbery problem, the suspects in particular.

The trolley station project represents a POP effort in which both reported crimes and the calls for service rates decreased within the target areas. The response was—as in the case of the Cucas—multidimensional, involving law enforcement and environmental design. The number of riders using these stations remained unchanged, but this is not surprising. People in the city who must rely on mass transit are not able to change patterns easily. They are likely to continue using the trolley even if the surroundings are unpleasant and fearful. The indicators in this case suggest that the POP approach improved the circumstances for those who use the stations and reduced the police workload at these locations.

In addition to the findings that relate to impact in each of the cases, there are relationships and patterns that emerge from the data on the problem-solving process and officer behavior. It is clear that multiple problems tend to coincide. At the beat level, there are no pure cases in which the problem can be captured under a single classification. The range of problems is wide, with each one presenting unique circumstances. Given the complexity of individual problems it is not surprising that the responses also tended to be complex. We were able to discern an average of seven tactics for each of the 16 problems, with two of the case study examples also showing multifaceted approaches. Most of the responses combined law enforcement and nonenforcement strategies, with the non-law enforcement measures often involving cooperation with other city agencies or community groups. All of these interagency contacts were instigated by the police.

The problem identification stage typically involves a variety of sources. Seven of the 16 cases came to police attention from sources outside the department, with 6 of them coming from citizens. It is interesting to note that when citizens brought a problem to an officer's attention, it was a public order or quality-of-life problem, whereas police always identified a specific crime as the problem. Beyond the initial identification of the problem, citizens were consulted or involved in some way with defining the problem in 11 of the 16 cases.

Although the public was involved in many of the problem-solving efforts, it is important to point out that the role played by citizens or citizens' groups in these projects was limited. As we noted earlier, there was only one example of direct public involvement in a response, and that involvement was similar to a Neighborhood Watch program. The public was most often used as a source of information to enable officers to carry out a response. The police tended to retain professional control of the problem-solving activity so residents did not often play active roles, particularly with respect to the design and implementation of responses. In practice, the officers apparently consider the public primarily to be a broader resource for the problem-solving efforts.

In addition, the analysis stage, intended to be a means for determining the scope and definition of the problem to be addressed, is weak and often nonexistent. As discussed earlier, officers tend to move directly from their original classification of the problem (usually a crime category) to a response without doing much analysis. This is, of course, consistent with the way police are accustomed to working under a traditional incident-driven framework. Police officers are trained to first gather information when they arrive at the site of an incident, and then take some ameliorative action based on that information. Moreover, when handling incidents on the street, police must take action quickly without time for reflection or detailed analysis. It is apparent that this style of behavior characterizes parts of the problem-solving process as well. These cases also provide some insight into the nature of problem-solving behavior employed by officers. There is little evidence of assessments of the POP efforts by officers or the department beyond the level of personal perception. This was true for the three examples highlighted in detail, and also characterized 10 of the remaining 13 cases we examined.

Notes

1. Although we examined 20 cases involving POP, 4 of them were not useful for analyzing impact. For various reasons, these 4 cases never developed to a point where a strategy was implemented. They are interesting examples of administrative and performance factors that interfered with the implementation of POP. (For a discussion of these cases see Capowich, Roehl, & Andrews, 1994.)

2. These include drinking alcohol in a controlled area, lodging without consent, open container, pedestrian blocking traffic, littering, and urinating in public.

References

Capowich, G. E., Roehl, J. A., & Andrews, C. (1994). *Evaluating problem-oriented policing: Assessing process and outcomes in Tulsa and San Diego.* Washington, DC: National Institute of Justice.

Cordner, G. W. (1986). Fear of crime and the police: An evaluation of a fear-reduction strategy. *Journal of Police Science and Administration, 14,* 223-233.

Eck, J. E., & Spelman, W. (1987a). *Problem solving: Problem-oriented policing in Newport News.* Washington, DC: Police Executive Research Forum.

Eck, J. E., & Spelman, W. (1987b). Who ya gonna call? The police as problem-busters. *Crime and Delinquency, 33,* 31-52.

Goldstein, H. (1979). Improving policing: A problem-oriented approach. *Crime and Delinquency, 25,* 236-258.

Goldstein, H. (1987). Toward community-oriented policing: Potential, basic requirements, and threshold questions. *Crime and Delinquency, 33,* 6-30.

Goldstein, H. (1990). *Problem-oriented policing.* New York: McGraw-Hill.

Goldstein, H., & Susmilch, C. E. (1982). *Experimenting with the problem-oriented approach to improving police service: A report and some reflections on two case studies.* Madison: University of Wisconsin, Law School.

Hoare, M. A., Stewart, G., & Purcell, C. M. (1984). *The problem oriented approach: Four pilot studies.* London: Metropolitan Police, Management Services Department.

McElroy, J. E., Cosgrove, C. A., & Sadd, S. (1989). *An examination of the Community Patrol Officer Program (CPOP) in New York City* [unpublished report]. New York: Vera Institute of Justice.

Roehl, J. A., Capowich, G. E., & Llaneras, E. (1991). *Evaluating the systems approach to crime prevention: Final report.* Washington, DC: Bureau of Justice Assistance.

Trojanowicz, R. C., & Bucqueroux, B. (1989). *Community policing: A contemporary perspective.* Cincinnati: Anderson.

Wilson, J. Q., & Kelling, G. L. (1989, February). Making neighborhoods safe. *The Atlantic Monthly,* pp. 46-52.

The Impact of Community Policing on Police Personnel

A Review of the Literature

ARTHUR J. LURIGIO

DENNIS P. ROSENBAUM

COMMUNITY POLICING is typically defined in terms of "problem solving" and "community engagement." At the operational level, these concepts translate into specific practices that are expected from the police officers engaged in such programs. The difficulty with the expectations is that they are frequently beyond the present capacities of most officers and the traditional roles for which they were selected and trained and the standard performance indicators on which they are evaluated. Therefore, an argument can be made that police departments will not be prepared to achieve effective problem solving and community partnerships until the beliefs, perceptions, attitudes, and behaviors of individual officers become more compatible with the redefinition and enlargement of their jobs as prescribed by the community policing model. To ignore police personnel and the organizational constraints placed on their activities is to risk program failure due to apathy, frustration, resentment, perceived inequity, fear of change, and other factors that militate against the successful implementation of community policing.

Most community policing programs are created—either implicitly or explicitly—to offer several fundamental advantages to participating officers (e.g., Skolnick & Bayley, 1988). The advantages are supposed to produce a "new breed" of officers through fundamental changes in cultural climate, organizational structure, decision-making strategies, management techniques, police roles, training curricula, and reward systems (Kelling & Moore, 1988). These changes are designed to lead to greater officer knowledge and expertise in problem solving and community engagement activities. Also, they attempt to encourage officers to make better use of community and police resources and to develop more favorable attitudes toward alternative police approaches and community involvement in the reduction of crime and the promotion of order (Moore, 1992). As a consequence, officers should experience greater job satisfaction, self-worth, and productivity, and the public should recognize significant improvements in the quality of police services and contacts. However, as Wycoff (1988) indicates, most of the benefits of community policing for officers have been based more on conjecture than on credible empirical evidence. Indeed, the bulk of studies on community policing have focused on its impact on the community or on the police organization; few investigations have examined its direct effects on individual police personnel.

In this chapter we address a very simple but important question, namely, what has research revealed about the impact of community policing on police officers' attitudes, beliefs, perceptions, and behaviors? Our review is limited to studies that involve quantitative surveys of police staff, which elicit line officers' self-reports about their job, community policing, and the community. These studies commonly include surveys of the community, which explore residents' satisfaction with police performance and contacts. Substantial variation exists among the investigations with regard to their conceptualizations of the programs, the strength of their research designs, the kinds of data-collection strategies they employ, and the nature of the hypotheses that they test and the outcomes that they measure. Unfortunately, the specific components of the programs, which may impact police personnel, are often poorly explicated because of the overriding attention given to the expected effects of the program on community-level variables, such as crime rates, fear of crime, calls for services, and perceptions of disorder. The majority of studies we have reviewed also include measures of community-based outcomes. We have chosen to report only citizen data relevant to police personnel.

The chapter has two basic sections. The first describes the programs and their evaluations in roughly the chronological order in which they were published. We present only those results that relate to the impact of community policing on police officers. The second summarizes the research findings, and discusses the general limitations of the studies and their conclusions.

A Review of the Literature

San Diego (1975)

From July 1973 through September 1974, the San Diego Police Department implemented an innovative patrol project called Community Profile Development, which was an antecedent to the city's problem-oriented policing program. The purpose of the project was "to improve the delivery of police services by (a) increasing the patrol officer's awareness and understanding of the community the officer serves; and (b) by improving his or her response to area problems through the development of new patrol strategies" (Boydstun & Sherry, 1975, p. 18). In an evaluation of the project, an experimental group of patrol officers and sergeants were randomly selected and specially trained to utilize the Community Profile Approach in responding to calls for service and in conducting self-initiated patrol activities during a 10-month field test. A second set of patrol officers and sergeants implemented a more traditional approach to patrol practice while working in the same beats at the same time as the experimental group.

Boydstun and Sherry (1975) employed several measures to assess the impact of the Community Profile Approach on the attitudes and behaviors of experimental officers. Among others, they tested the hypotheses that the profile-trained patrol officers, when compared to traditional patrol officers, would:

- change their perception of the police officer's role in relation to the community
- demonstrate greater beat accountability and service to the community
- show a higher level of job satisfaction
- draw on social service agencies and other community resources more often when handling problems on their beat

A five-part patrol officers' survey was the principal source of data for the study. Questionnaires were administered to both experimental and control groups at baseline (before the field phase of the project), at the midpoint of the project, and at the close of the field phase of the project. The project lasted approximately 12 months.

At baseline, the experimental and control groups were highly comparable. The impact of the program on experimental officers was mixed, however. Specifically, the experimental group showed an overall decline in the percentage of officers reporting service referral activity and a slight decline in the mean number of referrals per officer. Both groups evidenced a slight but nonsignificant decline in satisfaction with their current assignments. With respect to day-to-day work activities, experimental officers were more likely to report that their job was interesting and less likely to report that their job was frustrating. Furthermore, the experimental group demonstrated, through several indicators, an expanded conception of the police officer's role and a significantly greater increase in knowledge of their beats. Finally, experimental officers attached a higher value to community relations activities and expressed greater confidence in the community's support for law enforcement.

Cincinnati (1977)

Cincinnati's Community Sector Team Policing (COMSEC) program was one of the most thoroughly evaluated team policing projects, which were quite prevalent during the late 1960s and early 1970s (Walker, 1992). The program began in March 1971 and was reorganized 2 years later with the assistance of the Police Foundation. COMSEC was implemented in police District 1, which had a serious crime problem and was made up of diverse neighborhoods. To institute the program as planned, District 1 was divided into six sectors that included: two predominantly African American, high-crime, low-income residential areas; a low-income, mixed residential and business area; a predominantly white, middle-class residential area; a racially mixed, low-income, high-crime, largely residential area; and the central business district (Schwartz & Clarren, 1977).

COMSEC was designed according to a few basic principles of neighborhood team policing. A team of permanently assigned officers performed the full range of police services within a relatively small, demographically and geographically defined neighborhood. Thus each team represented an autonomous and decentralized operational unit and was responsible for the "unified delivery of all police services. The development of a 'generalist' role for officers was encouraged—a role in which they perform both investigative and patrol functions" (Schwartz & Clarren, 1977, p. 4). The overarching goals of COMSEC were to reduce crime and to improve police-community relations.

To evaluate the impact of COMSEC on police officers, the Police Foundation administered self-report surveys at baseline, and at 6 months (September 1973), 12 months (March 1974), 18 months (September 1974), and 30 months (September 1975) after the onset of the program. The police survey measured officers' job satisfaction and their attitudes toward the community and their work. A stratified random sample of officers was selected and randomly divided into two groups of approximately 90 each. One group participated in the first and third waves of surveys, the other in the second and fourth waves. Another group of officers was randomly selected for the fifth wave of surveys. Sergeants and lieutenants were overrepresented at all waves. COMSEC officers' responses were compared at each wave to those of equal numbers of officers and supervisors from outside District 1. In addition, interviews were conducted with citizens inside and outside District 1 who had recently received police services; the purpose of the interviews was to assess their experiences with and attitudes toward the police (Schwartz & Clarren, 1977).

During the evaluation, COMSEC's officers reported favorable changes in job breadth (i.e., more responsibilities and tasks), independence, and influence over decisions. Some aspects of job satisfaction, such as the correspondence between what officers were able to do and what they wanted to do, also initially increased. Nonetheless, little evidence was found that COMSEC enhanced officers' job satisfaction or that the program moved officers' views closer to those of citizens on selected issues of community concern (e.g., drug use, recruitment of minority officers, and civilian review boards). Furthermore, many of the positive changes documented in the early stages of the evaluation were lost by 18 months reportedly because of managerial problems that undermined the effectiveness of the program. As Schwartz and Clarren (1977, p. 5) noted:

Management decisions made during the latter half of the first 18 months eventually, whether purposely or not, undermined the integrity of the program and blurred the distinction between District 1 and the rest of the city. The program drifted away from an emphasis on decentralization and autonomy toward greater control by headquarters.

After COMSEC began, citizens in District 1 who had received police services reported fewer instances in which the police failed to arrive after being called, observed the increased visibility of police on foot patrol, and were more likely both to recognize the officers who worked in their neighborhoods and to endorse the concept of team policing. Comparable changes were not found outside District 1. However, citizens' overall satisfaction with police services and their belief in the honesty, impartiality, and courtesy of the police remained quite high, but did not increase, during the evaluation. After 30 months, some of the favorable trends continued, but citizens less often noticed officers providing services and believed that they had less influence with the police (Schwartz & Clarren, 1977).

Flint (1983, 1985, 1986)

Flint, Michigan's experimental Neighborhood Foot Patrol Program (NFPP) was initiated with funds from the Charles Stewart Mott Foundation and was conducted in 14 areas of the city between January 1979 and January 1982. For 2 years prior to the NFPP's onset, citizens participated in its planning and implementation through citywide neighborhood meetings. The program was designed to alleviate three long-standing problems: "(a) the absence of comprehensive neighborhood organizations and services; (b) the lack of citizen involvement in crime prevention; and (c) the depersonalization of interactions between officers and residents" (Payne & Trojanowicz, 1985, p. 4). NFPP officers provided full law enforcement services as well as problem solving and social service referrals. Among the program's 10 basic goals were the decrease of crime and the enhancement of community awareness of crime problems and crime prevention strategies (Trojanowicz, 1983). According to Trojanowicz (1983):

> The foot patrol officers in the Flint program were expected to function as catalytic agents of community organization. They were expected to encourage citizens to work together—either in neighborhood associations, citizen watch groups, or some other form of organization—for their mutual support and protection. (p. 411)

Trojanowicz and his associates conducted an evaluation of the NFPP (see Trojanowicz, 1982, 1983, 1986). Over a 3-year period, they interviewed residents, police officers, and community representatives; analyzed crime statistics, calls for service, and media reports; and documented patrol officer activities. Major findings showed that a significant percentage of community respondents were aware of the program and knew the role of the foot patrol officer.

In a 1981 survey, citizens in Flint were asked to compare foot and motorized patrol officers on six major police activities including: preventing and investigating crime, responding to and following up on complaints, working with juveniles, and encouraging citizens to protect themselves against crime. Trojanowicz (1986) reported that community respondents rated foot patrol officers as significantly more effective in four of the six areas, that is, preventing crime, working with juveniles, following up on complaints, and encouraging citizen self-protection. Motorized patrol officers were rated superior only in the area of responding to complaints.

During the 3 years of the evaluation, panel surveys indicated that foot patrol officers, when compared to motorized patrol officers, were more likely to report the following as important law enforcement activities: preventing crime, knowing community residents, helping victims, teaching citizens to report crime, conducting special crime-related classes for residents, and becoming involved with the community.

Trojanowicz and Banas (1985) interviewed 64 foot patrol and 50 randomly selected motorized officers in a posttest-only control group design. The two groups of officers were compared on measures of job satisfaction, opportunities for advancement, and attitudes toward work. Results demonstrated that foot patrol officers were more likely to perceive that they were doing an important job in the department and in their patrol areas, improving police-community relations, performing a job that the police department views as important, and working as part of a police team. Furthermore, foot patrol officers felt more enthusiastic about their positions, which they were more likely to view as increasing their chances for career advancement. Both foot and motor patrol officers reported that the latter had "more difficulty maintaining high morale and achieving job satisfaction" (Trojanowicz & Banas, 1985, p. 10).

Baltimore County (1985, 1987)

Hayeslip and Cordner (1987) examined police officer job satisfaction in Baltimore County, Maryland's community policing program, known as the Citizen Oriented Police Enforcement (COPE) project. In the early 1980s, the COPE project was developed primarily to alleviate citizens' fear of crime, which had been fueled by a recent surge in stranger-to-stranger murders. The program attempted to increase police-citizen contacts through neighborhood canvasing and "stop, walk, and talk" tactics, and to encourage citizen cooperation with police through police-citizen crime prevention and problem-solving efforts (see Goldstein, 1979). An evaluation of COPE found small to moderate reductions in fear (Cordner, 1986).

In an earlier investigation of the effects of COPE on officer's job satisfaction, perceptions of the police role, and attitudes toward the community and the COPE strategy, Hayeslip and Cordner (1987) administered self-report surveys to COPE and non-COPE officers at four points in time: June 1982 (at the beginning of the COPE project), January-February 1983, November 1983, and March 1985. Findings indicated that COPE officers, when compared to non-COPE officers, had a higher level of job satisfaction, which only slightly diminished over time; developed more positive attitudes toward citizens; and continued to regard the program very favorably throughout the investigation.

Hayeslip and Cordner (1987) conducted further analyses of these data to explore the potentially confounding effects of the background and personal characteristics of officers on observed officer changes. The investigation included several dependent measures (at Time 4) of job satisfaction, and of attitudes toward the community, the police role, and the COPE strategy. These measures were regressed on age, department tenure, assignment tenure, and COPE/control assignment.

The COPE variable (i.e., a dummy-coded variable indicating membership in the experimental or control group) significantly predicted 12 of the 16 outcome measures, and was the only significant predictor of 8 of the outcome measures. According to the researchers, "those officers who participated in COPE had higher levels of reported job satisfaction, more cooperative and service-oriented attitudes about the police role, more positive attitudes toward the community, and more positive evaluations of the COPE project's effects than did officers in the control group" (p. 115). Hence, the influence of personal and background variables did not explain away COPE's favorable impact on officers' attitudes and perceptions (Cordner, 1988).

Houston and Newark (1986)

The Police Foundation performed evaluations of two community policing programs in Houston and Newark, known collectively as the Fear Reduction Project (see Skogan, 1990; Skolnick & Bayley, 1986, for descriptions of the programs). Houston's program was initiated by the Houston planning task force; it was designed and implemented by patrol officers and a sergeant from the planning division of the department, and was staffed by a combination of patrol officers, civilian community service officers, and a civilian office manager. The program contained a number of components. Police-community stations were located in storefronts to "close the gap between citizens and the police" (Skogan, 1990, p. 96), a community organizing response team tried to organize neighborhoods and to empower residents to solve local problems, and a citizen contact effort involved door-to-door informal visits by the police to increase the frequency and quality of interactions between citizens and the police and to identify neighborhood problems and solutions to those problems.

Newark also planned and implemented a series of special policing programs under the rubric of community policing (Skogan, 1990). In contrast to Houston's approach, Newark's program was developed from the "top down" by the command staff of the police department and outside experts (Skogan & Lurigio, 1991), and incorporated more traditional enforcement tactics to reduce physical and social disorder. Efforts to alleviate disorder were part of an intensive enforcement program that included street sweeps to combat loitering, public disturbances, and drug sales; foot patrols to maintain order on the sidewalks; radar checks to enforce traffic ordinances; roadblocks to identify individuals driving without a license, under the influence of alcohol, or in possession of a stolen vehicle; and intensified city services to facilitate garbage collection and other cleanup projects. The community policing package to reduce fear and to improve police-citizen relations contained some of the same components as those found in Houston, such as community stations and citizen contact patrols.

The evaluations of Houston and Newark's programs were quite extensive (Pate, Skogan, Wycoff, & Sherman, 1986). Different elements of each program were implemented in different areas of the cities, and a comparison (no-program) area in Houston and Newark, which was matched with the program areas on a number of key demographic variables, was included as a benchmark for program change. The evaluation encompassed a variety of methods to test for program effects in a before-after control design that involved interviews with residents and police officers, observations of program activities, and analyses of administrative data.

Overall, the Houston program appeared to be effective. Citizens were likely to report that police performance improved, that is, they generally rated the police as more polite, helpful, and fair in their dealings with people in the area. However, program impact was mostly confined to nonminority, home-owning residents, that is, "those [citizens] at the bottom of the local status ladder were severely underrepresented in terms of awareness and contact with the programs, and were unaffected by them. In short, the better-off got better off, and the disparity between area residents grew deeper" (Skogan, 1990, p. 107). The results from the Newark evaluation also showed that the programs increased ratings of police performance. In Newark, no differential program impact was found along racial or class lines, primarily because of the homogeneity of the areas targeted by the project.

Wycoff (1988) reported that the researchers in Houston observed a number of positive changes in the officers who designed and implemented the program, including the recognition that most citizens welcome the opportunity to interact with police and that policing can be approached in a variety of ways; the realization that patrol work can be stimulating and challenging; a growing sense of pride, efficacy, and competence in their work; and a greater identification with the police profession. These reports are anecdotal.

New York (1988, 1993)

Weisburd, McElroy, and Hardyman (1988) focused on the effects of community policing on line supervisors as part of the Vera Institute's exploratory study of New York's Community Patrol Officer Program (CPOP). CPOP was designed as a means to introduce the concepts of community policing into New York without a massive restructuring of the city's patrol force. The CPOP model required each community patrol officer (CPO) to be a planner, problem solver, community organizer, and information link (see Farrell, 1988; Weisburd & McElroy, 1988). At the time of the study, CPOP was a pilot project in its first year of operation. Weisburd et al. interviewed CPOs and sergeants and directly observed them on the streets. The investigators reported that sergeants had to adjust their supervisory styles and behaviors in a number of fundamental ways in order to fulfill the tenets of CPOP.

Weisburd et al.'s findings addressed three areas of supervisory adjustment. The first adjustment involved monitoring officers' time on patrol, which emphasized the shift in sergeants' perceptions of the value of citizen contacts. The second adjustment involved overseeing proactive patrol strategies and tactics, which discussed CPOP efforts to combat neighborhood signs of disorder, in particular, street-level drug sales. The third adjustment involved monitoring police-citizen contacts to prevent corruption, which underscored the importance of sergeants' trust as a factor motivating officers to avoid compromising situations.

In a more recent investigation of CPOP, which examined CPOs' perceptions and behaviors, McElroy, Cosgrove, and Sadd (1993) interviewed program officers at two points in time (T_1 and T_2) over a 6-month data collection period. No comparison group was interviewed. A total of 51 CPOs participated at both T_1 and T_2; they had been assigned to CPOP for an average of one year before the study began. Results showed that officers' retrospective impressions regarding their potential for career advancement did not change from the time they joined CPOP to the time of the first interview: 56% believed CPOP would advance their careers, 23% believed CPOP would reduce their career options, and 20% believed that CPOP would have no influence (either positive or negative) over their career advancement.

CPOs were asked at T_2 to estimate the number of hours they spent on 13 different police activities (both CPOP and non-CPOP). According to McElroy et al. (1993), an average of nearly one third of the officers' activities was spent on general patrol, 22% on handling priority problems, 11% on paperwork, and the remaining third on the other 10 activities, such as going to court, organizing community groups, and attending CPOP meetings. CPOs rated working as a unit, maintaining beat visibility, and solving priority beat problems as the most important CPOP activities; they rated conducting security inspections and victim surveys, and completing the Beat Book as the least important CPOP activities.

The study also assessed T_1 to T_2 changes in CPO attitudes toward being a cop, the CPOP program, the community, and the New York City Police Department. Most of the respondents reported no attitudinal changes in any of these areas. However, when change was reported, their attitudes toward CPOP, the community, and being a cop became more positive, whereas their attitudes toward the department became more negative. Finally, from T_1 to T_2, officers' aspirations regarding their future rank in the department rose somewhat.

Edmonton, Canada (1989)

In 1987, the Edmonton's Police Department decided "to incorporate the philosophy and implement the practice of community-based policing" (Hornick, Burrows, & Phillips, 1989, p. 1). The project was called the Neighborhood Foot Patrol Program (NFPP) and was conducted in 21 neighborhood beat areas. The NFPP was designed to prevent crime and to identify "problems that damage the quality of life, then work through the community as a whole to find and apply solutions to those problems" (Cassels, 1988, p. 5).

The program had a variety of specific objectives: for example, to reduce the number of repeat calls for service, to increase officers' job satisfaction, and to improve the public's satisfaction with the police. Its basic strategies included: (a) targeting police services to "hot spots," (b) moving (decentralizing) police services to storefronts in each beat area, (c) increasing police visibility through foot patrols, (d) fostering officer autonomy and problem-solving ability, (e) encouraging the police to involve the community in defining and solving local problems through daily contact with neighborhood residents and businesspersons, and (f) broadening officers' overall knowledge of the community (Hornick et al., 1989).

Hornick et al. conducted a comprehensive process and impact evaluation of the NFPP during its first year of operations. In their impact evaluation, they employed quasi-experimental designs that examined the program's effects on the police and residents. The police study involved pretest-posttest surveys of officers, which were administered at baseline (shortly after the inception of the NFPP—May 1988) and again one year later (May 1989). Program officers' attitudes on several issues were compared to those of a random sample of patrol officers. The instrument asked about officers' attitudes regarding the patrol function, police performance issues, job satisfaction, personal motivation, and feelings toward work. The residents' study involved surveys of citizens 5 to 6 months after they had contact with foot patrol (program) and motor patrol (non-program) officers. Respondents were asked to rate officers on a number of factors, such as their level of satisfaction with the investigating officer; how well they remembered the investigating officer; and whether they found the investigating officer to be polite, helpful, and attentive.

Findings that compared pretest and posttest measures showed that program officers gave more positive ratings than nonprogram officers to work compensation, organizational policy and procedures, job growth and satisfaction, and internal work motivation. Results also demonstrated that citizens rated foot patrol officers more positively on nearly all the items in the resident survey. Specifically, individuals who had contact with program officers were more likely to remember and to be satisfied with the investigating officer; to rate the officer as more polite, helpful, and understanding; to report that the officer increased their confidence that the situation would be resolved and helped them to feel more relaxed and comfortable after the incident; and to indicate that the officer had engaged in satisfactory follow-up procedures.

Philadelphia (1989)

Community Oriented Police Education, known as Project COPE, is a police-community relations program in Philadelphia that began in 1980 with a grant from the Ford Foundation. The purpose of COPE is to encourage community crime prevention activities, to facilitate understanding and communications between the police and citizens, and "to improve police officers' affective attachment to the communities in which they are assigned" (Greene, 1989, p. 173). COPE involves 16 weeks of intensified classes, small group discussions, and role playing sessions—each attended by police officers and community residents from several Philadelphia neighborhoods. The content of the program has varied; however, several basic features and themes have remained constant, such as race relations, community resources, police use of power and authority, crime prevention strategies, and the need to relieve tension between police and citizens. Over the years, the program "has retained a strong emphasis on bringing police and community residents together to discuss and hopefully resolve 'community' problems" (Greene & Decker, 1989, p. 110).

Greene and Decker (1989) reported findings from an evaluation of COPE that examined its effects on police officers and residents who participated in two full sessions of the program—one conducted from April to June 1985, the other from September 1985 to January 1986. A total of 50 police officers and 24 citizens completed pre-post questionnaires measuring their perceptions of one another and one another's role in crime control and prevention. These perceptions were combined into seven indices of police-community relations. Police officers also responded to three questions exploring job satisfaction.

A number of significant findings (pre-post changes) appeared with regard to police perceptions and job satisfaction. On the positive side, officers perceived less direct citizen antagonism toward the police, a more involved role for citizens in community crime prevention and control efforts, and more visible citizen participation in community crime prevention activities. On the negative side, police viewed citizens as less supportive, believed that the quality of their interactions with citizens had diminished, and were less likely to emphasize citizen-police relations as part of their job. All three job satisfaction items also changed in the negative direction. After COPE, officers were less satisfied with their police career and direct assignment, and were less likely to see their job as providing challenges and opportunities for self-initiative.

Madison (1992)

The Madison Police Department implemented a community-based policing program in January 1987 following an employee planning group's recommendation to "get closer to the people we serve" (Reno, 1990, cited in Wycoff & Skogan, 1993, p. 195). The program is administered by a team of neighborhood officers who are assigned to "the Experimental Police District (EPD), a geographical area constituting one-sixth of the city in which officers devise strategies for communicating with citizens, learning citizens' perceptions of problems, and working with citizens to solve problems" (Wycoff, 1988, p. 114). The EPD provides three police functions, that is, neighborhood patrol, motorized patrol for emergency calls and traffic duties, and follow-up investigatory services (Madison, Wisconsin, Police Department, 1988). According to Wycoff (1988), the EPD planning team hypothesized (among other effects) that officers in the program would have greater concern for citizens' problems, higher self-esteem, and more organizational commitment.

Wycoff and Skogan (1993) employed a pretest-posttest, nonequivalent control group design, and measured changes in police attitudes and behaviors using a comprehensive survey with more than 100 questions embedded in numerous multi-item scales. Measurements on both program and control group officers (i.e., officers working in the rest of the city) were taken before the program began (Wave 1), and again at one (Wave 2) and two years (Wave 3) following program implementation. Most analyses compared Wave 1 and Wave 3 measures within each of the groups. In addition, residents across the city, including the EPD, were interviewed to examine their attitudes toward the police and ratings of police-citizen contacts.

Wycoff and Skogan (1993) reported several significant findings. From 1987 to 1989, officers in the EPD became more likely to: believe that quality police leadership was being provided, that the patrol function fosters community support, and that citizens regard them highly; feel more satisfied with the organization as a place to work, more task identity or wholeness, and more satisfied with the kind of work they do; perceive greater participatory management; and report greater organizational support for problem solving, less sick leave, and closer working relationships with other officers, their supervisors, and detectives. However, many of the measures did not show changes from Wave 1 to Wave 3. For example, officers were *not* more likely to perceive greater success at problem solving, to believe that citizens should be involved in problem solving, and to report more time available for proactive work.

Few significant findings emerged from the resident survey. For example, EPD respondents were no more likely than non-EPD respondents to report knowing the name of an officer who works in their area and being more satisfied with their last self-initiated contact with the police. Nonetheless, EPD respondents were more likely to rate the police as very helpful during their most recent officer-initiated contact with the police. Wycoff and Skogan (1993) noted that some of the nonsignificant findings in the resident survey could be attributed to "ceiling effects," that is, citizens' ratings of the police were already so positive that further improvements were unlikely. Also, the officers most enthusiastic about community policing were younger, lower seniority officers and therefore more likely to work the night shift, where they would have less citizen-initiated and more officer-initiated contacts.

Aurora and Joliet (1993)

With substantial external funding and two innovative police chiefs, the cities of Aurora and Joliet, Illinois, engaged in a cooperative effort to develop and implement the Neighborhood-Oriented Policing and Problem-Solving Project. The first year of the program (1991) focused on building resources and capacity within the police organizations, which was similar to the preparatory process pursued in Madison. Police personnel in both departments received considerable training from the Police Executive Research Forum; a problem-solving philosophy and model were at the core of their education. Planning and implementation teams were formed, but participation from the rank and file achieved only partial success. Furthermore, the traditional organizational police structure imposed some barriers to adequate supervision and support in both departments, especially in Aurora. Rather than attempting department-wide implementation the first year, Aurora and Joliet deployed special units of officers to conduct the programs in selected areas of the cities. In the field, community policing officers engaged in foot patrol and problem-solving efforts. Aurora also opened a mini-station (small trailer) in the target area.

To evaluate the programs, Rosenbaum and Wilkinson (in press) employed a pretest-posttest, nonequivalent control group design, with one posttest approximately 10 months after the pretest. (A second wave of posttest data are currently being collected.) A control group (Evanston, Illinois) was selected from a pool of 13 police departments in the Chicago area of similar size and population characteristics. An extensive police survey was modeled after Wycoff and Skogan (1993) and administered at pretest and posttest to both program and nonprogram officers in Aurora and Joliet and to control group officers in Evanston. More than 85% of the surveyed officers in all three cities participated in the pretest and posttest. Program effects were tested in two ways: first, program officers were compared to nonprogram officers in both cities; and second, officers as a whole group (including program and nonprogram officers) in Aurora and Joliet were compared to officers in the comparison department (i.e., Evanston).

In Aurora, program officers, when compared to nonprogram officers in the city, reported more opportunities to work closely with other employees and more familiarity with problem-oriented policing. When compared to Evanston officers, Aurora officers reported more familiarity with problem-oriented policing and more hours spent on foot patrol per week. However, they also reported that they were *less* satisfied with opportunities for communication with detectives and with the feedback they receive from supervisors and peers, that *fewer* problems were being addressed via problem-solving techniques, and that *fewer* meetings were being held with community groups and citizens.

The results in Joliet were similar. Program officers there reported more opportunities to work closely with other employees, more familiarity with problem-oriented policing, more frequent interaction with citizens, and more hours spent on foot patrol. When compared to Evanston officers, Joliet officers reported more familiarity with problem-oriented policing and more support for professional policing activities including conducting foot patrols, marketing police services, explaining crime prevention, and working with citizen groups. But they also reported addressing *fewer* problems via problem-solving techniques, using *fewer* nontraditional sources of information, and holding *fewer* community meetings for problem identification. In both cities, no differences in either the within- or between-department comparisons were found on most measures of job activity; management changes; job satisfaction; attitudes regarding community, professional, and traditional policing; and receptivity to change.

Summary and Conclusions

In this chapter, we have reviewed several studies examining community policing's impact on police personnel in 12 different locations. On balance, these studies have shown that community policing has exerted a positive impact on the police and on citizens' views of the police. From the police perspective, investigators have reported increases in job satisfaction and motivation, a broadening of the police role, improvements in relationships with co-workers and citizens, and greater expectations regarding community participation in crime prevention efforts. From the citizen perspective, officers engaging in community policing are rated as more visible, helpful, polite, and effective on a variety of job activities. Few researchers have reported negative changes in police or citizen-initiated measures; and even when investigators have presented adverse results, such findings have never been the primary or sole focus of any study.

Our interpretation of these generally favorable impact results—which are surely encouraging for program advocates—must remain cautious for several reasons. To begin, some of the research has been fraught with methodological and measurement flaws. Studies have employed research designs that are subject to serious threats to internal validity. (See Greene & Taylor [1988] for an excellent review of community policing evaluations and their shortcomings.) For example, several investigations did not include equivalent comparison groups or pretest measures to rule out competing explanations for findings. Without these design enhancements, observed results or changes cannot be confidently attributed to the program.

Selection biases and historical artifacts, which are especially problematic in the absence of pretests and control groups, have not been adequately addressed by researchers in this area. Hence some of the research designs described in this review were relatively weak and did not permit strong causal inferences. For example, with respect to selection confounds, community policing programs are often staffed by volunteers or newer officers who may already be more prone to engage in community contacts or problem-solving activities, or may be more satisfied with their jobs from the outset. In such instances, results can be a function of who is in the program and not of the program itself, or can be a product of the interaction between the program and the specially selected or self-selected officers, which would make it difficult to generalize the effects of the program to the rest of a department.

Few of the studies have incorporated measures with established reliability or validity. A number of researchers have attempted to quantify complex constructs such as job satisfaction or growth with single items instead of with previously validated or factor-analyzed scales. Moreover, a lack of uniformity or standardization in outcome measures has made it virtually impossible to compare or synthesize results across investigations (Greene, 1989).

For these reasons the studies should not be given equal weight when attempting to estimate the effects of community policing on police. Randomized experiments and quasi-experimental designs with carefully selected control groups suffer from fewer threats to validity, and thus deserve more serious attention. Similarly, studies with comprehensive measures and multi-item scales are more likely to yield reliable and valid measurement on key outcome variables.

Some recent evaluations have employed both solid research designs and validated measurement. However, because investigators have generally viewed programs as "black boxes," studies have yet to identify or test the relative contributions of various program components to observed outcomes. Without prespecified models of program impact, researchers cannot determine which features of community policing (e.g., foot patrol, crime prevention, decentralization, problem solving, community cooperation) are most or least efficacious in producing changes or how these factors operate to produce changes. Isolating the effects of program components is important for policy analysis and program replication. Although this task is difficult, some degree of success can be achieved by using more precise measures of the intervening variables that should be activated by various program elements.

Along these lines, perhaps the most troubling aspect of this research is the conspicuous dearth of conceptual or theoretical frameworks to drive the testing of hypotheses or to guide the interpretation of results. Only a couple of relatively recent evaluations have drawn on concepts and models from organizational behavior and job enrichment theory. Hackman and Oldham's (1976) job characteristics model, which includes aspects of job enlargement and job enrichment, would provide an excellent explanatory mechanism for understanding the influence of community policing on job satisfaction and motivation. Nonetheless, the focus of most evaluations has been on *community* impact (e.g., changes in citizens' perceptions and fears, crime rates, levels of disorder), and not on *officer* impact. As police organizations begin to realize that changes in police officers may be the first step toward the success or failure of community policing, such data have taken on new meaning. We hope this growing attention to police officers as clients (and not just program agents) will stimulate further interest in the processes of internal change—within both organizations and individuals—that must take place before community policing can become the prevailing policing paradigm in America.

References

Boydstun, J. E., & Sherry, M. E. (1975). *San Diego community profile: Final report.* Washington, DC: Police Foundation.

Cassels, D. (1988). *The Edmonton Police Department Neighborhood Foot Patrol Project: Preliminary report.* Edmonton, Alberta: Edmonton Police Department.

Cordner, G. W. (1986). Fear of crime and the police: An evaluation of the fear-reduction strategy. *Journal of Police Science and Administration, 14,* 223-233.

Cordner, G. W. (1988). A problem-oriented approach to community-oriented policing. In J. R. Greene & S. D. Mastrofski (Eds.), *Community policing: Rhetoric or reality?* (pp. 135-152). New York: Praeger.

Farrell, M. J. (1988). The development of the Community Patrol Officer Program: Community-oriented policing in the New York City Police Department. In J. R. Greene & S. D. Mastrofski (Eds.), *Community policing: Rhetoric or reality?* (pp. 75-88). New York: Praeger.

Goldstein, H. (1979). Improving policing: A problem-oriented approach. *Crime and Delinquency, 25,* 235-258.

Greene, J. (1989). Police officer job satisfaction and community perceptions: Implications for community-oriented policing. *Journal of Research in Crime and Delinquency, 26,* 168-183.

Greene, J. R., & Decker, S. H. (1989). Police and community perceptions of the community role in policing: The Philadelphia experience. *The Howard Journal, 28,* 105-123.

Greene, J. R., & Taylor, R. B. (1988). Community-based policing and foot patrol: Issues of theory and evaluation. In J. R. Greene & S. D. Mastrofski (Eds.), *Community policing: Rhetoric or reality?* (pp. 195-223). New York: Praeger.

Hackman, J. R., & Oldham, G. R. (1976). Motivation through the design of work: Test of a theory. *Organizational Behavior and Human Performance, 16,* 250-279.

Hayeslip, D. W., & Cordner, G. W. (1987). The effects of community-oriented patrol on police officer attitudes. *American Journal of Police, 4,* 95-119.

Hornick, J. P., Burrows, B. A., & Phillips, D. M. (1989, November). *An impact evaluation of the Edmonton Neighborhood Foot Patrol Program.* Paper presented at the annual meeting of the American Society of Criminology, Reno, NV.

Kelling, G. L., & Moore, M. H. (1988). *The evolving strategy of policing.* Washington, DC: National Institute of Justice and Harvard University.

McElroy, J. E., Cosgrove, C. A., & Sadd, S. (1993). *Community policing: The CPOP in New York.* Newbury Park, CA: Sage.

Moore, M. H. (1992). Problem-solving and community policing. In M. Tonry & N. Morris (Eds.), *Crime and justice: A review of research: Vol. 15. Modern policing* (pp. 99-158). Chicago: University of Chicago Press.

Pate, A. M., Skogan, W. G., Wycoff, M. A., & Sherman, L. W. (1986). *Reducing fear of crime in Houston and Newark: A summary report.* Washington, DC: Police Foundation.

Payne, D. M., & Trojanowicz, R. C. (1985). *Performance profiles of foot versus motor officers.* East Lansing: Michigan State University, School of Criminal Justice, National Neighborhood Foot Patrol Center.

Rosenbaum, D. P., & Wilkinson, D. L. (in press). The impact of community policing on police personnel: A quasi-experimental test in two cities. *Crime and Delinquency.*

Schwartz, A. I., & Clarren, S. N. (1977). *The Cincinnati team policing experiment: A summary report.* Washington, DC: The Urban Institute and Police Foundation.

Skogan, W. G. (1990). *Disorder and community decline: Crime and the spiral of decay in American neighborhoods.* New York: Free Press.

Skogan, W. G., & Lurigio, A. J. (1991). Multi-site evaluations in criminal justice: Structural obstacles to success. *New Directions for Program Evaluation, 50,* 83-96.

Skolnick, J. H., & Bayley, D. H. (1986). *The new blue line: Police innovation in six American cities.* New York: Free Press.

Skolnick, J. H., & Bayley, D. H. (1988). *Community policing: Issues and practices around the world.* Washington, DC: National Institute of Justice.

Trojanowicz, R. C. (1982). *An evaluation of the Neighborhood Foot Patrol Program in Flint, Michigan.* East Lansing: Michigan State University.

Trojanowicz, R. C. (1983). An evaluation of a neighborhood foot patrol. *Journal of Police Science and Administration, 2,* 410-419.

Trojanowicz, R. C. (1986). Evaluating a neighborhood foot patrol program: The Flint, Michigan, Project. In D. P. Rosenbaum (Ed.), *Community crime prevention: Does it work?* (pp. 157-178). Beverly Hills, CA: Sage.

Trojanowicz, R. C., & Banas, D. (1985). *Perceptions of safety: A comparison of foot and motor officers.* East Lansing: Michigan State University, National Neighborhood Foot Patrol Center.

Walker, S. (1992). *The police in America.* New York: McGraw-Hill.

Weisburd, D., & McElroy, J. E. (1988). Enacting the CPO role: Findings from the New York City Pilot Program in Community Policing. In J. R. Greene & S. D. Mastrofski (Eds.), *Community policing: Rhetoric or reality?* (pp. 89-102). New York: Praeger.

Weisburd, D., McElroy, J. E., & Hardyman, P. (1988). Challenges to supervision in community policing: Observations on a pilot project. *American Journal of Policing, 7,* 29-50.

Wycoff, M. A. (1988). The benefits of community policing: Evidence and conjecture. In J. R. Greene & S. D. Mastrofski (Eds.), *Community policing: Rhetoric or reality?* (pp. 103-120). New York: Praeger.

Wycoff, M. A., & Skogan, W. G. (1993). *Quality policing in Madison: An evaluation of its implementation and impact* (Final Technical Report). Washington, DC: The Police Foundation.

PART

IV

Impact on Community Residents
and Neighborhood Problems

The Impact of Community Policing on Neighborhood Residents

A Cross-Site Analysis

WESLEY G. SKOGAN

THIS CHAPTER EXAMINES one important aspect of community policing, its impact on neighborhood residents. Community policing is not a clear-cut concept, for it involves reforming decision-making processes and creating new cultures within police departments, rather than being a specific tactical plan. It is an organizational strategy that redefines the goals of policing (Goldstein, 1990; Moore, 1992). In general, community policing relies upon organizational decentralization and a reorientation of patrol in order to facilitate two-way communication between police and the public. It assumes a commitment to broadly focused, problem-oriented policing and requires that police are responsive to citizen demands when they decide what local problems are and set their priorities. It also implies a commitment to helping neighborhoods solve crime problems on their own, through community organizations and crime prevention programs.

These principles underlie a variety of policing programs. Under the rubric of community policing, American departments are opening small neighborhood substations, conducting surveys to identify local problems, organizing meetings and crime prevention seminars, publishing newsletters, helping form Neighborhood Watch groups, establishing advisory panels to inform police commanders,

AUTHOR'S NOTE: Supported under award 92-IJ-CX-0008 from the National Institute of Justice, Office of Justice Programs, U.S. Department of Justice. Points of view in this chapter are those of the author and do not necessarily represent the official position of the U.S. Department of Justice.

organizing youth activities, conducting drug education projects and media campaigns, patrolling on horses and bicycles, and working with municipal agencies to enforce health and safety regulations.

Can these programs live up to the expectations of their supporters? The answer to this is not clear, for there have been relatively few systematic evaluations of community policing programs. There is more hyperbole than solid evidence about the wisdom of community policing, and a great deal of "hype" behind many claims about new policing styles. Many researchers are professionally skeptical of claims about community policing, despite their general inclination toward it. A volume on policing edited by Jack Greene and Stephen Mastrofski (1988) included several chapters lamenting the dearth of good evidence on the effects of policing generally and community policing in particular. The contribution by Greene and Taylor (1988) criticized the implicit theories of community that lie behind the assumption that police can intervene in defense of neighborhoods by such tactics as foot patrol; David Bayley's (1988) contribution took a critical stance vis-à-vis the resurrection of traditional police order maintenance activity that it recommends.

This chapter describes several evaluations of community policing and summarizes some of their results. Most of the evaluations contrasted the impact of community policing programs with the effects of intensive enforcement programs, as well as against what happened in control areas representing "normal" styles of policing. Since the mid-1980s, these enforcement programs have had a special focus on drugs. The community policing evaluations examined here point to some significant successes, but illustrate that evidence that community policing can significantly reduce the crime rate remains elusive. They also point out many difficulties in actually implementing community policing.

Community Policing Experiments in Six Cities

Baltimore, Maryland

Two versions of community policing were tested in Baltimore. Each was implemented in two areas of the city, in white and African American neighborhoods of comparable income level and housing quality. *Foot patrols* were assigned to walk through the areas approximately 25 hours each week. They choose their own routes, concentrating on busy commercial areas and recognized trouble spots. They talked frequently with residents, business owners, and people on the street. In one area the officers put more stress on law enforcement and order maintenance; they spent much of their time dispersing groups of youths on street corners and looking for drug transactions and other legal infractions. The officer who conducted most of the foot patrols in the other area focused more on talking with residents and merchants. Surveys conducted after one year indicated that about 15% of the residents of each area recalled seeing an officer walking on foot within the past week; the comparable figure among residents of a control area was only 2%.

In two other areas, *ombudsman police officers* were assigned to work with neighborhood residents to solve local problems. They walked foot patrol, attended community meetings, and spent a great deal of time talking to merchants and residents about local problems. They developed a questionnaire that measured what residents thought were the most serious problems in the area, what caused them, and what could be done to solve them. Officers were to record how they had reacted to each problem, and their handling of them was reviewed by their supervisors. The officer serving one area was aggressive in his approach to possible drug dealers, broke up groups loitering on the street, and gave many traffic tickets. He spent most of his time in busy commercial areas of the neighborhood. The officer in the other target area spent more time meeting with area residents, working to solve juvenile problems, conducting a neighborhood clean-up campaign, and organizing a block watch program. He also involved other municipal agencies in these efforts. He arranged for abandoned cars to be towed away, trees to be trimmed, and empty buildings to be sealed. He also worked closely with the department's traffic, vice, and narcotics units when out of public view. Surveys at the end of the evaluation period found that 64% of the residents of one area, and 75% in the other, recalled officers coming to their home; the officer who emphasized local service had been seen by 33% within the past week (see Pate & Annan, 1989).

Oakland, California

Two policing programs were evaluated in Oakland, both aimed at reducing levels of drug trafficking and related crime and fear. Each program was implemented in its own target area, and both were implemented together in a third area. A special *drug enforcement unit* conducted traditional police operations in its target neighborhoods. They went undercover to make buy-bust arrests, and they used informants to buy drugs and identify distributors. They also mounted an aggressive, high-visibility program of stopping and searching motor vehicles and conducting field interrogations of groups of men whenever they gathered in public places. The team was extremely active, made a large number of arrests, and apprehended a number of major drug traffickers in the target area.

This traditional policing program was contrasted to a program of *home visits*. Officers in the experimental community policing area and in the combined target areas went door to door, introducing themselves to residents. Their job was to inform people in the target neighborhoods of the department's new emphasis on drug enforcement, to give them pamphlets on crime and drug programs, and conduct brief interviews asking about neighborhood problems. Their goal was to make contacts that might lead to useful information, alert the community to the drug problem, and perhaps deter potential offenders due to their presence and visibility in the community. These door-step interviews were conducted in about 60% of the households in the target areas, a high percentage. About 50% of those interviewed indicated that drugs were a major problem in their community. (In many places this kind of activity is known now as "directed patrol," because officers conducting this form of foot patrol have specific tasks to carry out as they walk through an area.) Unlike the enforcement program, however, it proved difficult to sustain the interest of Oakland officers in these home visits. It had little support from the district commander, who did not believe it could work. An energetic officer saw to it that many interviews were conducted, but there was no follow-up problem solving. None of the intended problem-solving policing was ever accomplished, and nothing was done with the information gathered in the door-step interviews (see Uchida, Forst, & Annan, 1990, 1992).

Birmingham, Alabama

Three programs were evaluated in Birmingham. As in Oakland, a special *drug enforcement unit* was formed to crack down on open drug dealing in dilaudid and cocaine. The team concentrated on undercover operations. They made a series of videotaped purchases from street dealers and then returned to the target area to make warrant arrests. Officers also posed as dealers and made videotaped drug sales to outsiders who were driving into the target area to make drug purchases. Throughout, they paid careful attention to the legality of their activities to ensure that their cases could be successfully prosecuted. Ten officers were involved in this program for a 6-month period, but although they made a number of arrests, it was unlikely that their efforts would be very visible in the community surveys.

In another area, officers were to make *home visits* in order to pass out crime and drug prevention pamphlets and conduct interviews with area residents. They developed a questionnaire that asked residents about neighborhood crime problems and the whereabouts of drug trafficking. They eventually completed interviews at 60% of the occupied housing units in their target area. Although they completed a large number of interviews, no effort was made to follow up on the information that was gathered. It was envisioned that they would do team-oriented problem solving with the information that they gathered, but events conspired to undermine the program. A rise in calls for service in their area of the city came at the same time that the Christmas holiday season left the district understaffed. Under pressure to respond to the resulting deterioration in police response to 911 calls, officers who were to conduct the community policing program were reassigned to traditional patrol.

The third Birmingham program was instituted in the evaluation's control area after 11 people were shot there in a short period, just after the beginning of the research project. In response to community demonstrations, a *police substation* was opened, staffed 24 hours per day by eight police officers. They greatly increased the visibility of police in the community. The substation unit assisted in a cleanup of the public housing project that dominated the area. In follow-up interviews, 72% of residents thought the substation was effective in reducing drug-related crime (see Uchida et al., 1990, 1992).

Madison, Wisconsin

Madison attempted to develop a "customer orientation" in providing police services by radically restructuring the police department and the way in which it was managed. It began as a traditional, hierarchically organized department. To reform the organization, an *innovative management structure* was put in place that emphasized teamwork and employee participation in decision making, as well as peer supervision. Police were to work as teams to identify and solve problems, with their managers working for them to secure the outside assistance and resources that they required to carry out their plans. A decentralized *police substation* was opened to experiment with these ideas in a district that covered one sixth of the city. The team worked flexible hours and took responsibility for managing their own activity. They developed a plan for "value added policing" that called for spending more time on calls for service and follow-up contacts with victims. They responded to most of the calls for service that originated from the area and attempted to analyze them to identify community problems.

The surveys that were conducted after the program had been in operation for 2 years found almost 70% of the residents of the target area knew about the police substation. Compared to the rest of the city, the surveys indicated a modest improvement in perceptions of the police among residents of the target area. The perceived quality of police-initiated encounters improved in the special district and especially the perception that officers were helpful. There was also a mild increase in police visibility that could be linked to the program, and more residents of the experimental area reported they thought police were focusing their attention on preventing crime and on important community problems. Residents of the target area reported a decrease in neighborhood problems, while those elsewhere thought they got worse.

Most of the effects of the program seemed to be internal to the department. Interviews with all of the city's police officers were conducted at three points in time over the 2-year reorganization experiment. They revealed, compared to those assigned elsewhere, that officers in the experimental district saw themselves working as a team, that their efforts were being supported by their supervisors and the department, and that the department was really reforming itself. They were more satisfied with their job and more strongly committed to the organization. They were more customer oriented, believed more firmly in the principles of problem solving and community policing, and felt that they had a better relationship with the community. In addition, department records indicated that disciplinary actions, absenteeism, tardiness, and days off sick went down more in the experimental area (see Wycoff & Skogan, 1993). These changes accord with Wycoff's (1988) summary of the results of interview studies of officers assigned to community policing. Compared to others, they have been found to think their work is more important, interesting, and rewarding and less frustrating. They feel they have more independence and control over their jobs, important determinants of job satisfaction. Finally, they tend to take a more benign and trusting view of the public.

Houston, Texas

Three programs were evaluated in Houston. The first was a neighborhood *police substation*. The program team located space in a small commercial building with good parking. The office provided a place for people to meet with police. Officers took crime reports and gave and received information from the public, and some community meetings were held there. Officers assigned to the station were freed from routine patrol for much of their daily shift. The office was their base of operations for getting acquainted with neighborhood residents and business people, identifying and helping solve local problems, seeking ways of delivering better service to the area, and developing programs to draw the police and community closer together. The staff quickly developed programs that extended into the immediate neighborhood, including a series of large community meetings in a nearby church. Station officers organized *special patrols* in area trouble spots, and they met regularly with local school administrators. Area churches and civic clubs were invited to select members to ride with officers patrolling in the neighborhood. Finally, on five occasions during the evaluation period the station staff distributed approximately 550 *newsletters* throughout the neighborhood. The newsletters advertised the station's programs and other community events, and printed articles about crime prevention. The station provided a direct test of several aspects of community policing. It provided the officers who ran it a great deal of management autonomy as well as flexibility in allocating their own time and effort. They responded by developing community-oriented programs that were virtually unheard of in Houston's police department, and they invented a variety of new ways in which police and citizens could meet and exchange information and discuss their priorities. Surveys conducted at the conclusion of the evaluation found that 65% of area residents knew about the substation (see Skogan, 1990; Wycoff & Skogan, 1987).

The *Community Organizing Response Team* (CORT) attempted to create a local crime prevention organization in a neighborhood where none existed. The team's immediate goal was to identify a group of residents who would work regularly with them to define and help solve neighborhood problems. Its long-term goal was to create a permanent organization in the community, one that would remain active after CORT left the area. To test the CORT concept, the task force first tried to become familiar with the area's problems. To do this they conducted their own door-to-door survey of the neighborhood. CORT members questioned approximately 300 residents about problems that they felt merited police attention, and whether they might be willing to host meetings in their homes. The survey told them a great deal about the nature of area problems and resulted in invitations to hold such meetings. They then organized small meetings to introduce themselves to area residents. Thirteen neighborhood meetings were held, each attended by 20-60 people. At these meetings CORT members identified a group of leaders who met regularly with their commander to discuss community problems and devise solutions involving both the police and residents. The group eventually held elections and formed committees, and by the end of the evaluation period it had 60 official members. During the evaluation period special newsletters were mailed each month to all residents who had been contacted in the survey or who had participated in an activity. The CORT program tested the ability of police departments to assist in the development of community self-help organizations.

Houston's *Home Visit* program was to help patrol officers to become more familiar with the residents of their areas and to learn about neighborhood problems. Officers in one target area were freed from routine patrol assignments for part of each daily shift. During this time they visited households in the area. Typically, officers in the program would visit an apartment building or a group of homes, introduce themselves to whomever answered, explain the purpose of the visit, and inquire about neighborhood problems. They recorded these on a small "citizen contact card," along with the name and address of the person they interviewed. The officers left personal business cards, indicating that if there were further problems they should be contacted directly. A record of these visits was kept at the district police station to guide further contacts. It also served as a mailing list for a newsletter tailored for the area, which was distributed each month to those who had been contacted. During the 10 months of the program, team officers talked to approximately 14% of the adult residents of the area. Visits also were made to commercial establishments in the area, and after 10 months about 45% of the merchants had been contacted. About 60% of the people who were interviewed had something to complain about. Conventional crimes were most frequently mentioned, but about one quarter of the residents mentioned a problem that might fall into the disorder category, including disputes among neighbors, environmental problems, abandoned cars, and vandalism. The officers took numerous actions in response to problems they identified during these visits (see Skogan, 1990).

Newark, New Jersey

Two programs were evaluated in Newark. In one area police attempted to suppress crime and street disorder using traditional *intensive enforcement* tactics. They conducted extensive "street sweeps" to reduce loitering and public drinking, drug sales, purse snatching, and street harassment by groups of men who routinely gathered along commercial streets in residential areas of the city. Congregating groups were broken up by police warnings and large-scale arrests. Foot patrol officers walked the areas in the evening; they were to become familiar with local problems, establish relationships with local merchants, disperse unruly groups, and ticket illegally parked cars. Special efforts were made to enforce traffic regulations in the area using radar units and by making frequent traffic stops to check for alcohol use. Random roadblocks were set up to check drivers' credentials, check for drunken driving, recover stolen vehicles, and arrest drivers with outstanding tickets and arrest warrants. There was also an attempt to clean up area parks and vacant lots and to deliver better city services. This program tested the ability of the police to reassert their faltering authority, demonstrate that they controlled the streets of Newark, and crack down on forms of disorder thought to lead to serious crime.

In another area of Newark the police implemented a variety of *community policing* projects at the same time. The test area for the community policing project was in the most densely populated and crime-ridden part of Newark. The evaluation tested the ability of an ambitious multi-intervention program to affect crime and fear of crime in an extremely difficult area. Police opened a *substation* that took crime reports, distributed crime prevention information, gathered complaints about city services for referral to other municipal agencies, and answered questions. Local groups held meetings in the station during the evening, and about 300 people used the substation each month. At the end of the evaluation period, 90% of the residents of the area knew about the substation. As in Houston, police also conducted *home visits* in the area. Officers visited homes and filled out brief questionnaires concerning neighborhood problems. The teams also distributed crime prevention information, told residents about block watch programs, and advertised the substation. During the course of the evaluation they questioned residents of 50% of the homes in the area, and in the evaluation surveys 40% of area residents recalled being interviewed. The sergeant supervising the team reviewed the questionnaires, and either his team dealt with the problems that residents identified or he passed them on to the special enforcement squad for their attention. The team also organized a *neighborhood clean-up program* and distributed a police *newsletter;* 43% of area residents recalled receiving one when they were later surveyed. As in the enforcement area, a special squad targeted street disorder in the area (see Skogan, 1990; Skolnick & Bayley, 1986).

Evaluation Findings

Each of the programs described here was evaluated using a systematic research design. The programs were conducted in test areas, while another matched area was designated as a control area where no new policing programs were begun.

Surveys of area residents were conducted in the target and control areas before the programs began, and again after they had been in operation for 10 months. Between 80 and 330 people were reinterviewed in each area. A variety of other kinds of data were collected as well, and the actual implementation of the program was monitored in all the cities. In Birmingham, this research design broke down; the control area was the subject of a wave of random violence and shootings shortly after the evaluation began and community pressure forced the opening of a police substation in the area to serve as the operations center for a new police team. In some other cities the evaluations indicate that community policing programs were only partly implemented, reducing our expectations regarding their impact.

Table 9.1 presents a summary of some of the findings of the evaluations. Each project had a number of goals, but this analysis focuses only on the results of the surveys, and not on aspects of the programs that were evaluated using other procedures. Table 9.1 also confines its attention to program outcomes that were common across the cities, to facilitate this cross-site analysis. The evaluations all shared common questionnaire measures of four outcomes. *Fear of crime* was measured by questions about worry and concern about personal and property crime in the neighborhood. The impact of the programs on *disorder* was assessed by questions concerning loitering, public drinking, begging, street harassment, truancy, and gang activity. These disorders did not all involve illegal activity, but they are closely linked to fear of crime and neighborhood decline. Between them, the fear and disorder questions assessed the extent to which residents felt they lived in a secure environment. The prevalence of *victimization* was measured by questions about respondents' experiences with burglary, robbery, and assault. These survey measures provide a better estimate of the extent of crime than official statistics, especially when police programs are being evaluated. *Police performance* was measured by questions about how good a job police did at a variety of tasks (preventing crime, helping victims, and keeping order), and how fair, helpful, and polite they were. The *availability of drugs* was measured by questions about the extent of drug trafficking in their neighborhood (questions about drug availability were not included in the Houston and Newark evaluations). In every case, responses to these questions were combined to form multiple-item scales for statistical analysis.

Except in Birmingham, the effects of each program were assessed by comparing changes in these measures in the target areas to comparable shifts in control areas, using multivariate statistical analyses that took into account many other factors. Because the survey respondents were interviewed twice, one important control factor was what they saw or felt before the programs began. Judgments about Birmingham are based on before-after changes in what became the three program areas, after the emergency implementation of a program in the intended control area. In Table 9.1, an "up" entry indicates a statistically significant increase in an outcome that probably was due to the program, and a "down" entry indicates a statistically significant decrease in an outcome that probably was due to the program. An "OK" entry for assessments of policing indicates that the outcome measures were *not* affected by enforcement programs that *could* have actually heightened tensions

TABLE 9.1 Summary of Community Policing Evaluation Findings

	Fear of Crime	Disorder	Victim-ization	Police Service	Drug Availability
Oakland					
enforcement	down	—	—	OK	down
home visits	down	—	down	up	down
enforcement and home visits	down	—	—	OK	down
Birmingham					
enforcement	—	—	—	OK	—
home visits	—	—	down	up	—
substation	down	—	—	up	—
Baltimore					
foot patrol	—	—	—	—	—
ombudsman	down	down	—	up	—
Madison					
substation	—	—	—	up	—
Houston					
home visits	—	down	down	up	n/a
substation	down	down	—	up	n/a
organizing	—	down	—	up	n/a
Newark					
enforcement	—	down	—	OK	n/a
multiple community policing	down	down	—	up	n/a

NOTE: "up" and "down" indicate significant program effects. "OK" indicates that possible negative program effects were avoided. "n/a" indicates there was no outcome measure for that evaluation. No entry indicates there was no significant program effect.

between the police and the community; in this case, the absence of a negative shift in opinion was also a positive outcome.

The overall picture presented by Table 9.1 is mixed. Discounting the five areas for which there were no data on drug availability, Table 9.1 reports the results of 65 before-after changes that could have been affected by community policing or intensive enforcement programs. There were significant positive changes that probably were the effects of the programs in 28 of 65 comparisons, and 4 other instances in which potentially negative effects were avoided. It is apparent that these programs had the most consistent effect on attitudes toward the quality of police service. In the 14 project areas, significant positive changes in views of the police were recorded in 9 instances, and in an additional 4 enforcement areas (one mixed with home visits) there were no negative shifts in opinion; this is a respectable 93% success rate. Fear of crime was down in 7 of 14 areas (50%), and perceptions that neighborhoods were disorderly were down in only 6 of 14 (43%). Drug availability went down only in Oakland (3 of 9 cases), and victimization was down only in 3 of 14 instances (interestingly, these were all home visit programs).

Table 9.1 indicates that enforcement programs did not do quite as well as community policing at meeting their goals; they were successful in only 6 of 14 opportunities (43%), whereas the community policing programs succeeded in 27 of 51 opportunities (53%). Relative to how many of them there were, the combination of home visits and community organizing (which must have looked like very similar programs to most neighborhood residents) was the most successful. This was followed closely by interventions combining intensive enforcement and community policing tactics. Next came neighborhood stations, followed by the combination of foot patrols and ombudsmen officers.

Challenges to Community Policing

Implementation

The first challenge to community policing is amply illustrated by the evaluations described above. Implementation problems plagued even these closely monitored projects. They were defeated by at least three challenges: Some were disbanded in the face of a rise in 911 calls, in order to restore traditional service levels; others were discredited by mid-level managers who resented their loss of authority to lower ranking personnel; and some failed to endure because they did not succeed in changing the organizational culture of the department.

In particular, successful community policing programs must not ignore the "911 problem." Since the volume of telephone calls to big-city departments skyrocketed in the mid-1970s, police commitment to respond to these calls as quickly as possible has absorbed the resources of many departments. In effect, many departments are being managed by the thousands of citizens who call the police, not by their commanders. In the home visit area of Birmingham, pressure to respond quickly to calls for service at a time when the police district was understaffed led to the abandonment of the problem-solving aspects of the program. The district commander responsible for devising the program was punished with an undesirable assignment for letting responses to calls for service slacken because of his commitment to the community policing experiment. At about the same time, Houston's citywide community policing effort was halted following charges that police had allowed responses to calls for service to deteriorate, because (it was charged) officers were being freed from this responsibility in order to carry out the program. The program had powerful enemies among lieutenants and other mid-level supervisors in the department; the Chief of Police was soon fired and little remains of her program.

In other cities, community policing has floundered in the face of the crime-fighting culture of traditional departments. In Oakland there was little enthusiasm for community policing among officers assigned to the program. Although a few hardworking officers carried out the most easily monitored tasks—making home visits and conducting interviews—they did nothing to follow up on the information that they gathered. Their immediate supervisor dismissed the effort as "social work" and did nothing to ensure that the community policing program developed in the Chief's office actually was implemented in the field. One officer conducting home visits actually quit his job because he was so frustrated by the lack of support for his efforts. In Baltimore, officers pulled from routine assignments to replace the foot patrol officers while they were on vacation were unenthusiastic about the assignment. One of the ombudsman police officers preferred giving out traffic tickets to interviewing citizens and attending meetings.

Effectiveness

As the evaluations described above also indicate, proponents of community policing must develop better answers to the question, "Does it work?" As already indicated, the evidence is mixed. The most consistent finding of evaluations to date is that community policing improves popular assessments of police performance. This is certainly an accomplishment, especially in the African American and Hispanic neighborhoods in which many of these projects took place. However, it is vulnerable to the charge that this is merely a triumph of public relations, for rarely is there good evidence that crime has been reduced. As depicted above, the evaluations indicate that assessments of policing improved in 13 of 15 opportunities, but victimization was down significantly in only 3 of 15 cases. I do not know of an evaluation of foot patrol that can point to reduced levels of conventional crime. If more of the projects had demonstrated reductions in crime, critics could also have pointed to the possibility that it was simply displaced to somewhere else rather than actually prevented, for none of these evaluations was designed to address that possibility.

To be fair, victimization is also very difficult to measure accurately. The evaluation surveys described here could not devote sufficient questionnaire space to measure it properly. Surveys are known to undercount certain kinds of crime (such as assault and domestic violence), and are of limited utility for others (drug trafficking, nonresidential vandalism). Neighborhood crime rates are quite sensitive to the level of repeat multiple victimization, something that surveys are not good at measuring under the best of circumstances. In this light, the fact that 6 of 11 community policing (or mixed) programs pointed to significant declines in measures of fear or worry about crime is hopeful evidence that these interventions are having effects on crime as well. (But alternately, it may be that the programs reduced fear by *reassuring* people, for in 5 of those 6 cases assessments of the quality of police service improved significantly as well.)

Equitable Policing

Community policing also threatens to become politicized. The evaluation of community policing in Houston reviewed above found that the way in which several of the programs were run favored the interests of racially dominant groups and established interests in the community. Houston's community station relied on existing community organizations to attract people to the station's programs. The groups chose who would ride along with the police and who would attend meetings with the local police district commander. The groups also helped organize community meetings that brought major figures such as the Chief of Police to speak to area residents. This approach worked well for members of those groups, but less affluent area residents did not hear about the programs and did not participate in them. The community organizing team held a number of small meetings to identify area leaders and begin their organizing efforts; almost all of them were held in the parts of the target area dominated by white residents owning single-family homes. The largely black residents of large rental buildings in the area were quickly identified as the source of problems in the community and became the targets of their activities. All of this was reflected in the findings of the evaluation, for the positive effects of the programs in both areas were confined to whites and home owners. The reasons for this were subtle, but important. Working on their own initiative, the officers in both areas focused their efforts in areas where they were well received. The community organizing team could hold meetings only where they were welcome, and the team working out of the neighborhood substation found that working through established groups made their task of quickly mobilizing community support much easier.

The Houston experience illustrates that policing by consent can be difficult in places where the community is fragmented by race, class, and lifestyle. If, instead of trying to find common interests in this diversity, the police deal mainly with elements of their own choosing, they will appear to be taking sides. It is very easy for them to focus "community policing" on supporting those with whom they get along best and share their outlook. As a result, the "local priorities" that they represent will be those of some in the community, but not all. Critics of community policing are concerned that it can extend the familiarity of police and citizens past the point where their aloofness, professionalism, and commitment to the rule of law can control their behavior. To act fairly and constitutionally and to protect minority rights, the police must sometimes act contrary to the opinion of the majority. As Stephen Mastrofski points out (1988, p. 65), community policing must develop a process by which officers can be given sufficient autonomy to do good without increasing their likelihood of doing evil.

Conclusion

Critics of community policing have been quick to claim that in reality it is just rhetoric. It is certainly true that it *involves* rhetoric, for community policing is an organizational strategy for redefining the goals of policing and providing a new vision of where departments should be heading. This calls for rhetoric, one of the tools of leadership. Community policing also calls for rhetoric because departments do not exist in a vacuum. They are dependent on the communities that they serve for financial support, so they must have public and political support for whatever direction they are going. Rhetoric about community policing informs the community about a set of goals that they are being asked to pay for.

The question is, is it *more* than rhetoric? The evidence reviewed in this chapter suggests that community policing is proceeding at a halting pace. There are ample examples of failed experiments and cities where the concept has gone awry. On the other hand, there is evidence in many evaluations that a public hungry for attention have a great deal to tell police and are grateful for the opportunity to do so. When they see more police walking on foot or working out of a local substation they feel less fearful. Where officers have developed sustained cooperation with community groups and fostered self-help, the public has witnessed declining levels of social disorder and physical decay.

This chapter also has not examined the full range of outcomes that might be attributed to community policing, including—for example—changes in officer attitudes and changes in how victims are treated. Many of these programs featured elements that could at best have had indirect and long-term impacts of community opinion (e.g., supervision changes in Madison's experimental police station), however important they might have been within the departments. Other intended outcomes (e.g., to alter departmental cultures) often prove difficult for evaluators to capture. The extensive combined enforcement and community policing experiment in Newark was conducted in one of the worst parts of the city, and the follow-up evaluation was probably conducted too quickly (after only 11 months) to let its full force be felt. Better evaluations and a more subtle and extensive set of outcome measures could reveal more about the intended benefits of community policing.

References

Bayley, D. (1988). Community policing: A report from the devil's advocate. In J. R. Greene & S. D. Mastrofski (Eds.), *Community policing: Rhetoric or reality?* (pp. 225-237). New York: Praeger.

Goldstein, H. (1990). *Problem-oriented policing.* New York: McGraw-Hill.

Greene, J. R., & Mastrofski, S. D. (Eds.). (1988). *Community policing: Rhetoric or reality?* New York: Praeger.

Greene, J., & Taylor, R. (1988). Community-based policing and foot patrol: Issues of theory and evaluation. In J. R. Greene & S. D. Mastrofski (Eds.), *Community policing: Rhetoric or reality?* (pp. 195-223). New York: Praeger.

Mastrofski, S. D. (1988). Community policing as reform: A cautionary tale. In J. R. Greene & S. D. Mastrofski (Eds.), *Community policing: Rhetoric or reality?* (pp. 47-67). New York: Praeger.

Moore, M. H. (1992). Problem-solving and community policing. In M. Tonry & N. Morris (Eds.), *Crime and justice: A review of research: Vol. 15. Modern policing* (pp. 99-158). Chicago: University of Chicago Press.

Pate, A., & Annan, S. (1989). *The Baltimore community policing experiment: Technical report.* Washington, DC: Police Foundation.

Skogan, W. (1990). *Disorder and decline: Crime and the spiral of decay in American cities.* New York: Free Press.

Skolnick, J., & Bayley, D. (1986). *The new blue line: Police innovation in six American cities.* New York: Free Press.

Uchida, C., Forst, B., & Annan, S. (1990). *Modern policing and the control of illegal drugs: Testing new strategies in two American cities* (Final technical report). Washington, DC: Police Foundation.

Uchida, C., Forst, B., & Annan, S. (1992). *Modern policing and the control of illegal drugs: Testing new strategies in two American cities* (Summary report). Washington, DC: National Institute of Justice; U.S. Department of Justice.

Wycoff, M. (1988). The benefits of community policing: Evidence and conjecture. In J. R. Greene & S. D. Mastrofski (Eds.), *Community policing: Rhetoric or reality?* (pp. 103-120). New York: Praeger.

Wycoff, M., & Skogan, W. (1987). Storefront police offices: The Houston field test. In D. Rosenbaum (Ed.), *Community crime prevention* (pp. 179-201). Newbury Park, CA: Sage.

Wycoff, M., & Skogan, W. (1993). *Quality policing in Madison: An evaluation of its implementation and impact* (Final technical report). Washington, DC: Police Foundation.

10

Foot Patrol Without Community Policing

Law and Order in Public Housing

GARY W. CORDNER

MUCH OF THE CURRENT ENTHUSIASM for community policing clearly derives from foot patrol studies completed in the early 1980s in Flint, Michigan (Trojanowicz, 1982) and Newark, New Jersey (Police Foundation, 1981), although prior developments in police-community relations, team policing, and crime prevention should not be overlooked (Greene, 1989). The discovery that foot patrol had beneficial effects on fear of crime and citizen satisfaction with police was made on the heels of the first wave of police effectiveness research that had suggested that "nothing worked" (Cordner & Trojanowicz, 1992). Interpretations of the foot patrol findings, including the "broken windows" thesis (Wilson & Kelling, 1982), attributed the beneficial effects of foot patrol primarily to closer police-citizen relationships and greater police attention to minor crime and disorder, pushing us toward what many now consider a new era and strategy of policing (Kelling & Moore, 1988).

Foot patrol and community policing are not synonymous, however. Many communities are geographically ill-suited for much foot patrol, yet they may implement community policing through other means, such as permanent geographic assignment of officers, increased use of mini-stations, greater citizen involvement in crime prevention, civilianization, and so forth (Skolnick & Bayley, 1986). Conversely, foot patrol may be employed as a patrol tactic without any particular emphasis on community-oriented policing. Foot patrol might be employed strictly for public relations purposes, for example, or merely to increase police visibility, or as part of an enforcement-oriented crackdown.

This chapter examines the effects of one such foot patrol program that was not particularly community oriented. The program was implemented within a public housing site in Lexington, Kentucky, in January 1991 and was continuing as of July 1993. Before describing the setting and presenting the results, though, a brief review of previous foot patrol research is presented.

Foot Patrol Studies

Evidence on the effects of foot patrol is, not surprisingly, mixed. Citizens do seem more likely to notice the presence or absence of foot patrol (Pate, 1989; Police Foundation, 1981) than corresponding fluctuations in motorized patrol (Kelling, Pate, Dieckman, & Brown, 1974). Whether this necessarily leads to higher citizen satisfaction with police is less clear. The initial Flint and Newark studies found improvements in citizen satisfaction, but two later foot patrol studies failed to replicate this finding (Esbensen, 1987; Pate, 1989). In some instances, very high baseline satisfaction with police service may make it difficult to achieve significant improvements with any strategy or program, including foot patrol.

The prevailing wisdom that foot patrol reduces citizens' fear of crime gets somewhat more consistent support. The Flint and Newark studies found such an effect. In Baltimore City, pre-post changes in six foot patrol beats were not statistically significant, but were generally in expected directions. Residents expressed reduced likelihood of crime victimization and increased perceptions of area safety. However, they also indicated becoming more worried about crime (Pate, 1989).

The view that foot patrol results in decreased disorder and minor crime gets mixed support. This effect was found, or at least postulated, in Newark. A study in Asheville, North Carolina, found that foot patrol was associated with a reduction in such public order offenses as vagrancy, disorderly conduct, and vandalism (Esbensen, 1987). In Baltimore City, disturbance calls and reported Part II crimes were reduced (though not by statistically significant amounts), while residents' perceptions were that disorder problems had *in*creased (Pate, 1989). A massive utilization of foot patrol in Boston did not produce any consistent order maintenance effects, however (Bowers & Hirsch, 1987).

The effect of foot patrol on the level of citizen calls for police service has been tested infrequently with inconsistent results. The Flint study reported decreased calls for service, while no effects were found in Boston (Bowers & Hirsch, 1987), Baltimore City (Pate, 1989), or New York (McElroy, Cosgrove, & Sadd, 1993). The Boston study also examined the possibility that utilization of foot patrol might encourage citizens to place calls for police service more often; no support for this stimulation effect was found.

Similarly inconsistent is the evidence concerning the effect of foot patrol on reported crime. Several studies in the 1950s and 1960s in England and New York found crime reductions associated with either the introduction or increased levels of foot patrol (Wilson, 1975, pp. 81-97). The Flint study claimed such an effect, and in the Baltimore City study recorded Part I and Part II crimes decreased, although not by statistically significant amounts (Pate, 1989). No effects on reported crime were found in Asheville (Esbensen, 1987), Boston (Bowers & Hirsch, 1987), or New York (McElroy et al., 1993), however.

Foot patrol has yet to be found to have statistically significant effects on actual crime victimization, but, oddly enough, the available evidence suggests such an effect. The Newark study found that pre-post changes in foot patrol beats were consistently more favorable than changes in control beats. In Baltimore City, victimization decreased in six crime categories and increased in just two. Also in Baltimore City, so-called vicarious victimization (awareness of crimes occurring in the area) decreased in seven crime categories and increased in just one. Five of the seven decreases in vicarious victimization were statistically significant (Pate, 1989).

Overall, the most defensible claims at this point are that citizens notice foot patrol and that it generally makes them feel safer. The possibility that foot patrol reduces crime victimization is intriguing but still lacks solid support. The effects of foot patrol on citizen satisfaction, disorder, calls for service, and reported crime have been inconsistent and consequently may depend on community characteristics and on variations in foot patrol as implemented by different officers and different police departments.

Setting

Lexington, Kentucky, is a merged city and county formally known as the Lexington/Fayette Urban County Government. It has a population of approximately 225,000 and a police department of about 400 sworn officers. Prior to 1991 the police department was not utilizing foot patrol except on special and limited occasions.

The Bluegrass-Aspendale public housing site in Lexington had 963 townhouse-style units until a downsizing and physical rehabilitation program was begun in 1988. Due to the razing of several buildings and renovation of others, the number of occupied units dropped to a low of 484 in July 1992 and climbed back to 609 as of December 1992. The vast majority of the residents are African American and about one quarter of the units are leased to elderly individuals or families.

As of early 1990 the Bluegrass-Aspendale site had become Lexington's primary "open-air" drug market. Runners, lookouts, and dealers occupied the sidewalks while customers' cars were driven slowly along the site's through streets. Elderly residents were reportedly wary of walking to stores or to the housing office, and parents restricted their young children from playing in common areas. By their own admission, the police largely ignored the area unless called to handle a specific complaint. The police knew the area as one characterized by high crime, drug sales, and heavy call-for-service workload. With the appointment of a new police chief in February 1990 the police department began to devote more attention to the Bluegrass-Aspendale area. A special 12-officer task force was assigned exclusively to the area from May through December 1990 and carried out a prolonged crackdown with high visibility. After December 1990 this special unit continued to assign some of its resources to the area. From January through December 1991 federal funds were used to deploy overtime foot patrols to the area. Typically, two-officer foot patrols were on duty from 2:00 p.m. through 2:00 a.m. each day. Since January 1992 the overtime foot patrols have been continued at a reduced level.

Because these foot patrols in Bluegrass-Aspendale were staffed by officers working on an overtime basis, little staffing continuity was achieved. More than 150 different officers had worked the foot patrol assignments as of October 1992. Some effort was made to limit the assignments to a smaller and more committed contingent as time went on, but it was still rare for any officer to work the overtime foot patrol in Bluegrass-Aspendale more often than once a week. Because no officer or supervisor in the police department had specific geographic responsibility for the Bluegrass-Aspendale area (or any other geographic area), efforts to coordinate the activities of the overtime foot patrol officers, to achieve a strong sense of identification with the area, and to create sustained problem solving efforts were largely unsuccessful.

In their defense, police department and housing authority officials did not envision a community policing or problem-solving role for the overtime foot patrol officers. To the extent that such efforts were expected, they were seen as the province of the special task force. The overtime foot patrols were primarily intended to establish a dependable and credible police presence in the area. It was hoped that they would be visible, that they would take enforcement action when appropriate, and that they would "maintain" the peaceful conditions established by the task force's earlier crackdown. Thus, the foot patrols were never intended as community policing (in fact, housing authority officials equated community policing with a soft, nonenforcement approach that they specifically did not favor).

Methods

The primary analysis presented in this chapter relies on police call-for-service data for the 4-year period 1989-1992. This data is gathered through the police department's computer-aided dispatching system. Analyses focus on three specific categories of calls (disorderly conduct, domestic violence, vandalism) and on total Priority 1-5 calls, which includes all calls requiring police action except those that are officer-initiated. Officer-initiated calls were deleted because they include both police business (such as traffic stops and field interviews), administrative duties (such as report writing), and personal business (such as meal breaks).

Call-for-service data for Bluegrass-Aspendale and for the entire jurisdiction are compared for each of the years from 1989 to 1992. The comparisons are made on the basis of calls for service per 100 occupied residences, in order to "normalize" the data. This was particularly necessary because of the widely fluctuating number of occupied units in Bluegrass-Aspendale during the study period. The estimated number of residences for the jurisdiction as a whole was obtained from the two utility companies servicing Lexington/Fayette County.

Multivariate time series analysis is also conducted for the 48-month study period. This analysis uses monthly Priority 1-5 calls for service in Bluegrass-Aspendale as the dependent variable and employs six independent variables: the number of occupied housing units; a variable representing the level of task force presence in the area; a variable representing the level of overtime foot patrol in the area; and three dummy seasonal variables.

Other data sources used peripherally for this chapter include firsthand observations of the area; walk-along observations of the foot patrols; interviews with police and housing authority officials; community surveys conducted in January 1991 and January 1992; and an officer survey conducted in October 1992.

Findings

Observations and interviews clearly indicate that Bluegrass-Aspendale is no longer an obvious open-air drug market and that the streets, sidewalks, and common areas are now routinely used by residents, including young children and the elderly. In the words of one housing official, "The site looks like a normal neighborhood." Police and housing officials attribute the change primarily to the task force crackdown in 1990 and the subsequent deployment of overtime foot patrols since January 1991. Another possible factor is the physical renovation of the site, which included street rerouting, improved off-street parking, and enhanced common areas. Also, population density in the site is more than one third lower than it was in 1988.

These readily apparent improvements in the level of drug dealing and street disorder in Bluegrass-Aspendale have not been matched by reductions in police calls for service or in numbers of drug arrests. Drug arrests in Bluegrass-Aspendale decreased by almost 50% from 1989 to 1990, but by 1992 had increased beyond the 1989 level. As shown in Table 10.1, call-for-service levels in Bluegrass-Aspendale in 1992 were equal to or higher than those in any of the preceding 3 years. Only with respect to domestic violence is the change from 1989 to 1992 better in the site than for the jurisdiction as a whole. If 1990, the

TABLE 10.1   Calls for Police Service Per 100 Residences, Bluegrass-Aspendale and Lexington/Fayette County, 1989-1992

	1989	*1990*	*1991*	*1992*	*Percentage Change 1989-1992*
Disorderly Conduct					
Bluegrass-Aspendale	67.3	81.2	76.0	81.3	+ 20.8
Lexington/Fayette	16.3	19.0	19.4	18.1	+ 11.1
Domestic Violence					
Bluegrass-Aspendale	17.6	10.2	11.3	18.1	+ 2.8
Lexington/Fayette	3.0	3.0	2.7	3.3	+ 10.9
Vandalism					
Bluegrass-Aspendale	16.5	26.6	20.6	29.1	+ 76.4
Lexington/Fayette	6.4	7.5	7.5	7.2	+ 12.2
Priority 1-5 Calls					
Bluegrass-Aspendale	263.3	282.6	248.7	282.0	+ 7.1
Lexington/Fayette	131.8	141.2	139.6	136.2	+ 3.3

year that the crackdown began, is used as the baseline, then changes in disorderly conduct, vandalism, and total Priority 1-5 calls have been negligible. Using that year as the baseline yields a 77% increase in domestic violence in 1992, however.

The trends in disorderly conduct, vandalism, and Priority 1-5 calls in Blue-grass-Aspendale have been similar over the 4-year period—up in 1990, down in 1991, back up in 1992. This pattern suggests that initial police efforts may have reaped some reward in 1991 but that these effects began to wear off in 1992. No obvious explanation has been found for the dramatic decrease in domestic violence calls in 1990 and the equally dramatic increase in 1992.

Comparison of the rates of calls for service in Bluegrass-Aspendale and in the jurisdiction as a whole indicates a continuing high demand for police service in the public housing site. In 1992 the overall level of calls for police service in Bluegrass-Aspendale was about twice as high as the jurisdiction norm. Vandalism calls were four times the norm, disorderly conduct calls 4.5 times the norm, and domestic violence calls 5.5 times higher than the county-wide average.

Community surveying done in January 1991 and January 1992 provides some corroboration for the reduced levels of calls for service in 1991. Residents reported reduced crime victimization, heightened awareness of police presence, increased contacts with the police (both positive and negative), and improved satisfaction with police service. However, fear of crime increased marginally and resident assessments of neighborhood conditions were largely unchanged. Unfortunately, the results of the 1993 community survey, which pertain to experiences and changes in 1992, are not yet available.

Multivariate time series analysis was used in an attempt to further sort out the relative impacts on calls for police service of (1) the task force crackdown, (2)

TABLE 10.2   Multivariate Analysis of Monthly Priority 1-5 Calls for Police Service in Bluegrass-Aspendale, 1989-1992 (48 months)

Independent Variables	Beta Weights With Constant	Beta Weights Without Constant
Occupied Units	.51*	.75*
Special Task Force	−.15	−.02
Overtime Foot Patrol	−.29*	−.14
Winter	−.20*	−.18
Spring	.15	.19
Summer	.41*	.45*
R Squared	.77	.73
F Statistic	22.27	28.40
Probability	.00	.00

NOTE: * Statistically significant at the .05 level or better.

the overtime foot patrols, and (3) the downsizing of the Bluegrass-Aspendale housing site. Results are presented in Table 10.2 for two such analyses, differing only in the use of a constant. An argument in favor of employing a constant term would be that any area generates some level of calls; thus this term estimates the constant demand for police service regardless of the number of occupied units and the presence or absence of special police efforts. An argument for omitting the constant term would be that if nobody lived in the area and no police units patrolled the area the level of calls would probably be minuscule and, at any rate, would be determined by other factors not presently operating or in the regression equation. In lieu of choosing between these two arguments, both analyses are presented.

The results of the two analyses are fairly consistent. In each case, the independent variable most strongly related to monthly calls for service is the number of occupied housing units. As one might expect, the more occupied units, and thus the more people living in the housing site, the more calls for police service. The independent variable with the next largest coefficient in both analyses is the dummy variable for summer. The coefficients are positive, indicating that summer months (June, July, and August) had more calls for service. The beta weights for the occupied units and summer variables were the only ones that were statistically significant in both analyses.

The variables for overtime foot patrol and winter had negative coefficients in both equations that were statistically significant only when the constant term was employed. The coefficients for both of these variables lost strength to the occupied units variable when the constant term was omitted. In either case, though, the negative coefficients indicate that winter months had fewer calls and that deployment of the overtime foot patrols was associated with reduced calls for police service. The special task force variable also had negative coefficients in both analyses, but its relationships with monthly calls for service were considerably weaker and not statistically significant.

The two regression equations had overall r squares of .77 and .73, indicating that the combined relationships of the independent variables with monthly calls for service in Bluegrass-Aspendale were quite strong. Both relationships were statistically significant.

Discussion

The analysis of calls for police service in the Bluegrass-Aspendale public housing site indicates no overall reduction in levels of such calls despite a sustained crackdown in 1990 and extensive overtime foot patrols since January 1991. The multivariate analysis suggests a possible modest impact for the overtime foot patrols, but the strongest determinants of monthly calls for service are seasonal fluctuations and the number of occupied housing units.

It is likely that the year 1991 is the source of the moderate coefficient for overtime foot patrol found in the multivariate analysis. During that year the foot patrols were concentrated exclusively in Bluegrass-Aspendale and calls for service went down by 12%. In 1992 the level of foot patrol at the site was reduced and calls for service went back up to 1990 levels.

During 1991, while so much police attention was focused on Bluegrass-Aspendale, calls for police service increased in Charlotte Court and Pimlico Park, Lexington's two other largest public housing sites, by 8.1%. When foot patrols were reduced in Bluegrass-Aspendale in 1992 they were added to these two other sites. Calls for service (per 100 residences) then went down in these two areas by 14.3% in 1992 while they went up in Bluegrass-Aspendale by 13.4%.

What all this suggests is a short-term impact for the overtime foot patrols but perhaps not much long-term impact, at least not on levels of calls for police service. In this regard the effects of the overtime foot patrols in Lexington may be more analogous to those of crackdowns (Sherman, 1990) than to those of more full-fledged community policing programs. It will be important to examine call-for-service levels in Charlotte Court and Pimlico Park for 1993 to see whether the reductions achieved in 1992 were maintained or lost.

Observations and interviews confirm the closer correspondence of the overtime foot patrols with crackdowns than with community policing. Police and housing officials primarily want visibility and enforcement from the overtime foot patrols, and that is mostly what they get. The officers carrying out the foot patrol assignments vary substantially in their individual styles and knowledge of the community, but they generally lack any strong sense of identity with or specific responsibility for Bluegrass-Aspendale. Surveys indicate that Lexington officers agree that the foot patrols prevent crime, reduce fear of crime, and improve police-community relations, and that officers who have worked the foot patrols agree more strongly than those who have not. But their performance seems to be guided more by professional and legal norms than by any strong commitment to community norms or substantive problem solving. Also, the department has not developed a system to create any extensive information sharing or continuity of effort among the many different officers who work the overtime foot patrol assignments.

Conclusion

The overtime foot patrols in the Bluegrass-Aspendale public housing site in Lexington, Kentucky, have succeeded in maintaining public order improvements initially achieved by a concerted crackdown, and they have led to some modest improvements in police-community relations in the area. Their effects on calls for police service, the primary focus of this chapter, have apparently been short-lived, however. In their implementation these overtime foot patrols have more resembled traditional policing and crackdowns than community policing or problem-oriented policing. This illustrates the important point that foot patrol does not necessarily equate to community policing.

References

Bowers, W. J., & Hirsch, J. H. (1987). The impact of foot patrol staffing on crime and disorder in Boston: An unmet promise. *American Journal of Police, 6*(1), 17-44.

Cordner, G. W., & Trojanowicz, R. C. (1992). Patrol. In G. W. Cordner & D. C. Hale (Eds.), *What works in policing: Operations and administration examined* (pp. 3-18). Cincinnati: Anderson.

Esbensen, F. (1987). Foot patrols: Of what value? *American Journal of Police, 6*(1), 45-65.

Greene, J. R. (1989). Police and community relations: Where have we been and where are we going? In R. G. Dunham & G. P. Alpert (Eds.), *Critical issues in policing: Contemporary readings* (pp. 349-368). Prospect Heights, IL: Waveland.

Kelling, G. L., & Moore, M. H. (1988). *The evolving strategy of policing* (Perspectives on Policing, No. 4). Washington, DC: National Institute of Justice.

Kelling, G. L., Pate, T., Dieckman, D., & Brown, C. E. (1974). *The Kansas City preventive patrol experiment: A summary report.* Washington, DC: Police Foundation.

McElroy, J. E., Cosgrove, C. A., & Sadd, S. (1993). *Community policing: The CPOP in New York.* Newbury Park, CA: Sage.

Pate, A. M. (1989). Community-oriented policing in Baltimore. In D. J. Kenney (Ed.), *Police and policing: Contemporary issues* (pp. 112-135). New York: Praeger.

Police Foundation. (1981). *The Newark foot patrol experiment.* Washington, DC: Author.

Sherman, L. W. (1990). Police crackdowns: Initial and residual deterrence. In M. Tonry & N. Morris (Eds.), *Crime and justice: A biannual review of research* (Vol. 12, pp. 1-48). Chicago: University of Chicago Press.

Skolnick, J. H., & Bayley, D. (1986). *The new blue line: Police innovations in six American cities.* New York: Free Press.

Trojanowicz, R. C. (1982). *An evaluation of the Neighborhood Foot Patrol Program in Flint, Michigan.* East Lansing: Michigan State University.

Wilson, J. Q. (1975). *Thinking about crime.* New York: Basic Books.

Wilson, J. Q., & Kelling, G. L. (1982, March). Broken windows: The police and neighborhood safety. *The Atlantic Monthly,* pp. 29-38.

11

The Hartford COMPASS Program

Experiences With a Weed and Seed-Related Program

JAMES M. TIEN

THOMAS F. RICH

IN 1990, the City of Hartford launched the Cartographic Oriented Management Program for the Abatement of Street Sales (COMPASS) program. COMPASS represented a new approach by the city in its attempts to improve the quality of life, especially in those areas in the city hard hit by crime and drugs. A basic premise of the program is that street-level drug sales are a key factor in the declining quality of life in urban neighborhoods and that the best approach to reversing this decay is through the combined efforts of the police, other city agencies, and the community. More specifically, COMPASS employed a reclamation and stabilization approach, which is synonymous with the "weed" and "seed" model for improving neighborhoods. That is, the police—with the community's input and help—reclaim a target area, first by performing a drug market analysis (which could include the use of a computer-based mapping tool that

AUTHORS' NOTE: COMPASS was partially funded by Grant No. 90-IJ-CX-0010 and 91-DD-CX-K054, provided by the National Institute of Justice (NIJ), U.S. Department of Justice. Points of view or opinions stated in this document are those of the authors and do not necessarily represent the official position or policies of the U.S. Department of Justice. The authors would like to acknowledge contributions of the Hartford Police Department (HPD), particularly Lieutenant James P. Donnelly.

192

was developed as part of the COMPASS project) and then by employing a variety of community policing and other antidrug tactics to weed out the underlying drug problem in the target area. Once an area is weeded, the stabilization phase attempts to seed the target area with businesses and activities that can replace the weeded out drug businesses and activities—this phase requires a strong partnership between the community, the city, and the police.

Actually, the ideas of weeding and seeding were not new to Hartford. In the mid-1970s Hartford was one of the first cities to implement an NIJ-funded Crime Prevention Through Environmental Design (CPTED) project. (In fact, this project was implemented in the Asylum Hill neighborhood, one of the four COMPASS target areas.) As advanced by Tien and Reppetto (1975), CPTED focuses on the interaction between human behavior and the (physically) built environment. It is hypothesized that the proper design and effective use of the built environment can lead to a reduction in crime and fear and, concomitantly, to an improvement in the quality of urban life. Operationally, CPTED is based on the neighborhood-oriented weeding and seeding approach, that is, reclaiming the neighborhood from crime and violence and then stabilizing it against a return to crime and violence.

Approach

In carrying out the weeding phase of COMPASS, the Hartford Police Department (HPD) engaged in several activities. To begin, target areas were selected. Although the criteria by which target areas were selected evolved over the program period, in the beginning there were three basic criteria used in selecting the COMPASS target areas. First, the area had to have a serious drug problem, one that involved open-air drug sales. Second, the area had to have a Community Service Officer (CSO) assigned to the area, inasmuch as the seeding efforts would revolve around this officer. And third, the area had to have a viable community organization that could also be active in both the weeding and seeding efforts. Once the area was selected, weeding activities began with an undercover operation, wherein undercover officers attempted to obtain arrest warrants on persons involved in the area's drug trade. Execution of these warrants coincided with a press conference announcing the presence of the COMPASS program in the target area. At this point, the visible phase of the weeding effort began with the deployment of the HPD's Crime Suppression Unit (CSU). The CSU performed a variety of tactics in the target areas, including high visibility tactics such as roving patrol, foot patrol, and vehicle safety checks, and undercover tactics such as reverse sting operations and buy-busts. It should be noted that the CSU officers were not dispatched to routine calls for service; thus, they were able to devote all their time to the weeding efforts. The intent was to have the CSU remain in an area for several months before migrating to another target area.

The COMPASS seeding activities were to involve a variety of groups in the target area, including target area residents, community groups, institutions, businesses, the HPD, other city agencies, and especially the CSO. In general, it was hoped that the CSO would assist target area residents, businesses, institutions, and organizations in their seeding activities and facilitate communication between the police department and city agencies on the one hand and the target area residents, businesses, institutions, and organizations on the other hand.

Also critical to area seeding efforts are the non-police city agencies, which could provide needed services to the COMPASS target areas. By the end of 1989, the City of Hartford became actively involved in the COMPASS program. The city government saw COMPASS as an opportunity to try a new approach to improving the quality of life in Hartford's neighborhoods. By January 1990, 3 months before weeding efforts began in the first two target areas, the city had formed a Reclamation Steering Committee to oversee and coordinate the program. At that time, the Hartford City Manager was vocal in his support of the program.

A complete discussion and analysis of the COMPASS program can be found in the report by Tien, Rich, Shell, Larson, and Donnelly (1993). This chapter is based on that report; it should not be considered a summary of the report, as it only focuses on the weed and seed aspects of the report.

COMPASS Implementation

From 1990 to 1992, COMPASS was implemented in four target areas—Charter Oak Terrace, Milner, Frog Hollow, and Asylum Hill.

Charter Oak Terrace is contained in a small area (0.11 square miles) of Hartford, consisting almost exclusively of public housing buildings. Its residents are among the poorest in Hartford. The area is geographically isolated, bounded by an industrial section of the town of West Hartford, a river, a railroad, and Interstate 84. This relative isolation, combined with the fact that everyone lives in the same housing project, created the sense of a well-defined community.

The Milner target area is contained in a 16-block area carved out of a large street grid in the north central part of Hartford. A major east-west highway bisects Milner. The area is centered around the Milner elementary school, but the school does not give the area an identity; for example, if one were to ask individuals living in the Milner target area in what section of Hartford they lived, one would get a variety of answers. Residential housing in the area includes a mix of multifamily apartment buildings and houses.

Frog Hollow, an area in the city's south end, is the largest of the four target areas with 11.2% of the city's population. Geographically, Frog Hollow is six times larger than Charter Oak Terrace and three times larger than Milner. Frog Hollow contained what many in the HPD believed were some of the city's largest drug markets, particularly those surrounding Park Street, a narrow, heavily congested commercial street with a carnival-like atmosphere.

Asylum Hill, which is physically the same size as Frog Hollow but has one-third fewer residents, is one of Hartford's most diverse neighborhoods. Several important cultural institutions and some of the largest insurance companies in the country are in the Asylum Hill area. Compared to the other COMPASS target areas, the neighborhood has a more middle-class quality to it.

As proposed by Tien (1979, 1990), four sets of evaluation measures—input, process, outcome, and systemic—were used in assessing the impact of COMPASS in these target areas. The collected evaluation data included police records (i.e., drug arrests, calls for service, and crime data), survey data (i.e., CSU surveys and community attitudinal surveys), and qualitative data obtained through interviews with program participants and on-site monitoring. Tables 11.1, 11.2, and 11.3 summarize key police records and community survey results. In reviewing these exhibits and the findings discussed below, it should be remembered that each target area is different, particularly in terms of geographic, demographic, and drug market characteristics. In addition, the length of time that COMPASS was active in each of these areas, the intensity of the police presence, the mix of tactics used, the time of year during which the weeding occurred, and a number of other factors make it difficult to evaluate precisely the impact of COMPASS as a whole.

It should be noted that the "during" periods in Table 11.1 correspond to those periods in which the CSU was deployed in the respective areas; that is, April 1990 to March 1991 for Charter Oak Terrace and Milner, April 1991 to December 1991 for Frog Hollow, and January 1992 to May 1992 for Asylum Hill. In June 1992, after the formal evaluation period ended, the CSU returned to Frog Hollow.

Charter Oak Terrace and Milner

In February 1990, the weeding's undercover phase began in both Charter Oak Terrace and Milner areas. On April 19, 55 arrest warrants for persons selling drugs in the two target areas were executed. This sweep coincided with a symposium on drug enforcement efforts held in Hartford and attended by several leading officials from the city, the state, and the NIJ. Extensive, and very positive, publicity regarding COMPASS appeared on local television, radio, and print media. On April 22, the visible phase of weeding began, as the Crime Suppression Unit (CSU) was deployed in both target areas. With overtime funding from the State of Connecticut, the CSU was initially able to establish a 6-day-a-week, 16-hour-a-day (8 a.m. to midnight) presence. Visibility decreased as of July 1990, when 5 of the 21 CSU officers were reassigned.

While the CSU was performing weeding tactics in Charter Oak Terrace, a number of other seeding-related activities were being carried out in that area.

TABLE 11.1 Average Monthly Police Statistics by Target Area and Period

| | Charter Oak Terrace | | | Milner | | | Frog Hollow | | | Asylum Hill | | |
| | Number Per Month[a] | | | | | | | | | | | |
	Before	During	After	Before	During	After	Before	During	After	Before	During	After
Calls for Service												
Gun	5.8	2.3	3.6	15.9	10.0	8.2	17.0	12.7	12.4	15.7	8.2	(c)
Loitering	0.2	0.5	0.8	9.5	14.1	24.6	11.6	23.3	27.0	10.4	15.0	(c)
Reported Crimes												
Drive-By												
Shootings	(b)	0.2	0.6	(b)	0.8	1.1	3.0	1.1	1.0	2.1	0.8	(c)
Burglaries	4.1	4.1	6.0	15.9	9.7	10.5	59.2	28.3	78.6	43.8	31.6	(c)
All Part I												
Crimes	19.1	18.1	36.4	57.6	45.3	58.1	196.9	94.3	336.2	178.2	158.4	(c)
Arrests												
Drug Offenses	19.4	5.6	1.6	29.5	18.8	15.9	72.1	71.1	43.6	20.8	33.6	(c)

NOTES: a. Before, during, after periods as follows:
Charter Oak Terrace: before—1/89-3/90; during—4/90-3/91; after—4/91-5/92
Milner: before—1/89-3/90; during—4/90-3/91; after—4/91-5/92
Frog Hollow: before—1/89-3/91; during—4/91-12/91; after—1/91-5/92
Asylum Hill: before—1/89-12/91; during—1/92-5/92; after—after project period, data not collected
b. Prior to COMPASS, the PD did not have an incident code for drive-by shootings.
c. The after period in Asylum Hill occurred after the end of the formal evaluation period.

TABLE 11.2 Comparison of Community Survey Results in Charter Oak Terrace and Milner (in percentages)

(1) Do you think there is less violent crime in your neighborhood than there was three months ago?[a]

	Charter Oak Terrace (N = 184)	Milner (N = 195)
Yes, there is less violent crime	83.7	38.5
There has not been any change in violent crime	15.8	46.2
There is more violent crime now	0.5	15.4
Total	100.0	100.0

(2) Do you think there are fewer people selling drugs in your neighborhood than there were three months ago?[a]

	Charter Oak Terrace (N = 183)	Milner (N = 197)
There are fewer people selling drugs	84.7	31.5
There has not been any change	13.7	44.2
There are more people selling drugs	1.6	24.4
Total	100.0	100.0

NOTE: a. Survey conducted in October 1990

TABLE 11.3 Comparison of Community Survey Results in Frog Hollow and Asylum Hill (in percentages)

(1) How concerned are you about crime in your neighborhood?

| | Frog Hollow | | Asylum Hill | |
	Before[a] *(N = 265)*	*After*[b] *(N = 262)*	*Before*[c] *(N = 238)*	*After*[d] *(N = 215)*
Very concerned	81.1	47.3	81.1	75.3
Somewhat concerned	18.1	24.4	14.7	14.0
Not concerned at all	0.8	28.2	2.5	8.4
Don't know	0.0	0.0	1.7	2.3
Total	100.0	100.0	100.0	100.0

(2) Do you think the drug problem is improving, staying about the same, or getting worse in your neighborhood?

| | Frog Hollow | | Asylum Hill | |
	Before[a] *(N = 249)*	*After*[b] *(N = 257)*	*Before*[c] *(N = 235)*	*After*[d] *(N = 215)*
Improving	17.7	21.4	9.8	21.4
Staying about the same	48.2	32.2	23.4	34.0
Getting worse	34.1	46.3	40.9	33.5
Don't know	0.0	0.0	26.0	11.2
Total	100.0	100.0	100.0	100.0

NOTES: a. Survey conducted in March 1991.
b. Survey conducted in June 1992.
c. Survey conducted in December 1991.
d. Survey conducted in June 1992.

Eighty Charter Oak Terrace residents participated in an area-wide clean up in May 1990. The Connecticut Probation Department set up an office in Charter Oak Terrace for their probation officers to meet with area residents sentenced to probation. A reduced caseload for the probation officers meant that they could meet weekly, rather than monthly, with their clients. The local YMCA was also rehabilitated. The CSO assigned to Charter Oak Terrace spearheaded an effort to rid the area of stray dogs and abandoned cars, which had been serious problems in the area. Later, the *Hartford Courant* ("Revolution at Charter Oak Terrace," 1990, p. C-14) would highlight the importance of the Charter Oak Terrace CSO, whom they noted "has arranged for the removal of abandoned cars and rat-infested dumpsters. He has mediated family feuds, dealt with troublesome youths and helped organize a youth basketball team [and he has] visited almost every one of the project's 900 households. The personal touch has paid off more than once."

Soon CSU officers began hearing from arrested drug sellers that dealers were leaving Charter Oak Terrace "because they can't make any more money." The number of drug arrests the CSU made in the area dropped dramatically after the first month of the weeding efforts (see Table 11.1). In fact, all parties involved in the COMPASS program were surprised at how quickly drug activity decreased in Charter Oak Terrace. The small geographic area, the well-defined geographic boundaries, the isolation of the area, and the fact that there are few legitimate reasons to be in the area made this neighborhood ideal for high visibility police tactics such as vehicle safety checks and intensive patrol. The CSU Commander felt that vehicle safety checks were by far the most effective tactic. As one CSU officer put it, "this area was made for a crackdown."[1] These early weeding successes in Charter Oak Terrace led to very positive feedback from target area residents. The CSU received many letters from residents, which in turn created high morale among the officers. The community survey results shown in Table 11.2 also reflect a high degree of satisfaction with the COMPASS efforts in Charter Oak Terrace.

At the same time, an important systemic problem appeared, a problem perhaps best symbolized by the CSO's efforts to improve Charter Oak Terrace's playground. At the start of COMPASS, this playground had one slippery slide and a basketball court with no nets on the hoops. There were no swings and the court was covered with broken glass. Given the large number of children in Charter Oak Terrace, fixing up this playground became a priority for the CSO, and he formed a committee of target area adults and youths to develop ideas on how to improve the playground. Yet the CSO ran into delay after delay in working with the responsible city agencies. No doubt the CSO was viewed as "just another police officer," rather than the key point person in a priority weed and seed program. The CSO's having promised a new playground to the residents, the delays damaged the CSO's credibility and fostered renewed cynicism among residents that the city could not deliver on their promises. Two years later, the playground is still in its dilapidated state.

Nevertheless, the events in Charter Oak Terrace were deemed a "revolution." In an unsolicited August 1990 editorial, the *Hartford Courant* ("Revolution at Charter Oak Terrace," 1990) noted:

> On one sweltering summer day recently, Charter Oak Terrace in Hartford was at peace. No corner drug dealing. No gang warfare. In fact, some youths were painting rusted dumpsters sky blue and earning money for it. Only one car was abandoned there overnight. Police received but two serious calls: one involving a family feud and another about a child who was left alone for too long.
>
> Compared with the federal housing project's notorious past, it was a slow day. (p. C-14)

Nearly 2 years after this editorial, long after the CSU migrated from the area, Charter Oak Terrace is still seen as a success. According to police officials and residents, although the neighborhood has slipped some since the CSU migrated from the area, the vast majority of drug dealing in the area occurs indoors and there is still little or no open-air drug dealing.

By contrast, drug activity remained high in Milner despite the presence of the CSU. Some locations, particularly vacant lots at intersections along the area's main thruway, seemed immune to enforcement efforts. As one CSU officer put it, "It doesn't matter what we do, there's always somebody selling at certain locations." At the same time, CSU officers complained of some hostility from a few of Milner's residents, in marked contrast to the basically warm reception the CSU received in Charter Oak Terrace. Some residents complained that "they [the CSU] didn't understand the area or the people or their problems [and that] they were just going through the motions to get their paycheck." This is not to say that residents of Charter Oak Terrace liked the police and residents of Milner did not. Indeed, many officers in the CSU felt that there was more support for the police from Milner area residents than Charter Oak Terrace residents before the COMPASS program began. Better support for the police in Charter Oak Terrace was no doubt largely due to the initial success in reducing drug activity. Milner residents did not see significant early successes. This fact, coupled with the residents' high expectations for the program (brought about by the program's extensive publicity), may explain a lack of support for the police in Milner. Again, the community survey results shown in Table 11.2 reflect the lower level of success in Milner, particularly as compared to Charter Oak Terrace.

The Milner area also lacked a dominant community-based organization that could help lead the seeding efforts. It had been hoped that these efforts would evolve around the Milner elementary school; however, the school was looking for a new principal and its Parent Teachers Association had few active members. Even if the community groups in Milner had been organized, the larger question is whether the community as a whole could become involved in the weed and seed efforts. One incident that occurred early in the weeding phase illustrated the scope of problems in Milner and how difficult community organizing would be in this area. One afternoon the CSU commander and a half dozen CSU officers were in the hallway of a six-unit apartment building in Milner setting up for a reverse sting operation. Not wanting to frighten the residents, the CSU commander knocked on the doors of the apartments and told the residents what they were doing. One of the residents, an elderly woman, was obviously alarmed at the sight of all the police officers and quickly shut the door after speaking to the CSU commander. A few seconds later she opened the door again and, wanting to take advantage of the situation, asked, "While you are here, do you mind if I come out and sweep the hallway?"

Meanwhile, the city and its Reclamation Steering Committee acknowledged that the service delivery piece of the seeding effort "was still getting organized"—through establishing lines of communication and defining and prioritizing needs. In addition, other elements of the Steering Committee's program were stalled. State and city budget crises prevented funding of major seeding initiatives, such as a residential drug treatment center for Milner. Delays, organization problems, and lack of understanding of roles in the seeding process led the city to acknowledge in June 1990 that the community would not be ready to take over the seeding efforts once the CSU migrated to a new target area and that the seeding timetable had become completely divorced from the weeding timetable. To make matters worse, the key accomplishment of the seeding efforts—having the City Manager make the COMPASS program a top priority—dissolved, because in June 1990 the City Manager resigned amid allegations of corruption. A new City Manager was appointed in September 1990 and, perhaps not wanting to be associated with a program championed by the ex-City Manager, largely ignored the COMPASS program until February 1991, when he appointed an assistant to oversee the city's role in the program. Thus, by mid-1990, COMPASS largely became a "police-only strategy," something that the COMPASS planners desperately wanted to avoid. Whether this would have happened if the original City Manager had not resigned is impossible to say, but the resignation of the City Manager clearly marked a turning point for COMPASS. Through mid-1992, COMPASS remained largely a police-only effort, in large part because of continuing changes in key leadership positions in the city—in November 1991, eight of the nine members of the City Council were replaced, and new City Managers were appointed in December 1991 and June 1992.

Despite the lack of involvement of the other city agencies in the seeding efforts, Charter Oak Terrace today remains significantly better off than it was prior to COMPASS. The Milner area, on the other hand, is thought to be no better off now than it was prior to COMPASS.

Frog Hollow

By late 1990, the HPD began to feel they had reached the point of diminishing returns in Charter Oak Terrace and Milner. The CSU felt there was basically nothing left to do in Charter Oak Terrace. Fewer and fewer arrests were being made. And boredom among the CSU officers began to set in. Discussions began on selecting the next major COMPASS target area. In this regard, two key lessons of Charter Oak Terrace and Milner impacted the selection of the next target areas. First, the experience in Milner underscored the importance of an existing strong community group that can facilitate seeding efforts. The second key factor was the need for a well-defined target area, in terms of both geographic boundaries and a general "sense of neighborhood"—two characteristics present in Charter Oak Terrace but absent in Milner. Actually, the first factor—a strong community organization—was the most important reason in selecting the Frog Hollow and Asylum Hill target areas. In these two areas are two of Hartford's most vocal and well-organized community groups. Both areas were promised that COMPASS would come to their areas sometime in 1991. The HPD had planned to go to Frog Hollow first.

Weeding efforts began in the Frog Hollow target area in March 1991, when the HPD's Vice and Narcotics Division started their undercover activities. Just prior to the April 22nd press conference announcing the start of the visible phase of the COMPASS program, the 77 warrants obtained during the undercover phase were executed. Initial weeding results were extremely positive. The CSU commander felt that the buy-bust tactic was particularly effective because it was easy for plainclothes CSU officers to make buys from any of a number of drug sellers operating in the area. Two weeks after the start of the visible weeding phase, the CSU commander received a standing ovation at a community meeting. CSU officers felt that drug sellers and customers were in a state of shock over the high police visibility and the aggressiveness of the CSU officers. No doubt the drug sellers were accustomed to patrol officers who were too busy responding to calls for service to notice them, and not to police officers who were freed from the 911 system and had the time to enforce laws aggressively. In this atmosphere, drug sellers became very cautious and there was a general feeling among the CSU officers that drug sellers and customers had suspended their activity or had moved to other parts of Hartford.

Unfortunately, the state overtime funds began to run out, and the CSU gradually began to cut back on overtime hours. By June 1991, these funds were depleted and delays in the state's announcement of the follow-up grant program meant that no overtime would be available for the CSU until October. Thus, the reduced coverage and visibility came during the summer months, when the level of drug activity is believed to peak. CSU officers complained that "there were just too many people in the drug trade" in the area, and "taking out a hundred sellers barely makes a dent in the drug trade, since another hundred just take their place."

The effectiveness of the weeding tactics may also have been hurt because of the drug sellers' and the customers' greater awareness of the program. As when COMPASS started in Charter Oak Terrace and Milner, the press conference announcing the start of COMPASS in Frog Hollow generated broad coverage by local newspapers, radio stations, and television stations. Drug sellers and customers no doubt knew that the CSU was therefore in Frog Hollow and, perhaps just as important, not in any other area. Based on the Charter Oak Terrace and Milner experience, they knew the CSU would be in Frog Hollow for several months. This phenomenon highlights the fact that publicity was a double-edged sword for COMPASS: Publicity generated public support of and involvement in COMPASS, but also informed drug sellers and customers of where the HPD had a heightened presence—and where it did not.

In Frog Hollow, COMPASS continued to be largely a "police-only" effort, as problems continued in trying to get the city involved with the seeding efforts. Inaction on the part of the non-police city agencies resulted in an increasing number of complaints from Frog Hollow residents and, in particular, from the key community organizations. Finally, in October 1991, the city responded to these complaints by creating the Quality Neighborhood Task Force (QNTF). Early efforts of the QNTF focused on identifying streets that needed paving, sidewalks that needed repairing, street lights that needed fixing, and vacant lots that needed cleaning. Still, months later, community leaders complained that the QNTF was "just rhetoric" and nothing concrete had been accomplished.

Meanwhile, in December 1991, the HPD fulfilled its promise to Asylum Hill by beginning COMPASS undercover operations in that area. As the CSU prepared to migrate to Asylum Hill in January 1992, they had a strong sense that drug activity in Frog Hollow would quickly return to the way it was prior to COMPASS. As one CSU officer put it, drug sellers and customers "were just waiting for us to leave." If that was the case, then the television, radio, and newspaper coverage of COMPASS's move to Asylum Hill in January let the Frog Hollow drug sellers and customers know that they could resume their old ways. By spring 1992, most HPD officials believed that Frog Hollow was in no better condition than before COMPASS, despite the drop in Part I crimes (see Table 11.1). The before and after community survey results (see Table 11.3) indicated mixed results: While a much lower percentage of respondents were "very concerned" with crime, a high percentage of respondents felt that the drug problem was "getting worse."

In late June 1992, the CSU returned to Frog Hollow. Fortunately, this return coincided with the renewed commitment from the Office of the City Manager to the seeding aspects of COMPASS. Unlike the prior efforts in 1991, the Assistant City Manager assigned to Frog Hollow was aggressive and determined to use all of the municipal resources at his disposal for seeding the neighborhood. This included the Public Works, Parks and Recreation, Fire, Licenses and Inspections, and the Social Services departments in addition to the HPD. Biweekly meetings were held with the key neighborhood organizations and the heads of the affected departments were required to attend. This level of support was supplemented by the extensive institutional support from institutions in the Frog Hollow area. Also attending and committed was the State's Attorney for Hartford County. In short, this group represented the broadest commitment to a focused neighborhood seeding since the inception of COMPASS in Charter Oak Terrace 3 years earlier.

In addition, this new effort was marked by increased participation and support from neighborhood organizations and residents. Of interest is the fact that the key neighborhood organization was manually maintaining a substantial amount of data on each building in the target area (e.g., housing code violations, broken windows, abandoned vehicles). Although the quality of some of this data was poor in that the source information was incomplete, it was interesting to note that the community group itself saw the value of maintaining such records for developing remedies to these problems. These initiatives have provided a psychological boost to the residents and institutions in the area. A key neighborhood organizer indicated that the neighborhood went from an "organizing mode to a problem-solving mode." He further indicated that the visual impact on the neighborhood has been astonishing. Nonetheless, the drug problem has not been eradicated. Even though the visibility of the drug market has been reduced substantially and the transactions are off-street and far more covert, there is a tacit recognition that the market still exists.

Asylum Hill

In December 1991, the HPD's Vice and Narcotics Division began their undercover operation in Asylum Hill. As a result of this operation, 44 warrants were obtained. These warrants were executed immediately before the January 10th press conference announcing the arrival of COMPASS in the Asylum Hill area. At the press conference, the president of Asylum Hill Organizing Project (AHOP) spoke on behalf of that organization, noting the tremendous "psychological difference" that the knowledge that COMPASS was coming had made on Asylum Hill residents. Importantly, she and other community organizers appeared to understand that COMPASS's success depended on them, as well as the HPD. Community leaders agreed that "we need to get organized."

As before, the CSU began a series of high-visibility tactics in the days immediately following the press conference, including vehicle safety checks and park and walks in the various pockets of drug activity in the target area. Because the Asylum Hill drug markets were isolated throughout the target area, and each market typically was limited to a single street segment, the CSU was able to focus on these hot spots and greatly reduce the level of drug activity. Some CSU officers, however, felt that the publicity of COMPASS alone—news of the press conference and the initial sweep was carried by all local television stations—drove many drug sellers out of the target area. The downside of the success in reducing drug activity in the target area was keeping the CSU officers motivated. Many CSU officers "hated" going to Asylum Hill because, they complained, "there was nothing to do."

The dramatic impact of the weeding efforts over the whole target area is perhaps best illustrated by an event that took place in Asylum Hill in May 1992. Every year AHOP, the key community organization in Asylum Hill, holds a convention to celebrate the previous year's accomplishments and to set priorities for the coming year. In the past, the conventions were always held in the afternoon, because of the fear of crime and drugs. As one AHOP organizer noted, "no one would show up if we held it in the evening." But this year, sensing a renewed confidence in the neighborhood, AHOP held the convention in the evening for the first time—and a record number of more than 300 people attended the convention.

HPD officials were more optimistic regarding the potential for seeding successes in Asylum Hill than in any of the other target areas. This area contained some very powerful institutions, which have a stake in improving the neighborhood. Asylum Hill, Inc. (AHI), had been organized by these institutions for this express purpose. Moreover, AHOP had enthusiastically embraced COMPASS and had given it rave reviews in the January press conference. Unfortunately, neither organization had a plan in place prior to the start of the weeding efforts. As noted above, the head of AHOP noted at the kick-off press conference that "we need to get organized." In addition, a leader of AHI felt that the HPD should postpone bringing COMPASS to Asylum Hill because there were no plans in place. Thus, instead of using the weeding period to implement their seeding plan, and so "really be ready when the CSU leaves the area," more time was spent formulating rather than implementing a seeding plan.

Asylum Hill residents and community organizations and the HPD, however, continued to express frustration with the city's lack of commitment to the COMPASS program. Asylum Hill residents nevertheless played a key role in the seeding efforts, particularly in one of the area's key drug hot spots. Spurred by the changes brought on by the CSU's efforts, residents on that street and the Asylum Hill CSO organized a neighborhood clean up at the end of February. Despite temperatures in the twenties, about 50 residents picked up trash and broken glass, raked yards, and removed fallen branches in the area. As one resident put it, "I wanted to help the community be a better place. The street looks nicer, it's cleaner, and it's finally safe" (Stansbury, 1992, p. C-7). Land-lords of apartment buildings located on the street further assisted by attaching floodlights to the tops of these buildings to discourage drug dealing at night.

As the end of the formal evaluation period coincided with the end of the weeding period in Asylum Hill, no "after" period police records were examined to assess COMPASS's impact on crime. However, surveys of community residents (see Table 11.3) support the apparent improvement in the area brought about by the CSU's presence.

Conclusions

Based on the experiences in the four COMPASS target areas, several general conclusions can be reached regarding the COMPASS weed and seed effort:

- The COMPASS program generated extensive positive publicity for the city, at least initially, and particularly for the HPD. Drugs were viewed as a serious threat to the community, and the public saw COMPASS as a new and innovative attempt to control drugs and improve neighborhoods. Although the publicity enhanced community support in the target areas for COMPASS, knowing where the CSU was and was not no doubt helped drug sellers and customers adapt their behavior and in the end may have lessened the effectiveness of weeding tactics.

- Geography can significantly increase the effectiveness of weeding tactics. Well-defined boundaries help define the target area and a limited number of roads in to and out of the target area helps the police control access to the area. Also, the police can obviously achieve higher visibility in smaller target areas.

- Weeding success spawns community support and participation in the ensuing seeding efforts. Visible and active community involvement, in turn, increases the effectiveness of weeding tactics and is critical for longer term success in seeding.

- The seeding component of COMPASS was largely not implemented, primarily because of turmoil in city government and a budget climate that made funding for new seeding programs difficult. COMPASS therefore became largely a police-only weeding program.

• Despite the lack of an effective seeding program, COMPASS has shown that an intensive and coordinated police effort can positively impact some of the poorest areas of the community. Nevertheless, without an effective criminal justice system and seeding programs that offer alternatives to persons involved in the drug trade, it is difficult to affect long-term improvements to an area.

For other cities implementing or contemplating weed and seed programs, a number of suggestions are offered.

• The city—meaning both city administrators and community (including business) leaders—must cooperate and coordinate program planning and implementation, so that the resultant program is a citywide program and not just a police-only effort.

• For each target area, the police department must initially commit resources for a several-month period. These resources should not be tied to the 911 system, so that they can focus exclusively on weeding operations.

• The heads of the pertinent non-police city agencies must pledge their commitment to the program and promise to give priority to problems identified in selected target areas.

• Police officers involved in the seeding efforts—such as community service officers—must be empowered so that problems identified by them can be given immediate attention.

• The city must develop specific criteria for selecting target areas. These criteria should include the degree of commitment from organizations, businesses, and residents in the area; the "sense of community" within the area; and the degree of geographic isolation and identification of the area. Whether geographic barriers or isolation can be created in the area is also a consideration.

• Detailed program plans, and in particular seeding plans, must be developed prior to the start of the weeding phase. Community organizations and city agencies must know in advance what their specific roles and objectives are with respect to both the weeding and seeding phases of the effort.

In sum, the COMPASS experience suggests that the neighborhood-oriented weed-and-seed approach can be effective, provided that a viable neighborhood, especially one with obvious geographic boundaries, does indeed exist. In light of the increasing popularity of the weed-and-seed model for improving neighborhoods, it is hoped that this chapter can be useful to jurisdictions contemplating such programs.

Note

1. See Caulkins, Rich, and Larson (1993) and Tien, Rich, Shell, Larson, and Donnelly (1993) for an in-depth discussion of how geography enhanced the success of police weeding tactics in Charter Oak Terrace.

References

Caulkins, J. P., Rich, T. F., & Larson, R. C. (1993). The impact of geography on focused drug enforcement operations. *Journal of Socio-Economic Planning Sciences, 27*(1), 119-130.

Revolution at Charter Oak Terrace. (1990, August 24). *Hartford Courant,* p. C-14.

Stansbury, R. (1992, March 1). Neighborhood cleanup day caps year's effort to sweep out drugs. *Hartford Courant,* p. C-7.

Tien, J. M. (1979). Towards a systematic approach to program evaluation design. *IEEE Transactions on Systems, Man and Cybernetics: Special Issue on Public Systems Methodology, SMC-9,* 494-515.

Tien, J. M. (1990). Program evaluation: A system and model-based approach. In A. P. Sage (Ed.), *Concise encyclopedia of information processing in systems and organizations* (pp. 382-388). Elmsford, NY: Pergamon.

Tien, J. M., & Reppetto, T. A. (1975). *Elements of CPTED.* Cambridge, MA: Urban Systems Research and Engineering.

Tien, J. M., Rich, T. F., Shell, M. C., Larson, R. C., & Donnelly, J. P. (1993). *COMPASS: A drug market analysis program final report.* Hartford, CT: Hartford Police Department.

PART

Community Policing in Other Countries

Community Policing in Canada

An Overview of Experience and Evaluations

BARRY N. LEIGHTON

Current Status of Canadian Community Policing

As Canadian policing moves toward the 21st century, community policing is firmly established as the dominant orientation or philosophy. Indeed, the preponderance of Canada's 400 or so police agencies have either officially endorsed or otherwise support community policing as the most appropriate approach for contemporary policing. In addition to this generalization, a number of other observations may help to situate the Canadian experience of the 1990s, particularly with respect to the American experience and to the late-1980s when Greene and Mastrofski (1988) and their colleagues assessed the condition of community policing in North America (see also Bayley, 1988, 1992; Friedmann, 1992; Murphy, 1988b; Skolnick & Bayley, 1988).

First, the overwhelming public rhetoric of Canadian police chiefs indicates they are committed to the paradigm shift, in principle and philosophy, if not yet in practice. Many chiefs obtained their position by making sweeping promises to implement community policing—whatever their understanding of the philosophy may have been at the time—and are publicly committed to following through. Whereas earlier observations indicated that community policing may be used in Canada as an excuse or metaphor for organizational change or reform (Murphy, 1988b), this is less likely to be the case now.

Moreover, the public—as the consumers of police services—together with the media, have responded to the appeal of community policing by affirming it as a progressive step in the language of public discourse. Through elected officials, political institutions, and the governing bodies of policing, it is now politically fashionable if not expedient to champion community policing at the local level. But, having "gone public" as the conventional wisdom, there are raised expectations over what can be delivered and there is less room to renege on promises made.

Third, the gap has largely been closed between community policing as a broad philosophy or strategy and its operationalization through a transformed organizational structure, accompanied by specific tactics of daily police operations. Consequently, the debate has moved well beyond those earlier paralysing discussions on what community policing really is, whether all policing is really just community policing, or whether policing has always been community policing.

Fourth, although the distinction between problem-oriented policing and community policing appears to be common in the United States (e.g., Moore, 1992), this contrast is seldom made in Canada, where problem solving, as promoted by Herman Goldstein (1990), is viewed as a fundamental component of the latter. However, because problem solving can occur without community involvement, it is sometimes seen as an initial strategy for implementing in the more traditional police agencies, to soften them up before embarking on the broader based community policing enterprise. A more common Canadian conundrum is the contrast between crime prevention and community policing.

Fifth, compared with their American counterparts, Canadian police services have a great deal of breathing room in which to implement community policing, despite some looming constraints such as a fiscal crisis. Indeed, as David Bayley (1991) has so cogently observed, Canadian police do not face a real "crime problem" in comparison with their southern neighbors. Nor is there any sign of a withdrawal of "consent" by the public to be policed. As a result, there is now a greater willingness by police chiefs to experiment with a full implementation rather than just an "add-on" program and to risk failure as a trade-off against the possibility of a successful implementation.

Sixth, despite the lack of evaluations, Canadian police leaders are becoming far more confident about the merits of their community policing efforts, particularly when compared with their American, English, and Australian counterparts. Having done the tour of American community policing "hot spots," Canadian police chiefs are now less likely to look exclusively south of the border for inspiration, less likely to call upon American academics to legitimate their efforts, and more likely to advertise their own successes. Indeed, a few police agencies are learning how to blow their own horns, such as the Edmonton Police Service report on community policing, *Working the Beat* (Koller, 1990).

Finally, the competition among police chiefs is no longer about who has always been doing it or who did it first, but about who can successfully demonstrate they are doing community policing on a department-wide basis. They are no longer able to make unsubstantiated claims for success in community policing and it is increasingly being recognized that this demonstration must be an empirical one, involving evaluations designed to produce proof against both the traditional performance criteria and the new community policing criteria.

Despite this positive picture, there are some serious weaknesses and misgivings. First, progress in advancing the implementation of community policing is hampered by lack of practical guides for use at the operational level. Second, yet to be developed are comprehensive criteria for fully implemented, department-wide community policing (i.e., in addition to client satisfaction, level of fear, level of repeat calls for service, etc.) that are practical alternatives to the traditional police agency performance measures. This has led to a void whereby pressures remain to demonstrate success by reducing crime rates and/or clearance rates. Third, researchers have not yet agreed to standard research methodologies for evaluating the impact of community policing against even those criteria that have been developed to date. Fourth, regardless of whether the results are used for promotion or for "officer coaching," appropriate individual officer performance evaluation and reward systems have yet to emerge.

Nonetheless, compared with 5 years ago, Canadian policing shows it is located firmly in the community policing paradigm and is working vigorously toward its wider implementation.

Influences on Canadian Community Policing

It is not clear why Canadian police leaders have been so eager to embrace community policing. There is no demonstrated crisis in crime (Bayley, 1992) and no tradition of police corruption (Leighton, 1991) that might have pushed police agencies toward the "professional model" (Kelling & Moore, 1988). The absence of a crisis is contrary to a widely held view that radical change in policing requires the catalyst of a crisis. What, then, were the influences on Canadian policing and community policing in particular?

Rather than merely succumbing to the overpowering influence of their American cousins (Murphy, 1988b), it is argued here that in adopting community policing, Canadian police simply returned to their 19th century origins that, for municipal police departments, lie in the Metropolitan London Police and, for the Royal Canadian Mounted Police (RCMP), are found in the Royal Irish Constabulary (both being Robert Peel inventions). The return to their roots occurred when, after a few decades of flirting with the professional policing model, it was proven to be ineffective. That is, Canadian police retained much of their original features, especially in medium to small police departments and in the RCMP as the dominant police force, instead of completely adopting the professional model by imitating "US-tested and proven police innovations" (Friedmann, 1992). Hence, rather than being fully swayed by the American trend and then shifting back to community policing, Canadian police largely stayed the course.

The few decades of flirting with professional policing can be partly explained by the lack of a national research institute and a critical mass of independent, university-based academics conducting research on policing in Canada (Murphy,

1988b) that could provide police practitioners with a critique of passing fashions in policing and a lesser tendency to imitate U.S. police. Nonetheless, in the absence of such a capacity, the research work of the Washington-based PERF, Police Foundation, and other major U.S. research initiatives (e.g., Eck & Spelman, 1987; Kelling, Pate, Dieckman, & Brown, 1974; Pate, Ferrara, & Kelling, 1981) has been influential in nudging Canadian police back on track toward community policing. Much of this research is studied by the federal government department responsible for policing, which has tended to shape the Canadian research agenda in policing through its funding priorities.

Whatever the reason that community policing has gained ground in Canada, it is consistent with trends in other public service institutions in which total quality management and other innovations are flourishing. Further, it is compatible with the resurgence in popularity of crime prevention in Canada. Adopted in the early 1970s, crime prevention and "preventive policing" set the stage for problem-oriented policing and, eventually, for community policing. The more recent version of crime prevention is, however, driven by the fiscal crisis of the state, which fosters the downloading of responsibility (and costs) for individual protection and public safety from public institutions to individuals and local communities. Perhaps this trend, together with influence of American police practitioners and academics spilling across the 49th parallel, is what is currently shaping Canadian policing.

Community Policing in Canada

A brief overview of the structure of policing in Canada provides a backdrop for a review of community policing. In 1991, there were 56,774 police officers in just over 420 police forces across Canada, supported by 19,000 other personnel. This translates into one police officer for every 476 Canadians, at a per capita cost of $197 and a national cost of 5.3 billion Canadian dollars. Of the total number of officers, about one quarter (15,555 or 27%) are members of the Royal Canadian Mounted Police (RCMP), and 16% work for the three provincial police forces (Ontario Provincial Police or OPP, Sûreté du Québec or SQ, and Royal Newfoundland Constabulary, with 185, 113, and 4 detachments, respectively). From another viewpoint, 62% are members of municipal or regional urban police forces (416 independent municipal forces plus 192 RCMP and 24 OPP detachments under contract to municipalities). Canada's five largest police forces (RCMP, OPP, SQ, Metro Toronto Police, and Montreal Police) account for more than 60% of all officers.[1]

The RCMP has three major roles, which result in the delivery of police services to 21.5% of the population through 720 detachments. First, it is the federal police service, enforcing federal statutes such as those relating to drug trafficking, through all its detachments (including 64 exclusively federal ones located in Quebec and Ontario and at airports). Second, it serves as a provincial police service under contract with eight provinces (excluding Quebec, Ontario, and parts of Newfoundland) and the two territories, serving in more than 300 small town and rural detachments. Third, it acts as a local police department, under the same provincial contracts, in more than 300 towns and municipalities. In its provincial and municipal role, the RCMP enforces the federal *Canadian Criminal Code,* provincial statutes, and municipal by-laws.

Police governance is articulated through provincial legislation, which has established 175 provincial and municipal boards and commissions for each police service, consisting of members appointed by elected officials combined with elected municipal politicians. One of the defining features of Canadian policing is the nature and scope of civilian oversight and public accountability mechanisms (Watt, 1991).

The structure of Canadian policing appears to fall somewhere between those of the United States and England and Wales. If the United States has anywhere from 15,000 to 20,000 independent forces with overlapping jurisdictions (Moore, 1992) that perform a highly complex and nonintegrated law enforcement role, then the 43 independent forces of England and Wales form a *de facto* national law enforcement force by virtue of a common policy direction and leadership cadre (Reiner, 1991). By contrast, Canadian policing is a mix of the two, by virtue of being dominated by the RCMP, OPP, and SQ detachment systems and by a few large municipal police services, a domination that facilitates the delivery of relatively homogeneous, high-quality police services across the country.

With respect to how Canada's police services provide policing, as indicated earlier the vast majority have accepted community policing as the appropriate approach to their responsibilities for crime and order maintenance. Evidence for this conclusion is found at various levels of the policing and law enforcement institution and takes the form of legislation, government reports, public endorsements by police chiefs and their governing bodies, police agency plans and other documents, operational programs, and, in a few police agencies, social science studies.

The broad criteria for assessing the presence of a community policing initiative include evidence of: (1) organizational commitment to the community policing philosophy or strategy, particularly of a partnership or joint ownership with the community for local crime and disorder problems; (2) problem identification and problem solving with community involvement; and (3) the presence of ongoing community policing tactics such as community consultative committees, locally based allocation of human resources, foot patrols, mini-stations, use of volunteers, and so forth. However, the evidence is clouded by the competitive rhetoric, proclamations, and claims of police chiefs; by the lack of relevant statistics and other concrete information; by a general lack of documentation of police practices; and by the general absence of evaluation studies. Nonetheless, there are a number of valuable descriptive studies of pilot projects or of attempts to implement elements of community policing.

To begin this review at the national level, the federal government department responsible for the RCMP and "national leadership" in policing, has formally endorsed the approach (Leighton & Normandeau, 1990; Normandeau & Leighton, 1990).[2]

A recent development is the creation of First Nations police services on reserves, resulting in eight new policing agencies to date and others in negotiation, all premised on community policing principles inherent within First Nations cultures.

At the provincial level, many governments have officially incorporated community policing into their public safety strategy while others have done so on a *de facto* basis, with two provinces standing out in terms of the level of commitment. The 1990 Police Services Act of the province of Ontario articulates community policing principles in its preamble as the philosophy guiding all policing within the province. This is noteworthy, because it is the only federal, state, or provincial legislation to do so in North America. The Ontario government department responsible for policing is actively promoting the approach through training and an inspectorate system with respect to provincial standards of policing (parallel perhaps to the accreditation system).

British Columbia has recently released a provincial review of community policing (British Columbia, 1993a), a report that continues a theme running through a recent examination of the policing arrangements (British Columbia, 1990) and that is expected to be supported in a commission inquiring into the state of provincial policing (British Columbia, 1993b). The provincial Police Academy, part of the Justice Institute of British Columbia, offers the first province-wide, intensive, problem-oriented policing course in Canada.

Third, the RCMP, as the federal police force and the largest police force in the country, has formally adopted community policing through an elaborate strategic plan as "a philosophy of policing and a method of service delivery" (RCMP, 1993). However, the standard response from the RCMP Commissioner on down through the lesser ranks has tended to be that the RCMP, as a police force serving a predominantly rural and small town constituency, has always been doing community policing, is currently doing it, and plans to continue doing it in a systematic way. The first recent step began with the RCMP Commissioner's 1989 annual Directional Statement on policy to all RCMP officers (somewhat akin to a "state of the nation" address) in which all detachments over 12 in size were directed to establish Community Advisory Committees. That this directive was not yet grounded in a rationale or plan to implement community policing did not seem to detract from its impact. Subsequent strategic planning exercises and other policy statements have reinforced community policing as a "strategic priority" (e.g., the 1990 Directional Statement). In addition to establishing community advisory committees, problem-solving courses are widely taught, and basic recruit training is increasingly oriented toward community policing. Further, a number of detachments are seen as being particularly innovative, despite the pressure toward conformity that is inevitably generated by a large institution.

The OPP in Ontario and the SQ in Quebec, as the other large, detachment-based, rural police services in Canada, have also made a business out of endorsing and working at implementing community policing. The OPP is actively promoting community-based policing, particularly in small towns, through training and an Action Plan that has been implemented and through the monitoring of its implementation, which reveals a high level of activity. Similarly, the SQ is encouraging change in the culture and professional practice of policing through training.

At the municipal level, a number of city police departments are widely recognized as having made significant progress toward implementation of the current philosophy (see also Kennedy, 1991). Moving the review from the east coast to the west coast, the Halifax, Nova Scotia, police department has been reorganized on the basis of three zones for team policing, with community consultative committees, and "village constables" (i.e., foot patrol officers) working out of storefront mini-stations in core urban areas (see Clairmont, 1990, 1992). This service has also decentralized criminal investigation as well as crime analysis and direct patrol, and has expanded crime prevention. The initial momentum may have been slowed as a result of the apparent inability to establish nontraditional, community policing performance appraisal and reward systems for police officers. Also located in the Atlantic provinces, Fredericton, New Brunswick, is well known for an innovative, multiagency storefront operation (the Devon Storefront) run out of a community center in support of a local neighborhood in a low-income housing project. However, it has not yet been evaluated.

Within the province of Quebec, the Montreal Urban Community Police (Le service de police de la communauté urbaine de Montréal, with 4,407 officers) has established storefront offices and a program for patrol officers to visit all residences to help establish positive community relations (see also Cartier, Grenon, & Rizkalla, 1987). In late 1986 the first stage was implemented of a zone community police service designed to prevent crime by getting closer to the residents of communities with high crime rates (Cartier et al., 1987). Nonetheless, with a relatively youthful officer corps confronted by growing racial incidents, community policing faces a rough ride. Evaluations of some programs have been conducted but there has been no systematic examination or comprehensive evaluation of community policing in Montreal.

Toronto, like Montreal, is another large North American city that is faced with rapidly rising crime, drug problems, violence, and a large minority population. It supports the largest municipal police agency in Canada, at 5,637 officers. Community policing has been a formal objective of the Metropolitan Toronto Police Department since the early 1980s (Lambert, 1988). One distinctive feature is the annual public discussion of policing priorities conducted by its governing body, the Metro Toronto Police Commission, including proposed police and community priorities for the coming year and a review of the year's performance against the previous priorities. Fortunately, part of the community policing experience has been documented by research that describes the history and development of Toronto's mini-stations (Lambert, 1988). A survey conducted in the Jane-Finch and Parkdale communities of Toronto examined citizen satisfactions with the police, knowledge of police services, particularly of the mini-station, and citizen identification of local crime problems (Murphy, 1988a; Murphy & de Verteuil, 1986). Although the mini-stations were well received by local residents, the researchers found it difficult to evaluate the impact of the mini-stations because their objectives and community crime and disorder problems were not clearly identified.

Halton Regional Police Force, working in an area neighboring on Toronto, is another police service that has introduced community policing innovations, including zone and beat policing, mini-stations, and "village constables" (Loree, 1988). Informal reports by the police chief indicate that half the budget is devoted to community policing, resulting in a halving of the crime rate.

In Ottawa, the nation's capital city, zone policing was implemented during the 1970s. However, it has only been in recent years that further community policing tactics were implemented in the Ottawa Police Service. Five mini-stations have been established during the past 2 years, the delivery of services has once again been reorganizing around zones and beats, and community consultation committees have been established.

Although the Winnipeg Police Department initiated a pilot project in 1988, with four experimental beat patrols in the city core and at least one beat constable working out of a mini-station (Linden, 1989), subsequent plans to implement community policing on a district- and then citywide basis seem to have fallen through. This may be as a consequence of commissions of inquiry into misconduct and systemic racial bias toward Aboriginal persons. Now in a form of managerial receivership under a former RCMP officer, community policing appears to be one avenue for reform by providing a renewed direction, a not unusual use of community policing in Australia, where it was adopted in New South Wales and Queensland following widespread corruption in state police forces.

In the western provinces, Calgary and Edmonton city police stand out. Initiated in 1973 with zones and beat policing, Calgary's experimentation with community policing is described in a report (Hornick, 1993a) as part of a federally sponsored research series entitled *Police Services of Excellence in Community Policing,* which reviews police agency experiences with community policing. Its Alberta partner, Edmonton, has pioneered a demonstration project on neighborhood foot patrol based in mini-stations (see below), and is also considered a "police service of excellence" (see Hornick, 1993b).

Finally, British Columbia plays host to the Victoria Police Service, which is well known for its mini-stations (see below). Elsewhere, a range of municipal forces and RCMP detachments (e.g., Delta, Prince George) are pursuing community policing, often in conjunction with crime prevention activities, for which the province is also well known.

Overview of Two Key Evaluations

Despite its wide acceptance as the dominant ideology, much rhetoric, and a number of promising programs, there has been little in the way of comprehensive, rigorous evaluations of community policing in Canada. Indeed, there are only two formal impact evaluations of community policing that have been published to date: one in Victoria, British Columbia, and the other in Edmonton, Alberta.

The Victoria Community Police Stations Project

The West Coast city of Victoria introduced "community police stations" ("CoPS.") into the 160-officer police department between late 1987 and early 1989. One CoPS station was located in each of five police districts, accompanied by a 3-year formative program evaluation and concluding with a summative or impact evaluation.

The purpose of these mini-stations was to "bring the police and community more closely together to work in making Victoria a safer and better place to live" (C. Walker, Walker, & McDavid, 1992), with two specific outcome objectives of reducing crime and fear of crime and six implementation objectives of problem solving, increasing accessibility to police services, increasing community involvement, increasing service delivery to both the elderly and to school children, and increasing the reporting of intelligence. The evaluators also provided "formative advice" to the Chief Constable through annual progress reports containing recommendations, many of which were subsequently implemented.

The traditional criterion of crime rate reduction was examined through official statistics, pre- and posttest telephone surveys of residents in each district, a survey of mini-station volunteers, and a survey of police personnel. Fear of crime and perceptions of safety were studied through telephone surveys of the districts and mini-station daily diaries and client logs.

Detailed results of this evaluation study are reported elsewhere (Walker, 1987; Walker & Walker, 1989; C. Walker et al., 1992; S. Walker & Walker, 1992). With respect to reducing official levels of crime, crime rates decreased in five categories but increased for business break-and-enter and total thefts. Although the vast majority of mini-station volunteers perceived crime rates as decreasing as a direct result of the program (a not surprising finding, given their investment of time), 62% of the police officers did not agree, possibly reflecting the rift between officers working out of the mini-stations and those on regular patrol. According to community surveys, one quarter of neighborhood residents tended to side with the police officers by viewing crime as increasing, whereas two thirds saw crime as staying the same, even though they also reported a decline in personal property victimizations. Only 8% believed that crime had declined and fewer still attributed the decline to the program or to the crime- and problem-solving capabilities of their local police.

A 1987 community survey found that the majority of respondents were aware of their local community station and that, although only 9% had been victims of crime, some 11% had called the station. A subsequent community survey showed that the majority of respondents were aware that a neighborhood community station existed and a significant proportion of them had also contacted the local station.

In terms of reducing fear of being personally victimized, the study showed little impact on the levels of fear in each of the five neighborhoods.

The Edmonton Neighborhood Foot Patrol Project

In 1988, the Edmonton Police Service began piloting and then arranged for an evaluation of its Neighborhood Foot Patrol (NFP) Program. This program consisted of 21 NFP officers in each of 21 neighborhoods or beat areas that were identified as "hot spots" of crime by an analysis of repeat calls for service and crime incident data. Working out of strategically located storefronts in each area, both traditional reactive policing and additional community policing services were provided on foot and by marked patrol car.

The program goals were to prevent crime, to provide proactive policing services based on problem solving, and to provide a community-based service involving the community in identifying and solving problems, with the NFP officers serving as "team leaders" for the community. The program objectives were: (1) to reduce the level of repeat calls for service in the beat areas significantly; (2) to improve public satisfaction with the police service; (3) to increase the job satisfaction of police officers; (4) to increase reporting of police intelligence on crime in the area; and (5) to solve community problems. Translating these objectives into operational strategies involved: (1) targeting police services to the "hot spot" neighborhoods; (2) decentralizing police services to the beat areas using storefront offices; (3) using foot patrol to increase police visibility and community contact; (4) increasing the officers' autonomy and problem-solving capability; (5) problem identification with community involvement; (6) problem solving with community involvement; and (7) increasing NFP officers' knowledge of the community. In addition to taking regular calls for service, specific community policing tactics included using: (1) patrol, mainly on foot; (2) a storefront office; (3) volunteers in the office; (4) a community consultative committee; and (5) problem solving techniques.

Conducted by Joe Hornick and his associates (see Hornick, Burrows, Tjosvold, & Phillips, 1990) from the Canadian Research Institute for Law and the Family in Calgary, this evaluation is one of the most comprehensive and rigorous evaluations of a community policing program undertaken in North America. The evaluation used an "exploratory, one-shot comparison group" research design to gather pretest and posttest data over a 2-year period, making comparisons between the group of NFP officers and a matched sample of motor patrol (MP) officers. Within-group comparisons were also made between the downtown and non-downtown NFP officers. Research instruments examined: (1) officer time allocation, using time budgets; (2) officer travel time; (3) users of police services, using a survey; (4) officer satisfaction; (5) repeat calls for service; (6) NFP officers' attitudes, and so forth; and (7) problem-solving cases.

These instruments produced a wealth of findings on how well the program was implemented and on the program impact in terms of its effectiveness. Because these are reported in detail elsewhere (Hornick, Burrows, Tjosvold, & Phillips, 1990; Hornick, Burrows, Phillips, & Leighton, 1991; Hornick, Leighton, & Burrows, 1993), only two types of findings are summarized here: repeat calls for service and public satisfaction with the police.

Over the test period, the total number of repeat addresses declined by 2.4% and, at the beat level, two thirds of the beats had significant decreases in the numbers of repeat addresses. More importantly, the total number of calls for service declined by 6.6% overall in the 21 study areas between the pretest and posttest studies. Moreover, an analysis of the number of repeat calls per repeat address showed that the total number of repeat calls declined significantly in 7 beats, with 2 beats showing a significant increase, and with a significant decrease overall in the number of repeat calls. Because new foot patrol and storefront office tactics are initially expected to increase the volume of direct calls for service from the public (but not central dispatch calls), the modest decline by virtue of reducing repeat calls from repeat addresses is noteworthy.

Changes in the level and nature of calls for service were attributed to the problem-solving activities. Time budgets reveal that a significant proportion of NFP officers' time was spent on "doing" problem-solving activities, but links to reductions in the number of repeat calls from specific addresses were made only on an aggregate basis. Nonetheless, support for the success of problem solving was produced by case study reports on specific success stories.

Not surprisingly, the public rated the NFP officers more highly on satisfaction scales than officers patrolling in cars, a rating that tended to have a halo effect on all areas of police work. This is a finding consistent with studies of community "ownership" of their own police force in contrast with user satisfaction with local detachments of larger police forces.

Conclusions from the evaluation indicate the NFP program in the 21 areas met the five program objectives. However, the researchers also concluded that the program was particularly applicable to residential areas but, with the exception of problem solving, it is not well suited to downtown or business/nonresidential settings. Most of the recommendations accompanying the evaluation report were subsequently adopted and community policing is now being implemented on a department-wide basis. Interestingly, the first step in implementation that was conducted toward the end of the evaluation study was a complete organizational overhaul of the police agency or, in the words of Superintendent Chris Braiden, "a bureaucratic garage sale" (Braiden, 1987).

In addition to this evaluation, an excellent qualitative evaluation report was produced as a parallel exercise at the request of senior police executives (Koller, 1990), apparently as a means of hedging their bets in case the quantitative evaluation results were not favorable. Taken together, these evaluations contribute significantly toward the chief's objective of becoming the "Mayo clinic of community policing."

These studies display some important similarities and differences. Both evaluate "add-on" programs rather than department-wide ones, although the Edmonton project subsequently led to plans for a full implementation, which is now in process. Whereas at the time of the study the Victoria program was not integrated into the routine operations of the police department because it did not handle calls for service from central dispatch, the Edmonton project handled centrally dispatched 911 calls for service and lightened the overall departmental workload in the pilot areas. Further, although within-group comparisons were made in both studies, only the Edmonton study used a control group. Finally, though both examined fear of crime, the Victoria study used traditional crime rates as a major criterion for success in contrast to the Edmonton research, which used the more innovative problem-solving measure of reduction in repeat calls for service from repeat addresses.

Conclusions and Future Direction

This selective review of the current state of community policing in Canada shows that this strategy is increasingly characterizing the organization and operational tactics of most progressive police services. There is a growing number of police agencies that have implemented at least some of the core tactics, such as foot patrol in zones or beats, storefronts or mini-stations, and community consultative committees. Nonetheless, some issues and concerns remain.

One of the main issues facing Canadian police executives at this time is how to implement community policing in a systematic way and on a department-wide basis. Once implemented, however, the next challenge is how to sustain the approach through a changed reward system, training, and other avenues. As well, police executives need to have on hand the performance criteria and research methods for evaluating how well community policing works. Consequently, community policing in Canada clearly invites attention by scholars intent on conducting evaluation studies.

Why are there so few evaluations of Canadian policing? First, there are a few academics involved with police research and fewer still pursuing evaluations of policing. Second, by the very nature of community policing, it is difficult to prove that a philosophy works. It is also difficult to achieve closure to the implementation of a fundamental organizational and operational change that would then allow for an appropriate impact study.

Regardless of the success of evaluations, Canadian community policing will increasingly be faced with two rigorous tests of its robustness as a policing strategy. One is its ability to withstand the fiscal crisis confronting all public institutions, a threat that will create unparalleled pressures in policing toward cost-efficiencies. Consequently there is the potential for backsliding toward the professional policing model by sacrificing effectiveness for traditional crime fighting.

Perhaps the major test for community policing in the future will be its ability to overcome its inherent bias toward local problems and local solutions, a local bias that facilitates "sand-box policing" (Leighton, 1991). The challenge is how the locally driven agenda of problem solving can be linked up with the regional, national, and international levels in an increasingly globalized context for crime and disorder problems.

Notes

1. For a more detailed overview of the structure of Canadian policing, see Canadian Centre for Justice Statistics (1986, 1992), Leighton and Normandeau (1990), and Bayley (1991, 1992).

2. The majority of Canada's 55,000 police officers received a copy of Leighton and Normandeau (1990), which, for the first time, provided a Canadian-authored rationale for and description of community policing.

References

Bayley, D. H. (1988). Community policing: A report from the devil's advocate. In J. R. Greene & S. D. Mastrofski (Eds.), *Community policing: Rhetoric or reality?* (pp. 225-238). New York: Praeger.

Bayley, D. H. (1991). *Managing the future: Prospective issues in Canadian policing* (User Report No. 1991-02). Ottawa: Ministry of the Solicitor General of Canada.

Bayley, D. H. (1992). Comparative organization of the police in English-speaking countries. In M. Tonry & N. Morris (Eds.), *Crime and justice: A review of research: Vol. 15. Modern policing* (pp. 509-545). Chicago: University of Chicago Press.

Braiden, C. (1987). *Community policing: Nothing new under the sun.* Edmonton, Alberta: City of Edmonton Police Service.

British Columbia, Ministry of Solicitor General. (1990). *Policing British Columbia in the year 2001, report of the Regionalization Study Team.* Victoria: Ministry of Solicitor General (now Ministry of Attorney General).

British Columbia, Ministry of Attorney General. (1993a). *Community policing advisory committee.* Victoria: Ministry of Attorney General.

British Columbia, Ministry of Attorney General. (1993b). *Policing in British Columbia Commission of Inquiry: Interim report.* Victoria: Ministry of Attorney General.

Canadian Centre for Justice Statistics. (1986). *Policing in Canada, 1986.* Ottawa: Statistics Canada.

Canadian Centre for Justice Statistics. (1992). Police personnel and expenditures in Canada—1991. *Juristat Service Bulletin, 12*(20). Ottawa: Statistics Canada.

Cartier, B., Grenon, S., & Rizkalla, S. (1987). *Prevention Communautaire du Crime: Les citoyens visites et les policiers non-intervenant s'expriment sur le programme.* Montreal: Societe Criminologie de Quebec.

Clairmont, D. (1990). *To the forefront: Community-based zone policing in Halifax.* Ottawa: Canadian Police College.

Clairmont, D. (1992). *Policing in the uptown.* Halifax: Atlantic Institute of Criminology, Dalhousie University.

Eck, J. E., & Spelman, W. (1987). *Problem-oriented policing in Newport News.* Washington, DC: Police Executive Research Forum.

Friedmann, R. R. (1992). *Community policing: Comparative perspectives and prospects.* New York: St. Martin's.

Goldstein, H. (1990). *Problem-oriented policing.* New York: McGraw-Hill.

Greene, J. R., & Mastrofski, S. D. (Eds.). (1988). *Community policing: Rhetoric or reality?* New York: Praeger.

Hornick, J. P. (1993a). *Community policing in Calgary.* Ottawa: Ministry of the Solicitor General of Canada.

Hornick, J. P. (1993b). *Community policing in Edmonton.* Ottawa: Ministry of the Solicitor General of Canada.

Hornick, J. P., Burrows, B. A., Phillips, D. M., & Leighton, B. N. (1991). An impact evaluation of the Neighbourhood Foot Patrol Program. *Canadian Journal of Program Evaluation, 6*(1), 47-70.

Hornick, J. P., Burrows, B. A., Tjosvold, I., & Phillips, D. M. (1990). *An evaluation of the neighbourhood foot patrol program of Edmonton Police Service* (User Report No. 1990-09). Ottawa: Ministry of the Solicitor General of Canada.

Hornick, J. P., Leighton, B. N., & Burrows, B. (1993). Evaluating community policing: The Edmonton project. In J. Hudson & J. Roberts (Eds.), *Evaluating justice: Canadian policies and programs* (pp. 61-92). Toronto: Thompson Educational Publishing.

Kelling, G. L., & Moore, M. L. (1988). From political to reform to community: The evolving strategy of police. In J. R. Greene & S. D. Mastrofski (Eds.), *Community policing: Rhetoric or reality?* (pp. 3-25). New York: Praeger.

Kelling, G. L., Pate, T., Dieckman, D., & Brown, C. E. (1974). *The Kansas City Preventive Patrol Experiment: A summary report.* Washington, DC: The Police Foundation.

Kennedy, L. W. (1991). The evaluation of community-based policing in Canada. *Canadian Police College Journal, 15*(4), 275-289.

Koller, K. (1990). *Working the beat: The Edmonton Neighbourhood Foot Patrol.* Edmonton: Edmonton Police Service.

Lambert, L. R. (1988). Police mini-stations in Toronto: An experience in compromise. *Royal Canadian Mounted Police Gazette, 50*(6), 1-5.

Leighton, B. N. (1991). Visions of community policing: Rhetoric and reality in Canada. *Canadian Journal of Criminology, 33*(3-4), 485-522.

Leighton, B. N., & Normandeau, A. (1990). *A vision of the future of policing in Canada: Discussion paper.* Ottawa: Ministry of the Solicitor General of Canada.

Linden, R. (1989). *A report on the Winnipeg City Police Community Officer Program.* Winnipeg: University of Manitoba, Criminology Research Centre.

Loree, D. J. (1988). Innovations and change in a regional police force. *Canadian Police College Journal, 12*(4), 205-239.

Moore, M. H. (1992). Problem-solving and community policing. In M. Tonry & N. Morris (Eds.), *Crime and justice: A review of research: Vol. 15. Modern policing* (pp. 99-158). Chicago: University of Chicago Press.

Murphy, C. J. (1988a). Community problems, problem communities, and community policing in Toronto. *Journal of Research in Crime and Delinquency, 25*(4), 392-410.

Murphy, C. J. (1988b). The development, impact, and implications of community policing in Canada. In J. R. Greene & S. D. Mastrofski (Eds.), *Community policing: Rhetoric or reality?* (pp. 177-189). New York: Praeger.

Murphy, C., & de Verteuil, J. (1986). *Metropolitan Toronto community policing survey.* Ottawa: Ministry of the Solicitor General of Canada.

Normandeau, A., & Leighton, B. N. (1990). *A vision of the future of policing in Canada: Background document.* Ottawa: Ministry of the Solicitor General of Canada.

Pate, A., Ferrara, A., & Kelling, G. L. (1981). *The Newark foot patrol experiment.* Washington, DC: Police Foundation.

Reiner, R. (1991). *Chief constables: Bobbies, bosses or bureaucrats.* Oxford: Oxford University Press.

R.C.M.P. (1993). *Strategic action plan update, Royal Canadian Mounted Police, 1992-1995.* Ottawa: R.C.M.P., Community and Aboriginal Policing Directorate.

Skolnick, J. H., & Bayley, D. H. (1988). *Community policing: Issues and practices around the world.* Washington, DC: National Institute of Justice.

Walker, C. R. (1987). The community police station: Developing a model. *Canadian Police College Journal, 11*(4), 273-318.

Walker, C. R., & Walker, S. G. (1989). *The Victoria community police stations: An exercise in innovation.* Ottawa: Canadian Police College.

Walker, C. R., Walker, S. G., & McDavid, J. C. (1992). *The Victoria community police station program: A three year review.* Ottawa: Canadian Police College.

Walker, S. G., & Walker, C. R. (1992). The process of developing a program evaluation of a community policing initiative. *Canadian Journal of Program Evaluation, 7*(2), 25-42.

Watt, S. (1991). The future of civilian oversight of policing. *Canadian Journal of Criminology, 33*(3-4), 347-362.

Community Policing on the Ground

Developments in Britain

TREVOR BENNETT

OVER THE PAST 10 YEARS the police service in Britain has undergone a substantial program of reform. This process has been based on a reform agenda drawn up by both the police and the government, who share a common objective of improving the quality of police service and customer satisfaction. Although the publications and official declarations relating to this process use the term *community policing* fairly infrequently, they contain many references to the concept of a greater working partnership between the police and the public.

The impetus for reform can be seen as deriving from a number of different sources. In particular, recent changes can be viewed as the product of the actions and wishes of at least three key groups: (1) the public, (2) the police, and (3) the government.

The Public

The current process of reform can be traced back at least as far as the riots in Brixton, London, in April 1981, which stimulated a substantial reappraisal of the nature of the relationship between the police and the public. This included an official inquiry set up by the Home Secretary and chaired by Lord Scarman to look into the causes of the disorder. The report that followed (the Scarman Report) concluded that some of the cause of the riots in Brixton lay with the police: in particular, unnecessarily "hard" policing in sensitive, multiracial areas and failure to consult the local community over policing matters. The report recommended that statutory liaison committees should be established in all police force areas in order to guard against making the same mistakes again (Scarman, 1986).

The widespread belief (stimulated in part by the Brixton and other riots in Britain during the early 1980s) that public confidence in the police might be declining was confirmed in a supplementary report of the 1988 British Crime Survey (BCS) on the public view of the police (Skogan, 1990). The report noted on its first page that public confidence in the police had declined successively across the last three British Crime Surveys. The surveys of 1982, 1984, and 1988 reported, respectively, that 92%, 90%, and 85% of respondents thought that the police were doing a "good" or "very good" job.

Additional information has been included in recent publications to attempt to confirm the apparent trend in public confidence. Evidence from a survey conducted by the Royal Commission on the Police in 1962 showed that at the time 83% of people interviewed said that they had a "great respect" for the police and most informants said that their opinions had not changed over the last 10 years (HMSO, 1962). Whereas, a recent public survey conducted by an independent research company (MORI) in 1993 revealed that 46% of respondents reported that they had "great respect" for the police ("Crime Wave Boosts Respect," 1993).

These findings and the subsequent discussion have been taken seriously by the police and reaffirmed their belief that a reappraisal of the quality of policing not only was desirable but also would be expected.

The Police

Since the middle of the 1980s police reform has been based on a complex interaction between police and government agendas. The police and the government share a central element of police reform known as the "quality of service" initiative that aims to pay due attention to the wishes and concerns of the public as the "customers" of the police service. However, there is not full agreement on the way in which this should be implemented. The government views quality of service as one element of a broader package of reforms that creates an efficient and effective police service over a range of activities and within a specified budget. The police view quality of service as a major objective of policing that should take priority over financial concerns.

The police emphasis on quality of service as a priority has found expression in two important police publications. The first was a report by the three main police staff associations called the *Operational Police Review* (The Joint Consultative Committee, 1990), which argued that the government's philosophy of economy, efficiency, and effectiveness was undermining the service role of the police. In particular, the report was concerned about the growing importance given to detection rates and response times as major performance indicators of police effectiveness and too little weight given to the less-easy-to-measure service functions of policing.

The second publication was the *ACPO Strategic Policy Document* (ACPO, 1990), which proposed a program of reform as a means of addressing some of the problems revealed in the *Operational Policing Review*. The report made various recommendations including the adoption of a nationwide "statement of common purposes and values" that stressed the police commitment to the core functions of policing, including a willingness to reflect the priorities of the public in the actions they take.

The work of the police on the "quality of service" initiative is continuing (at the time of writing this chapter). In addition to the development of a "statement of common purposes and values" the Association of Chief Police Officers is currently working on a "statement of ethical principles," quality of service performance indicators, and quality of management techniques and training.

The Government

The process of police reform as far as the government is concerned began in the early 1980s with what was referred to as the "Financial Management Initiative," which addressed the issues of efficiency and effectiveness within the public sector services and the extent to which public services were achieving their objectives and "value for money." The general principles of this initiative were applied directly to the police service through a Home Office Circular No. 114/1983 titled "Manpower, Effectiveness, and Efficiency in the Police Service" (Home Office, 1983).

In 1991 the government published a White Paper titled *The Citizen's Charter* (HMSO, 1991), which pledged a commitment to providing quality of service and value for money across a range of public sector services, including the police. In the White Paper the government reported its commitment to community policing and to its aim to provide a police service that met the expectation of the public. It also noted its support for the new managerial approach to policing that required that police managers set (in consultation with the local community) clear priorities and objectives and developed measurable standards to determine the extent to which these objectives had been met.

In June and July 1993 (at the time of writing this chapter), three government sponsored reports were published that aimed to set the character of policing for the 21st century.

The first of these was a White Paper called *Police Reform* that summarized a wide-ranging program of change to the police service (HMSO, 1993b). The report included a number of indirect references to community policing, including a direct statement of support for community policing and its principles. It noted that the government intended to build a partnership between the police and the public and placed crime prevention and reassurance of the community within the main aims of the police service. The main vehicle for implementing this change noted in the report was the enhancement of existing local police authorities that they proposed should elicit the views of the local community about policing priorities and involve the community in collaboration with the police in preventing crime.

The second publication is a report titled *Inquiry into Police Responsibilities and Rewards* (HMSO, 1993a), produced by a government review body chaired by Sir Patrick Sheehy. The report primarily concerned the pay and employment conditions of the police, and its main recommendations included a reduction in the number of ranks, performance-related pay, and fixed-term appointments. Although these proposals are of less direct relevance to community policing than the proposals contained in the White Paper, they have indirect relevance as a result of police reaction to them. The whole report has been strongly criticized by the police at all levels on the grounds that it will serve to undermine the service functions of policing and will result in a reduction in the quality of police service provided to the community. The most recent comments on the progress of reform suggest that it is unlikely that all of the principal recommendations of the report will be implemented ("Police Chiefs Confidant," 1993).

The third publication, the report of the *Royal Commission on Criminal Justice* (HMSO, 1993c), is less directly relevant to the debate about community policing as it concerns primarily criminal procedure rather than on-the-street policing. Nevertheless, it is indirectly relevant in relation to its proposals for reducing the miscarriages of justice and safeguarding the rights of suspects.

It should also be noted that there is currently pressure from the Treasury on the Home Office to privatize some aspects of policing that are not considered "core functions." Some of the measures currently being considered by the government (apart from the existing process of civilianization of office duties) are: hiring private security firms to patrol high-crime housing estates, contracting out some aspects of offense investigation (e.g., interviews with the victims of crime), and hiring private companies to conduct some traffic duties such as motorway surveillance ("Treasury Touts Police Carve-Up," 1993). While these developments may appear unrelated to community policing they are important elements of the current debate about the future of policing in Britain and have served to strengthen the resolve of the police to obtain the support of the community.

What Is Community Policing?

There appears to be some convergence of opinion in the recent literature that community policing is fundamentally a philosophy of policing or a policing paradigm (Ericson, 1992; Trojanowicz & Bucqueroux, 1990). The philosophy is converted into practice through compatible organizational structures and operational strategies. It is generally agreed that these organizational structures and operational strategies do not in themselves represent community policing as they could exist equally well within the context of a different policing philosophy or policing paradigm (Skolnick & Bayley, 1987). However, when they are implemented within a community policing paradigm they become community policing structures and strategies (Trojanowicz & Bucqueroux, 1990).

Some insight can be gained into the philosophy of community policing by looking at what has been said in the literature on the subject. In a general sense the philosophy of community policing is described as a new kind of relationship between the police and the public (Skolnick & Bayley, 1987). The idea that the philosophy should in some sense be "new" is helpful as it distinguishes community policing from preexisting philosophies of policing. For example, community policing should be conceptually distinct from "democratic policing," otherwise it would not justify a new concept to describe it. The idea of the philosophy being based on a kind of relationship between the police and the public is also helpful as it provides guidance on where to look in an attempt to disaggregate (or deconstruct) the concept.

The literature offers a large number of descriptions of the nature of the relationship between the police and the public within community policing. These comments can be categorized into two types of relationship: The first refers to kinds of consultation between the police and the public and the second refers to kinds of collaboration between the police and the public.

The idea of the police consulting members of the public covers a number of policing issues. It can mean that the police listen to the community in order to improve the quality of police service without necessarily affecting operational policing policy (e.g., using the public as a barometer to determine how well they are performing) (Wasserman & Moore, 1988). It can mean that the police listen to the community as a means of determining policing priorities and operational policy (e.g., responding to public concerns and wishes about local problems) (Goldstein, 1990). It can mean that the police listen to the community within a formal system of public accountability (e.g., they explain their actions to the local community) (Skolnick & Bayley, 1987).

The idea of the police collaborating with the community refers to a relationship between the police and the public in which they work together to achieve common goals. The popular expression of this approach in Britain at the moment is the idea of a "partnership" between the police and the public (Home Office, 1991). This concept matches closely the idea of the police and the public becoming "coproducers" of public safety (Skolnick & Bayley, 1987).

The principal elements of the philosophy of community policing as found in the literature are presented in Table 13.1. The table aims to summarize some possible connections between the conceptual and practical elements of community policing. It is proposed in the table that the philosophy of community policing can be subdivided into two key principles: consultation and collabora-

TABLE 13.1 Community Policing Philosophy and Practice

Philosophy	Principles	Goals	Organizational Strategies	General Operational Strategies	Specific Operational Strategies
		Consent			Consultative groups
	Consultation			Community meetings	
		Accountability			Foot patrols, Contact
				Community contact	patrols, Community
Community			Decentralization		constables, Police
policing		Problem			shops, Police surgeries
ideology		identification			
	Collaboration			Community crime	Neighborhood watch,
				prevention	Property marking,
					Security surveys,
					Partnerships
		Problem solving		Proactive policing	Problem-oriented
					policing, Targeted
					patrols

tion. These two principles can then be subcategorized into the primary goals of consultation (which include public consent and accountability) and collaboration (which include problem identification and problem solving).

Hence, on the basis of the descriptions of the relationship between the police and the public found in the literature, the main elements of a community policing philosophy might be summarized in a single sentence as a belief or intention held by the police that they should consult with and take account of the wishes of the public in determining and evaluating operational policing and that they should collaborate with the public in identifying and solving local problems.

The second component of community policing is the police organizational structure. It is widely reported in the literature that some organizational structures are more compatible with community policing than others (Murphy & Muir, 1985). Compatible organizational structures include supportive career and management structures that reward community policing and police attitudes and occupational cultures that accept community policing as a legitimate and desirable form of policing.

One of the most frequently reported organizational structures compatible with community policing is decentralization. It is believed that small command units that have small areas of operation will deliver community policing more effectively than large units with large areas of operation. Despite the fact that the concepts of "small areas" and "large areas" are relative terms (as is the concept of decentralization), it is presumed in this line of thinking that command units that are small enough to police individual communities are better placed than larger units to provide consultation and collaboration with local people.

The final components of community policing are the operational strategies used to implement community policing on the ground. The term *on the ground* is used here to refer both to the practice of the police in Britain to refer to their area of geographic responsibility as "the ground" and also to highlight the fact that police reforms at some point hit "ground level" (at least they should) and address the practical realities of policing.

It has been argued in the literature that there are no policing strategies that are intrinsically community policing strategies. This point has been made by Skolnick and Bayley, who argue that foot patrols need not represent community policing if they are implemented because they are cheaper than vehicle patrols (Skolnick & Bayley, 1987). Nevertheless, there are some programs that are frequently identified by police forces and by police spokespersons as compatible with community policing, including community consultation arrangements, community contact strategies, community crime prevention, and problem-oriented policing.

A hypothesized link between community policing philosophy, organizational structure, and operational strategy is proposed in Table 13.1. The principle of consultation between the police and the public and the related goals of policing by consent and police accountability to the public are logically connected to operational strategies that provide some kind of consultation arrangements for the police and the public. Similarly, the principle of collaboration and the related goals of problem identification and problem solving are logically connected to operational strategies that concern crime prevention and proactive policing. However, the connections between community policing principles and goals and operational strategies are more complex than this, as many operational strategies include elements of both consultation and collaboration.

The aim of this section has been to identify some of the key components of community policing in order to generate a structure for the remainder of the discussion. The following section examines the three main elements of community policing (philosophy, organizational structure, and operational strategies) and considers the extent to which community policing has been implemented in Britain and the extent to which what has been implemented has been effective in achieving its goals.

Community Policing Philosophies

It was suggested in the preceding section that a community policing philosophy might be identified through evidence that the police held a belief or intention that they should consult with and take account of the wishes of the public in determining and evaluating operational policing and should collaborate with the public in identifying and solving local problems. In order to determine whether there is community policing in Britain it would be necessary to determine whether British police held these beliefs or intentions.

One way of identifying policing philosophies is to analyze documentary evidence published by the police, such as police mission statements and police annual reports. Since the publication of the *Operational Policing Review* (The

Joint Consultative Committee, 1990) and the *ACPO Strategic Policy Document* (ACPO, 1990) it is common practice for British forces to publish a mission statement that reflects their overall philosophy of policing. A corporate "statement of common purposes and values" for the whole police service was included in the ACPO document and included a declaration that the police should reflect the priorities of the public in the actions that they take (ACPO, 1990). The ACPO document also proposed that all forces devised their own mission statements that (among other things) emphasized the allegiance of the police to the public.

Police annual reports (published by all 43 police forces in England and Wales) typically include some reference to policing philosophy and (more recently) include a mission statement or police charter. A recent annual report by the Northamptonshire Police, for example, stated: "Our primary aim is to provide a community service which earns the satisfaction, confidence and active support of the public" and concluded, ". . . our approach to policing is a simple implicit contract with the public . . . we are the people who care about people" (Northampton Police, 1990). Another report published by the City of London Police reported that one of the aims of the police was, "To provide a high quality police service . . . and, in cooperation with the community . . . seek to promote a safe, tranquil and crime-free environment" (City of London Police, 1991).

Declarations of support by the police for the principles of consultation and collaboration with the public are frequently made and can be found in most of the more widely distributed documents published by police forces. It is also important, however, to determine the extent to which the official rhetoric of community policing has actually permeated the police culture as a whole. There is no research in Britain that has tackled this problem directly, although there is some related research that suggests that a philosophy of community policing has not yet been fully assimilated.

A recent survey of chief constables of almost all police forces in England and Wales showed that 50% of officers had a broad view of the police role (which included the idea that the police should be concerned with community and social issues), 13% held a narrow view of the police role (which included the idea that the police should be concerned only with crime control and detection), and 35% claimed to stand between these two views. When asked specifically about community policing, 55% declared some support for the notion, whereas 45% thought that it was a meaningless expression. A common view of chief constables was that community policing was no more than traditional policing or "old wine in new bottles" (Reiner, 1991).

Another recent publication that examined police attitudes and behavior concluded that community beat policing was highly unpopular among police constables (McConville & Shepherd, 1992). A common complaint was that community beat work was boring, unglamorous, and disconnected from "real" policing. Many officers interviewed said that they did not want any closer involvement with the community as it would only give them more "hassle." Overall, policing was seen as a collective effort directed toward the restoration of law and order rather than servicing the particular needs of individual communities.

A similar point was made in a recent publication of an ethnographic study based on observations of the police in three police force areas that showed that the attitudes of the police and the dominant occupational culture were shaped primarily by the nature of the encounters that the police had on the street (Norris, 1989). The research reiterated the arguments made by Skolnick that a primary concern of police officers was the avoidance of "trouble" (Skolnick, 1966). Although most encounters with the public did not result in any kind of "trouble," the outcomes of these interactions with the public were unpredictable and any encounter could result in "trouble." As a result police officers tended to develop a view of the public that enabled them to be alert to and respond to unpredictable actions by them. Such attitudes tended to weaken the ability of the police to embrace fully a community-oriented philosophy of policing.

Overall, there is insufficient research evidence to arrive at a strong conclusion on the extent to which British police believe in a community policing philosophy of policing. The evidence that is available, however, suggests that while the philosophy of community policing is widely and publicly proclaimed as a central principle of policing in Britain, the philosophy has not yet become fully integrated into police thinking and beliefs.

Community Policing Organizational Structures

There are a wide range of organizational factors compatible with a community policing philosophy, including participatory management, cultural change, compatible reward structure, awareness training, monitoring and evaluation, compatible rank structures, supervision, and so on. In this section I will discuss just one of these structures that is most frequently reported in the literature as compatible with community policing: decentralization.

In one sense, Britain has always had some kind of decentralized policing. The division of the country into police force areas comprising divisions and subdivisions results in command units that typically cover areas small enough for police officers to get to know in some detail. It has also been common practice for police forces covering large rural areas to deploy detached beat officers to specific villages and other rural locations to work from a police house or other police base to provide a full police service to that area. However, current discussion on decentralization refers to reorganization of a force from large to small command units specifically as a means of improving the quality of policing in local areas (rather than for the administrative convenience of the police).

The main development in Britain over the past few years toward decentralization has been the implementation of sector policing. *Sector policing* is a term used here to cover a number of schemes with slightly different names including: zone policing, neighborhood policing, geographic policing, and grid-square policing. A recent national survey of community-oriented policing found that about one third of all forces had adopted at least one example of sector policing within its police force area (Bennett & Lupton, 1990). It should also be noted that in spring 1993 the Metropolitan Police implemented sector policing force-wide across the whole of the Metropolitan Police District (West, 1992).

In the early 1980s the Metropolitan Police organized a number of pilot programs that were referred to under the general heading of neighborhood policing. One of these schemes in Notting Hill in London was evaluated by the British Police Foundation (Irving, Bird, Hibberd, & Willmore, 1989). The research found substantial evidence of implementation failure at almost all levels of the program. The system of geographic responsibility was resisted by relief (response) officers on the grounds that it undermined reactive cover and manning levels and by home beat officers on the grounds that allocating proactive tasks to relief officers undermined and confused their position. The implementation of graded response was also disliked by lower ranking officers and was eventually abandoned along with the system of computerized management information that failed to be used by the police to inform operational policing. The outcome evaluation of the research showed no change in public attitudes toward the police or toward the area in which they lived. The report also showed that during the course of the experiment there was a slight increase in the number of victimizations and a substantial increase in the number of multiple victimizations. The report concluded that the program failed to overcome the issue of police conservatism and the self-interest of the various policing groups and failed to overcome the strong inertia to change among front-line police officers and junior managers (Irving et al., 1989).

Another independent study of area-based policing in two police forces in the north of England also found evidence that the programs were not fully implemented (Chatterton & Rogers, 1989). The authors reported that changes in the collection and use of information from a largely manual system to a computerized system had the effect of undermining the ability of lower ranking officers to conceal information about their behavior from their supervisors. As a result various resistance tactics were adopted in order to subvert the system, including the submission of brief reports and the use of generalized rather than specific descriptions of their activities.

Another independent evaluation of sector policing in Britain is the study by Bennett and Kemp of sector policing in the Thames Valley Police Force Area (Bennett & Kemp, in press). The evaluation consists of a pretest-posttest design with controls and includes (among other things) crime and public attitude surveys, questionnaire and interview surveys of the police, burglary victim surveys, activity surveys, observations, and telephone interviews with key public informants. The research is not yet completed although it is hoped that a research report will be available early in 1994.

On the basis of the small amount of research on sector policing available in Britain it appears that attempts at decentralization are experiencing similar problems as those experienced by team policing in the United States during the

1970s and 1980s (Sherman, 1990) and in Canada with zone policing during the 1980s and 1990s (Loree, 1988). It is unknown at this stage in the evaluation the extent to which sector policing in the Thames Valley Police Force Area can overcome the problems faced by these earlier schemes.

There are grounds to believe that decentralization in the absence of more fundamental change is unlikely to be effective in achieving either implementation or outcome objectives. This conclusion suggests that attempts to date to implement community policing have been conducted within organizational structures that have undergone either no reform or only partial reform. Although there is a view that community policing operational strategies can be effectively "bolted onto" quite different organizational structures, a more typical view is that in the absence of compatible and supportive organizational structures community policing is unlikely to be implemented effectively.

Community Policing Operational Strategies

There are many policing strategies and tactics that could be compatible with a community policing philosophy. In this section I consider only a small number of some of the most frequently cited examples of each of the four groups of strategies listed in Table 13.1.

Community Meetings

Community meetings constitute community policing (when part of a community policing philosophy) to the extent that they offer an opportunity for the police to consult the public about their policing needs and to account for actions taken by the police.

The recommendations of the Scarman Report to establish statutory liaison committees in all police force areas were enacted in *The Police and Criminal Evidence Act, 1984* (HMSO, 1984). Section 106 of the Act specified that, "Arrangements shall be made in each police area for obtaining the views of the people in that area about matters concerning the policing of the area and for obtaining their co-operation with the police in preventing crime in the area" (HMSO, 1984). In this sense community policing in general and community consultation in particular is a statutory requirement in Britain.

Although the Act did not specify the form of the consultation arrangements, guidelines were issued in the following year in a Home Office Circular that recommended that the police establish police consultative committees (Home Office, 1983). The major research on police consultative committees in England and Wales has been conducted by Morgan and Maggs (Morgan, 1986; Morgan

& Maggs, 1985). The authors concluded that all police authorities had followed Home Office advice and implemented some kind of consultative arrangement in their police force areas. Most police forces had a number of consultative committees with on average one for each division (or subdivision) or (in the case of the Metropolitan Police) one for each borough.

The research examined in detail consultative committees in nine police sub-divisions and showed that in many respects the committees were not working as planned. Meetings were usually poorly attended and were usually held on police premises rather than community premises. The meetings were generally open-ended and unstructured and had no secretarial support or means of taking minutes or notes of the meetings. The community members were disproportion-ately male, middle-class, middle-aged, and existing community activists. Many of the members had little experience of the police or current policing issues and were fairly ignorant of day-to-day policing methods and procedures. As a result the meetings typically took the form of the police educating the community representatives about policing. The majority of the time of the meetings was devoted to police reports about the state of crime in the area and the paucity of police resources. The police accounts were generally accepted by the members (who according to Morgan had no basis to challenge them) and the meetings were generally supportive and sympathetic to the situation of the police.

The consultative committees set up under the Police and Criminal Evidence Act comprise the main form of formal community consultation arrangements in England and Wales. Nevertheless, there are other opportunities for consultation that are less well documented in the literature but should also be acknowledged. All police forces have community involvement officers or race relations officers who are tasked with making contact with the community or specific sections of the community (Phillips & Cochrane, 1988). In addition, all forces operate some form of Neighborhood Watch scheme and many forces now have dedicated Neighborhood Watch liaison officers who coordinate Neighborhood Watch activities in their police force areas. Many forces also have generated mul-tiagency partnerships involving the police, agencies, and sometimes community representatives in devising and implementing crime prevention methods.

There is little research on these informal arrangements for consultation with the community. The national survey found that more than three quarters of all forces had some kind of liaison arrangements involving patrol constables (ar-rangements involving other officers were not recorded) and the community, local businesses, and other professional agencies (Bennett & Lupton, 1990). The police also obtain the views of the public (particularly about their crime con-cerns) through public attitude and victimization surveys and through the use of community profiling techniques that involve the collection and analysis of information reported by the public or from local intelligence gathered by com-munity constables or other officers. However, it is unknown to what extent these arrangements provide an effective forum for consultation between the police and the public.

Community Contact Programs

Community contact strategies span both community consultation and community collaboration. In this section I will comment on just four types of contact strategy that have been the subject of research: community constables, contact patrols, police shops, and police surgeries (similar to storefronts in the United States but operating only a few hours a week).

Community Constables

Community constables are dedicated police officers who are allocated to a particular area (usually a single beat) on a permanent or semipermanent basis with the specific task of providing a full police service to the local community of that area. In practice, their aims and job descriptions are unclear and tend to vary from one force to another. The names given to these officers also tend to vary from force to force and include: home beat officers, area beat officers, community officers, and permanent beat officers. However, there is some agreement in the literature that the work of community constables involves making contact with and speaking to members of the local community, getting to know their area, and generating good police-public relations. It is also acknowledged that some police functions, such as immediate response and some law enforcement work, are conducted in the beat area by general duty officers or by special units and not by community constables.

A recent national survey of community policing in Britain examined (among other things) the work of community constables (Bennett & Lupton, 1992b). The research found that community constables were widely used among forces with all forces reporting at least some officers allocated to these duties. In other respects, however, the community constable scheme suffered from varying degrees of implementation failure. Community constables were withdrawn from their beats for an average of one fifth of their working time to conduct other and unrelated duties in other areas. The results of an embedded activity survey showed that, when community constables were allocated to beat duties, more than one third of their time was spent inside the police station (which in some forces reached in excess of 50% of their total duty time) (Bennett & Lupton, 1992a). The research also found that when outside of the station only a small proportion of their time (less than 10%) was spent on community contact or preventive work.

Contact Patrols

Contact patrols have been included in this section mainly because they have recently been evaluated in two police force areas (Bennett, 1991). Apart from the experiment set up for the purpose of the evaluation there is little evidence of any other use of contact patrols in Britain (with the exception of a separate short-term trial in the Metropolitan Police district; see Murray, 1988).

The main impetus for the British evaluation was an attempt to replicate the citizen contact patrols experiment conducted in Newark and Houston and evaluated by the Police Foundation (Pate, Wycoff, Skogan, & Sherman, 1986). The primary aim of the evaluation was to determine the effectiveness of these programs in reducing fear of crime (as was the case with the Newark and Houston experiments). However, the evaluation also tested the effect of the programs on a range of other outcome variables, including victimization and public confidence in the police.

The contact patrols program was almost identical in the two experimental sites and involved the allocation of a team of four constables and one sergeant to provide a full police service to a single residential area. The two operational elements of the programs were continuous police presence and resident contacts. Continuous police presence involved at least one officer patrolling the area during at least two shifts a day (approximately 16 hours a day). Resident contacts involved the police knocking on the doors of residents in the area and conducting an agreed procedure that involved the officer introducing him- or herself, telling the resident that the police were getting to know people living in the area, asking the resident whether there were any problems in the area that the police might be able to help in solving, telling the resident that he or she could telephone the officer at the local station, and leaving a business card containing the name of the officer and the station telephone number (Bennett, 1991).

The analysis of the implementation effectiveness of the program showed that the program was implemented almost as planned. During the course of the experimental period (one year) the officers had contacted at least 87% of households in each experimental area (the goal was 100%) and had patrolled the area for an average of at least 10 hours a day (the goal was 16 hours a day).

The results of the outcome evaluation showed that the program had no statistically significant effect on crime or fear of crime. However, the evaluation indicated that public confidence in the police increased significantly in both experimental areas during the course of the experiment. In one area the percentage of residents who said that they were "very" or "fairly" satisfied with the police increased from 37% in the pretest survey to 65% in the posttest survey.

Hence, while the evaluation failed to show that contact patrols had a significant impact on crime or fear of crime, it showed that it was possible to implement contact patrols successfully and it was possible to improve public confidence in the police as a result.

Police Shops

The national survey found that more than half of police forces reported using some kind of police shop at the time of the research (Bennett & Lupton, 1990).

Police shops were mainly used in town center areas or in residential areas and had a number of functions.

Police shops used in town center areas (but not in town center shopping areas) typically comprised a base for advertising crime prevention advice or in promoting the latest police crime prevention campaign. The shops were often based in mobile or temporary offices such as caravans or trailers or temporary office accommodation. Police shops in shopping areas were more frequently based in shop or office accommodation within the shopping complex. The main objectives of the shops were to provide a contact point for the general public and to provide a base for policing the area. Police shops in shopping complexes tended to operate only during shopping hours and sometimes opened for just 1 or 2 days a week (e.g., Saturdays). Police shops in residential areas tended to differ from town center and shopping area shops. They were typically based in an empty dwelling or in empty office space within the residential area. Sometimes the accommodation was shared with other local agencies, such as social service departments or probation departments. The main objectives of police shops in housing estates was typically to provide a base for police officers who were permanently allocated to the area. They functioned partly as a mini-station and for the administrative convenience of the police and partly as a contact point for the local community.

There are no published evaluations (to my knowledge) specifically on the use of police shops in Britain. However, there is some evidence and anecdotal information on the use of estates policing strategies in generally (which often include police shops but also include a number of other strategies) and on the use of targeted patrols in shopping and town center areas. The available evidence suggests that policing strategies can be effective in reducing crime and disorder in residential and town center areas but does not disentangle the specific effect of setting up a police shop from other aspects of the program. (The evidence relating to targeted strategies is discussed later in the section on proactive policing.)

Police Surgeries

The national survey found that more than half of police forces reported using a police surgery (similar to storefronts in the United States) at the time of the research (Bennett & Lupton, 1990). Police surgeries differ from police shops to the extent that they are open for just a few hours a week and to the extent that they typically involve just one officer. The officer typically attends the surgery at specified times at which the public are encouraged to visit to discuss local problems. They are compared with doctors' surgeries because they involve the public visiting a particular location for a short period time in order to discuss a particular problem.

There is no evaluative research to my knowledge of the effectiveness of police surgeries. However, there is substantial anecdotal research that suggests that they are ineffective in providing a useful contact point for the public and an effective means of community consultation. It is my experience from conversations with police officers that many forces that have established police surgeries have abandoned them on the grounds that the public do not make use of them.

Overall, there is little evaluative research on community contact strategies and it is not possible to determine at this time the extent to which they are effective in providing an opportunity for effective consultation with the public or the extent to which they are effective in solving community problems (including community fears and perceptions of safety). Nevertheless, there is some research evidence that suggests that when the public are asked about policing priorities they typically request greater police presence and a greater number of foot patrols on the streets (The Joint Consultative Committee, 1990). The finding of the contact patrols evaluation that showed a substantial increase in public confidence in the police following greater contact with the police supports this notion and suggests that at least some outcome goals might be achieved by programs of this kind.

Community Crime Prevention

Community crime prevention is often regarded as the heart of community policing as it comprises a working alliance between the police and the public in the prevention of crime. Although the term may be taken to cover almost any area-oriented (compared with individual-oriented or nation-oriented) initiative, community crime prevention has become associated with just a small number of programs. The most commonly cited programs (when operated at the area level) are: Neighborhood Watch, citizen patrols, home security surveys, property marking, and partnerships between the community and other groups in the prevention of crime. In this section I discuss just one of these programs that has now become the single most prolific community-oriented crime prevention program in Britain: Neighborhood Watch.

At the time of writing it is estimated that there are more than 90,000 Neighborhood Watch schemes in England and Wales (McConville & Shepherd, 1992). The results of the third British Crime Survey (BCS) showed that 90% of the population of England and Wales had heard of Neighborhood Watch and it was estimated that at the beginning of 1988, 14% of households were members of a Neighborhood Watch scheme covering approximately 2½ million households (Mayhew, Elliott, & Dowds, 1989). The BCS report also noted that two thirds of respondents not currently members of a Neighborhood Watch scheme reported that they would be willing to join one if one were set up in their area.

The BCS report also showed that there were marked regional differences in the coverage of Neighborhood Watch schemes throughout the country. Schemes were most common in "affluent suburban areas" and "high-status non-family areas." Conversely, schemes were least common in "less well-off council estates" and in "poor quality older terraced housing" areas. The survey findings also suggest that Neighborhood Watch schemes tend to be most prolific in areas with little crime. High coverage areas tended to have lower burglary risks and low coverage areas tended to have higher burglary risks (with some anomalies in this trend). This latter finding gives some support to the argument that Neighborhood Watch is most frequently found in areas that need it least (although it is unclear what the phrase *need it least* means in this context).

Neighborhood Watch has been evaluated by both the police and by independent researchers. Police research in Britain has tended to produce favorable results in terms of both program implementation and outcome. Studies conducted in Bristol (Veater, 1984), Cheshire (Anderton, 1985), Merseyside (Jenkins & Latimer, 1987), and Stafford (O'Leary & Wood, 1984) each found some reduction in reported crime in the period following the implementation of Neighborhood Watch.

However, independent research in Britain has tended to produce less favorable results. The results of the detailed study of two Neighborhood Watch schemes in London showed that the programs had no impact on victimization rates, reporting rates, or police clear-up rates (although there was a reduction in worry about property crime in one of the Neighborhood Watch areas) (Bennett, 1990). The research concluded that the lack of program impact was a result (at least in part) of program failure and a weak program design that resulted in limited public involvement in it. Apart from attending the launch meeting and perhaps displaying a Neighborhood Watch sticker in their windows, local residents took little further active part in the scheme. The police found it difficult to service the increasing number of Neighborhood Watch schemes in their areas and little extra manpower or other resources were made available to conduct this task. Little encouragement was given to the public (beyond the initial launch meeting) to participate in policing their area, and few residents said that they looked out for anything suspicious or reported anything suspicious to the police.

Nevertheless, there was evidence that both the police and the public liked the schemes. The area coordinator of one of the schemes thought that it had improved the relationship between the police and the community and had brought the community closer together (which was confirmed by the survey analysis of the measures of social cohesion). Most of the street coordinators were convinced that crime had been reduced in their areas over the previous year (even though it had not) and believed that Neighborhood Watch had revitalized the community and had increased a sense of neighborliness. The local home beat officers who worked in the area and who helped administer the schemes enjoyed the fact they were now well known among the community and that the level of public contact had increased (although neither of them thought that the flow of useful information had increased) (Bennett, 1990).

The findings of this research tend to reflect the findings of anecdotal and related evidence. There is no strong evidence that Neighborhood Watch has prevented a single crime in Britain since its inception in the early 1980s, yet it continues to grow in popularity and is now the most widespread community-oriented crime prevention strategy in this country.

However, Neighborhood Watch (and other community crime prevention programs) might be evaluated differently when discussed in the context of the debate about community policing. Neighborhood Watch facilitates the two central principles of community policing: namely an opportunity for consultation and opportunity for collaboration between the police and the public. In this sense Neighborhood Watch helps achieve the related goals of policing by consent and of police accountability. It also helps achieve collaborative problem identification and collaborative problem solving (albeit the problem-solving aspect of the alliance appears at this point not to be helped much by community involvement).

Proactive Policing

Proactive policing (including problem-oriented policing and targeted policing) can be considered community policing when the problems tackled by the police have been discussed and agreed with the local community (at least within the definition of community policing used in this chapter). This might occur when local residents identify a problem and approach the local police (either through consultation arrangements or letter writing) to do something about it. It might also occur when the local police identify a problem and approach the local community in order to obtain their consent to tackle the problem.

The national survey of community-oriented policing identified a large number of strategies currently in use by the police as a means of targeting particular local problems (Bennett & Lupton, 1990). These strategies include "crackdowns" and "crime attack" strategies of the kind noted by Sherman (1986) and "focused" and "directed" patrols of the kind noted by Burrows and Lewis (1988). The national survey identified almost 500 strategies (including duplications) operating at the time of the research and reported to us by the police. Following the categorization used by Sherman (1992) it was possible to group these strategies into four categories: location-oriented strategies, offense-oriented strategies, offender-oriented strategies, and victim-oriented strategies.

Approximately half of these strategies could be described as location-oriented or "hot spots" strategies and covered five main types of locations (town center areas, residential areas, specific public places, out-of-town areas, and other high-crime areas. Town center strategies included patrols allocated to town center areas generally (such as high-profile patrols and late night saturation patrols) and patrols allocated specifically to shopping centers (such as police shops, police teams, and high-profile patrols). Residential area patrols comprised police teams, high-profile patrols, and general purpose patrols. Public place strategies typically involved the allocation of officers to specific high-risk locations such as single buildings or single locations (such as hospital complexes and public parks). Locational strategies aimed at out-of-town areas typically focused on specific villages and often focused on the village green area as a place where youths hang about. Other high-risk area strategies include all other location-oriented strategies that are directed at particular geographic crime clusters (e.g., a spate of robberies outside an underground railway station entrance).

There are very few evaluations of proactive or problem-oriented policing strategies in Britain. The only studies that could be found covered a rather wide and diverse field. One of the classic crackdown studies was conducted by Ross following the implementation of legislation in England and Wales in 1967 that allowed the police to take blood alcohol tests from drivers who were driving in a way that aroused police suspicion. The evaluation showed a substantial reduction in traffic deaths and serious injuries (Ross, 1981).

Other studies of targeted and problem-oriented policing strategies have shown some evidence of success. Matthews evaluated a policing initiative in the early 1980s in London that involved assigning a special vice unit to a residential area that had become the site for prostitutes to gather to pick up clients (Matthews, 1986). The author reported substantial reductions in "curb-crawling" and reductions in the number of prostitutes working in the area. A study of policing an alcohol-free zone in the city center of Coventry in England showed a reduction in the number of incivilities reported in the area (Ramsey, 1990). A recent policing strategy code named Operation Trident, which targeted a prominent drug dealing area of Notting Hill in London, resulted in drug dealers being driven from the area (Dorn, Murji, & South, 1992). A recent report of an attempt by Cambridge Police to target the local city-center shopping area to tackle the problem of drunks and drug users and "down-and-outs" who used the site as a place to congregate during the day showed a preventative effect. The police reported that following the implementation of the program the number of burglaries in the area was almost eliminated and the incidence of aggressive begging was reduced ("City-Centre Crime Squad a Success," 1992).

There are no published evaluations in Britain of problem-oriented policing of the kind discussed by Goldstein (1990) and Eck and Spelman (1987). However, the sector policing program in Thames Valley Police Force Area described earlier included problem-oriented policing as its operational arm and the evaluation of this program will include an assessment of this component and the specific programs that derive from it.

Although there are few evaluations in Britain of the effectiveness of proactive policing targeted at specific local problems, the small amount of research that is available provides some evidence of success in reducing crime and other problems. It is clearly too early to draw any strong conclusions from these findings. Nevertheless, on the basis of the available research to date, it does seem that strategies that involve the police working largely alone (e.g., targeted strategies) are more effective than strategies that involve the police working in collaboration with the community (e.g., Neighborhood Watch). It is possible that the contribution of the community to crime prevention and problem solving is not through collaboration arrangements whereby they engage in joint actions with the police but through consultation arrangements whereby they identify problems and provide the police with information that might assist them in their solution.

Conclusions

This chapter has considered the extent to which policing in Britain is community policing and the extent to which those elements considered to be community policing are effective in achieving useful outcomes.

The introduction to the chapter argued (in line with many contemporary discussions on this topic) that community policing is essentially a philosophy of policing. This philosophy can be converted into policing practice through compatible organizational structures and compatible operational strategies. The introduction also argued that the philosophy of community policing was based on the principles of consultation and collaboration between the police and the public as a means of informing and directing operational policing and as a means of making policing accountable and acceptable to the public.

The evidence suggests that at the level of official discourse and policing policy the philosophy of policing in Britain is strongly connected with the principles of community policing despite the fact that the phrase is hardly ever used in official publications. There is less evidence, however, that community policing is part of the police working philosophy or occupational culture.

Despite this slowness in assimilating community policing philosophies into the police occupational culture, there is some evidence that the police in Britain have implemented organizational structures and operational strategies compatible with community policing. Recent experiments in sector policing have resulted in police command units small enough to provide a local police service to the sector area. In addition, evidence from the national survey of the use of operational strategies shows that British police are using a wide range of programs typically associated with community policing.

Evaluations of the level of implementation of these programs and the degree of effectiveness that they achieve in terms of achieving policing outcomes have been disappointing. The more advanced systems of sector policing that require substantial restructuring of forces and ultimately change in the culture of policing have tended to be resisted or even sabotaged by front-line and lower ranking officers. Perhaps as a direct result of this there is little evidence to date of decentralization leading to any useful outcome goals.

The evidence relating to operational strategies is more mixed. The newer and more innovative programs (such as statutory community liaison arrangements) have proved to be difficult to implement effectively (although in terms of numbers they have been implemented well). Research on community contact strategies and community crime prevention has tended to show that while the police and the public like them and feel that there are a number of benefits to be derived from them they have rarely been found (in Britain) to have any major impact on crime or fear of crime. Research on proactive policing has tended to produce more encouraging findings with many of the published evaluations showing some crime preventive effect.

From the research evidence available it is not possible to arrive at any strong conclusions on the state and prospects of community policing in Britain. Nevertheless, it is possible to draw some tentative conclusions from the research to date. These conclusions would almost certainly have to be modified as more and better research becomes available.

First, it is questionable from the research cited whether collaboration between the police and the community (in the sense of working together) is able to prevent crime. There is little research evidence that shows that the public can control crime at an area level. Second, the review of policing strategies suggests that the greatest recorded successes appear to have come from strategies involving the police working without community collaboration. These strategies involve a combination of traditional law enforcement policing methods and more innovative problem-oriented approaches. Third, one of the most important benefits of contact strategies and community crime prevention strategies appear to be the subjective experiences of the process of contact and consultation rather than more objective outcomes. Fourth, imposed consultation arrangements appear to be implemented less well and work less well than locally generated and voluntary arrangements.

On the basis of these four conclusions (and bearing in mind their limitations) it could be argued that some components of community policing are more feasible and more productive than others. It would appear that community policing can work well as a means of providing contact and consultation between the police and the public and as a means of identifying community problems and providing a policing agenda that can be assessed and approved by the local community. However, there are fewer grounds to believe that the public can work with the police in an effective way in terms of devising problem-solving strategies or in terms of engaging in joint actions with the police in implementing them.

References

ACPO. (1990). *ACPO strategic policy document: Setting the standards for policing: Meeting community expectations. Report of an ACPO Working Party.* London: Author.

Anderton, K. J. (1985). *The effectiveness of home watch schemes in Cheshire.* Cheshire: Cheshire Constabulary.

Bennett, T. H. (1990). *Evaluating neighbourhood watch.* Aldershot: Gower.

Bennett, T. H. (1991). The effectiveness of a police-initiated fear reducing strategy. *British Journal of Criminology, 31*(1), 1-14.

Bennett, T. H., & Kemp, C. (in press). *An evaluation of area-based problem-oriented policing in Thames Valley Police Force area* (Report to the Home Office Research and Planning Unit). Cambridge: Institute of Criminology.

Bennett, T. H., & Lupton, R. (1990). *National review of community-oriented patrols: Report* (Report to the Home Office Research and Planning Unit). Cambridge: Institute of Criminology.

Bennett, T. H., & Lupton, R. (1992a). A national activity survey of police work. *The Howard Journal of Criminal Justice, 31*(3), 200-223.

Bennett, T. H., & Lupton, R. (1992b). A survey of the allocation and use of community constables in England and Wales. *British Journal of Criminology, 32*(2), 167-182.

Burrows, J., & Lewis, H. (1988). *Directing patrol work: A study of uniformed policing* (Home Office Research Study 99). London: HMSO.

Chatterton, M., & Rogers, M. (1989). Focused policing. In R. Morgan & D. J. Smith (Eds.), *Coming to terms with policing* (pp. 64-81). London: Routledge & Kegan Paul.

City-centre crime squad a success. (1992, December 30). *Cambridge Weekly News,* p. 12.

City of London Police. (1991). *Annual report 1991.* London: Author.

Crime wave boosts respect. (1993, July 25). *Sunday Times,* New Review Section, p. 6.

Dorn, N., Murji, K., & South, N. (1992). *Traffickers: Drug markets and law enforcement.* London: Routledge & Kegan Paul.

Eck, J. E., & Spelman, W. (1987). *Problem solving: Problem-oriented policing in Newport News.* Washington, DC: Police Executive Research Forum.

Ericson, R. (1992, September). *Community policing as communications policing.* Paper presented at a conference at the University of Heidelberg, Heidelberg, Germany.

Goldstein, H. (1990). *Problem-oriented policing.* London: McGraw-Hill.

HMSO. (1962). *Royal Commission on the Police 1962: Final report* (Command 1728). London: Author.

HMSO. (1984). *Police and Criminal Evidence Act, 1984.* London: Author.

HMSO. (1991). *The citizens charter: Raising the standard* (Government White Paper, Command 1599). London: Author.

HMSO. (1993a). *Inquiry into police responsibilities and rewards. Report* (Vol. 1) (Command 2280.I). London: Author.

HMSO. (1993b). *Police reform: A police service for the twenty-first century* (Government White Paper, Command 2281). London: Author.

HMSO. (1993c). *The Royal Commission on Criminal Justice. Report* (Command 2263). London: Author.

Home Office. (1983). *Manpower, effectiveness and efficiency in the police service* (Circular 114/1983). London: Author.

Home Office. (1991). *Safer communities: The local delivery of crime prevention through the partnership approach* (Morgan Report). London: Standing Conference on Crime Prevention.

Irving, B., Bird, C., Hibberd, M., & Willmore, J. (1989). *Neighbourhood policing: The natural history of a policing experiment.* London: The Police Foundation.

Jenkins, A. D., & Latimer, I. (1987). *Evaluation of Merseyside home watch.* Liverpool: Merseyside Police.

The Joint Consultative Committee. (1990). *Operational policing review.* Surrey: Author.

Loree, D. (1988). Innovation and change in a regional police force. *Canadian Police College Journal, 12*(4), 205-239.

Matthews, R. (1986). Policing prostitution: A multi-agency approach. London: Middlesex Polytechnic, Centre for Criminology.

Mayhew, P., Elliott, D., & Dowds, L. (1989). *The 1988 British crime survey* (Home Office Research Study 111). London: HMSO.

McConville, M., & Shepherd, D. (1992). *Watching police watching communities.* London: Routledge & Kegan Paul.

Morgan, R. (1986). Policing by consent: Legitimating the doctrine. In D. J. Smith & R. Morgan (Eds.), *Coming to terms with policing* (pp. 217-234). London: Routledge & Kegan Paul.

Morgan, R., & Maggs, C. (1985). Setting the P.A.C.E.: Police community consultation arrangements in England and Wales. Bath: University of Bath, Centre for the Analysis of Social Policy.

Murphy, C., & Muir, G. (1985). *Community based policing: A review of the critical issues.* Ottawa: Solicitor General of Canada.

Murray, J. D. (1988). Contact policing and the role of the constable. *Police Journal, 61*(1), 76-90.

Norris, C. (1989). Avoiding trouble: The patrol officer's perception of encounters with the public. In M. Weatheritt (Ed.), *Police research: Some future prospects* (pp. 89-106). Avebury: Aldershot.

Northampton Police. (1990). *Annual report 1989.* Northampton: Author.

O'Leary, J. M., & Wood, G. (1984). *A review of the experimental Neighbourhood Watch Scheme Holmcroft/Tillington.* Stafford: Staffordshire Constabulary.

Pate, A., Wycoff, M. A., Skogan, W., & Sherman, L. W. (1986). *Reducing fear of crime in Houston and Newark: A summary report.* Washington, DC: Police Foundation.

Phillips, S. V., & Cochrane, R. (1988). *The role and function of police community liaison officers* (Home Office Research and Planning Unit Paper 51). London: Home Office.

Police chiefs confident of compromise over Sheehy. (1993a, April 28). *Guardian,* p. 6.

Ramsey, M. (1990). *Lagerland lost: An experiment in keeping drinkers off the streets in Coventry* (Home Office Crime Prevention Unit Paper 22). London: Home Office.

Reiner, R. (1991). *Chief constables.* Oxford: Oxford University Press.

Ross, H. L. (1981). *Deterring the drinking driver: Legal policy and social control.* Lexington, MA: D. C. Heath.

Scarman, L. G. (1986). *The Scarman report: The Brixton disorders 10-12 April 1981.* London: Penguin.

Sherman, L. (1986). Police communities: What works? In A. Reiss & M. Tonry (Eds.), *Crime and justice: A review of research: Vol. 8. Communities and crime* (pp. 343-386). Chicago: University of Chicago Press.

Sherman, L. (1990). Police crackdowns: Initial and residual deterrence. In M. Tonry & N. Morris (Eds.), *Crime and justice: A biannual review of research* (Vol. 12, pp. 1-48). Chicago: University of Chicago Press.

Sherman, L. (1992). Policing and crime control. In M. Tonry & N. Morris (Eds.), *Crime and justice: A review of research: Vol. 15. Modern policing* (pp. 159-230). Chicago: University of Chicago Press.

Skogan, W. G. (1990). *The police and public in England and Wales: A British crime survey report* (Home Office Research Study 117). London: HMSO.

Skolnick, J. H. (1966). *Justice without trial.* London: John Wiley.

Skolnick, J. H., & Bayley, D. H. (1987). Theme and variation in community policing. In M. Tonry & N. Morris (Eds.), *Crime and justice: A biannual review of research* (Vol. 10, pp. 1-37). Chicago: University of Chicago Press.

Treasury touts police carve-up. (1993, April 7). *Guardian,* p. 2.

Trojanowicz, R., & Bucqueroux, B. (1990). *Community policing: A contemporary perspective.* Cincinnati: Anderson.

Veater, P. (1984). *Evaluation of Kingsdown Neighbourhood Watch Project Bristol.* Bristol: Avon and Somerset Constabulary.

Wasserman, R., & Moore, M. H. (1988). *Values in policing. NIJ.* Washington, DC: Government Printing Office.

West, A. (1992). *Briefing note: Sector policing* [Press release.] London: Metropolitan Police.

PART

VI

Current Issues and Concerns

(14)

Can Today's Police Organizations Effectively Implement Community Policing?

ROY R. ROBERG

THE PURPOSE OF THIS CHAPTER is to briefly examine whether police organizations in the United States can effectively implement community policing in the near future. It is clear that a definitional problem exists, thus making it difficult to determine who is actually "doing" community policing and how it has been (and will be) evaluated. Thus, some common definition regarding the concept must be determined if one is rationally to discuss its chances for success.

Although the problem of definition will not be debated here, it is recognized that community-oriented and problem-oriented policing are two distinct strategies, with the former more concerned with establishing a working relationship with the community and the latter more concerned with identifying and solving community problems (Moore & Trojanowicz, 1988). It is believed, however, that in order for community policing to be a truly effective approach the police must do both, that is, *work in close cooperation with the community in an attempt to solve mutually defined problems.* In other words, the community must participate with the police in identifying its problems and in suggesting solutions to these problems. It is from this framework that community policing will be defined and its potential for successful implementation analyzed.

Assumptions About Community Policing

In order to address this topic adequately, it is further important to understand the foundation, or underlying assumptions, on which the community policing concept is based. In a review of the literature, Riechers and Roberg (1990) identified 10 assumptions for the successful implementation of community policing. Several of these assumptions have serious implications for police-community interactions and community control, including whether the police should be responsible for actively helping to define and shape community norms, and whether community policing can be accomplished without violating the political neutrality of the police. Several other assumptions relating to the police organization itself were discussed; these included whether paramilitary police agencies can adapt to the more flexible organizational structure and managerial style that is required and whether the current qualifications of personnel—especially with respect to higher education—are sufficient to meet the increased demands and complex skill levels required by community policing.

In this analysis, only those assumptions relating directly to the police organization itself will be discussed. This does not mean, however, that the other assumptions, especially those of defining community, shaping community norms, and political neutrality, should not be addressed and resolved by the police and the communities they serve.

Obstacles to Implementing Community Policing

There are several internal factors that pose serious challenges for the police in their attempt to implement community policing. There is tremendous variety in the nation's police forces with respect to size, structure, and quality of personnel. In general, however, they are paramilitary in structure with highly bureaucratic managerial orientations, their training curricula and reward structure are based primarily on law enforcement activities and emphasize strict adherence to rules and regulations, and they require only a high school diploma for the initial selection of their personnel.

Police Organization and Management

Given the history of traditional policing practices, whether police agencies can adapt their paramilitary structures and bureaucratic managerial orientations to accommodate the requirements of a community policing approach is of paramount importance. Community policing requires a significant change in the philosophy and culture of policing, toward a more open and democratic orientation, and a redefinition and broadening of the police role. Such an orientation requires an organic organizational design (i.e., low-structured, nonauthoritarian) and participatory management style (i.e., one that empowers line personnel). Role emphasis would focus on defining community problems and creative ways in which to solve these problems, with significant input from the community in this process.

The reward structure in most contemporary police departments will also need to be substantially altered if community policing is to be viable; problem-solving and order maintenance activities will need to receive as much, if not more, attention as law enforcement functions. Concomitantly, strict adherence to rules and regulations will need to give way to rewarding innovative thinking and creative ways of working with the community and solving problems. Some agencies that have adopted community policing concepts have already moved in this direction. In the Newport News Police Department (Virginia), for instance, first-line supervisors incorporate problem-solving activities by patrol officers into their performance evaluations (Goldstein, 1990).

Training curricula, which currently emphasize law enforcement activities, will need to be redefined, with a greater emphasis placed on problem identification, program development and evaluation, and the management of community groups and resources. Furthermore, training methodologies tend to be dominated by a pedagogical teaching style, emphasizing a one-way transfer of knowledge based on lectures, memorization, and "absolute solutions" to problems based on the memorized materials. Undoubtedly, substantial movement will need to be made toward a more andragogical style of teaching, which emphasizes a two-way transfer of knowledge (i.e., between the student and trainer) based on analytical reasoning, alternative decision making, and problem solving (Roberg, 1979). Such training relies heavily on group or seminar style discussions and role playing.

Police Personnel

In undertaking the complex job of community policing, officers are expected to have the skills to identify problems and to help find solutions to these problems by using both department and community resources, including those of other governmental agencies. The skills required for such an approach include problem conceptualization, data collection (primarily through surveys) and analysis, development of action plans, program evaluation, and the communication of results. Skills such as these are undoubtedly enhanced by, and may even require, a college education. One national study (Carter, Sapp, & Stephens, 1989) indicated that only 14% of the reporting agencies required any education beyond the high school level. Of course, many departments have a substantial number of officers with college degrees (22.6% of the officers in the above survey had degrees). However, it could be persuasively argued that if community policing is to have any chance at national success—and the field is to become a true profession—a college degree will need to become more than just a "nicety" for upwardly mobile police officers. While arguments can be made that such a requirement might hamper minority recruitment, there are many ways in which this potential dilemma can be addressed, while progressing toward the goal of a college educated force (Carter et al., 1989).

In discussing any change toward community policing it must be recognized that the average line officer has been recruited, trained, and socialized in a traditional law enforcement orientation. In other words, they have a strong "stake" in maintaining the status quo in the organization. This does not suggest that there would not be many officers who would welcome their "new" role, and even relish the changes, as the possibilities for job enrichment are substantial. However, it is likely that there would also be many with a strong law enforcement orientation who would be much harder to persuade. In addition, there is a strong socialization process that has spawned a "street cops" culture (Reuss-Ianni, 1983) that tends to be distrustful of management and consequently may work against the implementation of any new philosophies or programs proposed by management.

Successful implementation of community policing will depend on how well mid-level police managers, most of whom have based their careers on traditional policing, accept such changes. It has been well documented that the team policing experiments failed, to a large extent, because of mid-level managers' reluctance to accept the proposed changes in philosophy and operating style (Schwartz & Clarren, 1977; Sherman, Milton, & Kelley, 1973). Although, as Eck (in press) points out, current managers have the advantage of the popular management literature that is more supportive of flattening police hierarchy and decentralizing authority, and other types of constructive changes associated with contemporary corporate management practice.

Mid-level police managers may also have some concerns, as did team policing managers, with respect to the loss of control, accountability, and potential for corruption. In addition, because many departments have been undergoing some type of organizational or operational "change" since the mid- to late 1960s, additional changes—especially of the magnitude required by community policing—may be viewed by today's police managers with a degree of cynicism, or a "here we go again" attitude. Although this would not be too surprising, it does not mean that such attitudes cannot be overcome. But it should be recognized that where a general attitude of cynicism with respect to organizational change has developed, the process will simply be that much more difficult. Because the degree of change is so great, these managers will need to do more than simply "buy into" this new style of policing; they will also need to become effective change agents and "cheerleaders," promoting innovation and the philosophy and principles of community policing.

Finally, the critical role played by training personnel, who must be open to innovative training methods promoting the techniques and ideals of community policing, should not be overlooked. A new philosophy and culture in policing simply cannot evolve if the proper foundation is not laid through recruit and in-service training.

Implementing Changes Required by Community Policing

Attempting to implement changes of the magnitude described above in those agencies that are highly structured and bureaucratic in nature will be a painstaking, long-term undertaking; such departments will most likely require 10 or more years for full implementation (including changes in philosophy and culture). This suggests that such changes will need to be well planned and incremental in nature; "quick" changes toward a community policing "style" just to be in vogue will ultimately fail. And it is problematic whether police executives can sustain the new course of action for the necessary period of time.

Perhaps due to the amount of time required to change police organizations to the degree necessary to implement community policing properly and/or the manner in which it has been implemented, the scant amount of empirical evidence available on the topic tends to be negative in nature. For instance, Greene and Taylor's (1988) review of the major studies on the effectiveness of community policing indicated no support for either reducing crime or the fear of crime, and Skogan (1990) makes the point that community organizing efforts are least likely to help those communities that need it the most (i.e., the most disorganized and deteriorated). In addition, Mastrofski (1983) discovered that citizens are more likely to be pleased with police responses to non-crime-related incidents (e.g., order maintenance) and are more likely to be displeased with police responses to serious crime incidents. Because low-income minority communities are often characterized by serious crime problems, there may be a limit to which the police, regardless of their approach, can satisfy low-income communities.

Evaluations of major programs in the Houston and New York Police Departments provide further evidence of the difficulty of attempting to implement community policing in a relatively short period of time. In Houston, an independent audit by Cresap Management Consultants of Neighborhood Oriented Policing (NOP), noted a number of operational problems, including: officers being torn between immediate reports of crime and preventive work required by community policing, being unprepared for their new tasks, too few supervisors, and skepticism and even hostility by many departmental members toward the program's aims. The report stated that it is unlikely that the department can recruit a force in which most officers have the level of complex skills required to do community policing, particularly at current pay levels. The president of the Houston Police Officers Association, Doug Elder, agreed that many officers were having difficulty incorporating the philosophy of community policing into their daily work. Elder stated, "I think most officers feel it's a hoax, renaming things and using a lot of buzz words and the like," and "I think a lot of officers probably feel they're expected to be more like social workers than police officers" ("Study Criticizes Community Policing," 1991, p. B2).

The evaluation of New York's Community Police Officer Program (CPOP) indicated many of the same types of problems as addressed by the Houston report (McElroy, Cosgrove, & Sadd, 1993). For instance, under recommendations for improving CPOP the authors suggest the following: intensify training for CPOs (community police officers) and CPOP sergeants; disseminate information about successful problem-solving strategies; encourage the involvement of a representative body of citizens within each beat; help strengthen the capacity of the community to participate actively; strengthen the integration of CPOP in the precincts; and ensure that the principles of CPOP are made a prominent part of training, testing, and performance assessments. The authors noted the importance of mid-level managers in the change process and stated that while they believed community policing is the desired direction, that police administrators "embarking on this course should know that, however they enter the process, they will be forced to think through its impact on *every element* of the organization" (McElroy et al., 1993 p. 186, emphasis added).

Indicating just how accurate this statement is, a critical report by a Brooklyn community group in New York's model community policing precinct, said that residents were frustrated because officers were frequently removed from their beats to respond to emergencies or reassigned to other duties ("NYC's Community Police Officers," 1993). Furthermore, it was becoming clear that officers had not received adequate training. Although current recruits receive workshop training in community policing at the academy, officers hired prior to 1991 have only had an orientation course and must attempt to learn from fellow officers and supervisors, many of whom have also not received any in-depth training. The deputy commissioner for training said she plans to take officers off the streets for 2-day classroom instruction on community policing ("NYC's Community Police Officers," 1993). This example indicates the difficulty departments have in providing time to train personnel in community policing concepts; it goes without saying that a substantially greater amount of time would be necessary in order to train officers adequately for community policing responsibilities.

On a more optimistic note, there have been some positive evaluation results from departments implementing community policing concepts in experimental areas or beats, for example, in Baltimore County (Hayeslip & Cordner, 1987) and Baltimore, Maryland (Pate, 1989), and Seattle, Washington (Fleissner, Fedan, Stotland, & Klinger, 1991). In Newport News, Virginia, a problem-oriented approach was implemented agency-wide with encouraging results (Eck & Spelman, 1987). In addition, a report issued on the community/quality policing experiences of the Madison, Wisconsin, department appears promising (Couper & Lobitz, 1991). And there are literally hundreds, if not thousands, of police accounts throughout the country—provided by various types of in-house publications—reporting their successes with community policing. It is important to consider, of course, how well such reports would hold up under serious evaluation.

Implications for the Future

Interestingly, despite the obstacles and empirical evidence cautioning against rapid progression toward a new paradigm, community policing, in one form or another, appears to be a "done deal." For example, President Clinton's fiscal year budget proposal for 1994 calls for $50 million to provide assistance directly to state and local governments and police agencies to promote and implement community policing (Drug Enforcement Report, 1993). The proposed budget also provides for $25 million to establish a Police Corps by providing educational assistance to students interested in pursuing a career in law enforcement. This type of program, along with the more professional approach inherent in community policing, should help to attract more highly educated individuals into the field and thus facilitate the transition of departments to community policing.

Because the community policing "movement" has become so strong, the question of whether it can be effectively implemented becomes a crucial one. This question is important because if departments attempt to implement community policing too quickly, without establishing a proper foundation, the results may create problems for both the department and the community. From the agency's perspective, organizational chaos and dysfunctional behavior could occur, and from the community's perspective, unequal norm enforcement or lack of political neutrality could result (e.g., see Short [1983] for her experiences with these problems in England).

Because the community policing movement is already well established, and because of the potential benefits such an approach offers, not only to the field of policing but to society as well, it should undoubtedly be encouraged—but with *caution*. Due to the potential harmful effects of misguided efforts, either intentional or unintentional, community policing should be supported only if it is properly defined, implemented, and evaluated (preferably by outside sources). It is important for police scholars, police executives, and community members to realize that some departments are more advanced than others (i.e., more organic in nature with more highly educated personnel), and that the more advanced departments can begin implementing community policing more quickly. Other, less advanced departments will need to be more cautious and move more slowly, while still other departments should maintain the status quo until they become more organic in nature before attempting any movement at all. Due to the potential serious side effects that may accrue from unprepared departments attempting to move too quickly into community policing, it is crucial to understand that, in general, "going slow" in order to establish a proper foundation is a necessary requirement for successful change.

This suggests that although the "implementation" of community policing appears to be a done deal, we should keep in mind that the development and quality of this approach will be uneven over the coming years. In the short term, with the definition of community policing used here, most departments throughout the country are not yet ready to assume the responsibilities required from such an approach. It is likely that a continuum of departments will develop. For those departments that are not ready to move fully into community policing, but think they are, definitional problems will surely abound, since they will be "doing" community policing according to their (e.g., the chief's) definition. Such a situation is potentially harmful because the police role will continue to be based on a "crime fighter," "we versus they" mentality, but cloaked in a "new" approach to policing. In other words, "traditional police agendas could continue to be pursued at the expense of developing genuine community rapport and problem solving capabilities" (Roberg & Kuykendall, 1993, p. 442).

It appears that the bottom line with respect to the successful implementation of community policing, as defined, can be tied directly to the amount of progress made toward: (a) organic organizational designs and managerial styles, (b) higher educational standards, and (c) redefinition of the training and reward structures. In the final analysis, the answer to the question of whether today's police organizations can effectively implement community policing is: "It all depends." It all depends on how advanced the department is at this particular point in time; the more advanced the department, the more quickly it can adapt a community policing approach.

Given the high skill levels and innovative methods required by community policing, however, until the field adequately addresses the requirements listed above, this approach can be effectively implemented by only a small number of "elite" departments throughout the country. The departments that do not address these requirements and are therefore unable to change their philosophy and culture will continue with the status quo; they may be able to achieve limited, programmatic efforts toward community policing, but they will not be able to transition to a "true" community policing model.

References

Carter, D. L., Sapp, A. D., & Stephens, D. W. (1989). *The state of police education: Policy directions for the 21st century.* Washington, DC: Police Executive Research Forum.

Couper, D. C., & Lobitz, S. H. (1991). *Quality policing: The Madison experience.* Washington, DC: Police Executive Research Forum.

Drug enforcement report. (1993). President proposes federal and state law enforcement partnerships. April 23.

Eck, J. E. (in press). Alternative futures for policing. In E. Weisburd & C. Uchida (Eds.), *Police innovation and control of the police.* New York: Springer.

Eck, J. E., & Spelman, W. (1987). *Problem-solving: Problem-oriented policing in Newport News: Research in brief.* Washington, DC: National Institute of Justice.

Fleissner, D., Fedan, N., Stotland, E., & Klinger, D. (1991). *Community policing in Seattle.* Washington, DC: National Institute of Justice.

Goldstein, H. (1990). *Problem-oriented policing.* Philadelphia: Temple University Press.

Greene, J. R., & Taylor, R. B. (1988). Community-based policing and foot patrol: Issues of theory and evaluation. In J. R. Greene & S. D. Mastrofski (Eds.), *Community policing: Rhetoric or reality* (pp. 195-223). New York: Praeger.

Hayeslip, P. W., Jr., & Cordner, G. W. (1987). The effects of community-oriented patrol on police officer attitudes. *American Journal of Police, 6,* 95-119.

Mastrofski, S. (1983). The police and non-crime services. In G. P. Whitaker & C. C. Phillips (Eds.), *Evaluating performance of criminal justice agencies* (pp. 33-61). Beverly Hills, CA: Sage.

McElroy, J. E., Cosgrove, C. A., & Sadd, S. (1993). *Community policing: The CPOP in New York.* Newbury Park, CA: Sage.

Moore, M. H., & Trojanowicz, R. C. (1988). *Corporate strategies for policing.* Washington, DC: National Institute of Justice.

NYC's community police officers aren't adequately trained for their new mission. (1993, March). *Law Enforcement News,* p. 15.

Pate, A. M. (1989). Community-oriented policing in Baltimore. In D. J. Kenney (Ed.), *Police and policing: Contemporary issues* (pp. 112-135). New York: Praeger.

Reuss-Ianni, E. (1983). *Two cultures of policing: Street cops and management cops.* New Brunswick, NJ: Transaction Books.

Riechers, L. M., & Roberg, R. R. (1990). Community policing: A critical review of underlying assumptions. *Journal of Police Science and Administration, 17,* 105-114.

Roberg, R. R. (1979). *Police management and organizational behavior: A contingency approach.* St. Paul, MN: West.

Roberg, R. R., & Kuykendall, J. (1993). *Police and society.* Belmont, CA: Wadsworth.

Schwartz, A. T., & Clarren, S. N. (1977). The Cincinnati team policing experiment: A summary report. Washington, DC: Police Foundation.

Sherman, L. W., Milton, C. H., & Kelley, T. V. (1973). *Team policing: Seven case studies.* Washington, DC: Police Foundation.

Short, C. (1983). Community policing—Beyond slogans. In T. Bennett (Ed.), *The future of policing* (pp. 67-81). Cambridge: Institute of Criminology.

Skogan, W. G. (1990). *Disorder and decline: Crime and the spiral of decay in American neighborhoods.* New York: Free Press.

Study criticizes community policing. (1991, August 8). *The New York Times,* p. B2.

15

The Future of Community Policing

ROBERT C. TROJANOWICZ

COMMUNITY POLICING is being touted as the cure-all for the problems within and without the criminal justice system. It is not a panacea. There are many obstacles and challenges in order for community policing to become a viable catalyst for changing public policy in the near future.

The future of community policing includes both its past and its present. There is much to be learned from the past: values that were conducive to mutual help and assistance, sustained personal relationships because of common interests, and a vision of achieving the "American dream" through hard work and perseverance.

The theories that form the basis for community policing, Normative Sponsorship Theory and Critical Social Theory, were more easily operationalized in the past: Normative Sponsorship Theory emphasizing problem solving through shared values and a *community of interest,* and Critical Social Theory requiring *enlightened* and *empowered* citizens and police officers, so that *emancipation* results (Fay, 1987; Sower, 1957; Trojanowicz, 1992).

The present has taught us that social problems are complex, communities are diverse, and problem solving is driven by social upheaval within the context of economic hard times.

Community policing's future is dependent on the government and the governed coalescing to identify needs that can be addressed through a combination of government resources and citizen activism and volunteerism.

Community policing can be the catalyst for stimulating the partnership between the government and its citizens. The personalized, decentralized, and long-term relationship between the police and the people has proven effective, but the police cannot do it alone. There needs to be the commitment from all the "Big Five," the police, the community, social agencies, political leaders, and the

258

media. Citizens need to do more for themselves and volunteer to help rejuvenate their neighborhoods; social agencies need to do their share; political leaders need to provide long-term commitment and support; the media needs to educate the public; and the police cannot conduct "business as usual."

Research by the staff of the National Center for Community Policing has verified that community officers are so well received that they often find themselves inundated with requests that go beyond the scope of traditional law enforcement. As problem solvers who act as catalysts for positive change, community officers routinely network with other social service providers, whose support is essential but whose participation is limited by the fact that they are not in the community each day alongside the community officers.

Cont

Community officers risk burnout trying to wear "too many hats." If we think back to those days when the old-fashioned beat cop patrolled city streets, we should remember that those were the days when an unofficial team of public service providers spent much of their time "making house calls." In that era, social workers routinely made home visits to see firsthand if children were neglected or abused. At the same time, the public health nurses might be out in the community visiting the homes of the young, the elderly, and the infirm. Probation and parole officers made scheduled and unscheduled home visits to ensure that their clients were living up to the terms of their release. Those were also the days when so-called truant officers were on the streets making sure that kids were not "playing hooky."

Among the unintended consequences of centralization and removing service providers (including the police) from the community is that it reduced opportunities for them to act as informal agents of social control.

The shift to centralization and the use of the formal system reduced opportunities for all relevant service providers to act as positive role models for the young. Perhaps it is no coincidence that the transition to centralization took place at the same time that rising crime rates also persuaded those members of the community who could afford to do so to flee to safer neighborhoods.

As a result of the centralization and the depersonalization of the service providers that stand in the way of making community policing work, we at the National Center for Community Policing have encouraged the establishment of *Neighborhood Network Centers* as a way to operationalize the Big Five functioning together.

These centers seek to apply the decentralized and personalized model of community policing to the delivery of other public and private services. This operationalizes the interaction of the Big Five and allows social service providers such as social workers, public health nurses, mental health professionals, drug treatment counselors, education specialists, and probation and parole officers to join the community officer in the neighborhood on a part-time or full-time basis. This new community-based team of professionals and community volunteers operates from a facility located in the target neighborhood. We are observing and evaluating four Network Center sites; the primary one is in Lansing, Michigan.

BIG FIVE —

The community officer is the key professional because he or she serves as the vanguard and informal leader of this new group of community-based problem solvers and volunteers. There are several reasons why the community officer is the leader: First, the officer knows the community intimately, its strengths and weaknesses. Second, the community officer has already established a bond of trust with the people in the community, which can serve as a foundation for the other service providers. Third, the community officer acts as the protector for the other professionals who follow his or her lead back into the community, just as the community officer is the protector of the private citizens and the volunteers in the beat area. Fourth, the community officer has the broadest range of options, ranging from a pat on the back for a job well done to the use of deadly force in dealing with the problems that the community may face.

The objective of the Neighborhood Network Center is to allow the personalized and decentralized professionals to work together, to intervene with troubled individuals and families and their social and physical environment with the goal of helping to make the neighborhood a better and safer place in which to live and work.

The Network Center in Lansing is being evaluated on whether it can make a positive impact on problems as diverse as crime, disorder, substandard housing, neighborhood decay, child neglect, substance abuse, or any other of the host of ills plaguing neighborhoods today.

The Neighborhood Network Center concept not only recognizes what is already happening on many community policing beats as community officers turn to others for help, but advances the idea further by enhancing relationships among the community-based team of problems solvers and by establishing that they should work together—part time or full time—from an office in the community. The opportunity to network with and engage other service providers and volunteers can often make the difference between the success and failure of many community policing initiatives, not only because it involves more concerned people who can apply their talents to the challenges, but because it allows others to share the load, thereby allowing community officers to preserve their main role as peace keepers.

There is not enough experience yet with the Neighborhood Network Center approach to identify all of the potential problems that may arise. The major question for the future of community policing is: Can the Network Center concept expand upon the community policing model and survive the bureaucratic regime of centralization and depersonalization?

Other Questions for the Future of Community Policing

In order for community policing to survive and flourish and the Neighborhood Network Center orientation to operationalize the delivery of neighborhood service in support of community policing, many challenges must be met. This author has serious reservations about the future of community policing. In addition to the question of whether a Neighborhood Network Center-type approach will become common, there are several other unanswered questions related to the future of community policing.

1. Will police departments embrace community policing as a department-wide philosophy and a citywide strategy, resisting the temptation to make it another "program" that comes and goes?

2. Will police departments revise their policies, specifically those concerning recruiting, selection, training, performance evaluation, and rewards, to reflect a commitment to the philosophy and practice of community policing?

3. Can and will departments find ways to free up patrol time so officers can engage in proactive community-based problem solving rather than reacting to problems after they occur?

4. Will there be critical problem analysis and long-term solutions to problems rather than moving from problem to problem without officer decentralization and permanency?

5. Will citizens be willing to do more for themselves and be patient with the trade-offs necessary with community policing, such as increased response time for non-life-threatening situations and the need to be activists and volunteers in their neighborhoods?

6. If police departments do their part, will the rest of the Big Five, the community, elected officials, social agencies, and the media, provide the sustained support that community policing needs?

7. Will chiefs be provided the job security that they need to take risks and embrace innovation?

8. Will the trend toward two separate police systems—private security for those who can afford it and public policing for the poor—continue?

9. Will there be appropriate, quantitative, and qualitative measures to evaluate community policing so that there is not a lapse back to an overemphasis on meaningless numbers like citations given and response time?

10. Will uncertainty about the future draw us together so that we work collectively to solve our problems or will it pull us apart so that we selfishly attempt to protect only ourselves?

Conclusion

For community policing to not only survive but flourish in the future, all relevant groups need to do their part. A Neighborhood Network Center-type of approach may be the necessary supportive structure to operationalize a broad-based orientation to identify and solve the myriad problems that lead to crime and disorder.

The police cannot do it alone. The Big Five are critical to the future of community policing. Citizens need to get involved, ranging from providing information to prevent and solve crime to volunteering for neighborhood projects. Social agencies need to become partners to help deal with the conditions that lead to crime and to deal with both victims and perpetrators. Political leaders can both support long-term policies that are needed to prevent and control crime and provide job security for Chiefs of Police so that they are willing to be innovative, take risks, and be agents of change. The media needs to educate everyone about the complexity of social problems and the necessity that everyone become involved in the problem-solving process. The future of community policing is in the hands and hearts of more than just the police.

References

Sower, C. (1975). *Community involvement: The webs of formal and informal ties that make for action*. Glencoe, IL: Free Press.

Trojanowicz, S. (1992). *Theory of community policing*. Unpublished master's thesis, Michigan State University.

The Community Role in Community Policing

WARREN FRIEDMAN

"PROBLEM-SOLVING PARTNERSHIPS" captures, in a phrase, two ideas central to community policing: a focus on patterned, repetitive crime and disorder, and the need for police to have allies in solving these problems. Considerable thought has gone into understanding the conditions that are necessary for a police department to be more responsive to the community. Criminal justice scholars and police officials meet at conferences. Studies are funded through the National Institute of Justice. Ideas are exchanged in police and scholarly journals. A multimillion-dollar national dialogue about the fate of communities is being conducted among professionals.

The dialogue is replicated at the local level. Departments hire consultants. Committees meet. Community policing is defined by professionals and presented to the citizens. Little space has been created for community participation in either the national or local dialogue. Little thought has been given to the conditions necessary for effective community participation and almost no resources are committed to the community role. Yet, to the degree community policing reaches beyond a problem-solving methodology toward "partnership," it is a coordinated strategy, and the role, knowledge, and effectiveness of the partner is critical to its success. In community policing, the quality of the community's participation is decisive. If community policing is to contribute to the reduction of crime and disorder and the improvement of a neighborhood's quality of life, more than dialogue between professionals and even more than real police reorganization is necessary.

The community must have a voice in the forums that define community policing itself, must be a ready and knowledgeable ally to the forces of reform, and, in the neighborhood, where the benefits are supposed to be delivered, must have a serious part in implementing solutions as well as nominating problems.

There is not a great deal of experience with full community participation in the city or the neighborhood, but, as Chicago launches its community policing prototypes in five police districts, we will be able to watch one version of this participation unfold. This might be called a community organizing version of participation. While individuals within the department, including the present superintendent, were in favor of change, in its initial stages the impetus for reform came from outside the department and the city administration. Change was resisted. It required citizen organizing and mobilization to bring the issue to broader public attention. Finally, the city hired a management consultant. The company issued a major report and community policing was on the city's agenda.

Much about the following narrative is historically specific to Chicago. Nevertheless, there are lessons to be learned from it: about how community leadership can be developed to participate in the defining policy dialogue, about the partnership role of the community in problem solving, about the conditions for this partnership participation, and about the economics of this partnership. Perhaps thinking about and following Chicago's development, its successes and failures, will focus attention on the community and help to introduce a new and necessary voice into the discussion of community policing's future.

The Campaign for Change

Since the 1988 release of *Police Service in Chicago,* by the Chicago Alliance for Neighborhood Safety (CANS), community policing has increasingly become the goal of a broad spectrum of community organizations. CANS's initial impetus to involvement grew out of its experience in the early 1980s with the Urban Crime Prevention Program (UCPP) and the shortcomings of community crime prevention when done in the context of an incident-driven department. During the UCPP, complaints from block watch participants mounted. Lack of police responsiveness became a regular theme in meetings between CANS and community groups. This dissatisfaction led to the search for alternative models of policing, the writing and distribution of *Police Service,* and the launching of an effort, based on the report's recommendations, to move the department toward more "neighborhood-oriented alternatives."

The campaign to put community policing on the city's agenda was sustained through two police administrations and two mayors. The campaign involved thousands of people in educational forums and workshops, in the design of their own pilot project proposal, in explaining, organizing, lobbying, and testifying. Over the last 2 years this activity has involved a coalition of more than 60 community organizations working together in the Community Policing Task Force. The length, breadth, and depth of the effort—small and shallow in the context of the total task—accounts for Robert Trojanowicz's conclusion that, compared to other parts of the country, "Chicago is way ahead of any other city in terms of community participation."[1]

Getting "way ahead" took considerable energy and persistence, not only to wage a campaign, but to develop a core of community leaders who understood the ideas and felt a commitment to making them a reality in the city and their neighborhoods. The strategy to put community policing on the city's agenda had three components: (1) stimulating and participating in a policy-making debate about crime, safety, and policing; (2) drawing on Chicago's decade of experience with community crime prevention to emphasize the notion of the community's responsibility in neighborhood safety and civility; and (3) mobilizing community-based organizations as crucial agents of change in city policy and in the neighborhood implementation of that policy.

From the beginning, in addition to stimulating public discussion and pressuring for change, the strategy included setting up what Task Force members called "informal pilot projects" or "liaison projects." The strategy involved persuading a district commander to assign a police officer to work as a liaison with groups to solve one or more problems. This was seen as both a form of local pressure for change that paralleled the citywide campaign, and as a way of encouraging community responsibility and generating problem-solving experience in the community.

The Problem-Solving Partnership

A successful example of an informal pilot project took place in the 24th Police District on Chicago's far northeast side. The district is one of Chicago's most ethnically diverse, a mixture of moderately high- and low-crime areas, of middle income and poverty, renters and homeowners. The area of the project is a mixture of apartment buildings and single family homes adjacent to and under constant pressure from the district's highest crime area. That pressure increased when a building owner in the high-crime area ran out of patience. For some time he had been unable to get the phone company to remove a bank of phones in a storefront laundry leased from him. The phones were used by drug dealers to take orders. Finally, despairing of cooperation from the company, the owner ripped the pay phones from the wall.

By cutting off phone service, he deprived the drug dealers of a way of taking orders. In response, they moved their operations a few blocks south, to a convenient pay phone and an intersection that would handle the traffic. The relocation of the open drug market added to the neighborhood's growing problems. At about the same time, the management of one building in the neighborhood was becoming lax. The building was showing signs of deterioration. It was becoming a haven for drug dealing. Nearby, an absentee landlord purchased two other buildings. These buildings also became centers for gangs, loud parties, prostitution, and drug dealing.

Something similar to the problems occurring in this neighborhood were probably happening in dozens of other Chicago neighborhoods at about the same time. What was different here was the Jargowood Block Club (JBC). When the problems moved into their neighborhood, the Block Club was already organized and active on a variety of issues. It had the organizational structure in place to launch a 1½ year campaign against the increased dealing and disruption.

Almost as important, key leaders were involved in the Task Force campaign for community policing. Because of this, they had read about community policing, been to trainings and forums on the subject, and had, with other community people and several high-ranking Chicago police officers, visited New York and Seattle to see those cities' versions of the strategy. People understood key concepts of community policing and the failings of incident-driven policing. They were prepared to pursue alternatives to traditional policing.

In addition to educated leadership, the block club benefited from the work done by a community organization and the 6100-6200 Winthrop Block Club in the southern part of the district. Residents from this block group as well as leadership and staff from the community organization were also involved in CANS, the Task Force, and the campaign for community policing.

The Winthrop Block Club and the Commander had been at loggerheads for some time over what the Commander was interpreting as a demand from the residents for constant foot patrol in the area, a demand he felt he could not meet without slighting other areas. Block club members had asked for help from the local community group, the Edgewater Community Council (ECC), in order to break the stalemate. After working with the block club, ECC invited CANS's involvement.

At a meeting of CANS, ECC, and residents, the block club members decided to ask the Commander to appoint a liaison to work with them on solving the problems. The meeting with the Commander went well and, with the encouragement of a sympathetic and informed Neighborhood Relations Sergeant, a tactical officer was appointed to be their liaison in an "informal pilot project."

When the Jargowood Block Club requested help from the district, they were, in part, implementing a strategy agreed on by the Task Force and, encouraged by the success of another block club, they also asked for a liaison. The same officer who worked with the Winthrop Block Club served as their liaison. By the time he met with them, he had done some thinking about community policing. He suggested to the Jargowood residents at their first meeting that the dealers could be arrested, but they would be back. A longer term solution, he suggested, would necessarily involve community participation and creative thinking. Moved by the officer's suggestion and commitment, and the urgings of the local leadership who were involved in the citywide campaign, the residents accepted the challenge.

With the aid of the aldermanic office and a group of volunteers concerned with the effect slumlords were having on the community, block club members identified the owners of the problem buildings. They began meeting with one landlord and one building manager, urging eviction of key individuals and more effective tenant screening in the future. When friendly persuasion failed, the group increased the pressure. In the case of one owner, neighbors visited the bank that held his mortgage, stimulating pressure from the bank. They called his suburban home whenever tenant's parties disturbed them or illegal activity was spotted. They also pressured the city to inspect and write citations for building code violations.

JBC also targeted the company that owned the new pay phone that was being used for order-taking. Residents worked with the owner whose store it stood in front of. Their objective, using a tactic employed successfully by another participant in the citywide campaign, was to get the phone company to convert the phone so that it handled only out-going calls, once again cutting dealers off from orders.

As the campaign progressed, participants were strengthened by the experience of working together and their growing trust of the police officers with whom they worked. One result of this growing confidence was that for 6 weeks, 40 to 70 residents spent their evenings, Thursday through Saturday, loitering in the open drug market, taking the license plate numbers of customers and generally, by their presence, making it an uncomfortable place to do business.

From the first meeting with JBC, the police played a role in this campaign. As part of the pressure on the open market, they occasionally made sweeps, arresting visible dealers. After an early show of support involving officers from the Tactical Squad, Gang Crimes, and Narcotics, police presence was reduced considerably. From time to time, officers loitered with the residents to make clear to the dealers that this was a joint effort and that intimidation of the residents would not be tolerated. In addition, as part of the pressure on the landlords, they made the two drug-related arrests on the property, which is required in Chicago to get a building into housing court as a public nuisance. By midsummer, the problem-solving partnership was having an effect. There had been evictions and pressure on disruptive tenants to change their behavior, one building had been sold to a more responsible landlord, and all the buildings were quieter. They were also in better repair because of code citations. The street corner drug dealing was gone, and, one year later, the area remains quiet.

Lessons

Of course, circumstances are different in different parts of Chicago and the country. There are not always grassroots organizations through which volunteers can participate. Sometimes there are organizations, but the leadership is not well informed. Sometimes the staffed community-based organizations in the area are mostly social service agencies, concerned with serving clients and not with organizing people and acting on local concerns. Often, there are community organizations without a strong block-level constituency, or there are block groups with no umbrella organization supporting them and knitting them together. Sometimes, instead of being motivated by a challenge to save the neighborhood, residents, feeling powerless, withdraw further because they feel the neighborhood is already lost.

None of this invalidates the general principles underlying the Jargowood example. Without denying the individuality of every neighborhood, if problem-solving partnerships are to be effective, there must be: (1) grassroots organization through which volunteers can work and be educated; (2) informed local leadership; (3) the presence of independent, staffed organizations that can support local efforts and provide them with training, education, and technical assistance; and (4) an appropriate problem-solving target, in this case, a chronic problem area that residents have a strong stake in clearing up and that, because of its relative stability, offers an opportunity for organizing, planning, and partnership building, and thus for maximum community participation.

The Jargowood effort was sustained by the community with only occasional, though crucial, police intervention. The largest investment of time and resources came from community volunteers and, secondarily, staff members of not-for-profit organizations. The Jargowood example also suggests, therefore, that (5) when the community is an organized, informed, and active partner, the problem-solving process is not so labor intensive for the police as some have asserted.

Policy Implications

If partnership is crucial to community policing and informed organizations are crucial to the partnership, then support for community organizing and education must be part of the planning and thinking about community policing. This is especially important if, as the Jargowood story indicates, effective partnership heightens the impact of short-term problem solving, sets the stage for consolidating gains, and lowers costs to police departments and, ultimately, the taxpayer.

Where will this support come from? Police officers can help, but they are not community organizers and, for the most part, lack the desire, time, and skills to do the job. They are also more expensive than community organizers. However, even if large numbers of officers had the desire and skills, and it were the most economical way to go about the job, it would still not be a good idea. The independence of organizations is crucial to ensure that the police are and remain responsive to community concerns and have an effective partner in solving problems. Independent, competent organizations are also important because in the long term, the fight for community safety is much more than a criminal justice concern. Only independent organizations that are run by and responsive to the community can advocate on issues like community investment and jobs that are crucial to community health and safety.

If organized and informed partners are crucial to the success of police efforts in crime reduction, and to the long-term possibilities of revitalizing high-crime, low-income neighborhoods, education, training, organizing, and investment are critical. There is precedent for policy and investment that supports the growth of community organizations and community capacity as part of a national and local strategy for public safety. Community crime prevention, supported by the Law Enforcement Assistance Administration (LEAA) in the 1970s and early 1980s, was designed to accomplish this. Unfortunately, it built grassroots partners before police departments were ready to cooperate. It would be foolish to repeat the error in reverse.

One mechanism for supporting this is in place now, Volunteers In Service To America (VISTA). It played a major role in LEAA's Urban Crime Prevention Programs and could be called upon again to support low-income communities with VISTA volunteers. The national service program about to be instituted could also devote resources to this effort (VISTA may be merged into the new service program by the time you read this). This is not enough, however. There must be resources for training and education, for bringing communities together, nationally and locally, to share experiences. Perhaps the Community Policing Assistance Act, if it passes, can provide help in funding these activities as well as community efforts, but this is still inadequate. There needs to be a fund for the development of community capacity that can be called upon to support the building of independent organizations in high-crime and at-risk neighborhoods where they do not exist, or strengthening them when they are not strong enough to be effective partners.

Police, prosecutors, and prisons provide only a small part of the answer to crime and disorder. The whole criminal justice system and all the criminal justice scholars cannot, without an organized, informed community, make significant progress toward safer, friendlier neighborhoods. It is crucial that the country acknowledge this by deeds and dollars. It is crucial that those who have the privilege of participating in the dialogue begin to say this loudly in the public forums that they occupy.

Note

1. Speech to the Community Policing Task Force delivered in Chicago, June 17, 1993.

The Limits of Community

MICHAEL E. BUERGER

THE RHETORIC OF COMMUNITY POLICING ascribes to "the community" a great power to regulate itself, shake off its fear of crime by forming "partnerships" with the police, and reestablish community norms that regulate behavior and successfully resist the encroachments of the criminal element. Unfortunately, early returns from the field suggest that its successes in this regard are modest and that community policing initiatives have so far failed to tap the great wellspring of "community" believed to lie waiting for the proper catalyst.

Little attention has been given to a definition of *the community* commensurate with the vast promise embedded in the community policing rhetoric. Even less has been spared for defining the role that can be reasonably expected of "the community," howsoever it should be defined. Though some departments and localities are engaged in honest efforts to make the promises a reality, community policing by and large remains a unilateral action on the part of the police.

"Community" participation seems to be limited to four primary roles (singly or in combination), of which three are police related. First and foremost, the community is expected to act as the "eyes and ears of the police," providing information about crime and criminals, suspicious persons, and undesirable conditions in their neighborhoods. The citizen contribution to the "partnership" is legitimization for police actions in individual incidents.

Cheerleading, frequently intervening on behalf of the police in the political arena, tends to be a collective role: answering surveys on citizen satisfaction with the police and staging demonstrations in support of the police generally, or in support of particular actions. Community support legitimizes the overall strategies of the police.

A third publicly supportive role augments approval with monetary assistance. The most well-known example is the collective action of the taxpayers in Flint,

Michigan, passing two successive tax measures to fund foot patrol. More recently, such participation has tended to be more modest and comes largely though not exclusively from the business community: donating space for mini-stations, paying for equipment for bicycle patrols or special outreach programs, and so forth.

The fourth role of the community is statement-making, which can be exercised independently or in concert with police action. Statements are *symbolically confrontational:* implicit in the statement is an "or else," the threat of opposition and sanctions for continued misconduct. Statements directed at the disreputable elements, that certain behaviors will not be tolerated, may be short-term events—vigils and demonstrations such as the annual Take Back The Night rallies—or activities with more lasting effects, such as posting "Drug-Free School Zone" or Neighborhood Watch signs. Some statements are made to select respectable targets, such as the Court Watches that threaten public embarrassment or political opposition in retaliation for lenient rulings that the community regards as improper. Still others are cast like bread upon the waters to the silent and retreatist residents of the neighborhoods, encouraging them to enlist in the collective effort.

Ironically, it is those statements that are directed at the nominal servants or allies of the community that get the greatest response. Respectable targets are far more amenable to community action than disreputable ones, but such actions only indirectly affect the criminal and disorderly elements. There is little evidence that the criminal element is disposed to respond positively (though they may shift locales temporarily as a convenience), and none that retreatists are listening at all.

A potential fifth community role, that of *actual confrontation* of criminal or disorderly activities—whether attempting to move loiterers or drunks off one's property or interposing one's self between a drug seller and a potential buyer—runs the risk of eliciting an equally direct, physically violent response. Many police departments actively discourage direct citizen intervention into illegal activities for exactly this reason. As a result, community-based "statements" directed at nonrespectable targets tend to be merely symbolic, talismanic phrases uttered in hopes of warding off evil manifestations.

For all the rhetoric about empowering the community or the community "taking responsibility" for itself, when it comes down to cases the police establishment assigns to the community a role that simply enhances the police response to crime and disorder. Rather than "empower" the community to act in its own interest, this model calls upon it to help focus police crime-fighter activities. Proponents may correctly argue that it is impossible to engage in cohesion-building while under siege and that system responses are necessary to clear the ground for planting seeds of hope, but experience teaches us that the seeds only rarely take root.

The question of regulation of behavior actually turns on the still unanswered question of Rosenbaum's Implant Hypothesis: whether or not a group of dedicated individuals can implant a set of social values that will make a ragged neighborhood viable again. Though initial efforts to implant social cohesion produced negative results, the catalyst role of the police—both in terms of their ability to mobilize citizen participation and in their greater leverage with other agencies—may conceivably tip the balance in a positive direction. Community groups have had success mobilizing city agencies on particular problems, be they derelict buildings, abandoned cars, street prostitution, or crack houses. It remains an open question of how much social cohesion can be expected from these tactics alone.

With sufficient community-group pressure (which sometimes moves first the media and only then the government structure), bureaucracies are roused from their lethargy to effect a crackdown on a small, locally defined problem. The community group then "celebrates its small successes," trying to increase the hope of those whose hopelessness kept them from being involved, enlisting their support for the next project. Each new success is supposed to generate more participation, until a critical mass is reached. But rarely is that critical mass achieved: The norm of community mobilization is a small segment of the community, with varying degrees of dedication, and limited success in building upon its initial achievements. Small successes are not enough to establish a stake in a geographically defined community with none of the attributes of a more capable community.

The vast number of the silent members of the community are neither disposed nor prepared to respond to clarion calls. They may have seen past successes celebrated to no great effect; they may know at firsthand the costs of taking an activist role. Without a greater stake in the geographically defined community they will likely ignore all symbolic statements directed at them.

The nostalgic sense of community embedded in the language of community policing is largely absent in the neighborhoods beset by crime. Despite all the problems related to doing so, reversing an area's economic decline may be a necessary precursor to restoring the sense of community; at the very least, some mechanism other than "crime prevention" is needed to galvanize the uncommitted.

Future research and programs need to leave the realm of the hypothetical to grapple with the real questions of what the community can *do*. There is sufficient documentation that the transformation from small organizational groups to cohesive community does not occur automatically even when the pump is primed with small anticrime successes. One possible avenue is to shift community efforts away from symbolic interactions that are easy to do but have little overall impact, into long-term interactions with public and private agencies that have the power to rebuild the infrastructure vital to community.

Though crime and disorder must be resisted simultaneously, it is time to stop thinking in terms of crime as the only barrier to community well-being. An alternative cognitive framework for community activities might regard crime prevention as a result of other activities rather than as an independent activity in its own right. Efforts should be brought to bear on the conditions in the same order that they occurred: If the broken windows theory is correct, it was community decline that signaled the availability of the area to the dissolute and the criminally minded. It may be unrealistic to expect neighborhood activism alone to correct conditions created by exploitive practices of slumlords and redliners among the banking and insurance industries, or the relocation of industry. Merely sweeping the vulgar from the streets will not correct that basic problem, and sooner or later the tide of undesirables will flow back again.

Success requires more than different target selection. Building community is not a matter of monthly or weekly meetings, but of day-to-day caring. It requires demonstrations of caring that have meaning in terms that are understood by the persons cared about—the neighbors, who may very well be persons difficult to like—more than in terms meaningful to those showing the caring spirit. That is a formidable task, difficult to conceptualize in the quantitative terms that dominate social science and one that places the direct burden on the shoulders of those with the fewest resources, financial or personal. But it is in filling *that* void that the community-based organizations have the greatest chance for success, in mobilizing agencies with a positive rather than a punitive agenda. Keep the feet of the police to the fire, by all means, but recognize that enforcement (whether by arrest or citation for building code violations) is but a bandaid. The real community healing must be done by outreach, by pouring into a seemingly bottomless hole of need those things that are taken for granted in the nostalgic "community" we allude to: teaching *everyone's* children a sense of self-worth, seeing that they do not go hungry, or without medical care or an adequate education; insisting on economic opportunities for all members of the community, support services for those who need it, and most important, membership in "the community," which is bestowed, not earned by trial.

Evaluating Community Policing

Role Tensions Between
Practitioners and Evaluators

DAVID WEISBURD

PRACTITIONERS WHO IMPLEMENT and run community policing programs and researchers who evaluate them are likely to enter the evaluation process with the assumption that they agree on the basic questions and methods that underlie such studies. What they often neglect to take into account are the role conflicts that exist between program evaluators and practitioners and the extent to which these are exacerbated in the context of community policing programs. In this chapter I begin by outlining the source and nature of some of these conflicts and conclude with suggestions as to how to minimize their effect on the evaluation process.

The Source of the Conflict

At the source of the conflict lies the fact that "bad news" has a very different implication for researchers than for practitioners. Program managers, sponsors, and staff are likely to react with hostility to negative evaluations for the understandable reason that their work is judged by how well the program is doing (Rossi & Freeman, 1982, p. 310). In some sense, if the program fails, they fail, regardless of what they might be told to the contrary. The powerful protection of confidentiality given to subjects does not apply to practitioners. They are directly influenced and threatened by the statements of the evaluators. At the same time, their enthusiasm for the program can play an important role in motivating others to become involved. They cannot afford to be skeptics on the sidelines. Indeed, their enthusiasm often contributes to the successful operation of the program.

The evaluator, on the other hand, can be rewarded as much for negative as positive evidence. His or her commitment "is to knowledge, not the success of some program" (Empey, 1980, p. 146). Moreover, the evaluator does not want to be seen as "going native"—as becoming too much a part of the enthusiasm of the program process. From the perspective of practitioners this skepticism is often irritating.

The fact that evaluation results have different implications for evaluators and practitioners has a direct impact on the quality of their cooperation. Problems begin immediately with the focus of investigation. Practitioners know how difficult it is to implement community policing programs and want to understand how successes are created. They do not want there to be a focus on such "red flag" issues as abuse of authority and corruption. Merely their introduction into research view may threaten the future of the program.

The researcher, on the other hand, wants to document the wider story. Evaluators want to uncover processes that lead to failure as well as those that lead to success. They want to open up investigation in areas that are sensitive—but important—especially given the controversy that surrounds innovations in community crime control.

Defining Cooperation

It would seem that effective cooperation as the research develops would break down some of these conflicts. But importantly, even the definition of what *good cooperation* means is often a matter of controversy. Practitioners want to know everything they can about the program's operation. The more information they have, the more effective they can be in correcting program flaws or changing program personnel. Just as they would feel free to discuss program participants or problems they hope to correct, they expect the same feedback from evaluators.

Yet evaluators are caught in a bind. In the first case they are often constrained by promises of confidentiality. Those promises facilitate data collection and are required by professional norms. Unlike the practitioner, evaluators cannot openly discuss many aspects of their findings. They are especially constrained in their ability to use interviews or observations in identifying program troublemakers.

A second and perhaps more important constraint on cooperation comes from the evaluator's need to assess the impacts of the program fairly. If the evaluator provides information for managing or evaluating the program, an artificial research environment is created that is difficult to replicate in other settings. Is the evaluation part of the program? Will future programs enact a very expensive research effort to provide the same feedback? Most likely not. Accordingly, if the evaluator provides feedback to the program manager, he or she may make it impossible to generalize the findings from this program to others.

Who Will Disseminate Project Findings?

Finally, we come to conflicts over dissemination of research findings. In community policing there is often much at stake in the results of an evaluation. Community groups and the media focus a good deal of attention on such efforts—attention that makes the dissemination and interpretation of data a political problem that may have important ramifications for practitioners and public officials. Media interest in such programs also provides a degree of celebrity for those involved that often intensifies competition over dissemination of information about the program and its impacts.

In this highly charged environment, policy makers and the general public are likely to prefer unambiguous conclusions. And in this sense the most serious danger of an evaluation may be, as Ward Edwards (1980) has noted, not "inaccuracy" but "irrelevance" (p. 179). The fact that evaluation results are often complex and equivocal—that they may not provide a clear bottom line—leads to a vacuum in "actual evaluation" of the program, a vacuum that is all too easily filled by those with very strong vested interests in the program's success. Indeed, in many programs, program managers also produce reports. Naturally these are not hindered by the skepticism of the researcher. Such reports are likely to provide unambiguous descriptions about program successes, and thus program reports can leave a longer lasting impression on outsiders than the evaluation itself.

Resolving the Conflicts

It is important to recognize at the outset that the research process cannot be purged of role tensions altogether. If there is no tension then one of the parties is not carrying out his or her role very effectively. Rather there are steps that can be taken at the outset of an evaluation that can reduce tension and produce a more effective and better managed evaluation in the long run.

The research design must be carefully mapped out at the start, and in this process practitioners should be heavily involved. When will intervention be allowed? When not? How will confidentiality be defined? Good fences make good neighbors in research as well as communities. A clear definition in the research design of the boundaries that lie between evaluators and practitioners will allow the evaluator to avoid the label of being uncooperative or uninterested in the project's success later on.

Practitioners and evaluators should also clearly define what project success or failure means. How is it to be measured? What variables are most relevant to its measurement? Importantly, evaluators should make sure that realistic standards are created. They should get beyond the necessary rhetoric that accompanies new program development. Practitioners and evaluators should make sure that they are in fact speaking the same language.

Finally, evaluators and practitioners should clearly define at the outset how evaluation results are to be disseminated. What types of evaluation reports should be presented? What types of cooperation should there be between practitioners and evaluators in developing such reports? What data should appear in them? How are program reports, if they are also produced, to differ from research reports? Much like agreements over authorship in professional publications, practitioners and evaluators should clearly stake out their claim over how the project will be viewed by outsiders.

Overall, these suggestions demand a degree of communication at the outset of an evaluation that is time consuming and difficult to carry out. Yet attention at the outset to these details will avoid the much more difficult destructive conflicts that can arise from the role tensions that are inherent in the practitioner/ evaluator relationship.

References

Edwards, W. (1980). Multiattribute utility for evaluation: Structures, uses, and problems. In M. W. Klein & K. S. Teilmann (Eds.), *Handbook of criminal justice evaluation*. Beverly Hills, CA: Sage.

Empey, L. (1980). Field experimentation in criminal justice: Rationale and design. In M. Wilkins & K. S. Teilmann (Eds.), *Handbook of criminal justice evaluation*. Beverly Hills, CA: Sage.

Rossi, P. H., & Freeman, H. E. (1982). *Evaluation: A systematic approach*. Beverly Hills, CA: Sage.

International Differences
in Community Policing

DAVID H. BAYLEY

THE SUCCESS OF COMMUNITY POLICING will never be evaluated. The reason is simple. Community policing means too many things to different people. Its practices are so varied that any evaluation will be partial or challengeable as not being authentic "community policing." Furthermore, because the mix of practices is so great, any evaluation will be sui generis, making generalization to other situations problematic.

Around the world, I have heard community policing described as horse patrols, neighborhood police offices, the traditional practices of criminal investigation, intensified enforcement of drunk-driving laws, prompt response to emergency calls for service, tightened disciplinary procedures, statements of departmental values and objectives, liaison with ethnic groups, victim support, and foot patrols. Such is the virtue of "community policing" that everyone wants to be seen doing it.

Even the cognoscente talk in tongues. Lee P. Brown (1989), former commissioner of police in New York City and a founding father of community policing, talks about it as a philosophy that should shape what every police officer does. Mark Moore, like Brown a member of the Harvard Executive Session that did so much to popularize community policing, emphasizes that it is a new approach to managing police organizations, one that stresses collegiality in decision making, de-emphasis on formal hierarchy, experimentation, routinized evaluation, and the valuing of skills rather than ranks (Executive Session, 1991). Others, such as Jerome Skolnick and myself, believe that community policing is a dead letter if it does not change the delivery of police services (Bayley 1989;

Skolnick & Bayley, 1988). Our view is that even though community policing may not be a single program, it must produce change in operational behavior in order to become more than a trendy slogan.

Although different languages are being employed to describe what is central to community policing, I have found that certain operational elements recur again and again when police forces seriously attempt to improve the reality as well as the perception of public safety under the banner of community policing (Bayley, in press). They are Consultation, Adaptation, Mobilization, and Problem Solving (CAMPS). *Consultation* means asking communities regularly and systematically what their security needs are and how the police might more effectively meet them. *Adaptation* involves command devolution so that precinct and subdivisional commanders can decide how police resources should be mixed in order to meet the needs of specific areas. *Mobilization* refers to the active enlistment of non-police people and agencies, public as well as private, in addressing community security problems. *Problem solving* means remedying conditions that generate crime and insecurity. It involves conditions-focused prevention at local levels.

Consultation, Adaptation, Mobilization, and Problem Solving constitute an operational definition of community policing in practice around the world. They are what police forces do when community police rhetoric becomes operational reality. Community policing in this ostensible sense exists in New York City with the Community Police Officer Program and in Madison, Wisconsin; Denton, Texas; and Newport News, Virginia. In Canada, these elements can be found in Edmonton, Alberta, and in Australia in Toowoomba, Queensland, and throughout New South Wales. The CAMPS elements have become the dominant operating practices of the police in Japan and Singapore (Bayley 1989, 1991).

If CAMPS represent the operational face of community policing, then the job of evaluation would seem to be manageable. Unfortunately, this is not the case. There are major variations in the way these four programmatic elements are delivered, making the permutations in community policing mind-boggling.

1. Personnel. Community policing activities may be assigned to all operational personnel, as in Newport News, Virginia, or to only a specialized subset, as in New York City and New South Wales.

2. Organization. When community policing is specialized, a new command may be set up for it, as with Detroit's mini-stations, or it may be turned over to an existing command, as CPOP has been to uniformed patrol in New York City.

3. Basing. Specialized community police personnel may operate out of beats, as in Edmonton; precinct-based squads, as in San Diego; force-wide task forces, as in Baltimore County; or out of headquarters, as in Queensland.

4. Deployment. Community police officers may be deployed on foot (New York City), bicycles (Boston), motorcycles (Denver), motorcycles (Toowoomba), neighborhood offices (Houston), mobile mini-stations (Fort Worth), or cars and vans (San Diego).

5. Functions. Personnel doing community policing may do some but not all the elements of the operational definition. Edmonton's beat officers are responsible for consultation; Japan's *koban* officers are not, although that is changing. Patrol personnel are expected to solve problems in Newport News and San Diego; they are not in Japan and Great Britain. Furthermore, officers assigned to community policing may or may not be responsible for other forms of police work. CPOP officers in New York City must be visible and patrol on foot; Detroit's mini-station officers do not. Community police officers in Edmonton and Ontario must respond to radio calls for service; they do not in Detroit or Singapore, except when convenient.

6. Scope. Whether community policing becomes specialized or not, it may be introduced force-wide, as in New York City and Denton, Texas, or targeted on selected areas, as in Edmonton and in Madison, Wisconsin.

7. Consultation. It may be undertaken explicitly, under departmental guidelines, or ad hoc, as determined by local personnel. New South Wales, Australia, is an example of the former, the Ontario Provincial Police of the latter.

8. Coordination. Non-police resources may be mobilized through formal mechanisms coordinated at a designated command level, as in Thames Valley, Great Britain, or on a case-by-case basis at the initiative of local officers, as in Toowoomba, Australia.

9. Mobilization. The resources of communities are varied (physical, monetary, and human) and may be used in many ways (in policing, in support of policing, supplementary to policing). They may also be used either reactively or preventively. Finally, civilian personnel may be paid or volunteer.

The point to this survey of operational practice is that although the core element of meaningful community policing can be identified (CAMPS), either by inspection or the imposition of a preferred definition, the variations in experience are likely to be so great as to constitute major differences in "treatment."

My own conclusion, then, is that we should stop trying to evaluate community policing. To try to do so makes as much sense as evaluating "traditional policing." This does not mean, however, that we should stop evaluating what police are trying to do. On the contrary. We need to intensify that. Policing must develop an experimental mind-set, so that operational programs and strategies are repeatedly tested in order to determine what works best. Police must learn to innovate incrementally in a double sense: specific program by specific program and selectively in terms of coverage rather than force-wide. These programmatic lumps are the appropriate unit for evaluative analysis, not some mythical package with a trendy name.

In short, although I believe that community policing in the sense of CAMPS represents the most promising strategy for enhancing public safety by the police, I do not think it can be evaluated in toto. Innovations of any sort must be evaluated in terms of programs easily recognized by police personnel and according to criteria meaningful to local communities. Community policing may be a wonderful catalytic phrase, but it is an unmanageable focus for meaningful operational evaluation.

References

Bayley, D. H. (1988). Community policing: A report from the devil's advocate. In J. R. Greene & S. D. Mastrovski (Eds.), *Community policing: Rhetoric or reality?* New York: Praeger.

Bayley, D. H. (1989). *A model of community policing: The Singapore story.* Washington, DC: National Institute of Justice.

Bayley, D. H. (1991). *Forces of order* (rev. ed.). Berkeley: University of California Press.

Bayley, D. H. (in press). *The future of law and order.* New York: Oxford University Press.

Brown, L. P. (1989, August). Community policing: A practical guide for police officials. *The Police Chief,* pp. 72-82.

Skolnick, J. H., & Bayley, D. H. (1988). *Community policing: Issues and practices around the world.* Washington, DC: National Institute of Justice.

PART

Conclusions and Future Directions

Research Synthesis and Policy Implications

MARK H. MOORE

SOMETHING IS CLEARLY AFOOT in the field of policing. Throughout the country (even the world), police executives are committing their organizations to something called "community" or "problem-solving" policing (Kelling, 1988). Indeed, popular enthusiasm for these ideas is so great that in a few cases in which police executives have been slow to embrace them, communities have forced the ideas upon them.

Predictably, rhetorical commitments to these ideas have outpaced the concrete achievements. Still, as one looks across the country, one finds many examples of departments that have introduced important new operational programs and administrative systems that are consistent with the spirit of the wider reforms (and are often the important first steps in changing the operational philosophy of an entire department). As Eck and Rosenbaum observe, "Community policing has become the new orthodoxy for cops"; and "community policing is the only form of policing available for anyone who seeks to improve police operations, management, or relations with the public" (Chapter 1, this volume).

The Community Policing Movement

It is not hard to understand the attraction of the new ideas about policing. They seem to recognize and respond to what have come to be seen as the limitations of the "reform model" of policing: its predominantly reactive stance toward crime control; its nearly exclusive reliance on arrests as a means of reducing crime and controlling disorder; its inability to develop and sustain close working relationships with the community in controlling crime; and its stifling and ultimately unsuccessful methods of bureaucratic control (Sparrow, Moore, & Kennedy, 1990).

In contrast, the new ideas point to a new set of possibilities: the potential for crime prevention as well as crime control; creative problem solving as an alternative to arrest; the importance of customer service and community responsiveness as devices for building stronger relations with local communities; and "commissioning" street-level officers to initiate community problem-solving efforts (Sparrow et al., 1990). To many, these ideas seem more likely to ameliorate the wide variety of crime and disorder problems that are now tearing the heart out of America's communities.

Yet beneath the enthusiasm for this wave of reform is an undercurrent of doubt and concern. Those influential in shaping decisions about how to police cities— the "Big Five" alluded to by Robert Trojanowicz (the police, the community, political leaders, social agencies, and the media)—still hesitate to commit to the new forms of policing (Chapter 15, this volume). They worry that the new ideas sacrifice important aspects of policing's traditions (including its predominant focus on crime control and the achievement of high levels of performance in traditional police functions such as patrol, rapid response, and criminal investigation), and do so for quite uncertain gains in other less important and less substantial dimensions (such as fear reduction or improved community relations). They worry that policing is heading "back to the future" and that some of the important gains that the police have made in becoming less corrupt and more professional in their key law enforcement roles will be lost.

Academic experts (who might be expected to be more consistently enthusiastic about the reform movement) also express concerns (Bayley, 1988; Greene & Mastrofski, 1988). Many of them worry that the ideas are nothing more than empty rhetoric, embraced by police executives to curry favor with the public and defeat rather than enhance public accountability (Klockars, 1988). They also worry that the ideas are too vague to be tested either logically or empirically and consequently that the welfare of America's communities is being imperiled by the wholesale embrace of untested ideas. Finally, they worry that when properly understood, the ideas associated with community and problem-solving policing could not be implemented successfully in today's police organizations, for they were founded and have long operated on wholly different premises.

The reason for the hesitation, of course, is that we do not know whether community policing "works." Nor do we know whether it is possible to implement community policing in the form in which it works. Indeed, it remains at least somewhat uncertain what community policing is and what a proper test of its performance would be! Until these uncertainties can be cleared up, prudence counsels a hedged rather than whole-hearted commitment to the new ideas. As Roberg (Chapter 14, this volume) observes:

> Due to the potential harmful effects of misguided efforts, either intentional or unintentional, community policing should be supported only *if* it is properly *defined, implemented,* and *evaluated* (preferably by outside sources).

The Challenge to Police Researchers

Obviously, this situation presents a golden opportunity for police researchers. Society needs to know whether the new directions in which police agencies are now moving are valuable or not. In principle, police researchers are well positioned to provide the answers.

Yet the situation holds a dangerous temptation for police researchers as well as an important opportunity. The temptation is that the researchers will try too early to give a definitive answer to the key question of whether community policing "works." Alternatively, researchers might try to "rationalize" the untidy developments now occurring in the field, and bring them under some form of central control designed to ensure that the one best form of community policing is tested and implemented. In doing so, there is a real risk that the search for better ways to police America's communities might be aborted or crippled.

As the chapters of this book indicate, the concept of community policing is a complex one. At the moment, it is more a set of challenging, general ideas pointing to new frontiers to explore than it is an operational and administrative blueprint for a newly designed police department. Yet these general ideas seem to be challenging and inspiring the field. As a result, the field is experimenting (more or less formally) with a wide variety of particular operational and administrative ideas that might fill the void between the big, abstract, rhetorical ideas on one hand and the concrete operations of police departments and the street-level behavior of individual officers on the other.

Arguably, it is important both to society and to the police field that the current binge of innovation be allowed to go forward without too much regulation. Such an approach would ensure both the most intensive use of the field's own imagination and experience, and the widest possible search for interesting operational and administrative ideas. It would also ensure that the police field would continue to "own" and feel responsible for the developments that are now occurring.

The danger associated with too heavy-handed a research intervention is that by trying to learn too quickly and too systematically, society could actually shrink its capacity to learn what works. In trying to answer the question of whether community policing works before society and the field have had ample opportunity to explore the possibilities of the complex idea, we might unwittingly stop the prospecting just before we found gold. Similarly, in trying to channel the natural experiments now occurring into a few, well-structured experiments designed to test a small number of specific operational programs or administrative systems that are arbitrarily defined as the "essence" of community policing, the prospecting might be limited to areas where the real gold cannot be found. In short, by trying to act as the arbiter of the reform movement, the research community might end up killing it altogether.

The alternative, as Weisburd (Chapter 18, this volume) suggests, is for the police research community to play a quite different role: to play the role of commentator rather than arbiter. In this role, their job would not be to reach an early conclusion about whether community policing works or to seize control of the direction of experimentation. Instead, it would be to keep taking stock of developments in the field.

As commentators, the police researchers would keep asking questions designed to clarify the concept of community policing and to unearth the particular assumptions that were being made in establishing the plausible value of the new approach. They would report the results of experiments undertaken by the field, those that were observed both through the apparatus of the relatively formal methods of program evaluation, and through the more informal methods associated with case studies. The findings from such studies would be accumulated as they became available, and used to influence judgments about the meaning, value, and feasibility of community policing. But these reports would reflect the understanding that definitive results on the success of community policing would probably take a decade—perhaps a generation—to produce.

Through such work, society will ultimately learn what it needs to know about the developments now occurring in policing. The complex idea of community policing will gradually become clearer and the relationships among its constituent parts better understood, both theoretically and empirically. We will know better than we do now whether the complex ideas fit together into a coherent whole and whether the coherent whole works to achieve goals and objectives that society judges to be important and useful. And we will learn how hard it is to implement these ideas in the context of today's police organizations.

Yet all this will happen at a pace that allows the important experimentation and innovation now occurring within the field to carry on at its current rapid pace. And, most importantly, the professional field will continue to own the developments now taking place. Just as it took us a generation to develop and understand simultaneously the strengths and limitations of "professional policing," it may well take us a generation to develop and understand simultaneously the strengths and limitations of "community policing."

The Book as a Commentary on Community Policing

I am happy to say that this book represents an important example of police researchers, taking the role of commentator rather than arbiter of the developments now occurring in the police world. It is an extremely useful series of chapters on community policing. Inevitably, its coverage is a bit spotty—reflecting the uneven development of knowledge and experience in the field. Some important questions about community policing get some answers, but they are not definitive (e.g., the effects of community policing programs on such measures as community satisfaction with the police, fear reduction, crime prevention, and officer satisfaction). Perhaps as important, some new questions get raised (particularly about the justifications and difficulties associated with involving communities in problem definitions and solutions).

Inevitably, by reading these chapters one's judgment about whether the big bet that is now being made on community policing is justified or not is influenced. Like an investor reading an analyst's reports, one gains more or less confidence in the enterprise in which one has invested. Somewhat unexpectedly, I came away from reading these chapters a little more optimistic than I was before I read them.

Yet the far more important contribution of the chapters in this book is that they inform society and the field of policing about what is now known or suspected and what important questions we should be asking about the developing concept of community policing. It is in this way that these chapters help light the way forward—not necessarily to the effective implementation of a particular concept called community policing, but to better ideas about how to police our cities, which were initially suggested by the concept of community policing.

Let me set out in more detail what I think these studies and essays tell us about: (a) the concept of community policing; (b) the effectiveness of community policing; and (c) the feasibility of community policing. I will also take the liberty of concluding with some observations on what might usefully be done simultaneously to accelerate the development of community policing, learn from the accumulating experience what works and what does not, and determine the role that police researchers could usefully play in that effort.

Developing the Concept of Community Policing

A theme that runs through these essays and reports is continuing frustration with the problem of how to define community policing. On one hand, the writers seem frustrated—even a bit indignant—that the idea cannot be encapsulated in a few, well-defined operational programs or administrative systems. The concept seems to encompass a wide variety of programs and managerial systems, with no particular priority given to the individual elements.

On the other hand, the authors are also able to define community policing in terms of a small number of fairly abstract ideas that differ importantly from the way that policing is now being done. Bayley (Chapter 19, this volume), for example, defines community policing in terms of four elements: consultation, adaptation, mobilization, and problem solving.

The Utility of Ambiguity

So, it's clear that there is something to the concept. Yet it is also true that the concept is susceptible to multiple interpretations. This may be frustrating to those who want to work with simple concepts. But it is not at all clear that the ambiguity of the concept is preventing it from doing useful work in stimulating important innovations in the field of policing. Indeed, as Skogan (Chapter 9, this volume) observes:

> Community policing is not a clear-cut concept, for it involves reforming decision-making processes and creating new cultures within police departments rather than being a specific tactical plan. . . . Under the rubric of community policing, American departments are opening small neighborhood substations, conducting surveys to identify local problems, organizing meetings and crime prevention seminars, publishing newsletters, helping form neighborhood watch groups, establishing advisory panels to inform police commanders, organizing youth activities, conducting drug education projects and media campaigns, patrolling on horses and bicycles, and working with municipal agencies to enforce health and safety regulations.

In short, it is partly the ambiguity of the concept that is stimulating the wide pattern of experimentation we are observing. In this sense, it is important that the concept mean something, but not something too specific. The ambiguity is a virtue.

Operational Program, Management Style, or Overall Philosophy?

A second key issue in defining community policing is whether the concept refers to: (a) a particular kind or set of operational programs; (b) a particular kind or set of administrative reforms in the police department; or (c) an overall philosophy, or strategy, or style of policing that is meant to change the entire department's operations.

Of course, there is an important relationship among these different elements. Community policing may have begun as a set of new operational programs: for instance, the increased use of foot patrols, the development of mini police stations, surveys of citizens to find out what problems concerned them, increased attention to victims of crime, and so forth. Yet, to launch these efforts it was often necessary to make important administrative changes in the department: Special units were created, patrol schedules were rearranged, and personnel systems were adjusted to reflect the priority that was now being given to the new programs. Moreover, these programmatic and administrative innovations often suggested the possibility of wider strategic changes in the overall operations of the experimenting department.

Yet, both to clarify the concept and to keep accurate track of what we are learning about community policing, it is probably important to continue to distinguish among these different ideas and to understand the relationships among them. Ideally, community policing is meant to be an overall philosophy of policing that redefines the overall mission of policing as well as its operational methods and administrative form. In short, it is intended to be a strategic innovation.

In practice, no department has yet fully implemented community policing as an overall philosophy. The closest we have come is probably a small number of experiments with police districts or precincts that have incorporated many important aspects of community policing (e.g., the 72nd Precinct in New York, or the Experimental Police District in Madison) (Couper & Lobitz, 1991; Vera Institute of Justice, 1991). This is one of the reasons we are still a long way from knowing about whether community policing, understood as an overall strategy of policing, works or not. We cannot know this until a whole department tries it (Moore, 1992).

Consequently, what the field is now experimenting with is not the ideal of community policing as an overall philosophy, but instead a series of programmatic or administrative innovations that are thought to be consistent with the overall spirit of community policing, or important elements of the larger concept. And there are lots of examples of these. We now have pretty good information about the effects of foot patrol (Police Foundation, 1981; Trojanowicz, 1982) and some important examples of what problem-solving methods can do (New York City Police Department, 1993; Spelman & Eck, 1987) and how communities can be engaged effectively in the fight against street-level drug dealing (Kennedy, 1993; Weingart et al., 1992). We also have some important information about the effects of decentralizing operational decisions and empowering officers (Couper & Lobitz, 1991). This is important because this is thought to be a necessary if not sufficient administrative change to support community problem-solving policing.

What is perhaps most important, however, is that we now know enough to distinguish these different ideas of community policing. It is important to understand that *administrative* changes must be made in order to make changes in both *institutionalizing* and *widening* the effects of the new operational programs associated with community policing. Indeed, the key distinction between a department that is experimenting with operational programs and one that is committed to a strategy of community policing is the extent to which its administrative and operational systems have been adapted to accommodate the ideas of community policing (Brown, 1989): that is, the extent to which the department relies on differential police response to ensure that patrol resources are adequate to maintain "beat integrity" in dispatching calls and the extent to which the organization's personnel systems have been adapted to recruit, train, and reward officers for the kinds of behavior consistent with community policing. This represents an advance in our analytic thought about the concept of community policing, and allows us to see more clearly what is now known about community policing and what the challenges of implementing it will be.

The Role of Rhetoric

The field is also making progress in understanding what role the rhetoric about community policing might play in the implementation of community policing. It is fair to say that, at the outset, the academic community was quite skeptical about the rhetoric of community policing. They thought it was being used cynically to build the reputations of chiefs and departments and to obscure the actual operations being carried out by the department. No doubt, in many cases, their cynicism was justified.

Yet it was also clear that, if important changes in policing were to be made along the lines suggested by the concept of community policing, some leadership would be necessary, and that one of the important tools of that leadership would be rhetoric. As Skogan (Chapter 9, this volume) observes:

> Critics of community policing have been quick to claim that in reality it is just rhetoric. It is certainly true that it *involves* rhetoric, for community policing . . . [provides] a new vision of where departments should be heading. This calls for rhetoric, one of the tools of leadership. Community policing also calls for rhetoric because departments do not exist in a vacuum. They are dependent on the communities that they serve for financial support, so they must have public and political support for whatever direction they are going. Rhetoric about community policing informs the community about a set of goals they are being asked to pay for.

In short, as I have argued elsewhere, the rhetoric of community policing helps to establish the department's external terms of accountability, and in so doing stimulates community expectations that can actually help a chief successfully implement the reforms that are to be undertaken (Moore, 1990).

Evaluating Community Policing

Given that we now understand that a certain amount of ambiguity about the concept of community policing might be helpful to the field, and that it is important to distinguish programs and administrative systems that are consistent with the philosophy of community policing from the overall philosophy of community policing, and that the rhetoric of community policing might be an important tool in helping to implement community policing, one still wants to know what is known about whether community policing in any of its guises works. This turns out to be an important conceptual as well as empirical question, for one of the important issues about community policing is that it seeks to redefine the *ends* of policing as well as the *means*. Insofar as it does so, and insofar as the public embraces the redefinition of the ends, the standards for evaluating community policing must change from the way that policing has been evaluated in the past.

Redefining the Ends of Policing

In the past, it was relatively clear how operational innovations in policing should be evaluated: All one had to do was check to see whether or not they succeeded in reducing crime (as measured by UCR reports or by victimization surveys). That was because there was widespread agreement that the overall objective of the police was to reduce crime.

To some degree, however, community policing seeks to redefine the overall purposes and ends of policing. As Eck and Rosenbaum (Chapter 1, this volume) observe, community policing increases the emphasis given to such goals as responding to emergencies, reducing fear, mobilizing communities to take their part in controlling crime, and enhancing security.

What remains somewhat unclear, however, is whether these new goals are to be understood and evaluated as new ends of policing, important to achieve in and of themselves, or whether they should be viewed as important new means to the traditional end of crime control, important only insofar as they are also shown to be effective methods for improving police performance in controlling crime or apprehending offenders.

The reason this ambiguity exists is that one can make reasonable arguments for both positions. One can make the argument that it has always been a mistake to evaluate police departments solely in terms of their crime control effectiveness. It has long been a part of the police mission to "serve" as well as "protect," and it is plausible to imagine that the value of such activities is going up in today's cities. Moreover, reducing fear has long been associated with the goal of enhancing security, and that has long been seen as a valuable purpose of the police. So, it is clear that one can make an argument for the independent value of these "new" police activities.

Yet one can also make an argument for the value of these activities as the means of achieving more effective crime control. The argument is that it has long been apparent that most crime control is done informally by communities. It has also become clear that the traditional methods of policing (rapid response to calls for service and retrospective investigation of crimes) depend for their effectiveness on close relationships with local communities. Consequently, to the extent that activities undertaken by the police to reduce fears, or to provide emergency services to citizens, or to help organize a community's defenses are successful in building informal community control and effective crime control partnerships with the police, these activities could be justified as important means to the ends of reducing crime in the community.

The distinction matters in evaluating community policing initiatives because it determines how far one has to go in establishing the value of community policing efforts. If one views service provision, fear reduction, and community mobilization as important ends in themselves, one need go no further in evaluating community policing efforts than to show that these effects occurred. If, however, one sees these only as important means to the traditional end of crime control, one must go further and show that these activities actually work in the way they are theorized to do in producing these results. That is a far more difficult and longer term evaluation task.

At the moment, it seems that the research community remains somewhat divided on this important value question. The broader society and the individuals who call the police, however, seem much clearer about the point. They seem to value police departments that produce services and fear reduction even when they are not particularly effective in reducing criminal victimization. This may be because they are confused about these effects. If so, it may be important for the research community to point out the difference between them. But for now, it seems clear that the terms in which it is proper to evaluate police programs have been widened by the concept of community policing.

Proven Effects

Almost nothing is certain about the effects of community policing programs. The programs are so varied that it will be a long time before we can say something definitive about the whole set of programs, the individual elements of the set, and the particular features of particular programs. And it will obviously be a long time until we can say important things about the strategy of community policing as opposed to the operational programs (Moore, 1992).

Still, there are some trends that seem to be relatively robust—at least for the time being. It seems clear, for example, that citizens like community policing programs. As Skogan (Chapter 9, this volume) reports:

[T]here is evidence in many evaluations that a public hungry for attention has a great deal to tell police. When they see more police walking on foot or working out of a local substation, they feel less fearful.

Bennett (Chapter 13, this volume) also reports community policing programs adopted in England tend to be popular among citizens.

There is slightly less strong evidence indicating that the programs can be successful in reducing the fear of crime. For example, in reviewing the evidence on the effects of community policing programs in six sites, Skogan finds that fear of crime is reduced in five of the six sites. Bennett, however, reports that this effect is found less consistently in Britain.

There is even weaker evidence indicating that community policing programs can be successful in mobilizing communities to deal with problems of crime and disorder. Tien and Rich (Chapter 11, this volume) report on the basis of a program they observed in Hartford, Connecticut, that:

Weeding success [in disrupting street level drug markets] spawns community support and participation in the ensuing seeding [community development] efforts. Visible and active community involvement, in turn, increases the effectiveness of weeding tactics, and is critical for long-term success in seeding.

Yet, Sadd and Grinc (Chapter 2, this volume) seem to report opposite conclusions in their study of eight "Innovative Policing" sites. They observe that:

[The] forays into community policing . . . produced only minimal . . . effects on drug-trafficking, drug-related crime, and fear of crime.

And there is almost no evidence yet indicating that community policing programs can be successful in preventing or reducing crime and criminal victimization. The strongest evidence on potentially important preventive effects used to be the evidence indicating that the introduction of community and problem-solving techniques could reduce calls for service in the areas in which they are tried (Trojanowicz & Bucqueroux, 1989). But that finding, too, is now being challenged with some studies showing that calls for service are reduced and others showing that they are not. The only evidence that community policing programs can be successful in reducing actual criminal victimization is presented by Wycoff and Skogan (Chapter 4, this volume), who find some such evidence from their evaluation of Madison's experimental police district.

So, the jury is still out on the size and character of effects that community policing programs can have on citizen perceptions of the quality of police service, on fear, and on crime. It seems relatively clear that the programs are popular and can reduce fear, but much less obvious that they can prevent or reduce crime.

The Feasibility of Community Policing

An important part of the reason for the difficulties in producing consistent operational successes may have less to do with the correctness of the theory of community and problem-solving policing and much more to do with the difficulty of implementing those theories correctly. Indeed, the authors in this book who evaluated operational programs report universally that there were substantial difficulties in implementing the community policing programs in the ways that they were supposed to be done. Sadd and Grinc (Chapter 2, this volume), for example, report that the eight INOP sites they examined "experienced common implementation problems that hampered their ability to have the desired impacts." Cordner (Chapter 10, this volume) reports that the particular foot patrol experiment he evaluated "more resembled traditional policing and crackdowns than community policing or problem-oriented policing." Capowich and Roehl (Chapter 7, this volume) reported that two of the three problem-solving efforts they evaluated in San Diego were based largely on traditional methods of police work, and that these were largely ineffective.

The authors in this volume were particularly critical of the efforts that were made to involve community participants either in the design or the actual execution of the programs that were developed to deal with particular problems. Sadd and Grinc (Chapter 2, this volume) observed that:

In all eight sites, the police administrators were the initiators and formulators of the community policing programs. The involvement of police officers, city agencies, and community residents in program design was generally minimal.

[T]he education and training of community residents in their roles in community policing is almost nonexistent. Without meaningful involvement of patrol officers in the planning process, participation by all city agencies, and true community involvement, community policing will fail to realize its potential.

Buerger (Chapter 17, this volume) expressed the same concerns on the basis of his clinical experience.

For all the rhetoric about empowering the community, . . . when it comes down to cases the police establishment assigns to the community a role that simply enhances the police response to crime and disorder.

It is important to remember that these implementation problems are experienced even when leading-edge departments are trying to implement community policing programs. It should come as no surprise, then, that ordinary police departments are having difficulty implementing community policing as an overall philosophy. As Leighton (Chapter 12, this volume) candidly reports in sizing up developments in Canada:

There is a growing number of police agencies that have implemented at least some of the core tactics, such as foot patrol in zones or beats, storefronts or mini-stations, and community consultative committees. Nonetheless . . . one of the main issues facing Canadian police executives at this time is how to implement community policing in a systematic way and on a department-wide basis.

So, questions about effective implementation of both programs and philosophy remain important. What is clear from reading the chapters is that this is a major issue in efforts to further develop community policing. If we cannot reliably implement community policing programs, we cannot find out whether they work, and we know in advance that any grander plans are likely to be stillborn. If we cannot learn how to move from programs to an overall philosophy through the redesign of the department's culture and administrative systems, we cannot get the full benefits theoretically available from community policing.

The principal work that has been done so far on the questions of implementation concerns the potential for decentralization of operational initiative in the police department to street-level officers. That is thought to be important in the creation of an organization that is capable of undertaking community problem-solving initiatives. It is also thought to be important for enhancing the morale of officers generally and engaging their commitment to the changed strategy of policing.

What the evidence shows on these matters is that it is both important and possible to decentralize initiative in a police department and that the effects of doing so on officer morale are largely positive. Wilkinson and Rosenbaum (Chapter 6, this volume) report on the basis of observations of community policing initiatives in Joliet and Aurora that:

> [A] police organization that is heavily invested in the professional model of policing—with a centralized, hierarchical and bureaucratized command structure—will have difficulty creating an environment that is conducive to community policing strategies and that encourages creative problem solving.

Given this finding, it is important that Wycoff and Skogan (Chapter 4, this volume) conclude on the basis of an examination of an experiment in decentralization carried out in Madison that:

> It is possible to change a traditional, control-oriented police organization into one in which employees become members of work teams and participants in decision-making processes.

They would also be the first to point out, however, that this change takes a great deal of sustained effort.

There is also evidence from both the Wycoff and Skogan studies and from the Lurigio and Rosenbaum work that such efforts do enhance the satisfaction of officers who are involved—once they become intensely involved. Lurigio and Rosenbaum (Chapter 8, this volume) report, for example, that:

> On balance, these studies have shown that community policing has exerted a positive impact on the police and on citizens' views of the police. From the police perspective, investigators have reported increases in job satisfaction and motivation, a broadening of the police role, improvements in relationships with co-workers and citizens, and greater expectations regarding community participation in crime prevention efforts. (1994, 27).

This is all very encouraging, but as Leighton (Chapter 12, this volume) puts it, the challenge still remains to find means to "sustain the approach through a changed reward system, training, and other avenues." As to efforts to implement an organization-wide shift to community policing rather than simply achieve this result for some particular programs or in one particular district, Chapter 5 in this volume, by Greene, Bergman, and McLaughlin, offers a cautionary tale. Their description of a major top-down effort to implement community policing as a philosophy against entrenched, high-level opposition suggests that although progress can be made in such situations and, indeed, can accelerate, it is a very slow process.

In many respects, the question of how to implement community policing programs, and how to move from programs to an overall philosophy, and what the administrative systems of a mature community policing organization might look like, represents one of the important frontiers of research in this domain.

This raises the question of how we are likely to learn about such things. Importantly, Weisel and Eck (Chapter 3, this volume) offer a suggestion. They urge that the field adopt:

> [A] bias for action . . . [T]he most important activity in implementing change may be simply to move forward and avoid laboriously concentrating on process variables. Indeed, the single most important activity for changing the police agency and institutionalizing community policing may be simply to move ahead and get new people on board.

Toward the Future of Policing

It is in that spirit that I offer the following ideas about what should be done with the powerful movement that is now occurring within the field of policing. I recommend that it be allowed to proceed apace. There are enough theoretical arguments about the potential utility of the approach, and enough empirical evidence about the accuracy of the judgments (to say nothing of enough evidence about the limitations of our current methods) that the widespread search for improved methods of policing along the lines suggested by community policing is warranted.

There are two principal problems with the way things are now developing. One is simply that the field as a whole is not yet accumulating enough experience. The rate of programmatic and administrative innovation should be higher than it now is if the movement is not to slacken and is to provide the basis for learning what works. The rhetorical commitment must be matched by the operational commitment. The second is that police researchers are not well positioned enough now to maximize the learning that can come from the experience.

One way to solve both problems simultaneously would be for the federal government to use its current commitment to increasing police presence on the street to encourage a change in the style of policing and to support efforts to learn as efficiently as we can from the field's accumulating experience. This should involve three things: (a) an ongoing survey of the field of policing to determine to what extent community policing is moving from rhetorical to operational levels throughout the country; (b) the establishment of a small number of police departments that could become the nation's laboratories and resource centers in which many of the operational and administrative problems associated with implementing community policing as an overall philosophy could be worked out for the benefit of the field as a whole; and (c) the creation of a national award process that would give a cash award to any police department that developed an important operational or administrative innovation consistent with the principles and spirit of community policing. Police researchers should be closely involved in these activities so that they can reliably fulfill the role of commentator that is suggested by the publication of this book. Through these devices, we can not only get on with the implementation of community policing, but discover what we ought to mean by the concept.

References

Bayley, D. H. (1988). Community policing: A report from the devil's advocate. In J. Greene & S. Mastrofski (Eds.), *Community policing: Rhetoric or reality?* New York: Praeger.

Brown, L. P. (1989). *Community policing: A practical guide for police officials* (Perspectives on Policing, No. 12). Washington, DC: National Institute of Justice and Harvard University.

Couper, D. C., & Lobitz, S. H. (1991). *Quality policing: The Madison experience.* Washington, DC: Police Executive Research Forum.

Greene, J. R., & Mastrofski, S. (Eds.). (1988). *Community policing: Rhetoric or reality?* New York: Praeger.

Kelling, G. L. (1988). *Police and communities: The quiet revolution* (Perspectives on Policing, No. 1). Washington, DC: National Institute of Justice and Harvard University.

Kennedy, D. M. (1993). *Closing the market: Controlling the drug trade in Tampa, Florida. Program focus.* Washington, DC: National Institute of Justice.

Klockars, C. B. (1988). The rhetoric of community policing. In J. Greene & S. Mastrofski (Eds.), *Community policing: Rhetoric or reality?* New York: Praeger.

McElroy, J. E., Cosgrove, C. A., & Sadd, S. (1990). *CPOP The research: An evaluative study of the New York City Community Patrol Officer Program.* New York: Vera Institute of Justice.

Moore, M. H. (1992). Problem solving and community policing. In M. Tonry & N. Morris (Eds.), *Modern policing* (Vol. 15, pp. 99-158). Chicago: University of Chicago Press.

Moore, M. H. (1990). Police leadership: The impossible dream? In E. C. Hargrove & J. C. Glidewell (Eds.), *Impossible jobs in public management.* Lawrence: University Press of Kansas.

New York City Police Department. (1993a). *Problem solving annual for community police officers and supervisors: Disorderly groups.* New York: Author.

New York City Police Department. (1993b). *Problem solving annual for community police officers and supervisors: Drugs.* New York: Author.

Police Foundation. (1981). *The Newark foot patrol experiment.* Washington, DC: Author.

Sparrow, M. K., Moore, M. H., & Kennedy, D. M. (1990). *Beyond 911: A new era for policing.* New York: Basic Books.

Spelman, W., & Eck, J. E. (1987). *Problem-oriented policing. Research in brief.* Washington, DC: National Institute of Justice.

Trojanowicz, R. (1982). *An evaluation of the Neighborhood Foot Patrol Program in Flint, Michigan.* East Lansing: Michigan State University.

Trojanowicz, R., & Bucqueroux, B. (1989). *Community policing: A contemporary perspective.* Cincinnati: Anderson.

Vera Institute of Justice. (1991). *72nd Precinct Model Precinct Project: Initial development and implementation.* New York: Author.

Weingart, S. N., Hartmann, F. X., & Osborne, D. (1992). *Lessons learned: Case studies of the initiation and maintenance of the community response to drugs. Report to the National Institute of Justice.* Cambridge, MA: Harvard University, John F. Kennedy School of Government, Program in Criminal Justice Policy and Management.

Author Index

Subject Index

About the Contributors

David H. Bayley is a professor in the School of Criminal Justice, State University of New York at Albany. He is a specialist in international criminal justice, with particular interest in policing. He has done extensive research on the police in India, Japan, Australia, Canada, Britain, Singapore, and the United States. His work has focused on strategies of policing, the evolution of police organizations, organizational reform, accountability, and the tactics of patrol officers in discretionary law enforcement situations.

His most recent publications include *Forces of Order: Policing Modern Japan* (1991); *Patterns of Policing: A Comparative International Analysis* (1985); *Community Policing: Issues and Practices Around the World* (1988), with Jerome H. Skolnick; *A Model of Community Policing: The Singapore Story* (1989); and "The Organization of the Police in English-Speaking Countries" in *Crime and Justice: An Annual Review of Research* (1991).

Bayley has just finished a multiyear research project on the future of policing in Australia, Canada, Great Britain, Japan, and the United States. Publications from this project so far are "Toward Policing the Year 2000" (National Police Research Unit, Australia, 1990) and "Managing the Future: Prospective Issues in Canadian Policing" (Solicitor-General of Canada, 1991).

Trevor Bennett is currently Lecturer in Criminology at the University of Cambridge, Institute of Criminology, and a Fellow of Wolfson College. He is currently director of the M.Phil. program at the Institute of Criminology and also has overall responsibility for a new teaching program designed specifically for police officers. His research work includes a crime-specific analysis of the offense of burglary (published as *Burglary in a Dwelling*) and work with burglary offenders (published as *Burglars on Burglary*). He has conducted research on police involvement in crime prevention, including a project on neighborhood watch (published as *Evaluating Neighbourhood Watch*) and work on the impact of police contact patrols on crime and fear reduction. He has written widely on the topic of community policing and has recently completed a national survey of the community policing strategies in England and Wales. His current research includes a Home Office-funded evaluation of problem-oriented policing in Thames Valley Police force area.

William T. Bergman, Commander of the Philadelphia Police Department's South Operations Bureau, has been responsible for implementing strategic change within the police department for the past several years. He has been an advisor to three police commissioners regarding implementing institutional and organizational change in the Philadelphia Police Department and has served as Executive Officer to the Police Commissioner. He has also chaired the Implementation Committee for community policing in Philadelphia.

He is currently introducing victim's assistance and community-oriented policing into the department's patrol and investigative services. He completed a master's degree from St. Joseph's University and regularly teaches for Temple University and the Federal Law Enforcement Training Center.

Bergman has most recently served as a loaned executive to the School District of Philadelphia, where he evaluated school safety and security programs and designed initiatives to further school safety within the Philadelphia School system. He also regularly consults with state and local police agencies on matters pertaining to juvenile gangs and reducing youth violence.

Michael E. Buerger is a Visiting Fellow at the National Institute of Justice, on leave from the University of Wisconsin-Oshkosh where he is an Assistant Professor of Public Affairs. His Fellowship research at NIJ focuses on the impact of community policing initiatives upon the capacity of "the community" to establish cohesion and resist crime and disorder. He is developing case studies of such efforts in Minneapolis, Minnesota; Fort Worth, Texas; and city and suburban departments in the District of Columbia metropolitan area.

He was a police officer for 9 years and holds bachelor's degrees in English Literature (Dartmouth) and in Criminal Justice (St. Anselm), master's degrees in Criminal Justice (Rutgers) and Liberal Studies (Dartmouth), and a doctorate in Criminal Justice from Rutgers. He was the Director of the Minneapolis office of the Crime Control Institute during the RECAP (Repeat Call Address Policing) and Hot Spots of Crime Experiments. Buerger's research and publications in policing include studies of drug markets and street-level drug enforcement, problem-solving and problem-oriented policing, and handling of domestic violence. In addition, he has conducted various unpublished studies of police organizations' scheduling, case processing, jail operations, and planning processes for establishing community policing.

George E. Capowich is an independent criminal justice consultant specializing in organizational issues, system-wide policy questions, and program evaluation.

When he was with the Institute for Social Analysis he was a senior researcher on several projects, including an evaluation of the systems approach to crime prevention for the Bureau of Justice Assistance, an evaluation of an expedited civil arbitration program in the New Jersey state courts, and an evaluation of community-based drug prevention for the Office of Substance Abuse Prevention. Currently he is completing a final report of an evaluation of problem-oriented policing as a community policing strategy, a project he directed. In addition, he is writing a monograph that details program evaluation approaches for police administrators, and is consultant for a neighborhood-based project that is organizing inner-city residents for crime prevention in five cities. He is also a member of a policy action task force focusing on nonlegislative innovations in youth policy for the Center for Youth Development at the Academy for Educational Development in Washington, D.C. His current research interests include organizational behavior as a context for program operations, and the use of qualitative methods in process and impact evaluations.

Gary W. Cordner, Professor of Police Studies at Eastern Kentucky University, was editor of the *American Journal of Police* from 1987 through 1991 and now edits the new *Police Computer Review.* He has coauthored texts on police administration and criminal justice planning and is coeditor of the book *What Works in Policing?* (1992). He received his Ph.D. in social science/criminal justice from Michigan State University.

He began his police career as a police officer in Ocean City, Maryland, and later served for 3 years as police chief in St. Michaels, Maryland. In the early 1980s, he helped Baltimore County, Maryland, develop a repeat offender program and evaluate a community policing program. During the past few years he has worked on projects with the Police Foundation, the Rand Corporation, the Police Executive Research Forum, and the SEARCH Group, and has conducted police executive training programs in Maryland, Ohio, Kentucky, Illinois, Florida, and Texas.

Cordner is currently evaluating Drug Elimination Programs in the public housing authority in Lexington, Kentucky, and conducting a National Institute of Justice-funded study of the compatibility of community policing and police agency accreditation.

John E. Eck is the Associate Director for Research for the Police Executive Research Forum. He has conducted research on criminal investigations, problem-oriented policing, community policing, and police drug control strategies. He has served as a consultant on investigations management to the London Metropolitan Police and has taught courses on research methods at the Canadian Police College. He holds Master of Public Policy and Bachelor of General Studies degrees from the University of Michigan and currently is completing his doctoral dissertation at the Department of Criminal Justice and Criminology, University of Maryland. He is interested in how police organizations address community problems, crime places, how crime places develop, and methods for controlling crime in and around places.

Warren Friedman has for the past 12 years directed the Chicago Alliance for Neighborhood Safety (CANS). CANS is a multiracial coalition of community organizations from low- and moderate-income neighborhoods around Chicago. CANS has pioneered in community antidrug house and hot spot strategies and has been the leading advocate for a democratic version of community policing in Chicago. CANS works to prepare community groups for their role in community policing and trains and provides technical assistance to these organizations in programs such as neighborhood and school watch.

Friedman is coauthor of *Police Service in Chicago: 911, Dispatch Policy and Neighborhood-Oriented Alternatives,* and *Mapping Crime in its Community Setting: Event Geography Analysis.*

Herman Goldstein is the Evjue-Bascom Professor of Law at the Law School, University of Wisconsin-Madison. He joined the Wisconsin faculty in 1964 after serving as a researcher and analyst with the American Bar Foundation Survey of the Administration of Criminal Justice and, from 1960 to 1964, as executive assistant to O. W. Wilson when Wilson undertook, as superintendent, the reform the Chicago Police Department.

His earliest writings explored the discretion exercised by the police, the policy-making role of police administrators, and the political accountability of the police. He has also written extensively on the police function, police relationships with minorities, the control of police conduct, and police corruption. He is coauthor of the American Bar Association's *The Urban Police Function* (1973), the author of *Policing a Free Society* (1977), and, most recently, the author of *Problem-Oriented Policing* (1990).

Goldstein has been a consultant to numerous national and local groups, including the President's Commission on Law Enforcement and Administration of Justice, the National Advisory Commission on Civil Disorders, the National Institute of Justice, the Police Foundation, and the Police Executive Research Forum. He has also worked with numerous police agencies on specific problems and in introducing innovative programs.

Jack R. Greene, Ph.D., is the Director of Temple University's Center for Public Policy and Professor of Criminal Justice, conducting research and teaching on topics of organizational dynamics and the evaluation of police services. He received his Ph.D. in Social Science from Michigan State University in 1977. He was on the faculty of the University of Wisconsin-Milwaukee and Michigan State University prior to joining Temple's faculty in 1984.

He has conducted research and published extensively on matters pertaining to police efficiency and effectiveness, police management, and community-oriented policing, most particularly in urban areas. His most recent coedited book, an anthology of readings, *Community Policing: Rhetoric or Reality?* (1988) examines a major institutional change occurring in American policing.

Greene is a regular consultant to several criminal justice agencies where he has overseen projects to improve planned change strategies. He is currently providing consultant services to the Philadelphia and Los Angeles Police Departments on matters of implementing community-based policing. He has also been recently appointed to the Advisory Committee of the National Center for State and Local Law Enforcement Training.

Randolph Grinc received his Ph.D. in Sociology from New York University in 1989 and has been employed as a Research Associate at the Vera Institute of Justice since that time. He is currently involved in a project with the New York City Police Department to develop a performance measurement system for community policing. He also served as Deputy Director for Vera's NIJ-funded evaluation of BJA's Innovative Neighborhood Oriented Policing projects (INOP). Prior to the INOP research, he was responsible for developing, conducting, and analyzing the in-depth panel interviews of community leaders and residents for Vera's NIJ-funded research on the community effects of the New York Police Department's Tactical Narcotics Teams.

Barry N. Leighton is currently Adjunct Research Professor in the Department of Law, Carleton University, Ottawa, where he teaches current issues in policing. His full-time hobby is working as Manager of research and policy on community policing and police race-relations with the Ministry of the Solicitor General of Canada, in Ottawa. Previously, he was Senior Criminologist with the Department of Justice, Canada (1985-1988).

A New Zealander, he obtained his undergraduate degree, B.A. Honours, in 1973 from Victoria University of Wellington and his Ph.D. in 1986 from the University of Toronto. He authored "Visions of Community Policing: Rhetoric and Reality in Canada," *Canadian Journal of Criminology* (1991), co-authored *A Vision of the Future of Policing in Canada* (1990), and articles on the evaluation of community policing in Edmonton.

Leighton's current interests include the application of community policing to police-race relations issues; evaluating the effectiveness of community policing; the efficiency and economy of public policing; and the future of community policing in light of the fiscal crisis and the challenge to overcome its local bias as "sand-box policing."

Arthur J. Lurigio, a social psychologist, is currently Associate Professor of Criminal Justice at Loyola University and Director of Research for the Cook County, Illinois, Adult Probation Department. He was recently a Research Associate at the Center for Urban Affairs and Policy Research, Northwestern University and a Visiting Assistant Professor in the Psychology Department at Northwestern University. He received his doctorate from Loyola University of Chicago in 1984. Lurigio has been the lead researcher on a dozen federal, state, and local grant projects. His research interests include community crime prevention, criminal victimization and victim services, community policing, drugs and crime, intermediate punishments, monetary sanctions, decision making in sentencing, crime and mental disorders, and AIDS in the criminal justice system.

Among his most recent publications are three co-edited books: *Smart Sentencing: The Emergence of Intermediate Sanctions, Drugs and the Community,* and *Gangs and Community Corrections.*

Edward J. McLaughlin has been a Philadelphia police officer for the past 27 years. His responsibilities have progressively intensified across a wide range of police and community partnerships. He is currently the Commanding Officer of Operations Bureau North, coordinating all police services in approximately one half of the City of Philadelphia.

He is the recipient of the Gary P. Hayes Award from the Police Executive Research Forum, for "Outstanding initiative in furthering the improvement in the quality of policing." He is also a regular consultant to the Police Executive Research Forum on matters of police innovation. As a community policing/problem-solving advocate, he regularly provides consultation and instruction to several metropolitan law enforcement agencies. He is also an active member in several victim services and domestic violence agencies throughout Philadelphia and Pennsylvania.

McLaughlin has participated in academic and police training courses offered by Harvard University, Temple University, LaSalle University, and Northwestern University, while also participating in numerous professional development programs.

Mark H. Moore is the Daniel and Florence Guggenheim Professor of Criminal Justice Policy and Management. He is the Faculty Chairman of the Kennedy School's Program in Criminal Justice, and for a decade served as the Founding Chairman of the Kennedy School's Committee on Executive Programs. His intellectual interests lie in criminal justice policy, public management, and—in particular—the intersection of the two fields. He has led national "executive sessions" on the future of juvenile justice, policy, and prosecution. In the domain of crime policy, Moore is the author of *Buy and Bust: The Effective Regulation of an Illicit Market in Heroin* and the co-author of *Dangerous Offenders: Elusive Targets of Justice, From Children to Citizens: The Mandate for Juvenile Justice,* and *Beyond 911: A New Era for Policing.* In the domain of public management, he is the author of *Accounting for Change: Reconciling the Demands for Accountability and Innovation in the Public Sector* and the forthcoming *Creating Public Value: Strategic Management in the Public Sector;* his co-authored books include: *Inspectors-General: Junkyard Dogs or Man's Best Friend, Public Duties: The Moral Obligations of Public Officials,* and *Ethics in Government: The Moral Challenges of Public Leadership.*

Thomas F. Rich is a Senior Analyst at Queues Enforth Development (Q.E.D.), Inc., a Cambridge- (Massachusetts) based criminal justice consulting and software company. He has been at Q.E.D. since 1982 and has participated in a variety of criminal justice studies, primarily for the U.S. Department of Justice and for a number of New York agencies. His work at Q.E.D. also includes developing geographic information systems for public safety agencies, and he is currently Project Manager of a U.S. Department of Justice-funded evaluation of efforts to improve the status of criminal history records. Rich holds a B.A. in Mathematics from Cornell University and an M.S. in Engineering-Economic Systems from Stanford University.

Roy R. Roberg, professor in the Administration of Justice Department at San Jose University, has written extensively in the areas of police organization and behavior. Roberg has authored or co-authored numerous books on the police, the most recent of which are *Police Organization and Management* (1990) and *Police and Society* (1993). He is currently working on a second edition of the management text, to be titled *Community Police Management.*

Janice A. Roehl, Ph.D., has for the past 18 years concentrated her research and evaluation work in two areas: conflict resolution and prevention research. She has studied a wide range of dispute resolution mechanisms, particularly their achievements in procedural justice, disputant satisfaction, and system impact. Her prevention research interests and experience encompass community-based crime prevention and drug abatement efforts, conflict resolution and violence prevention in the schools, community policing, and substance abuse prevention. Roehl is Senior Vice President of the Institute for Social Analysis and the principal investigator of the national evaluation of the Weed and Seed program and a national assessment of community-based anti-drug efforts, both supported by the National Institute of Justice. She received her doctoral degree in Social Psychology from The George Washington University in Washington, D.C.

Dennis P. Rosenbaum is the Director of the Center for Research in Law and Justice and Associate Professor of Criminal Justice at the University of Illinois at Chicago. His primary research agenda is to better understand community, police, school, and media-based initiatives to prevent crime and drug abuse. He is presently conducting a longitudinal study of adolescent drug abuse, violence, and school-based drug education. He is currently assessing the process and impact of community policing reform in several cities. Rosenbaum's recent books include *Community Crime Prevention: Does It Work?* (1986), *The Social Construction of Reform* (1988), *Drugs and Communities* (1993), and the forthcoming *Fighting Back: Two Sides of Crime Prevention.*

Susan Sadd received her Ph.D. in Social Psychology from New York University and is currently the director of Research and Planning for the Bronx District. For the previous 16 years, she was employed at the Vera Institute of Justice, where she was involved in evaluations of police programs since 1986 and most recently worked on a project with the New York City Police Department (NYPD) to develop a performance measurement system for community policing. She also served as Project Director for Vera's NIJ-funded evaluation of the Innovative Neighborhood Oriented Policing (INOP) programs, and prior to that project, she was responsible for the household survey component of Vera's NIJ-funded research on the community effects of the New NYPD's Tactical Narcotics Teams. Sadd also shared major responsibility for Vera's study of the NYPD's Community Patrol Officer Program, which initiated the NYPD's movement toward community policing; the results of this study have been published as a book by Sage (*Community Policing: The CPOP in New York*). During her tenure at Vera she also directed studies on employment training for youth and detoxification for homeless alcoholics.

Wesley G. Skogan is Professor of Political Science and Urban Affairs at Northwestern University. His research focuses on the role of citizens as producers and consumers of safety. His recent Sage book, *Victims of Crime* (1989), reflects his continuing interest in criminal victimization. Another line of his research concerns neighborhood and community responses to crime. This includes work on fear of crime and individual behavior. His 1981 Sage book, *Coping With Crime,* deals with these issues. His third research focus is community policing. Sections of his 1990 book, *Disorder and Decline,* examine this movement. He has been a visiting scholar at the Max-Planck-Institut, the Dutch Ministry of Justice, the University of Alberta, and the National Institute of Justice. Skogan has served on the editorial boards of several journals, ranging from the *Journal of Criminal Law and Criminology* to *Evaluation Review,* and is a consultant to several governments.

James M. Tien received the B.E.E. degree in 1966 from Rensselaer Polytechnic Institute, Troy, New York, and the S.M., E.E., and Ph.D. degrees in systems engineering and operations research in 1967, 1970, and 1972, respectively, from the Massachusetts Institute of Technology.

He joined the Department of Electrical, Computer and Systems Engineering at Rensselaer Polytechnic Institute in 1977; he was appointed Acting Chairman of a then one-year-old interschool unit—the Department of Decision Sciences and Engineering Systems. Since August 1992, he has been the Acting Dean of the School of Engineering. Previously, he was a Member of the Technical Staff at Bell Telephone Laboratories, Holmdel, New Jersey (1966-1969), a Project Director at the Rand Corporation, New York, New York (1970-1973), an Area Research Director at Urban Systems Research and Engineering, Cambridge, Massachusetts (1975-1977), and a Vice President of Queues Enforth Development, Cambridge, Massachusetts (1977-present). His areas of research include the development and application of computer and systems analysis techniques to information and decision systems. He has published extensively, with more than 70 refereed publications to his credit. He has presented invited papers and lectures at numerous conferences and workshops.

Tien is a Fellow of the IEEE. He is listed in several *Who's Who* publications and is an Associate Editor of both the IEEE *Transactions on Systems, Man, and Cybernetics* and the *Journal of Information and Decision Technologies.* He has served the IEEE and the SMC Society in several capacities since 1980. He was a member of the IEEE Technical Activities Board (TAB), the President of the SMC Society, the Chair of the IEEE Society Presidents' Forum, and the Chair of the IEEE Research Initiation Grants Review Committee, and is presently the Chair of the IEEE Membership Structure Committee and of several other IEEE, TAB, and SMC committees.

Robert C. Trojanowicz was director of the National Center for Community Policing at Michigan State University, a Professor of Urban Affairs at Michigan State University, and a Research Fellow in the Program in Criminal Justice Policy and Management, Kennedy School of Government, Harvard University. He held a B.S. in police administration, an M.S.W. in social work, and a Ph.D. in social science, all from Michigan State University. Trojanowicz had experience with various police and social agencies. He was the author of several textbooks and contributed numerous articles to management and criminal justice journals.

David Weisburd is Associate Professor of Criminology at the Hebrew University Law School in Jerusalem and Director of the Center for Crime Prevention Studies at Rutgers University. He received his Ph.D. from Yale University and has served as a Research Associate at Yale Law School and the Vera Institute of Justice. He has been a Principal Investigator for a series of federally funded research programs in policing, including the Drug Market Analysis Experiment in Jersey City and The Minneapolis Hot Spots Patrol Experiment. Weisburd is author or editor of *White Collar Crime Reconsidered* (1992, with Kip Schlegel), *Police Control and Control of the Police: Problems of Law, Order and Community* (1993, with Craig Uchida), *Jewish Settler Violence: Deviance as Social Reaction* (1989), and *Crimes of the Middle Classes: White Collar Offenders in the Federal Courts* (1991, with others). He has also published numerous scholarly articles and reports.

Deborah Lamm Weisel is a senior research associate for the Police Executive Research Forum in Washington, D.C. She currently directs a national assessment of emerging drug enforcement tactics and a study exploring the links between criminal youth gangs and traditional and newly emerging organized crime groups. She has recently completed an 18-month national assessment of community policing and a project studying police responses to gang problems, reviewing alternative police responses to gang problems, and exploring the gang-drug nexus. She has participated in numerous other research projects studying police and crime, and has expertise in gangs, drugs—particularly street-level drug dealing—and alternative responses to crime-related problems in public housing communities. She is the author of *Tackling Drug Problems in Public Housing: A Guide for Police,* a resource widely used in the police and public housing fields.

Weisel is a graduate of the University of North Carolina at Chapel Hill and of North Carolina University and is a doctoral candidate at the University of Illinois at Chicago.

Deanna L. Wilkinson received her B.A. in sociology from Cornell College in 1990 and her M.A. in criminal justice from the University of Illinois-Chicago in 1992 and is currently a doctoral candidate at Rutgers University, School of Criminal Justice. She has served as project manager for the Aurora/Joliet Neighborhood-Oriented Policing and Problem Solving Evaluation. Wilkinson's research interests include organizational reform, citizen and police reactions to crime, substance abuse, and the cause of juvenile delinquency.

Mary Ann Wycoff has worked as a researcher for the Police Foundation since 1972. She is a Project Director, currently conducting a national survey on community policing under a grant from the National Institute of Justice. She has recently completed an evaluation of the implementation of Quality Policing in Madison, Wisconsin, and an evaluation of a personnel performance measurement system for community policing designed by the Houston Police Department. Wycoff's interests include community policing, organizational change, program implementation, and management and personnel issues. She is a doctoral candidate in sociology at the University of Wisconsin, Madison.

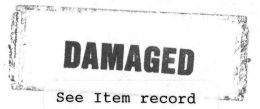